YELLOWSTONE, GRAND TETON & GLACIER ROAD TRIP

Carter G. Walker

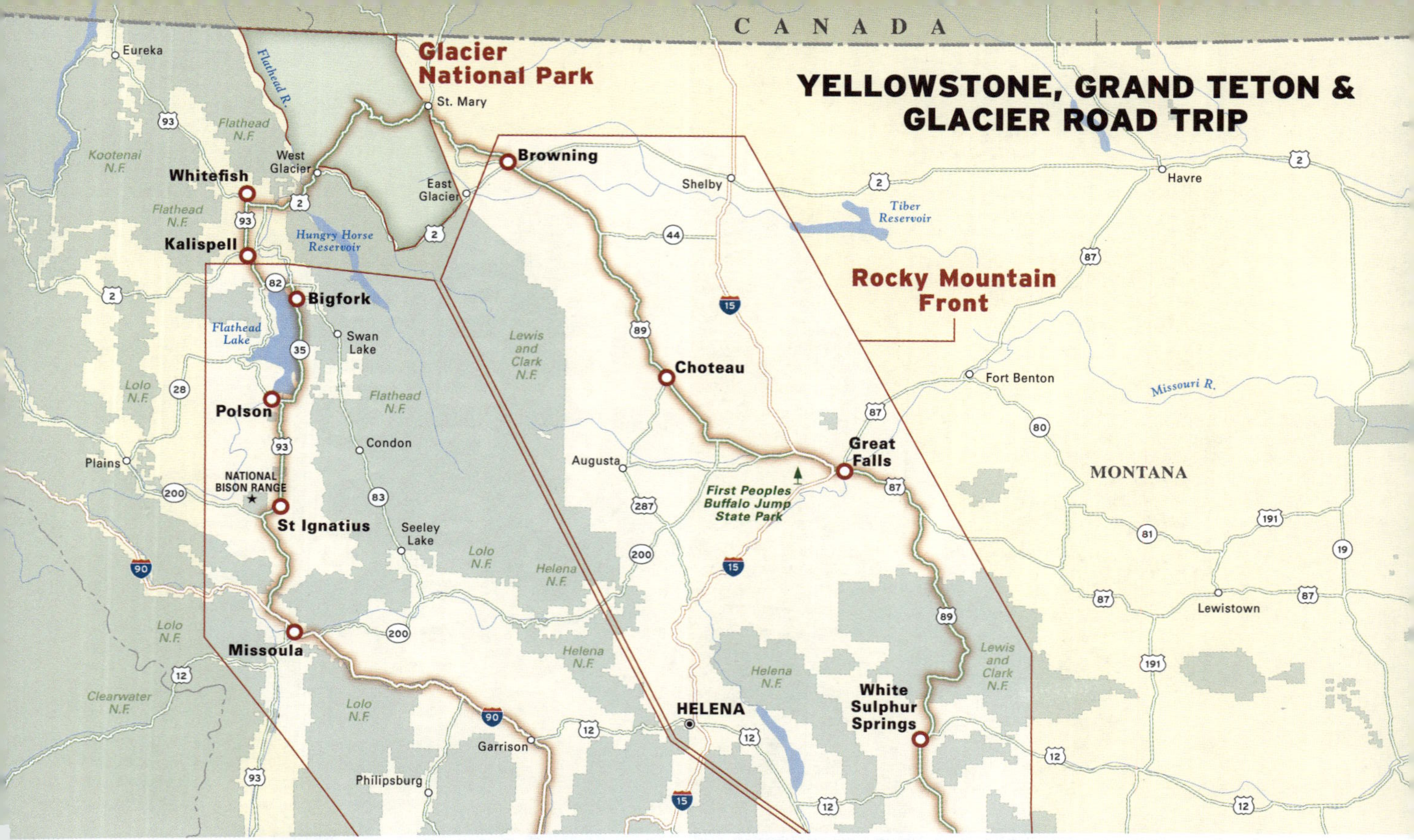

YELLOWSTONE, GRAND TETON & GLACIER ROAD TRIP

CANADA

Glacier National Park

Rocky Mountain Front

MONTANA

Eureka
St. Mary
Browning
Shelby
Havre
Flathead R.
Flathead N.F.
Kootenai N.F.
West Glacier
Whitefish
East Glacier
Tiber Reservoir
Flathead N.F.
Kalispell
Hungry Horse Reservoir
Bigfork
Flathead Lake
Swan Lake
Lewis and Clark N.F.
Choteau
Fort Benton
Missouri R.
Lolo N.F.
Flathead N.F.
Polson
Condon
Great Falls
Plains
Augusta
NATIONAL BISON RANGE
First Peoples Buffalo Jump State Park
St Ignatius
Seeley Lake
Lolo N.F.
Helena N.F.
Lewistown
Lolo N.F.
Missoula
Helena N.F.
Lewis and Clark N.F.
Helena N.F.
Clearwater N.F.
Lolo N.F.
White Sulphur Springs
HELENA
Garrison
Philipsburg

2 93 2 93 2 2 82 35 28 93 200 83 200 90 12 90 93 44 89 15 287 200 15 12 12 15 12 87 87 80 87 89 81 191 19 87 87 191 12 12 2 2

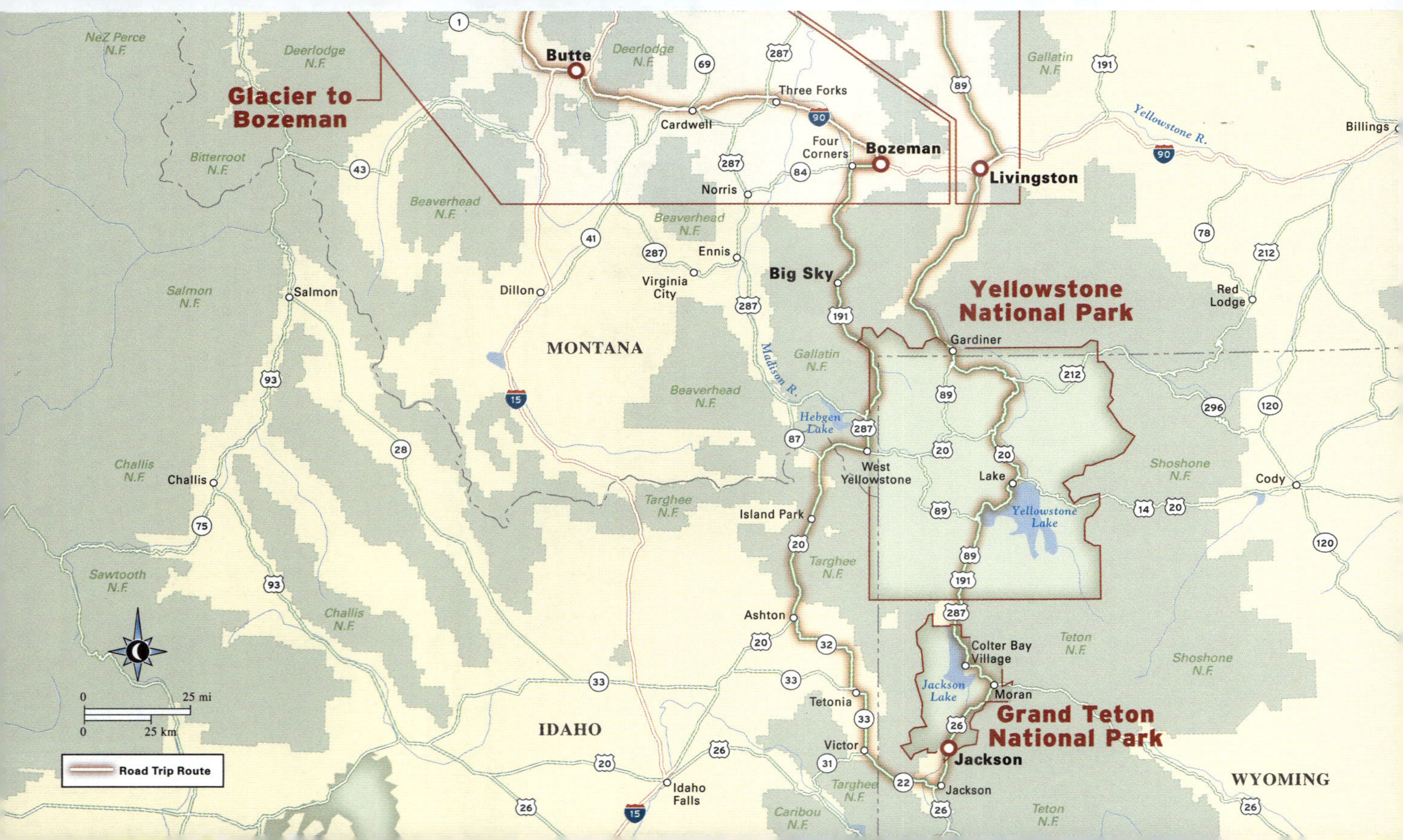
Glacier to Bozeman
Yellowstone National Park
Grand Teton National Park
Butte
Bozeman
Livingston
Big Sky
Jackson
Three Forks
Cardwell
Four Corners
Norris
Ennis
Virginia City
Dillon
Salmon
Challis
Gardiner
West Yellowstone
Lake
Island Park
Ashton
Tetonia
Victor
Colter Bay Village
Moran
Idaho Falls
Red Lodge
Cody
Billings
MONTANA
IDAHO
WYOMING
Yellowstone R.
Madison R.
Hebgen Lake
Yellowstone Lake
Jackson Lake
NeZ Perce N.F.
Deerlodge N.F.
Bitterroot N.F.
Beaverhead N.F.
Salmon N.F.
Challis N.F.
Sawtooth N.F.
Gallatin N.F.
Targhee N.F.
Caribou N.F.
Shoshone N.F.
Teton N.F.
0 25 mi
0 25 km
Road Trip Route

CONTENTS

WELCOME TO THE Yellowstone, Grand Teton & Glacier Road Trip

There is something quintessentially American about a road trip out West.

Amid long stretches of highway and wide-open country, with no evidence of civilization besides a far-off fence line, there's something about being out here that reminds us how a day works: the way the sun moves across the sky; the way your body gets tired when it takes you to the top of a mountain; the way a good burger ought to taste, first juicy bite in. Things are simpler here—and they are also beautiful beyond words.

Yellowstone, Grand Teton, and Glacier National Parks are the jewels in this humble crown. They are ineffable in their beauty and unknowable in their vastness and scale, from soaring mountainscapes and hulking grizzly bears to the tiniest wild orchid, purple against green. There is wildness here. You can feel it.

But there is civilization here as well. And culture. There are Native American reservations where you can experience the visual and auditory feast of a powwow. There are little towns that feel untouched by time. There are big towns, too, with museums and restaurants, with old theaters and new art galleries. You can be comfortable when you travel out here—a big bed, a good meal—but you'll find yourself humbled at being part of something much larger than any of us dare to imagine. Come out West, to these parks, to this landscape. Make your way between destinations by slowing down, by paying attention. If you honor what's here, and what came before, this place will change you.

8 TOP EXPERIENCES

1 **Spotting wildlife** throughout the region, including bears, bison, wolves, elk, bighorn sheep, and more (page 23).

2 Hiking to Glacier's historic **chalets,** including Granite Park Chalet and Sperry Chalet (page 212).

>>>

3 **Horseback riding** through the vast Western landscape (page 135).

>>>

4 **Floating the Snake River,** whether on a relaxed sunrise float or a white-knuckled paddle under the blazing sun—or both (page 133).

5 Attending a **powwow** and witnessing the time-honored celebrations (page 243).

6 Soaking in resort-style pools and thermally heated rivers in the wilderness or in towns built on **hot springs** (pages 45 and 156).

7 Driving **Going-to-the-Sun Road,** where the journey *is* the destination (page 192).

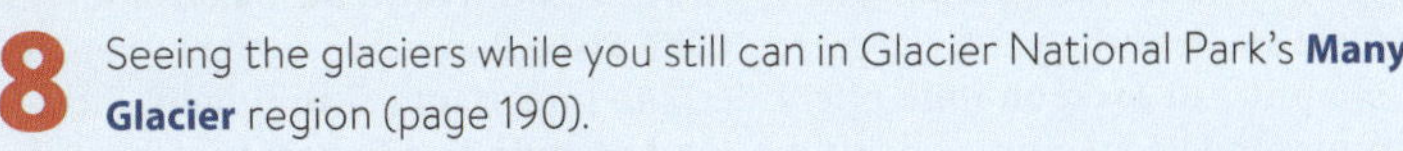

8 Seeing the glaciers while you still can in Glacier National Park's **Many Glacier** region (page 190).

PLANNING YOUR TRIP

Where to Go

Yellowstone National Park

This magnificent and dynamic place was the world's first national park. A natural wonderland, Yellowstone offers a rare and up-close view into one of the last large intact ecosystems in the Northern Hemisphere. See abundant wildlife, including **bison, elk, bears, and wolves;** marvel at geothermal features like **Old Faithful,** or swim in them at the **Boiling River;** hike the peaks, **Mount Washburn** for starters; and stay in historic lodges like the **Old Faithful Inn** and the rambling **Lake Yellowstone Hotel.** Perimeter communities, including **West Yellowstone, Gardiner,** and remote **Cooke City,** should not be missed.

Grand Teton National Park

Grand Teton packs a punch, particularly when it comes to mountain splendor. Twelve peaks in the Teton Range soar above 12,000 ft (3,658 m). And while there are only 152 mi (245 km) of paved roads in the park, there are nearly twice as many miles of **trails,** and more than 1,200 designated **campsites,** leaving hikers endless options for adventure at breathtaking spots like **Hidden Falls** and **Inspiration Point.** Favorite landmarks include picturesque **Jenny Lake,** vast **Jackson Lake,** drive-to-the-summit **Signal Mountain,** and serene **Oxbow Bend;** favorite ways to enjoy the beauty of the region include **hiking, biking,** and **rafting.** Just south of the park, the gateway community of **Jackson Hole** offers ritzy accommodations and a thriving culinary scene.

Rocky Mountain Front

The vast plains erupt into soaring peaks along the Rocky Mountain Front. History comes to life in the heart of **Helena,** in **Last Chance Gulch** and **Reeder's Alley.** Straddling the division between mountains and plains, **Great Falls** boasts two of the state's best museums: the **C. M. Russell Museum** and **Lewis and Clark National Historic Trail Interpretive Center.** Along the winding roads, there's **fishing** to be done, **bird-watching** opportunities, and an outstanding place to learn about **Blackfeet** history and culture.

Glacier National Park

Known as the "Crown of the Continent," Glacier National Park embodies the Montana you've always imagined: rugged mountains piercing the sky, crystalline lakes and plunging waterfalls, abundant wildlife, gravity-defying roads, and miles upon miles of trail. For now, the park still lays claim to 25 **glaciers** and offers excellent viewing opportunities for such wildlife as **mountain goats, bighorn sheep,** and even **grizzly bears.** There are an infinite number of ways to explore and enjoy this stunning landscape, including hiking the **Highline Trail** to **Granite Park Chalet,** picking huckleberries in season, swimming or boating on **Lake McDonald,** biking the twists and turns of the **Going-to-the-Sun Road,** or just relaxing porchside in **Many Glacier.**

Glacier to Bozeman

One of the best things about road trips out West is that the journey truly is just as worthwhile as the destination. This 6-hour drive from Glacier to Bozeman offers up abundant natural beauty—**Jewel Basin, Flathead Lake,** and the **CSKT Bison Range** for starters—plus access to important cultural hubs, including **Missoula** and **Bozeman,** where the arts flourish and excellent restaurants and hotels abound. There are wonderful

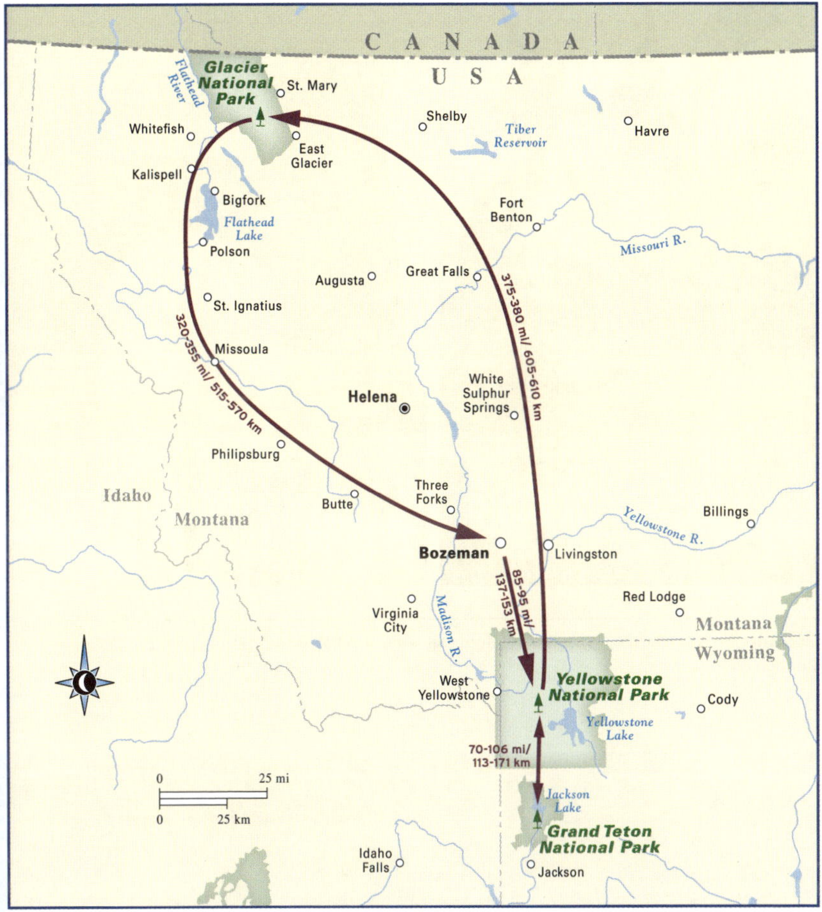

places to get your fill of mining history, including **Butte,** and the living ghost towns of **Virginia City** and **Nevada City.**

When to Go

Summer is the easiest and by far the busiest time to travel the roads, both into and out of the national parks. The roads are mostly open—save for rogue snowstorms that can happen at high elevations—but travel can be slowed by **traffic, animal jams** (particularly in Yellowstone), and **construction.**

Winter road travel can be challenging because of the inevitable storms and possible closures. With the exception of the road in Yellowstone between Gardiner and Cooke City, which stays open year-round for the residents of Cooke City, most of the roads in the three national parks are closed in winter. In Grand Teton National Park, the roads between Jackson and Flagg Ranch (US 89/191 and US 26/287) are plowed and open year-round. Winter travel in Glacier is limited to skis, snowshoes, and the occasional dogsled tour. In Yellowstone, snow coaches and guided snowmobile

Clockwise from top left: summer flowers; Roosevelt Arch at Yellowstone's north entrance; Mormon Row

tours are available when the roads are covered with snow.

The increasingly popular **shoulder seasons** can be a great time to travel in this region. The national parks are colorful and a bit less crowded in **autumn,** but keep in mind that winter comes very early at high elevations. There are also little-known ways to enjoy the parks by bicycle in the **spring,** before they open to cars. And as a bonus, less than half as many people visit the parks in May as do in July. Opening and closing times for the parks can vary by year (weather and federal budget, too), so make sure to check with the parks before you travel.

Before You Go

When it comes to staying in any of the three parks, advance planning is critical. In **Yellowstone,** more than 1 million people visit the park in July, with slightly fewer visiting in June, August, and September. Compare that to right around 45,000 people per month in Yellowstone from December through February. Statistics in **Glacier National Park** are similar, with nearly 800,000 people visiting in July, followed by August, September, and June. Winter numbers in Glacier range from around 20,000 visitors in December to nearly 44,000 in April. Statistical trends vary in **Grand Teton National Park,** with some 772,000 visitors in July, slightly fewer in June and August, and between 50,000-75,000 visitors per month in winter. As such, thoughtful planning and **advance reservations,** particularly for hotels and campgrounds, are essential in summer months. Even in perimeter communities, hotel rooms can be hard to find during peak summer months, especially around local events such as the Fourth of July celebration in Livingston or the Fall Arts Festival in Jackson Hole.

Rates for accommodations are generally lower and rooms more available when snow is on the ground—except around ski areas—but keep in mind that most of the accommodations in the parks are closed during the winter. The exceptions are the Mammoth Hotel and the Old Faithful Snow Lodge, both in Yellowstone.

More and more **campgrounds** in all the parks can (and must) be reserved up to six months in advance. In Yellowstone, 2,000 sites in 11 campgrounds can be reserved through www.yellowstonenationalparklodges.com and www.recreation.gov. In Grand Teton National Park, all park campgrounds must be reserved in advance through www.recreation.gov. In Glacier, 13 front country campgrounds offer more than 1,000 sites, at least some of which are open May to mid-October. With the exceptions of St. Mary and Fish Creek, half the individual and group sites at Apgar, and half the campsites at Many Glacier, all campgrounds are available on a first-come, first-served basis, with nightly fees ranging $10-23. You'll increase your chances of finding a site by showing up earlier in the day and scheduling your trip midweek rather than on the weekend. An excellent page on the National Park Service website (www.nps.gov/glac) shows updated availability at campsites across the park.

For now, there are no limits on the number of visitors allowed into the parks, so you do not need to order **park passes** in advance (although doing so can save you time in the entrance line). In an effort to deal with crowds and the problem of more cars than parking spots, Glacier has implemented a pilot **vehicle reservation program** requiring reservations for some places and roads at specific date ranges and times of day. Entry passes for all three parks are required and can be purchased upon arrival. If you arrive after hours, when rangers are not manning the entrance stations, you can pay when you leave the park.

Top: Teton Mountains and Oxbow Bend of the Snake River **Bottom:** Glacier National Park

Getting There

The most time-efficient way to see all three parks is to fly into **Jackson Hole Airport** (JAC) and see Grand Teton, Yellowstone, and then Glacier before flying out of **Glacier Park International Airport** (GPI) in Kalispell—or vice versa.

However, it's often much less expensive to fly into and out of the same city. In this case, you will have to cover some of the same ground twice. That's not a bad thing out here. You can build a fantastic itinerary around whatever city offers the best airfare.

Besides Jackson Hole, the airports closest to Yellowstone are **Bozeman Yellowstone International Airport** (BZN) and **Billings Logan International Airport** (BIL). After Kalispell, **Great Falls International Airport** (GTF) is closest to Glacier. **Missoula Montana Airport** (MSO) is about midway between Glacier and Yellowstone. **Helena Regional Airport** (HLN) is about 3 hours from Yellowstone and 3.5 hours from Glacier.

Driving Guide

Because the distances between the parks and towns are vast, you will need a private vehicle unless you book an all-inclusive tour. **Rental cars** are available at all of the major airports, with some additional rental agencies having off-airport offices in larger towns. In the busier airports, rental cars can sell out during holidays and peak vacation weeks, so be sure to book ahead. **All-wheel-drive vehicles** are recommended for back-road driving where higher clearance can come in handy. In the winter, all-wheel drive is practically mandatory at high elevations. **RVs** can be rented in most of the major towns including Bozeman, Billings, Missoula, and Kalispell, with both Bozeman and Missoula offering RV rentals from the airports.

While most of the interstates and highways across the region are in good shape, there is often **construction** happening in the snow-free months. Many of the smaller roads into recreation areas are dirt and gravel. There can be significant potholes any time of year, and roads can flood during spring runoff or heavy storms. Always carry a map and emergency supplies of food, water, and winter gear. Drivers should watch for wildlife, particularly at twilight and dark. For Wyoming road conditions, the **Wyoming Department of Transportation** (www.wyoroad.info) has a wealth of information. The Wyoming 511 app can also provide up-to-date road conditions and closures. Montana information can be found through the **Montana Department of Transportation** (800/226-7623 or 511; www.mdt.mt.gov/travinfo).

While most towns have taxi service, only the larger cities have public transportation. If you are planning to travel between cities by bus, check this book's individual town sections for information and consider making arrangements in advance. In Montana, train service is only available across the northern section of the state, known as the Hi-Line.

HIT THE ROAD

The 14-Day Yellowstone to Glacier Road Trip

This ambitious two-week, 1,150-mi (1,852-km) itinerary starts and ends in Bozeman, Montana, taking you through Yellowstone, Grand Teton, and Glacier National Parks. Most days require only 100 mi (161 km) or fewer of driving, so you can see and experience this breathtaking region without feeling stuck behind the wheel. For detailed driving directions for each leg of the trip, see the beginning of each chapter.

Day 1

BOZEMAN

Start your trip in bustling Bozeman, Montana, equal parts tourist hot spot, college town, and outdoors paradise. Fit in a trip to the **Museum of the Rockies** to explore the cultural and natural history of the region, with an emphasis on dinosaurs that roamed here. Throw in a hike up the **M,** just northeast of town, and end with a shopping stroll on historic **Main Street.** Enjoy a game of pool, a local brew, and a hearty meal at the popular **Montana Ale Works.** After a pre-bed ice-cream cone from **Airstream Ice Cream,** bed down for the night at **The Lark,** a hip and artsy hotel.

Day 2

BOZEMAN TO OLD FAITHFUL

120 mi (193 km), 3 hours

Start your morning with a hearty breakfast at **Feed Café** before you head into the **Gallatin Canyon,** toward **Big Sky Resort.** Adrenaline junkies can **raft the Gallatin** with **Montana Whitewater.** Grab a gourmet lunch at Big Sky's **Horn & Cantle** before continuing on to **West Yellowstone** to check out the critters at the **Grizzly and Wolf Discovery Center.**

Make your way into **Yellowstone National Park** and, on a warm day, stop to swim in the geothermally heated water of the **Firehole River.** Leave time to walk around the **Midway and Lower Geyser Basins**—don't miss the colorful **Grand Prismatic Spring**—before arriving at the **Old Faithful Inn** for the night. Make sure to see at least one eruption of its namesake geyser and check out the **Old Faithful Visitor Education Center** before you enjoy a meal in the hotel's lovely dining room and settle in for the night.

Day 3

OLD FAITHFUL TO JACKSON HOLE

100 mi (161 km), 3 hours

After breakfast and perhaps one more eruption of Old Faithful, head south toward **Yellowstone Lake,** stopping to explore the thermal features at **West Thumb Geyser Basin.** Take your time, cruising south through Yellowstone and into **Grand Teton National Park.** Dip your toes in the water, or just enjoy the scenery at various pull-outs.

You could have lunch at Colter Bay and visit the **Colter Bay Visitor Center,** which is home to the Indigenous Arts and Cultural Demonstration Program. Stretch your legs with a 2.2-mi (3.5-km) loop on the **Colter Bay Lakeshore Trail.** Continue on through Moran and down to Moose, where you'll want to get an overview of the park at the **Craig Thomas Discovery & Visitor Center.**

Settle in for three nights at the **Mountain Modern Motel** in Jackson. You're within walking distance to all of downtown and to **The Kitchen,** where you can sit outside and feast on flavorful comfort food with an Asian twist.

Days 4-5

JACKSON HOLE

With three nights in Jackson and two full days, you'll have time to pack in both

TOP EXPERIENCE

Where the Wild Things Are

The most obvious choice for prime wildlife-viewing is Yellowstone National Park, where animals have the right of way; just try telling a herd of migrating or rutting bison that you have to be somewhere. Grand Teton and Glacier National Parks are also great bets, although the restricted roads and dense forests can limit visibility. Still, this is the Wild West, and there are excellent opportunities to see wildlife almost anywhere.

Yellowstone National Park

- The **Lamar Valley** is known as the "Little Serengeti of North America," and for good reason. Time it right and you could see bison, elk, coyotes, foxes, wolves, bears, and even the occasional moose in this grassy, wide-open valley (page 51).
- In summer, the **Hayden Valley** is the gorgeous green stomping ground for hundreds, even thousands of bison. Seeing such big herds is an unforgettable sight (page 52).

Grand Teton National Park

- **Oxbow Bend,** between Moran Junction and Jackson Lake Junction, is an excellent place to look for moose, deer, birdlife, and the occasional bear. Dusk and dawn are the best times of day to see wildlife (page 107).
- Just outside Jackson, and south of the park, the **National Elk Refuge** is home to anywhere between 5,000-11,000 elk throughout the year (page 131).
- In Dubois, the **National Bighorn Sheep Interpretive Center** offers winter tours of the nearby Whiskey Mountain Habitat Area. Self-guided tours take visitors into prime sheep country, where raptors and moose can often be seen (page 132).

Glacier National Park

- Hikers on the **Grinnell Glacier Trail** often get a chance to see bighorn sheep, mountain goats, and the occasional moose (page 197).
- The trails to **Iceberg Lake** and **Avalanche Lake** are among the best spots in Glacier to look for grizzly bears in May and June. Mountain goats can also be spotted (pages 198 and 200).

Glacier to Bozeman

- In the **Jewel Basin,** there are 17 species of raptors. Hikers often see mountain goats and even grizzlies, especially during huckleberry season (page 233).
- Near St. Ignatius, the **CSKT Bison Range** is home to around 400 bison, along with white-tailed and mule deer, bighorn sheep, pronghorn antelope, and elk (page 244).

Clockwise from top left: Mammoth Hot Springs Terraces; Glacier's Iceberg Lake; a bike tour in Grand Teton National Park

culture and adventure. Make sure to visit **Town Square** for shopping, dining, or the **Jackson Hole Shootout.** Perhaps the first morning you could explore the **National Museum of Wildlife Art** before embarking on a white-water rafting adventure on the **Snake River** or taking the **aerial tram** up the mountain at **Teton Village** to take in the view or indulge in a waffle from **Corbet's Cabin.** Save just enough room and energy for an excellent meal in Jackson at **Wild Sage** if you're feeling fancy, or **The Merry Piglets** if you're not.

The next morning, pick up a picnic lunch at **Persephone Bakery** and plan to spend your second day back in Grand Teton National Park. Visit the **Chapel of the Transfiguration** and the historic buildings at **Menors Ferry** before you head to **Jenny Lake** for a picnic and a hike to **Hidden Falls and Inspiration Point.** Before you return to Jackson for another night on the town, you could take a tour of the **Murie Ranch** or visit the **Laurance S. Rockefeller Preserve.**

Day 6

JACKSON HOLE TO LAKE LODGE

65 mi (105 km), 2 hours

You can hit **The Bunnery** on your way out of town, heading north past **Antelope Flats** and **Mormon Row** to **Signal Mountain.** Drive to the top for a magnificent view or hike it if you want. Make a stop at **Oxbow Bend** to look for wildlife.

For a real treat, plan a **lunch cruise** from Colter Bay Marina to Elk Island, and then keep heading north and back into Yellowstone. From the Bridge Bay Marina, hike the 2.6 mi (4.2 km) roundtrip to **Natural Bridge,** but keep an eye open for grizzlies. Settle in for the night at **Lake Lodge** and enjoy dinner in the beautiful dining room overlooking the lake.

Day 7

LAKE LODGE TO PARADISE VALLEY

55 mi (89 km), 2 hours

After breakfast, make your way to the **Fishing Bridge Visitor Center** for a great exhibit on Yellowstone Lake's geology. Take a picture of the old bridge itself, which used to be one of the best fishing spots in the park. Head north into the wide-open **Hayden Valley,** where hundreds of bison can congregate in summer. Keep driving to the **Grand Canyon of the Yellowstone** and take in the scenic views. From there, plan on lunch and maybe an afternoon trail ride at **Roosevelt Lodge.**

From Roosevelt, continue north to **Mammoth Hot Springs** for a stroll around the boardwalks. When you exit the park, head to **Chico Hot Springs** for the night where you can soak, dine, and sleep to your heart's content.

Day 8

PARADISE VALLEY TO GREAT FALLS

234 mi (377 km), 3 hours 45 minutes

After a big breakfast and a morning dip at Chico, drive north to the hip, artsy town of **Livingston,** where you can browse galleries and shop until you work up an appetite for lunch at **Gil's Goods.** From there, head west on I-90 through **Bozeman** to US 287 North past Canyon Ferry Lake to **Helena.** Wander down Last Chance Gulch and get a cone at **Big Dipper.** From Helena, push north on I-15 past **Gates of the Mountains** to **Great Falls,** where you can have dinner at **The Union** before checking into the **O'Haire Motor Inn** and, if you have a bit more energy, watching the mermaid show at the hotel's one-of-a-kind **Sip-N-Dip** tiki lounge.

Day 9

GREAT FALLS TO EAST GLACIER

140 mi (225 km), 2.5 hours

Decide between art and history when you choose a morning at either the **C. M. Russell Museum** or the **Lewis and Clark National Historic Trail Interpretive Center**—you can't go wrong at either place. From Great Falls, make your way northwest on US 89 past Freezeout Lake and Choteau.

Arrive in Browning in time for a **Blackfeet Tour,** which can include a visit to the **Museum of the Plains Indian.** After the tour, pile back in the car and head toward East Glacier. Arrive in time for a juicy steak and a comfy bed with a view at the **Summit Mountain Lodge.**

Day 10

EAST GLACIER TO MANY GLACIER

60 mi (97 km), 1.5 hour

Fuel up with a big breakfast in town at the **Two Medicine Grill.** It's worth ambling the grounds of the stately Glacier Park Lodge before you drive north. As you head toward the park, you could stop for some recreation in the isolated **Two Medicine Valley:** Consider taking a 45-minute cruise on Two Medicine Lake, cutting 6 mi (9.7 km) off the hike to **Twin Falls.** Or continue farther north to **St. Mary** where cruises and cruise-hike combos are also available. You'll end up at the storied **Many Glacier Hotel,** where you can order bison tenderloin or wild mushroom stroganoff in the **Ptarmigan Dining Room,** serving French-American cuisine and considered to be the most elegant restaurant in the park.

Day 11

MANY GLACIER

Plan to spend the day adventuring around Many Glacier. Possible activities include an endless number of **hiking trails** and canoeing, kayaking, or cruising on **Swiftcurrent Lake.** One option is to combine a scenic cruise with a hike to **Grinnell Glacier.** The **Swiftcurrent Valley and Lookout** hike is a favorite and can last as long as your legs do. Other options include **ranger-led hikes** and **Red Bus Tours.**

Day 12

MANY GLACIER TO LAKE MCDONALD

65 mi (105 km), 3 hours

You'll head out of the park at Many Glacier and back in again at St. Mary to go up and over the magnificent **Going-to-the-Sun Road,** the drive you've been waiting for the entire trip, and maybe your whole life. Take the time to park at Logan Pass and take a hike—the **Highline Trail** is extraordinary.

Head down the pass for a refreshing dip in **Lake McDonald** and have a late lunch at **Russell's Fireside Dining Room** at **Lake McDonald Lodge.** In the afternoon, consider another short hike—**Rocky Point** is good; so is **Trail of the Cedars** and **Avalanche Creek Trail to Avalanche Lake**—or take a sunset cocktail cruise on a historic wooden boat. You've earned your time to relax and enjoy this place. If you have the energy to leave your hotel, a gourmet dinner at **Belton Chalet** will not disappoint.

Day 13

LAKE MCDONALD TO WHITEFISH

50 mi (81 km), 1 hour

Take your time getting out of the park—you're going to miss this place. Take a morning hike or a dip in the lake. It's okay to backtrack here and repeat your favorite hike. When it's time, travel through West Glacier and on to the resort town of **Whitefish,** where you can do a little shopping and settle in for the night at the **Garden Wall Inn** after dinner in town at **Wasabi Sushi Bar.**

Day 14

WHITEFISH TO BOZEMAN

320 mi (515 km), 6 hours

The longest day by far, there is a lot of ground to cover between Whitefish and Bozeman. Whatever your plan, you'll want to fuel up with a pie and lunch to go from **Loula's Café.** Head south to **Bigfork** and have a picnic on one of the lovely beaches that line **Flathead Lake.**

Drive through the **CSKT Bison Range** en route to Missoula, where you can stretch your legs on the riverside trail and grab coffee and a pastry at **Le Petit Outre.** From here, it's all highway driving east through Butte and on to Bozeman. You might stop in Three Forks for a hike at **Madison Buffalo Jump State Park.** By the time you roll into Bozeman, you'll be

Best Hikes

The best way to see the parks, and to really know them, is to get out and hike. Explore the wilderness. Climb the mountains. Run your fingertips along the bark of trees. Feel the whisper of high grasses on your legs. Earn the best view you've ever seen.

Glacier's Highline Trail

Yellowstone National Park

- Overlooking the vast Lamar Valley, **Specimen Ridge** is a strenuous 3-mi (4.8-km) round-trip trail that leads hikers to one of the largest petrified forests in the world, with fossils dating back 50 million years. It's a steep climb, but the views of the valley from the top are well worth the effort, particularly when there are bison in residence (page 62).
- Among the geysers in the Upper Geyser Basin is **Lone Star Geyser,** named for its lonely location about 5 mi (8 km) from Old Faithful. An old once-paved road leads to the geyser and makes a nice, level 5.3-mi (8.5-km) round-trip hike or bike trip. Lucky viewers will get to see a 30-50-ft (9-15-m) eruption, which happens every 3 hours or so and can last up to 30 minutes (page 63).

Grand Teton National Park

- The **Taggart Lake-Bradley Lake Loop** takes hikers to two glacially formed lakes at the base of the Tetons. With only 890 ft (262 m) of elevation gained over 5.6 miles (9 km), this moderate trail along water and through forest offers views of Nez Perce Peak, Middle and Grand Tetons, and Teewinot Mountain (page 114).
- **Hidden Falls Trail** offers the best of the park—access to Jenny Lake, pristine conifer forests, rushing creeks, soaring alpine views, and a chance to encounter wildlife. The moderately challenging trail is 4.9 mi (7.9 km), but can be shortened to 1 mi (1.6 km) by taking the shuttle across Jenny Lake (page 115).

Glacier National Park

- The **Highline Trail** is popular for good reason. Best in midsummer when the wildflowers explode with color, the shorter version of this strenuous hike climbs a total of 1,950 ft (594 m) over 11.4 mi (18.3km) from Logan Pass to Granite Park Chalet and on to the Loop and offers outstanding scenery, including a stretch along the Garden Wall, a ledge that will delight thrill seekers (page 200).
- A short and easy hike through alpine meadows known as the Hanging Gardens, the **Hidden Lake Overlook Trail,** also known as the Hidden Lake Nature Trail, offers extraordinary views of Clements Mountain, the Garden Wall, and Mount Oberlin. The 2.7-mi (4.3-km) round-trip trail crosses the Continental Divide and is often snow-covered, even in midsummer (page 202).

Clockwise from top left: Flathead Lake; Madison Buffalo Jump State Park; CSKT Bison Range

ready for a last big meal at **Montana Ale Works** and a comfy bed for the night at **The Lark.**

Indigenous Heritage

The culture and history of Indigenous people have powerfully defined the identities of both Montana and Wyoming. There are eight reservations between the two states, but only two of them lie close to the parks. The **Blackfeet Reservation** is just east of Glacier, and the **Flathead Reservation** is southwest of Glacier. But you don't have to be on a reservation to be exposed to Native American history and culture here. This region offers tremendous opportunities for those interested in learning about and experiencing Indigenous history, traditions, and contemporary culture. Here are just a few of the ways to engage with Indigenous culture.

National Park Attractions and Programs

In Grand Teton and set on Jackson Lake, the unassuming **Colter Bay Visitor Center** is home to the **Indigenous Arts and Cultural Demonstration,** where visitors can see various exhibits and meet the artists from mid-May to late September. Media include painting, weaving, pottery, beadwork, musical instruments, and more. Most Saturday nights at 7pm, visiting artists will give lectures and demonstrations at the Colter Bay Amphitheater.

One of the most noteworthy programs in Glacier National Park is **Native America Speaks,** where members from the Blackfeet, Salish, Kootenai, and Pend d'Oreille tribes provide campfire talks about their life, culture, and influence in Glacier. The speakers range from artists and musicians to historians who intersperse their talks with personal stories and Native American legends. These talks are given at the Apgar, Many Glacier, Two Medicine, and Rising Sun Campgrounds. During July-August, the St. Mary Visitor Center also hosts weekly Indigenous dance troupes.

Buffalo Jumps

Used by Native Americans for more than 5,000 years, buffalo jumps are rocky cliffs over which entire herds of bison were driven, causing mortal injury to the animals and providing the hunters with ample meat, fur, and bones to make into weapons, tools, and decorative objects. The jumps have become significant archaeological sites, with discoveries of bones and tools guiding scientists to a better understanding of the various cultures of people who hunted in this way. They can also be places of quiet contemplation.

Two of the most well-known buffalo jumps in the region can be found outside Bozeman and Great Falls. The **First Peoples Buffalo Jump State Park** in Ulm was used for more than 1,000 years before Lewis and Clark arrived in the area. The site, a mile-long sandstone cliff, is magnificent. Various buildings interpret the history and culture around the jump itself. Overlooking the Madison River between Bozeman and Three Forks, the **Madison Buffalo Jump State Park** was in use 2,000 years ago, and as recently as 200 years ago. Not nearly as large as the jump in Ulm, and with only a small outdoor interpretive display, this site boasts original tipi rings and the remains of eagle-catching pits. Both sites are beautiful and meaningful places to spend an afternoon.

Guided Tours

A fascinating way to learn about Blackfeet culture is by traveling with local Native guides who can interpret Native history and culture and the ways they have shaped and influenced the region. **Blackfeet Tours** offer guided tours around Great Falls—including the First People's Buffalo Jump—in the Badger-Two Medicine National Forest, on the

Best Non-Hikes

Because your legs can only take you so far, here are the top ways to spend an afternoon without putting miles on your feet.

A wrangler leads the way at a Wyoming guest ranch.

Yellowstone National Park

- No organization in the park helps people understand the wonder of nature better than the **Yellowstone Forever Institute,** with whom you can go on expert-led excursions, from day-long adventures to multiday vacations (page 44).
- Of the park's thousands of thermal features, only two are swimmable. The **Boiling River** (page 45) is a worthy adventure year-round, and the **Firehole River** (page 56) near Madison Junction is an ideal place to spend a warm summer afternoon.
- The **Old West Dinner Cookout** takes diners by horseback or covered wagon into Yellowstone's wilderness for a steak-and-potato dinner with all the fixings (page 71).

Grand Teton National Park

- The best way to get out and see wildlife is to go with someone who knows, and no one knows better than the **Wildlife Expeditions** guides from **Teton Science Schools.** The half-day, full-day, or multiday trips are guided by wildlife biologists (page 104).
- Leaving from Colter Bay Marina, the 3-hour **meal cruises** are a relaxing way to get out on the water and explore **Elk Island** (page 106).
- Whether it's a scenic sunrise float or a white-knuckle ride through such rapids as Lunch Counter and the Big Kahuna, there are many ways to get on the **Snake River** (page 133).

Glacier National Park

- Glacier's famed **Red Bus Tours** are the best way to see the park from the road without worrying about the driving (page 188).
- No matter what interests you—wolves, birds of prey, wildflowers, fly-fishing, photography—the **Glacier Institute** probably offers a class on it. There are amazing offerings for both kids and adults (page 188).
- Between late May and mid-September, **horseback rides** are available from the corrals at **Apgar, Lake McDonald,** and **Many Glacier.** Trail rides are an excellent way to get up into the high country (page 205).

Blackfeet Reservation, and in Glacier. From a fancy air-conditioned bus to a trusty steed, from half-day to multiday, there are options aplenty.

A number of tribes—including Cheyenne, Kiowa, Shoshone, Bannock, Blackfeet, Nez Perce, and Crow—have ancestral stories about Yellowstone, which was also called "The Place of Yellow Rock Water," that go back more than 10,000 years. Through **Go Native America** travelers can book two different Yellowstone day trips led by Indigenous guides that focus on the grizzly bear or wolf, and the prominence of both animals in Native culture.

A unique way to see Glacier on a comfortable coach tour is with **Sun Tours.** Its guides are all lifetime residents of the Blackfeet Reservation and provide outstanding narratives on everything from park history and wildlife information to medicinal plants and Blackfeet spiritual perspectives.

Museums

The best Native American museum in the region is the **Museum of the Plains Indian,** in Browning, on the Blackfeet Reservation. The museum exhibits the arts and crafts of the Northern Plains Indians. The permanent collection highlights the diversity of tribal arts and displays artifacts from everyday life, including clothing, weapons, toys, and household implements. Two galleries are dedicated to showcasing contemporary Native American artists. During summer, painted tipis are assembled on the grounds. Although it is not dedicated to Native American culture and history, the **Lewis and Clark National Historic Trail Interpretive Center** does a good job of portraying the importance of Indigenous people to the westward journey.

Flathead and Blackfeet Indian Reservations

One way to experience the tribal lands firsthand is by attending traditional celebrations open to the public. On the Flathead Indian Reservation, annual events include the **Arlee Celebration** and the **Standing Arrow Powwow,** which happens in mid-July at the Elmo Powwow Grounds in Elmo, Montana. In Pablo, Montana, **The Three Chiefs Culture Center** is a museum and gift shop where visitors can experience the cultural heritage of the Salish, Pend d'Oreille, and Kootenai tribes. Also on the Flathead Reservation, the **St. Ignatius Mission** tells a much darker story of abuse and betrayal of Native children taken from their families to be educated at the mission.

On the Blackfeet Indian Reservation, annual powwow celebrations include the **North American Indian Days,** held in Browning the second week in July for four days, and the **Heart Butte Society Celebration,** held over four days the second week of August in Heart Butte, 26 mi (42 km) south of Browning. Both events are open to the public and include contest dancing and drumming, games, sporting events, ceremonies, and plenty of food. Also on the reservation is the important **Museum of the Plains Indian,** which should not be missed by anyone interested in Native American culture and history.

Yellowstone to Glacier: The Fast Route on the Back Roads

Philosopher Simone Weil said it best, and most beautifully—"Attention, taken to its highest degree, is the same thing as prayer." I would argue vociferously that you cannot pay generous attention to anything going 80 mph (129 km/h) for long stretches of time. Slow down. That's the best advice I can offer you. This place is magic mostly because of its timelessness—eons-old geology, flora and fauna that have been here since time immemorial, and culture too that predates the arrival of European immigrants. So if you can give yourself some time and space to really see it, to appreciate it, you won't be sorry.

Still, this is the 21st century and hurried is the way we do most things. If you only have a few days, and want to fit both Yellowstone and Glacier into a short trip, there are a few ways of covering the ground between the parks.

St. Mary to Gardiner via the Rocky Mountain Front

378 MI (608 KM), 6.5 HOURS

The shortest and usually fastest route from St. Mary on Glacier's west side to the northern entrance of Yellowstone at Gardiner follows Highway 89 south along the dramatic Rocky Mountain Front through open ranch country, small towns, and then—via Highway 287—the cities of Helena and Bozeman. From St. Mary, travelers could stop in Browning at the **Museum of the Plains Indian** before heading on through tiny communities including Piegan, Dupuyer, and blink-and-you-miss it Pendroy. Stop for lunch in **Helena** before continuing along through to **Bozeman,** where there are museums and shopping galore. From Bozeman, take Highway 90 east to **Livingston,** then Highway 89 south through **Paradise Valley**—you might love a gourmet meal and a soak at **Chico Hot Springs**—before arriving at the north entrance to Yellowstone National Park in Gardiner.

West Glacier to West Yellowstone via Seeley-Swan Valley

388 MI (624 KM), 6 HOURS 45 MINUTES

From the west side of Glacier to the west entrance of Yellowstone, the shortest route also happens to be incredibly scenic and mostly on single-lane highways through towering mountains, dense evergreen forests, and open ranch land. From West Glacier, head southwest on Highway 2 to Columbia Falls, where you'll go south on Montana Highway 206 to 35, which will bring you to the edge of **Flathead Lake** and the resort town of **Bigfork.** From there, you'll drive east on 209 to 83, which takes you down through the **Seeley-Swan Valley** nestled in the evergreen forest between two impressive mountain ranges. If you can, have lunch or a quick dip at the **Holland Lake Lodge.** Continue south and east on 141 and US 90 through Avon, Garrison, and **Deer Lodge** to **Butte,** which offer fun restaurants and fantastic sightseeing including the **World Museum of Mining.** Take 287 South, along the Tobacco Root Mountains, to Ennis and on to West Yellowstone. There are mountain ranges along the way and only one stretch of freeway between Garrison and Cardwell.

Yellowstone
National
Park

Highlights

★ **Soaking in the Boiling River:** In a stretch of the Gardner River at the park's north entrance, hot water flows over waterfalls and via springs, mixing with the river water to create a perfect soaking temperature (page 45).

★ **Mammoth and the Mammoth Hot Springs Terraces:** The travertine terraces here look like an enormous cream-colored confection. Because the springs shift and change daily, a walk around the colorful terraces is never the same experience twice (page 45).

★ **Grand Canyon of the Yellowstone:** The sheer cliffs and dramatic coloring of this canyon have inspired millions of visitors. In the summer, get a rare bird's-eye view of several osprey nests (page 47).

★ **Watching the Wolves:** The wolves put on a spectacular show—with at least one reported sighting daily since 2001. The sagas of the 11 packs are dramatic, heart-wrenching, and captivating (page 49).

★ **Lamar Valley:** Known as the "Little Serengeti of North America," this scenic, glacially carved valley offers spectacular wildlife-watching year-round (page 51).

★ **Fly-Fishing in Slough Creek:** Yellowstone is a fishing paradise. Join other eager anglers as they cast dry flies for cutthroat trout in Slough Creek (page 51).

★ **Yellowstone Lake:** This beautiful lake was touted by early mountain men as perhaps the only place where you could catch a fish and cook it without ever taking it off the line (page 52).

★ **Old Faithful:** One of nearly 500 geysers in the park, and undoubtedly the most famous, this natural wonder erupts every 45-90 minutes (page 55).

★ **Swimming the Firehole River:** This river offers a stunning, heated swimming area surrounded by cliffs. The twists and turns of the cascading canyon are worth seeing even if you don't get wet (page 56).

★ **Hiking Mount Washburn:** Take one of two trails to reach the lookout tower at the summit of Mount Washburn. The views along the way and from the top are worth every step (page 58).

Yellowstone National Park is at the heart of our country's relationship with wilderness. It's also one of the largest nearly intact temperate-zone ecosystems on earth, and many of the species that have roamed this plateau are still (or once again) in residence.

Yellowstone was our nation's first national park. Signed into being in 1872 by President Ulysses S. Grant after a series of important and legendary scouting expeditions through the area, the region's history is lengthy and very much alive, from its prehistoric volcanic eruptions, to its occupation by the US Army in the 1880s, to the controversial reintroduction of wolves in the 1990s and the more recent snowmobile usage, bison, and grizzly delisting quagmires. The stories, both far-fetched and true, and characters that have emerged from the park are as colorful and compelling as the landscape itself.

A vast 2.2 million acres (890,000 ha), Yellowstone is indeed a wonderland, filled with steaming geysers and boiling mud pots, packed with diverse and healthy populations of wildlife, and crisscrossed by hundreds of miles of hiking and ski trails. A stretch of the park called the Lamar Valley is known as the "Little Serengeti of North America," and for good reason: At certain times of the year, in a single day, visitors can spot grizzly and black bears, moose, wolves, bison, elk, coyotes, bald eagles, and the occasional bighorn sheep or mountain goat. In fact, the opportunities for viewing wildlife in the park are unparalleled anywhere in the United States, and although Yellowstone may not be as picturesque as Glacier or the Tetons, it is magnificent in its wildness and uniquely American.

Seeing Yellowstone from the back of a cramped station wagon—or these days, a decked-out Winnebago—is almost a rite of passage in this country. What parent doesn't dream of hauling their children to see Old Faithful erupt or to catch a glimpse of a grizzly bear? And what kid doesn't want to swim in the Boiling River or lie awake in a sleeping bag, listening to the howl of coyotes? It is not exactly the last frontier it once was—there are convenience stores, beautiful old hotels, and even places to get a decent latte—but Yellowstone still occupies its own corner of our national imagination; classified somewhere between American wilderness and family vacations, it conjures foggy but perfect memories.

Getting to Yellowstone National Park

Keep in mind that while distances through the park may seem short in actual mileage, your drive time is often extended by lower speed limits, traffic congestion, and animal jams. In addition, most of the park roads are **closed in winter.** Flood damage can also impact access to the park.

Driving from Bozeman

North Entrance: 85 mi (137 km); 1.5 hours

From Bozeman to the park's north entrance at Gardiner is 85 mi (137 km) east on I-90 and south on US 89, a 90-minute drive.

West Entrance: 95 mi (153 km); 2 hours

It takes just under 2 hours to drive the 95 mi (153 km) south from Bozeman to the west entrance at West Yellowstone on the winding, two-lane US 191.

Driving from Jackson, Wyoming

50 mi (81 km); 1 hour

From the **Jackson Hole airport,** Yellowstone's south entrance, which borders Grand Teton National Park, is 50 mi (81 km) north on US 191, a 1-hour drive.

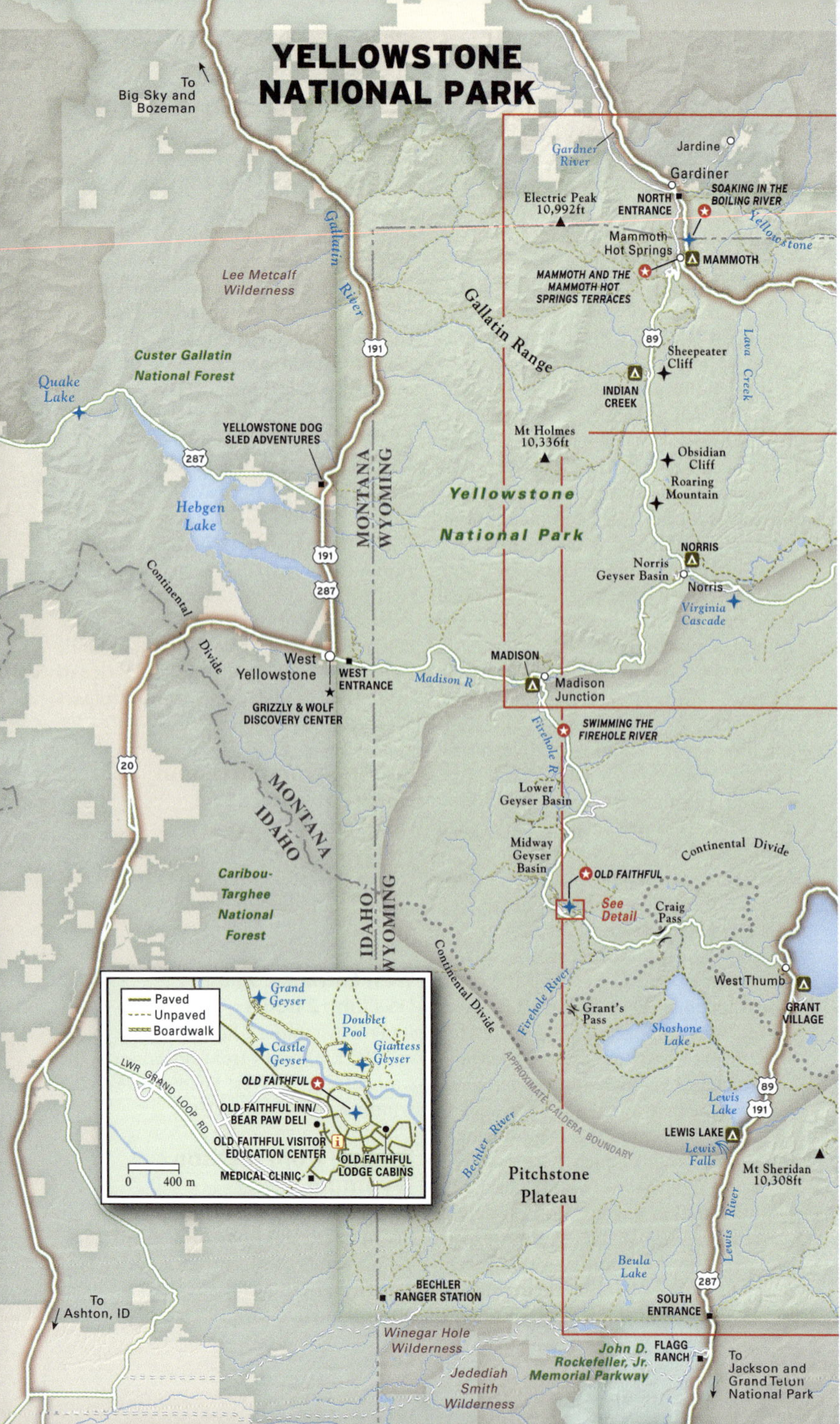
YELLOWSTONE NATIONAL PARK
To Big Sky and Bozeman
Gardner River
Jardine
Gardiner
Electric Peak 10,992ft
NORTH ENTRANCE
SOAKING IN THE BOILING RIVER
Yellowstone
Mammoth Hot Springs
MAMMOTH
MAMMOTH AND THE MAMMOTH HOT SPRINGS TERRACES
Gallatin River
Lee Metcalf Wilderness
Gallatin Range
Sheepeater Cliff
Lava Creek
INDIAN CREEK
Custer Gallatin National Forest
Quake Lake
YELLOWSTONE DOG SLED ADVENTURES
Mt Holmes 10,336ft
Obsidian Cliff
Roaring Mountain
Hebgen Lake
MONTANA
WYOMING
Yellowstone National Park
NORRIS
Norris Geyser Basin
Norris
Virginia Cascade
Continental Divide
West Yellowstone
WEST ENTRANCE
MADISON
Madison R
Madison Junction
GRIZZLY & WOLF DISCOVERY CENTER
SWIMMING THE FIREHOLE RIVER
Firehole R
MONTANA
IDAHO
Lower Geyser Basin
Midway Geyser Basin
Continental Divide
OLD FAITHFUL
See Detail
Craig Pass
Caribou-Targhee National Forest
IDAHO
WYOMING
West Thumb
GRANT VILLAGE
Firehole River
Grant's Pass
Shoshone Lake
Continental Divide
APPROXIMATE CALDERA BOUNDARY
Paved
Unpaved
Boardwalk
Grand Geyser
Doublet Pool
Castle Geyser
Giantess Geyser
LWR GRAND LOOP RD
OLD FAITHFUL
OLD FAITHFUL INN/ BEAR PAW DELI
OLD FAITHFUL VISITOR EDUCATION CENTER
OLD FAITHFUL LODGE CABINS
MEDICAL CLINIC
0
400 m
Lewis Lake
LEWIS LAKE
Lewis Falls
Mt Sheridan 10,308ft
Bechler River
Pitchstone Plateau
Lewis River
Beula Lake
To Ashton, ID
BECHLER RANGER STATION
SOUTH ENTRANCE
Winegar Hole Wilderness
John D. Rockefeller, Jr. Memorial Parkway
FLAGG RANCH
Jedediah Smith Wilderness
To Jackson and Grand Teton National Park
191
287
89
20

See "The Northern Loop" Map
Absaroka-Beartooth Wilderness
MONTANA
North Absaroka Wilderness
Cooke City
COLTER
NORTHEAST ENTRANCE
Silver Gate
212
Slough Creek
FLY-FISHING IN SLOUGH CREEK
River
Abiathar Peak 10,928ft
FOX CREEK
BEARTOOTH HWY
To Red Lodge
Petrified Tree
Tower Junction
SLOUGH CREEK
PEBBLE CREEK
212
YELLOWSTONE INSTITUTE
WYOMING
ROOSEVELT LODGE
Tower Fall
TOWER FALL
Specimen Ridge Trail
The Thunderer 10,554ft
296
CHIEF JOSEPH SCENIC HWY
LAMAR VALLEY
WATCHING THE WOLVES
Mount Washburn 10,243ft
HIKING MOUNT WASHBURN
Lamar Valley
Shoshone National Forest
North Absaroka Wilderness
Dunraven Pass 8,859ft
Mirror Plateau
Lamar River
Canyon Village
APPROXIMATE CALDERA BOUNDARY
GRAND CANYON OF THE YELLOWSTONE
Lower Falls
Howard Eaton Trail
Hayden Valley
Pelican Cone
Valley
Absaroka Range
Mud Volcano
Lehardy Rapids
Pelican
FISHING BRIDGE RV PARK
Elephant Back Mtn
See "The Southern Loop" Map
Lake Village
Lake Butte
BRIDGE BAY
BRIDGE BAY MARINA
Avalanche Peak 10,566ft
EAST ENTRANCE
To Cody
YELLOWSTONE LAKE
Sylvan Pass 8,530ft
14 16 20
Shoshone National Forest
Frank Island
Mt Doane 10,352ft
Mt Langford 10,774ft
Mount Stevenson 10,352ft
Washakie Wilderness
Southeast Arm
South Arm
The Promontory
Yellowstone National Park
Eagle Peak 11,358ft
Eagle Pass
Table Mountain 11,063ft
Heart Lake
Overlook Mountain 9,321ft
Two Ocean Plateau
Yellowstone River
0 10 mi
0 10 km
Snake River
Continental Divide
Road Trip Route
Teton Wilderness

Two Days in Yellowstone

Day 1

Start your whirlwind tour at the park's north entrance with a sunrise swim in **Boiling River** before the crowds descend. Then, on your way to the famed **Lamar Valley,** stop at the **Albright Visitor Center** in Mammoth for a quick park history lesson and a chance to find out from rangers about recent wildlife sightings. Wind your way through the Lamar, known as the "Little Serengeti of North America" for its abundant and diverse wildlife. Stretch your legs on a short but beautiful hike at **Trout Lake.**

Watch for bears, wolves, bighorn sheep, and mountain goats as you continue on to **Cooke City,** just outside the park's northeast entrance. Stop for lunch at the **Beartooth Café.** After lunch, retrace your route through the Lamar to Tower Junction, where you'll head south through the broad Hayden Valley to the **Grand Canyon of the Yellowstone.** Stop for ice cream and a fascinating exhibit on Yellowstone's volcanic eruptions at the **Canyon Visitor Center** before you hit one of the trails for an outstanding view of the canyon.

After your hike, make your way south to Fishing Bridge and settle in for the night at **Lake Hotel** with a cocktail on the porch and a gourmet dinner in the dining room.

Day 2

After a big breakfast, plan a scenic cruise or guided kayak tour on **Yellowstone Lake** before you hit the road for **West Thumb Geyser Basin.** Give yourself at least 30 minutes to stroll around the boardwalk and see the unique geothermal features. From there, make your way up the west side of the park to **Old Faithful,** where you can have lunch in the historic **Old Faithful Inn Dining Room** and walk through the geyser basin while you wait for one of the famed eruptions.

After lunch, head north to the **Firehole River** for a swim in the rocky canyon. Then continue north to explore both **Norris Geyser Basin** and the **Mammoth Hot Springs Terraces** before exiting the park at Gardiner and settling in for the night at **Chico Hot Springs.**

Driving from Glacier National Park

375-420 mi (605-676 km); 6-7.5 hours

The fastest route from Glacier Park's east entrance at **St. Mary** to **Gardiner,** the north entrance of Yellowstone, travels south on US 89 and US 287 for 375 mi (605 km) and should take just over 6 hours. The drive goes along the Rocky Mountain Front through Choteau, Augusta, Helena, and Bozeman. Just a few miles longer, the southbound route through Great Falls, White Sulphur Springs, and Livingston on US 89 is 380 mi (610 km), and should be a drive of 6 hours 20 minutes. This route also takes you to Gardiner.

From **West Glacier,** you can drive to Gardiner via US 93 South and I-90 East. The drive is roughly 420 mi (675 km) and will take approximately 7.5 hours without stops. The route takes you through Kalispell, Polson, Missoula, Butte, Bozeman, and Livingston.

From the west side of Glacier, it's also possible to take a route through the **Seeley-Swan Valley** to reach Gardiner. The drive follows MT-83 South (southeast of Kalispell), MT-141, US 12 East, US 287 South, I-90 East, and then US 89 South for a total of 395 mi (635 km) and will take roughly 7 hours.

Driving from Billings

125-175 mi (201-280 km); 3-3.5 hours

From the airport in Billings to the park's north entrance at **Gardiner** is 175 mi (280 km) southwest on I-90 West and US 89 South, a 3-hour drive.

The 125-mi (201-km), 3.5-hour drive from Billings through Red Lodge and over the **Beartooth Scenic Highway** (only open in summer) to the park's northeast entrance just beyond Cooke City travels via I-90 West and US 212 West.

Bus and Shuttle

Shuttle service with **Karst Stage** (800/845-2778, www.karststage.com) is available from Bozeman to West Yellowstone in winter ($120 pp one-way, $215 pp round-trip). In the summer, Karst offers day trips to Yellowstone for $190 per person with a four-person minimum. Private coaches (10-11 passengers, from $739/day) can also be arranged through Karst.

Air

The **Yellowstone Airport** (WYS; 607 Airport Rd., West Yellowstone; 406/646-7631; www.yellowstoneairport.org) is served by Delta with regular service to Salt Lake City, and is only open late May to late September.

Visiting Yellowstone National Park

Planning Your Time

One could quite literally spend a lifetime in Yellowstone without being able to cover every last corner of this magnificent wilderness, but the reality is that most visitors only have a couple of days, at best, to spend exploring the park. Something like 98 percent of visitors never get more than a mile from the road, but it's easier than you might think—and incredibly worthwhile. Three days in the park is ideal, but if you have less time, there are ways to maximize every minute.

One important consideration in planning your time in Yellowstone is to know the season you'll be traveling. Summer offers magnificent scenery, usually good weather, and the inevitable "bear jam," when drivers hit the brakes as soon as someone spots anything resembling a brown furry creature. Summer visitors to Yellowstone need to plan for traffic and often for road construction delays. Fall and spring are fantastic times to see wildlife, but the weather can change in a heartbeat—at Yellowstone's high elevation, blizzards can strike nearly any month of the year. Winter is a magical time in the park, but cars are only permitted on one road in the northeast corner. All other travel is done via snow coach, guided snowmobile tour, or on skis and snowshoes. There is no wrong time to visit the park, but knowing the advantages and disadvantages of the various seasons will help you manage your expectations.

Assuming you'll be in Yellowstone when the roads are open to car traffic, there are five entrances and exits to Yellowstone, making loop trips relatively easy. From Montana, you can enter or exit the park from the northeast at Cooke City, from the north at Gardiner, or from the west at West Yellowstone. From Wyoming, you can enter the park from the east entrance nearest Cody or from the south through Grand Teton National Park. If you're going from one state to the next, there is no more spectacular route than through the heart of Yellowstone.

A cursory glance at a Yellowstone map will reveal the main roads, which form a figure eight in the heart of the park, and the access roads leading to and from the entrances. The majority of the park's big-name highlights—**Old Faithful, West Thumb Geyser Basin, Fishing Bridge, Grand Canyon of the Yellowstone, Norris and Mammoth Geyser Basins**—are accessible from the main loops. Depending on your time and your plan for accommodations, you could easily spend a full day driving each of the two loops. A third day would permit an opportunity for deeper exploration—perhaps a hike—and a leisurely exit from the park.

If time won't permit even one night in the park, it is still well worth driving

Best Restaurants

★ **Old West Dinner Cookout, Northern Loop:** Accessed from the Roosevelt Lodge by either horseback or covered wagon, this steak-and-potatoes dinner in the wilds of Yellowstone is an unforgettable experience (page 71).

★ **Lake Yellowstone Hotel Dining Room, Southern Loop:** The dining room at Lake Yellowstone Hotel dishes up specialties like brown butter lobster sliders and grilled quail in an elegant setting—and the views make everything taste even better (page 73).

★ **The Corral, Gardiner:** The menu is small, the seating sparse, and the line often long, but the huge beef, bison, and elk burgers here are out of this world (page 73).

★ **Beartooth Café, Cooke City:** Housed in a beautiful old log cabin with a sprawling deck, this spot serves up delicious hand-cut steaks, burgers, pasta, salads, and more (page 74).

★ **Taqueria Las Palmitas, West Yellowstone:** Located in a converted white school bus parked in an alley, the "Taco Bus" serves authentic and outstanding Mexican street food—soft tacos, enchiladas, and burritos (page 75).

★ **Café Regis, Red Lodge:** A grocery store and restaurant known for organic fare, with fruits and vegetables grown in the back garden, Café Regis serves up hearty portions for reasonable prices (page 88).

★ **Horn & Cantle at Lone Mountain Ranch, Big Sky:** The restaurant here serves seasonal farm-to-table fare—think coffee-rubbed elk chop, crispy-skin Montana trout, and pork belly—with lovely, rustic ambience (page 94).

through, just to get a sense of this tremendously diverse place. Consider choosing one feature and pursuing it. To give yourself the best chance of seeing wolves, traveling between the north and northeast entrances is an excellent route during non-summer months. Geothermal aficionados will have no shortage of choices for seeing the park's impressive features, but to swim in them, try the **Boiling River,** a stretch of the Gardner River near Mammoth, which is swimmable year-round except during spring and early summer runoff. The **Firehole River** also offers excellent summer swimming not far from Old Faithful. Landlubbers might prefer a short hike into a less-famous geyser like **Lone Star,** just a few flat miles from Old Faithful.

The best advice is this: Get off the road, get out of your car, be smart, and come prepared to give yourself the opportunity to see and understand what makes Yellowstone America's first wonderland.

Entrances

Yellowstone National Park is open 365 days a year, 24 hours a day. There are five entrance stations: three in Montana and two in Wyoming.

- The **north entrance,** at Gardiner, Montana, is the only one open year-round to wheeled vehicles.
- The **northeast entrance** is near the small communities of Cooke City and Silver Gate, Montana, and generally open late May to mid-October, depending upon weather and road conditions.

Best Accommodations

★ **Roosevelt Lodge Cabins, Northern Loop:** Among the smallest and most rustic accommodations in the park, these tiny cabins are simple, charming, and set in the trees away from the madding crowds (page 76).

★ **Lake Yellowstone Hotel, Southern Loop:** With a variety of refurbished cabins and cottages and the grand historic hotel, the accommodations at Lake Yellowstone range from rustic to luxe, and the waterside setting is arguably the best in the park (page 77).

★ **Old Faithful Inn, Southern Loop:** This classic beauty is the most popular lodging in the park for its historic log-and-stone architecture, not to mention its location just steps from the famous geyser (page 78).

★ **Gardiner Guest House, Gardiner:** A sweet little bed-and-breakfast just outside the park's north entrance, this guesthouse is long on Victorian charm and Montana hospitality (page 79).

★ **Silver Gate Lodging, Cooke City:** Located just outside the park's northeast entrance, at the foot of the Beartooth Highway, this spot offers several pet-friendly cabins, motel rooms, and a big lodge (page 79).

★ **Yodeler Motel, Red Lodge:** Touting themselves as groovy and noncorporate, this budget- and pet-friendly motel in downtown Red Lodge is run by two former guides who will point you to all the best places (page 88).

★ **The Pollard Hotel, Red Lodge:** A historic railroad lodging in downtown Red Lodge, this charming redbrick hotel offers cozy accommodations, excellent dining, and an ideal location (page 88).

- The **west entrance,** in West Yellowstone, Montana, is open to wheeled vehicles generally from the third Friday in April until the first Sunday in November.
- The **south entrance,** 49 mi (79 km) north of Jackson, Wyoming, at the border between Grand Teton National Park and Yellowstone, is open to wheeled vehicles typically the second Friday in May through the first Sunday in November, and to snow coaches and snowmobiles mid-December to mid-March.
- The **east entrance,** 53 mi (85 km) west of Cody, Wyoming, is generally open to wheeled vehicles from the first Friday in May to the first Sunday in November.

All entrances can be closed at any time due to weather and unscheduled changes. Visit www.nps.gov/yell before your trip for up-to-date road information or call 307/344-2117 for recorded road and weather information.

Park Fees and Passes

Admission to the park is $35 per vehicle for seven days, $30 for motorcycles and snowmobiles, and $20 for hikers and bicyclists. An annual pass to the park costs $70. In 2024, entrance fees to the park were waived on six days, including Martin Luther King Jr. Day in January, the start of National Park Week in April, June 19 for Juneteenth, August 4 to celebrate the anniversary of the Great American Outdoors Act, the fourth Saturday in September for National

Public Lands Day, and Veterans Day on November 11. The park is open year-round, but during winter cars can only access the park through the north and northeast entrances.

Visitor Centers

There are 10 visitor centers in and around the park. Since days and hours vary seasonally and are often subject to staff shortages, it's a good idea to check the website (www.nps.gov/yell) before you go into the park.

Albright Visitor Center at Mammoth Hot Springs

Grand Loop Rd.; 307/344-2263; 9am-5pm daily

The Albright Visitor Center at Mammoth Hot Springs is open year-round and houses a bookstore, wildlife and history exhibits, and films on the park and its early visitors. Free Wi-Fi is also available. Fishers and backcountry campers can get permits in the basement backcountry office. And there are restrooms, perhaps the last for a while depending on your adventure.

Canyon Visitor Education Center

Canyon Village; 307/344-2550; 8am-6pm daily summer

The Canyon Visitor Education Center offers the best overview of the park's geology, including phenomenal volcano exhibits and a dynamic film. During the season, the bathrooms remain open 24 hours a day.

Fishing Bridge Visitor Center

East Entrance Rd.; 307/344-2450; 8am-6pm daily summer

The Fishing Bridge Visitor Center is home to a museum, a bookstore, and bird and wildlife exhibits, plus information on the lake's ecology. The building opened in 1931 and is a beautiful example of the "parkitecture"-type architecture.

Grant Village Visitor Center

Grand Loop Rd., west shore of Yellowstone Lake; 307/344-2650; 8am-6pm daily Memorial Day-Sept., 9am-5pm daily early Oct.

The Grant Village Visitor Center offers an outstanding exhibit on the integral role of fire in the Yellowstone ecosystem.

Madison Information Station and Trailside Museum

Madison Junction, halfway between Old Faithful and West Yellowstone; 307/344-2821; 9am-4:30pm daily early June-late Sept.

The Madison Information Station and Trailside Museum at Madison Junction provides a bookstore as well as detailed information on the **Junior Ranger** program. Another prime example of "parkitecture," the Trailside Museum opened in 1930.

Museum of the National Park Ranger

Grand Loop Rd.; 307/344-7353; 10am-4pm daily July-Aug.

The Museum of the National Park Ranger is 1 mi (1.6 km) north of Norris Geyser Basin and gives a good history of the park ranger profession. The log building was built in 1897 after a fire destroyed the original building, and was modified in 1908 to be used as soldier stations. The building was rebuilt again, log by log, after the 1959 earthquake.

Norris Geyser Basin Museum & Information Station

East of Norris Junction; 307/344-2812; 9am-5pm daily late May-early Oct.

The Norris Geyser Basin Museum & Information Station offers visitors an excellent overview of the park's hydrothermal features.

Old Faithful Visitor Education Center

Upper Geyser Basin; 307/344-2751; 9am-5pm daily mid-Apr.-late May, 8am-8pm daily Memorial Day-Labor Day, 8am-6pm daily Labor Day-Sept., 9am-5pm daily Oct. and mid-Dec.-mid-Mar., closed Nov.-mid-Dec. and mid-Mar.-mid-Apr.

The Old Faithful Visitor Education Center includes exhibits, information, and films on the park's hydrothermal features, plus a bookstore and geyser eruption predictions. A hands-on Young Scientist room is a hit with kids.

West Thumb Information Center

Grand Loop Rd. at West Thumb Geyser Basin; 307/242-7690; 9am-5pm daily late May-early Oct.

The West Thumb Information Center offers information about the West Thumb Geyser Basin on the shore of Yellowstone Lake. You can also sign up for ranger programs.

West Yellowstone Visitor Information Center

30 Yellowstone Ave.; 307/344-2876; 8am-8pm daily Memorial Day-Labor Day, 8am-5pm daily Labor Day-Memorial Day

In West Yellowstone, the West Yellowstone Visitor Information Center hosts a National Park Service desk, plus information and publications.

Services

Yellowstone National Park Lodges (307/344-7311; www.yellowstonenationalparklodges.com) is the official concessionaire of Yellowstone; all reservations for lodging, dining, and special activities can be made through them.

If you encounter an **emergency** in the park, dial 911, but be aware that cell coverage is spotty. Emergency medical services are attended to by rangers. There are three **urgent care facilities** inside Yellowstone.

Mammoth Medical Clinic

108 Grand Loop Rd.; 307/344-7965; 8:30am-5pm daily late May-late Sept., 8:30am-5pm Mon.-Thurs., 8:30am-1pm Fri. late Sept.-May

The clinic at Mammoth is open year-round and can offer routine care and such services as X-ray, lab, and pharmacy.

Lake Medical Clinic

1 Lake Station; 307/242-7241; 8am-8pm daily mid-May-late Sept., 8:30am-5:30pm Wed.-Sun. early Oct.-mid-Oct.

The Lake Medical Clinic is equipped for routine care and most medical emergencies with no appointments necessary.

Old Faithful Medical Clinic

Old Faithful Lodge; 307/545-7325; 8:30am-5pm Mon.-Fri. late Apr.-early May, 7am-7pm daily late May-late Sept., 8:30am-5pm daily late Sept.-mid-Oct., 8:30am-5pm Wed.-Sun. mid-Oct.-late Oct.

The Old Faithful Medical Clinic offers routine care options from spring into fall.

Getting Around

Private Vehicles

Your best bet to see the park on your own terms is to go by car. The nearest car-rental agencies are **Avis, Budget,** and **Big Sky Car Rentals** (406/646-9564), available seasonally in West Yellowstone. Cars can also be rented from airports in Billings, Bozeman, Cody, and Jackson Hole.

When planning your drive through Yellowstone, it is best to fill up your tank outside the park. Once inside, the gas prices you'll encounter tend to be extremely high, and options are quite limited. Gas stations are located within the park at Canyon, Fishing Bridge, Grant Village, Mammoth, Upper and Lower Old Faithful, and Tower Junction. They are generally open late spring-early fall.

One of the things that makes Yellowstone so wild and enchanting is its utter unpredictability—something that relates to wildlife, weather, and, unfortunately, road conditions. A 20-year, $300-million plan is currently afoot to address the structural deficiencies of Yellowstone's roads. Keep a close watch on road closures and delays that can happen at any time of year because of construction, bad weather, or even fire. For a 24-hour road report, check **Road Construction Delays and Closures** (307/344-2117; www.nps.gov/yell). Information on state roads is available from the **Montana Department of Transportation** (800/226-7623; www.mdt511.com) and **Wyoming Department of Transportation** (888/996-7623; www.wyoroad.info). **National Weather Service** (www.crh.noaa.gov) reports are available for Yellowstone and Grand Teton National Parks.

Tours

Depending on your particular interests, a range of companies outside and inside the park offer specialized tours of Yellowstone.

Xanterra/Yellowstone National Park Lodges

307/344-7311 or 866/439-7375; www.yellowstonenationalparklodges.com

Xanterra/Yellowstone National Park Lodges offers a variety of bus tours during the summer, including historic Yellow Bus tours that range 1-12 hours. The **Yellowstone in a Day** tour ($167-177) departs daily from Gardiner, Mammoth, and the Old Faithful Inn and covers the entire park in one day. Other options include early morning or evening wildlife tours, lake sunset tours, geyser gazers, Lamar Valley wildlife expeditions, photo safaris, boat tours, fishing trips, and custom guided tours.

Yellowstone Forever Institute

308 W. Park St., Gardiner; 406/848-2400; www.yellowstone.org

The only tour option inside the park is the outstanding Yellowstone Forever Institute. Courses are broken into summer and winter semesters. Single-day adventures start at $99 (open to ages 5 and up, lunch not included), and multiday field seminar fees begin around $168. Multiday tours with lodging are also available. The courses are taught by experts, using Yellowstone as their classroom and concentrating on "individual aspects of the ecosystem." During summer, you can take "Introduction to Wolf Management and Ecology," led by a wolf biologist, or "Mammal Signs: Interpreting Tracks, Scat, and Hair" with an animal tracker. There are several naturalist guide certificate programs offered in both summer and winter. Fall and winter field seminars include wildlife photography, wilderness first aid, and raptors over Yellowstone. The institute can provide unique (and inexpensive) lodging in its two field campuses, in Gardiner and the Lamar Valley. Or it can include standard hotel lodging at park hotels. If you take the time to browse through the course catalog, you will likely find something geared to your interests.

See Yellowstone

211 Yellowstone Ave., W. Yellowstone; 800/221-1151 or 800/646-7353; www.seeyellowstone.com

See Yellowstone is a full-service travel agency in West Yellowstone that can book everything from accommodations and tours to complete packages, including guided snowmobile trips, snow-coach tours, and all manner of summer tours.

Yellowstone Wild Tours

Gardiner; 406/224-0001; www.yellowstonewildtours.com

Yellowstone Wild Tours offers a fantastic array of public and private single- and multiday tours year-round. Owned by a wildlife biologist and staffed by naturalists, the focus will be on finding and observing wildlife. They offer special bear and wolf tours, family wildlife tours, hiking, thermal features, and winter tracking tours.

Sights

The Northern Loop

With striking panoramas, thermals, wildlife, and year-round vehicle access between the north and northeast entrances, the northern loop is one of the most underappreciated parts of the park. The accommodations and dining are not as fancy as elsewhere, but the crowds are more manageable. Highlights include Mammoth Hot Springs, the Lamar Valley, Tower Falls, Dunraven Pass, the Grand Canyon of the Yellowstone, and Norris Geyser Basin.

TOP EXPERIENCE

★ Boiling River

Halfway between Gardiner and Mammoth Hot Springs, straddling the Montana-Wyoming border and the 45th parallel, and halfway between the equator and the North Pole is the Boiling River, one of only two swimmable thermal features in Yellowstone. From the parking area, visitors amble upstream along a 0.5-mi (0.8-km) rocky path running parallel to the Gardner River. Where the trail ends and the steam envelops almost everything, a gushing hot spring called the Boiling River flows into the otherwise icy Gardner River. The hot and cold waters mix to a perfect temperature that can be enjoyed year-round. The area is open during daylight hours only, and all swimmers must wear a bathing suit. The Boiling River is closed each year during spring and early summer runoff, when temperature fluctuations and rushing water put swimmers at risk. Alcohol is not permitted.

★ Mammoth and the Mammoth Hot Springs Terraces

Just 5 mi (8 km) into the park and down the road from Gardiner is Mammoth, a park village with a small medical center, the most beautiful post office in the West, and a magnificent stone church. Once known as Fort Yellowstone, Mammoth was built by the US Army during its 1886-1918 occupation. Thinking they were on

Top to bottom: the Boiling River; Canary Spring; elk around Mammoth Hot Springs

The Northern Loop

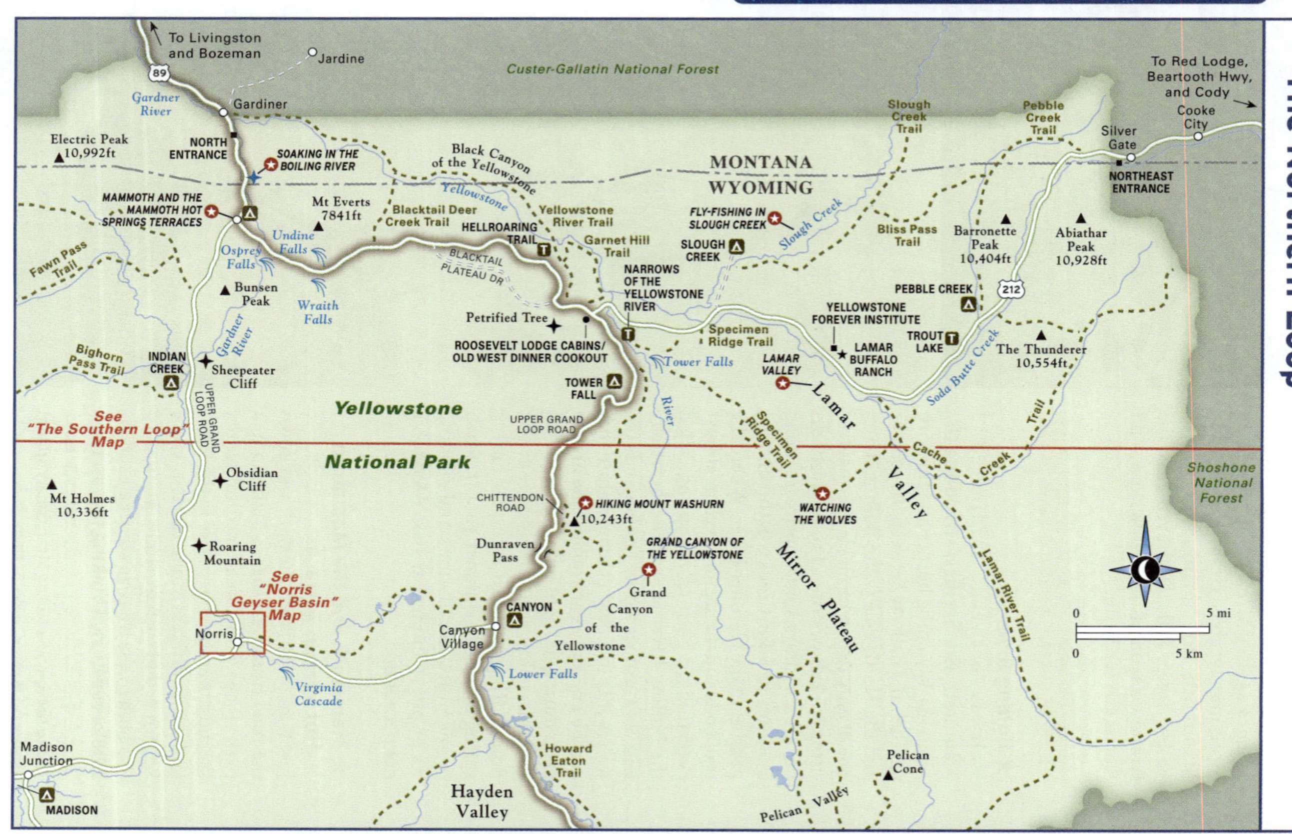

a temporary assignment, the soldiers erected canvas wall tents and lived in them through five harsh winters. In 1890, Congress set aside $50,000 for the construction of a permanent post, a stately collection of stone Colonial Revival-style buildings, most of which are still in use today.

The **Albright Visitor Center** (Grand Loop Rd.; 307/344-2263; 9am-5pm daily) offers films, history and wildlife exhibits, and an excellent selection of books and videos in the shop run by **Yellowstone Forever** (406/848-2400; www.yellowstone.org). Don't miss seeing some of the artwork produced during the 1871 Hayden Geological Survey of the park, including quality reproductions of painter Thomas Moran's famous watercolor sketches and original photographs by William Henry Jackson. Rangers on staff can usually give you up-to-date animal sightings and activity reports. The flush toilets downstairs are the last for a while.

The primary ecological attraction in Mammoth (other than the elk often seen lounging around and nibbling on the green grass) can be found on the **Mammoth Hot Springs Terraces.** Since the days of the earliest stagecoach trails into the park, they have been a visual and olfactory marvel for visitors. Beneath the ground, the Norris-Mammoth fault carries superheated water rich in dissolved calcium and bicarbonate. The mountain is continuously growing as travertine is deposited and then shifted as the cracks are sealed and the mineral-laden water emerges somewhere else. In addition to changes in shape and water flow, the colors at Mammoth can vary dramatically from day to day. Not only does travertine morph from bright white when it is new to cream and then gray as it is exposed to the elements, the cyanobacteria create fabulous color shifts too—from turquoise to green and yellow to red and brown, depending on water temperature, available sunlight, and pH levels.

Liberty Cap, at the base of the terraces, is an excellent example of a dormant spring, where all but the core cone has been eroded away. **Minerva Terrace** and **Canary Spring** are two other springs worth seeing. Their temperatures average around 160°F (71°C), and when they are flowing, they often put on marvelous color displays.

Tower Falls

Eighteen scenic miles (29 km) down the road from Mammoth—past the lookouts at **Undine Falls** and **Blacktail Plateau**—is Tower Junction, where you can continue south toward Canyon and the Lower Loop or east toward the Lamar Valley and Cooke City, and the breathtaking Tower Falls. The waterfall cascades 132 ft (40 m) from volcanic basalt. A popular spot just steps from the parking lot, this is not a place for solitude, but it is lovely.

Dunraven Pass

Between Tower and the dramatic Grand Canyon of the Yellowstone is one of the most nerve-racking and beautiful drives in the park. Climbing up the flanks of **Mount Washburn,** Dunraven Pass is the highest road elevation in the park, topping out at 8,859 ft (2,700 m) and offering views of Yellowstone's caldera rim. Eagle eyes can also spot the nearby Grand Canyon of the Yellowstone. Hikers will have no shortage of trailheads to start from. The whitebark pines that grow along the road are a critical and dwindling food source for grizzly bears, so keep your eyes open. Because of its extreme altitude and relative exposure, Dunraven Pass is one of the last roads to open in the spring and one of the first to close when bad weather hits. For current road information, call 307/344-2117.

★ Grand Canyon of the Yellowstone

Yellowstone's most recent volcanic explosion, some 600,000 years ago, created a massive caldera and subsequent lava flows in the area now known as the Grand Canyon of the Yellowstone. The 20-mi-long (32-km-long) canyon is still growing thanks to the forces of erosion, including water, wind, and earthquakes.

Before setting out for the canyon itself, visitors should stop at the **Canyon Visitor Education Center** (Canyon Village; 307/344-2550; 8am-6pm daily in summer) for its exhibit on Yellowstone's volcanic and geothermal activity.

On the **North Rim,** don't miss **Inspiration Point,** a natural viewing platform that gives a bird's-eye view up and down the river. Look down, if you dare, among the nooks and crannies of rock to try to spot nesting ospreys. Nathaniel Langford, the park's first superintendent, stood in the same spot with the Washburn Expedition in 1870. He wrote:

> Standing there or rather lying there for greater safety, I thought how utterly impossible it would be to describe to another the sensations inspired by such a presence. As I took in the scene, I realized my own littleness, my helplessness, my dread exposure to destruction, my inability to cope with or even comprehend the mighty architecture of nature.

Another phenomenal viewing platform can be found at **Lookout Point,** where visitors can gaze at the thundering Lower Falls of the Yellowstone. To get to the base of the falls at **Red Rock Point,** it's a 0.5-mi (0.8-km) trip one-way that drops more than 500 vertical ft (152 m). The smaller **Upper Falls** can be easily accessed at the **Brink of the Upper Falls.**

From the **South Rim,** visitors can see the Upper Falls from the **Upper Falls Viewpoint.** A trail that dates back to 1898, **Uncle Tom's Trail** takes hearty hikers to the base of the **Lower Falls.** The trail loses 500 vertical ft (152 m) through a series of 300 stairs and paved inclines, but what goes down must come up again. From **Artist Point,** one of the largest and most inspiring lookouts, visitors get a glorious view of the distant Lower Falls, which was long thought to be where Thomas Moran made sketches for his masterpiece *Grand Canyon of the Yellowstone.* More likely, say historians, he painted from a spot on the North Rim now called **Moran Point.**

Norris Geyser Basin

Both the hottest and the most unpredictable geyser basin in the park, Norris Geyser Basin is a collection of bubbling and colorful geothermal features. A 2.3-mi (3.7-km) web of boardwalks and trails leads through the basin. From the **Norris Geyser Basin Museum** (east of Norris Junction; 307/344-2812; 9am-5pm daily late May-early Oct.; free), which unravels the geothermal mysteries of the region, two loop trails wind through the basin. The 1930s log and stone building that houses the museum has been designated a National Historic Landmark.

Porcelain Basin is a stark, barren setting with a palette of pink, red, orange, and yellow mineral oxides. Some of the noteworthy features include **Africa Geyser,** which had been a hot spring in the shape of its namesake continent and started erupting in 1971. When it is active, **Whirligig Geyser** erupts in a swirling pattern for a few minutes at irregular periods with a roar and hiss. The hottest steam vent in the hottest geothermal basin in the park is **Black Growler,** which has measured 280°F (138°C). The second-largest geyser in Norris, **Ledge Geyser** erupts irregularly to heights up to 125 ft (38 m).

In Norris's **Back Basin,** the world's tallest geyser, **Steamboat Geyser,** can erupt more than 300 ft (90 m) in the air. Minor eruptions of 10-40 ft (3-12 m) in height are more common. The eruptions can last 3-40 minutes and be separated by days or decades (in the past, Steamboat has gone more than 50 years without an eruption, but in 1964, it erupted 29 times). A major eruption in September 2014 happened at 11pm and was witnessed by a park ranger.

Norris Geyser Basin

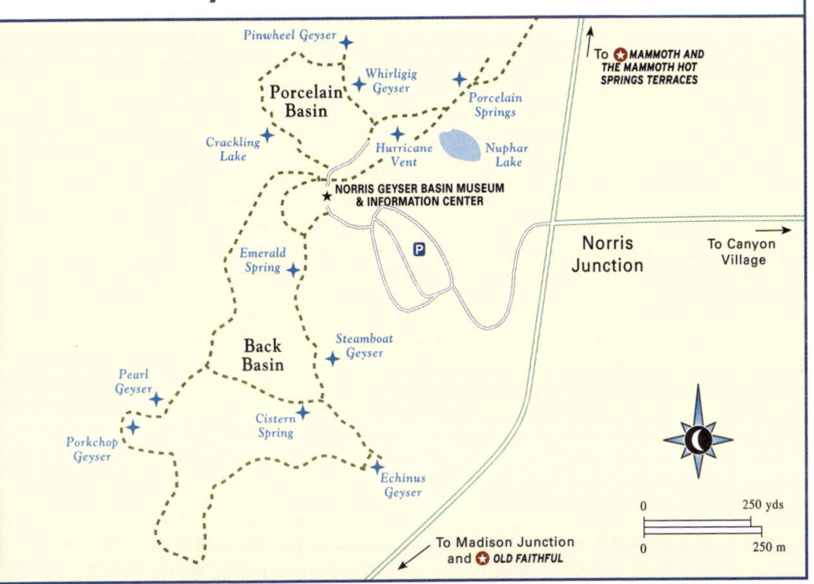

Prior to that, the last major eruption occurred in 2013, and before that in 2005. There were just four eruptions in 2024. Just down the boardwalk, **Cistern Spring** is linked to Steamboat Geyser and drains in advance of a major eruption. The color is a beautiful blue, enhanced by gray sinter. **Echinus Geyser** is the world's largest acid geyser and is almost as acidic as vinegar. Eruptions since 2007 have been rare and unpredictable, typically lasting about four minutes, but large ones have been known to reach heights of 80-125 ft (24-38 m).

Lamar Valley and the Northeast Corner

With the best wildlife-viewing in the park, especially in winter, this region is known as the "Little Serengeti of North America." The wide-open spaces of the Lamar Valley and much of the northeast corner also offer dramatic mountain vistas. There is excellent fishing and hiking, and just outside the park's northeast entrance is Cooke City, a cool little community with tremendous appeal to backcountry skiers and snowmobilers.

★ Watching the Wolves

When visitors list the animals they most want to see in Yellowstone, wolves often rank second, right behind grizzly bears. Since their return to Yellowstone in 1995, wolves have surprised park-goers and wildlife experts alike by being much more visible than anyone anticipated. In fact, since their reintroduction, wolves have been spotted in Yellowstone by at least one person nearly every day. Much of that is thanks to wolf researchers, including the indefatigable Rick McIntyre, who is out in the field an average of 11 hours per day, seven days per week, and the ever-passionate wolf watchers (who tend to follow Rick), armed with massive scopes and camera lenses that look strong enough to spot wildlife on other planets.

The bad news is that there are roughly 124 wolves in ten packs, plus a few lone wolves, roaming throughout Yellowstone, an area that is approximately the size of Connecticut. It's always a good idea to bear those figures in mind when you have only a couple of hours and a keen desire to spot one of these majestic canines.

But there's good news too. If seeing the wolves is a high priority, here are five ways to improve your odds:

- **Visit in winter.** Wolves are most active and most visible (nearest to the roads and against a white backdrop) in the winter when they have significant advantages over their prey, including elk and bison. Spring and fall can offer viewing opportunities as well, but summer visitors are at a disadvantage because the wolves are often way up in the high country, far from roads. Whenever you go, don't forget your binoculars.

- **Do your homework or hire a guide.** Stop at the visitor center in Mammoth in winter (or any of the visitor centers at other times of year) and inquire about recent activity. Rangers can often tell you where packs have been spotted, if kills have recently occurred, and so forth. You could also hire a guide that specializes in wolf-watching. **Yellowstone Wolf Tracker** (406/223-0173; www.wolftracker.com; $800/day for up to 3 people, $900 for 4-5 people, $1,000 for 6-8 people, $1,100 for 9-10 people) offers 6-8-hour tours led by wildlife biologists. The **Yellowstone Forever Institute** (406/848-2400; www.yellowstone.org) offers multiday courses that focus on wolves.

- **Visit the Lamar Valley.** The only road open to car traffic year-round takes visitors through the heart of some of the park's best winter wolf terrain. There are numerous pullouts along the road for viewing, but be sure to park safely out of traffic without blocking other visitors. In summer, along the stretch of road near the confluence of the

photographing wildlife

Lamar River and Soda Butte Creek, the road is often closed to stopping thanks to a wolf-denning site not far from the pavement. Your chances to see a wolf—even pups—are good.

- **Wake up early.** Like most wildlife, wolves are most active at the edges of day. Putting yourself in the heart of the Lamar Valley before sunrise greatly improves your odds of seeing the wolves. The same is true at sunset. In this game, patience pays.
- **Watch for the wolf watchers.** They often have significant advantages, including radio telemeters that allow them to track collared wolves. These people know much about the wolves and can regale you with dramatic sagas of individual animals and entire packs. Don't be shy about pulling over when you see them; they are often willing to let you peer through their scopes. But do be safe and courteous; turn off your engine and remain quiet.

★ Lamar Valley

One of my favorite corners of the park, the Lamar Valley is stunningly beautiful, with wide valleys carved by rivers and glaciers as well as views to the high, rugged peaks around Cooke City. It's generally less crowded than other parts of the park (save for the ever-growing number of bespectacled and bescoped wolf watchers), and some of the best hiking, fishing, and camping can be had at Slough Creek. And the wolf-watching, particularly in winter, is unrivaled anywhere else in the world. There are also grizzlies, black bears, mountain lions, coyotes, red foxes, elk, bison, bighorn sheep, and pronghorn in the area.

Lamar Buffalo Ranch

The Lamar Buffalo Ranch Field Campus of the **Yellowstone Forever Institute** (406/848-2400 or 307/344-8826; www.yellowstone.org/lamar-buffalo-ranch) is located away from the large crowds (of two-legged creatures, anyway) in the idyllic Lamar Valley. The institute offers field seminars at this private campus year-round. If you bring your own sleeping bag and pillow, you can stay at the ranch in one of its shared or private log cabins. Propane heaters, a communal bathhouse with individual showers, and a fully equipped kitchen are housed in the common building. It's comfortable enough, but not fancy. The best part is waking up in the Lamar Valley, an opportunity very few people have. You can also stay in a hotel or campsite of your choosing while taking a course at the ranch. Field seminars also take place at hotels throughout the park. The institute holds rooms up to 30 days before the course.

★ Slough Creek

A 25-mi-long (40-km) tributary of the Lamar River, Slough Creek flows from high in Montana's Absaroka-Beartooth Wilderness and into Wyoming and the park, where it converges with the Lamar River near Tower Junction. The creek winds through fir forests, sage flats, and grassland, making it prime habitat for a variety of animals, ranging from bison to coyotes to wolves to grizzly bears. A **campground** and 11 mi (18 km) of maintained and relatively flat trails provide excellent access to both hikers and anglers.

Slough Creek is known for its **dry-fly-fishing,** with abundant cutthroat trout being the prize. Within the park, the creek flows through big meadows and a few pocket water areas in small canyons. Only the top portion of Lower Meadow is accessible by car. The rest is earned with a hike. From the campground, anglers walk 1.5 mi (2.4 km) to VIP Pool at the end of Lower Meadow, where cutbows and rainbow trout are present and can be as big as 22-25 in (58.8-63.5 cm). It's 2.5 mi (4 km) to the First Meadow, 4 mi (6 km) to the Second Meadow, and 6 mi (10 km) to the Third Meadow. In each of these meadows, 14- to 16-inchers (35.5-40.6 cm) are common, with some fish up to 20 in (50.8 cm). The farther you go, the lower the fishing pressure, meaning less company for you and perhaps easier catching.

The Southern Loop

Plenty of the park's highlights are found in the southern loop, along with a significant number of visitors and abundant wildlife. There are a lot of trees, many of them burned, and not as much dimension to the land as elsewhere, but the terrain accessed by the Lower Loop Road is what many people picture when they think of Yellowstone: from the sweeping Hayden Valley and the otherworldliness of West Thumb Geyser Basin to the vastness of Yellowstone Lake and the hubbub around Old Faithful.

Hayden Valley

Northwest of the east entrance between Canyon and Lake Villages is the Hayden Valley, a sweep of grassland carved by massive glaciers named for the leader of the 1871 Hayden Expedition and occupied by wildlife that includes grizzly bears, wolves, and, in summer, thundering herds of bison. The Yellowstone River weaves quietly through the valley bottom, and because the soil supports grasses and wildflowers instead of trees, this is one of the most scenic drives in the park, especially during the bison rut in late summer. Besides driving, hiking is an excellent way to explore the valley, either on your own (pay very close attention for signs of bear activity) or with a ranger on weekly **guided hikes** (4-5 hours, early July-late Aug.; free). The hikes are limited to 15 people, and reservations must be made in advance at the **Canyon Visitor Education Center** (307/344-2550; 8am-6pm daily summer) in Canyon Village.

Fishing Bridge

What was once the epicenter of Yellowstone fishing is today a relic of the past and a touchstone for the ongoing struggle between nature and human meddling. Fishing Bridge was built in 1937 and for years was considered the best place to throw a line for native cutthroat trout. Humans were not the only ones fishing in the area, and human-grizzly encounters led to 16 grizzly bear deaths. To protect the bears and the fish, fishing in the vicinity was banned in 1973. Today, because of the sharp decline of cutthroat as a direct result of the introduction of nonnative lake trout, grizzlies are not seen as often fishing in the river.

There are some services—an RV park, a gas station, and a general store—and a 1931 log and stone structure that serves as the **Fishing Bridge Visitor Center** (East Entrance Rd.; 307/344-2450; 8am-6pm daily summer). On the National Register of Historic Places, the visitor center has stuffed bird specimens and an exhibit on the lake's geology.

★ Yellowstone Lake

Covering 136 sq mi, Yellowstone Lake is North America's largest freshwater lake

The Southern Loop

above 7,000 ft (2,134 m). In addition to being spectacularly scenic—both when it is placid and when the waves form whitecaps—the lake is a fascinating study in underwater geothermal activity. Beneath the water—or ice, much of the year—the lake bottom is littered with faults, hot springs, craters, and the miraculous lifeforms that can thrive in such conditions.

Aside from its geological significance, Yellowstone Lake also offers plenty of recreational opportunities, primarily in the form of boating and fishing. The water is bitterly cold, typically 40-50°F (4-10°C), and not suitable for swimming. Eighteen-foot, 40-horsepower outboards ($68/hour) can be rented mid-June to early September at **Bridge Bay Marina** (307/344-7311), just south of Lake Village or 21 mi (34 km) north of West Thumb. There is great fishing for native cutthroat trout as well. It's worth mentioning that early visitors to the park loved to tell stories about catching fish at the edge of the lake and then dipping their catch in the hot springs at West Thumb Geyser Basin to cook them without taking the fish off the line—a practice that would be seriously frowned upon today. Not to mention, what about the guts?

The rambling pale-yellow **Lake Yellowstone Hotel** was built in 1891 and is an elegant reminder of Yellowstone's bygone era. The lobby and deck overlook the lake and are worth seeing. Grab an iced tea and soak in the views. If you can, stay for a meal and enjoy the live piano music.

West Thumb Geyser Basin

On the western edge of Yellowstone Lake is the eerie West Thumb Geyser Basin, a collection of hot springs, geysers, mud pots, and fumaroles that dump a collective 3,100 gallons (117,300 liters) of hot water into the lake daily. An excellent boardwalk system guides visitors through the area, but there have been injury-causing bison and bear encounters on the boardwalk, so keep your eyes open.

Abyss Pool is a spring that transforms in color from turquoise to emerald green to brown and back, depending on a variety of factors. **Big Cone** and **Fishing Cone,** surrounded by lake water, are the features that led to the stories of fishing and cooking the catch in a single cast. Called "Mud Puffs" by the 1871 Hayden Expedition, **Thumb Paint Pots** are like miniature reddish mud volcanoes (depending on rainfall, after which they can get soupier) and are an excellent example of mud pots. Throughout the last several years, the mud pots have been particularly active, forming new mud cones and even throwing mud into the air. **Surging Spring** is fun to watch as the dome of water forms and overflows, unleashing a torrent of water on the lake.

pool in West Thumb Geyser Basin

Grant Village

On the West Thumb of Yellowstone Lake, Grant Village is a controversial development dating to the 1970s and built in the heart of grizzly bear habitat and among several cutthroat spawning streams. The architecture is ugly, and the location is better suited to wildlife than visitors. The **Grant Village Visitor Center** (west shore of Yellowstone Lake; 307/344-2650; 8am-6pm daily Memorial Day-Sept., 9am-5pm daily early Oct.) houses an exhibit dedicated to fire in the Yellowstone ecosystem, accommodations, a campground, and food services are available on-site.

★ Old Faithful

Though often crowded, the Old Faithful complex brings together so many of the phenomena—both natural and human-made—that make Yellowstone so special: the landmark geyser and the incredible assortment of geothermal features surrounding it, the wildlife, the grand park architecture of the Old Faithful Inn, and even the mass of people from around the world who come to witness the famous geyser. From Old Faithful, West Thumb is 20 mi (31 km) and Grant Village is 22 mi (36 km) southeast.

Known as the **Upper Geyser Basin,** the area surrounding Old Faithful is the largest concentration of geysers anywhere in the world. By far the most famous is Old Faithful because of its combination of height (although it is not the tallest) and regularity (although it is neither the most frequent nor the most regular). Intervals between eruptions are generally 60-90 minutes and can be predicted according to duration of previous eruptions, which can last anywhere from 90 seconds to five minutes. It spouts 3,700-8,400 gallons (14,000-32,000 liters) of hot water at heights of 106-184 ft (32-56 m). Signs inside the nearby hotel lobbies and the visitor center, an X feed (@GeyserNPS), and the NPS Yellowstone App keep visitors apprised of the next expected eruptions, of which there are an average of 17 in any 24-hour period. Keep in mind that Old Faithful doesn't stop being predictable just because people go to bed or the weather turns cold—some of the most magical eruption viewings can happen without crowds. Choose a full-moon night, any time of year, and be willing to get up in the middle of the night. The vision of Old Faithful erupting in winter with snow and ice, frost, and steam in every direction is unforgettable.

If you take the time to come to Yellowstone to see Old Faithful, take the time—an hour or more is ideal—to walk through the other features of the Upper Geyser Basin. **Giantess Geyser** can erupt up to 200 ft (61 m) high in several bursts. The irregular eruptions happen 2-6 times each year and can last 4-48 hours. **Doublet Pool,** a colorful hot spring with numerous ledges, is lovely and convoluted. You can actually hear Doublet vibrating and collapsing beneath the surface. Looking something like a fire hose

shooting 130-190 ft (40-58 m) in the air, **Beehive Geyser** typically erupts twice daily, each eruption lasting 4-5 minutes. **Grand Geyser** is the world's tallest predictable geyser, erupting every 7-15 hours, lasting 9-12 minutes, and reaching heights up to 200 ft (61 m). Visible from the road into the Old Faithful complex if you look back over your shoulder, **Castle Geyser** is thought to be the park's oldest. It generally erupts every 10-12 hours, reaches 90 ft (27 m) in height, and lasts roughly 20 minutes.

Old Faithful Visitor Education Center

Upper Geyser Basin; 307/344-2751; 9am-5pm daily mid-Apr.-late May, 8am-8pm daily Memorial Day-Labor Day, 8am-6pm Labor Day-Sept., 9am-5pm daily Oct. and mid-Dec.-mid-Mar.

An obvious stop at the Old Faithful complex is the Old Faithful Visitor Education Center, which showcases Yellowstone's hydrothermal features. The facility hosts more than four million visitors annually. Efficient travelers (who are fighting an uphill battle here most of the time) can call ahead for a recorded message about daily geyser eruption predictions (307/344-2751).

★ Firehole River

Since swimming in Yellowstone Lake is not an option, a dip in the heated (but far from hot!) waters of the Firehole River is one of the nicest ways to spend an afternoon. The designated swimming area is surrounded by high cliffs and fast-moving rapids both up- and downstream, so the area is not recommended for inexperienced or young swimmers. Water temperature averages 75°F (24°C). Though quite limited, parking is accessible from Firehole Canyon Drive, which leaves the main road south of Madison Junction, less than 1,000 ft (305 m) after crossing the river. There is a toilet

Top to bottom: Old Faithful; swimming in the Firehole River; Grand Prismatic Spring

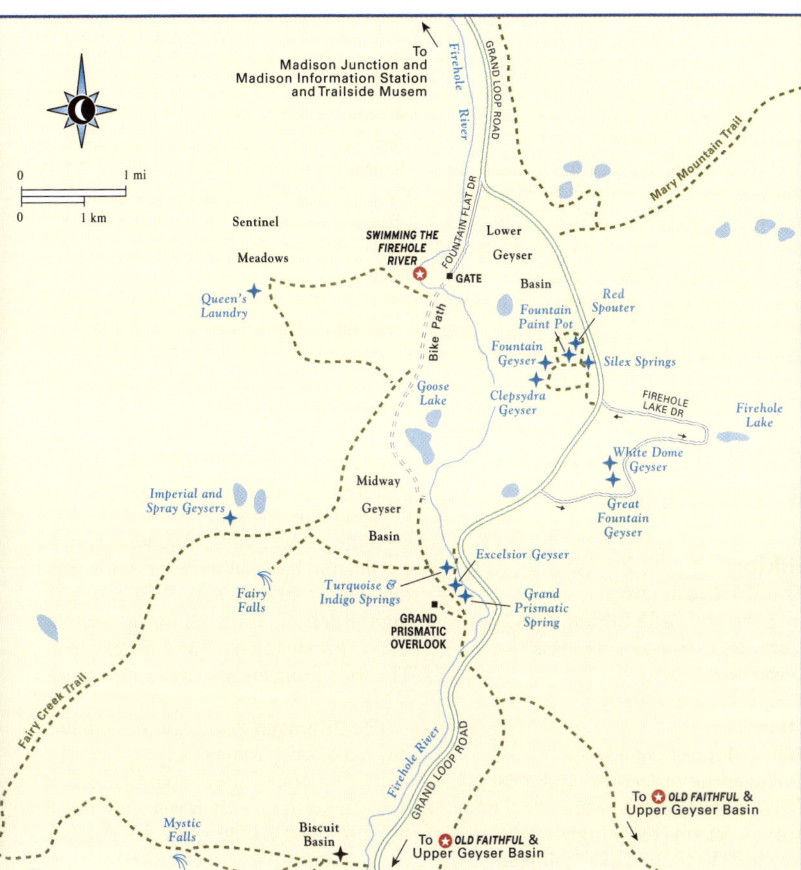

available but no lifeguards, so you will be swimming entirely at your own risk.

Midway and Lower Geyser Basins

Between Old Faithful and Madison Junction, along the pastoral Firehole River, are the Midway and Lower Geyser Basins, technically considered part of the same basin. In 1889, Rudyard Kipling dubbed Midway Geyser Basin "hell's half-acre" for its massive hot springs and geysers. Among the most significant features at Midway is **Grand Prismatic Spring,** a colorful and photogenic spring that was immortalized by painter Thomas Moran on the Hayden Expedition. It releases some 560 gallons (2,100 liters) of water into the Firehole River every minute. Grand Prismatic is the third-largest hot spring in the world and the largest in Yellowstone. Now dormant, **Excelsior Geyser Crater** was once the largest geyser in the world, soaring up to 300 ft (91 m) high. Major eruptions in the 1880s led to a dormancy that lasted more than a century. In 1985, Excelsior erupted continuously for two days but never topped 80 ft (24 m).

Compared to the smaller Midway Geyser Basin, the Lower Geyser Basin is enormous, spanning 12 sq mi (31 sq km) and including several clusters of thermal features. Among them are the notable **Fountain Geyser,** a placid blue pool that erupts on average every 4.5-7 hours for 25-50 minutes and sprays up to 50 ft (15 m) high; the temperamental **White Dome Geyser;** the almost-constant **Clepsydra;** and the **Pocket Basin Mud Pots,** the largest collection of mud pots in the park. **Great Fountain Geyser** is the only predictable geyser in the Lower Geyser Basin and erupts every 10 hours 45 minutes, give or take 2 hours, for up to an hour, reaching heights of 70-200 ft (21-61 m).

Adventure and Recreation

Hiking

The Northern Loop

Ice Lake and Little Gibbon Falls Trail

Distance: 3.9 mi (6.3 km) round-trip
Duration: 1.5 hours
Elevation gain: 249 ft (76 m)
Effort: Easy
Trail surface: Dirt, boardwalk
Trailhead: Ice Lake or Little Gibbon Falls

Drive east of Norris Junction 3.5 mi (5.6 km), or 8.5 mi (13.7 km) west of Canyon Junction, to the **Ice Lake Trailhead** on the north side of the road. A popular loop with minimal elevation gain, the entire trail to Ice Lake is wheelchair-accessible and leads to the only wheelchair-accessible backcountry campsite in the park. Avid hikers will want to continue on to **Little Gibbon Falls,** a 25-ft (7.6-m) waterfall that is not even on the US Geological Survey topographic map. The trail is not always obvious, and hikers will have to deal with downed trees, bugs, and creek crossings. Another way to see this hidden gem is to find the Little Gibbon Falls Trailhead 0.4 mi (0.6 km) east of the Ice Lake Trailhead. There is a small pullout on the south side of the road. The trail starts about 100 ft (30 m) east of the pullout on the north side of the road. From here, Little Gibbon Falls is a 1.2-mi (1.9-km) out-and-back hike.

★ Mount Washburn

Distance: 5.4-6.4 mi (8.7-10.3 km) round-trip
Duration: 4 hours
Elevation gain: 1,400-1,483 ft (427-452 m)
Effort: Strenuous
Trail surface: Roadbed, dirt, rocks
Trailheads: For the south trail: Dunraven Pass Trailhead parking area on the east side of Grand Loop Road, 5 mi (8 km) north of Canyon Junction. For the north trail: 10 mi (16 km) north of Canyon Junction; drive 1.3 mi (2.1 km) up Chittenden Road to reach the parking area.

At 10,243 ft (3,122 m), the Mount Washburn Lookout yields a 360-degree panorama with big views. On a clear day, you can see Yellowstone Lake and even the Tetons. The Chittenden Trail is steeper and has a bit more elevation gain than the Dunraven Pass Trail, but both high-elevation trails climb up switchbacks in a steady plod on former roads. The elevation makes this a strenuous hike.

The **Dunraven Pass Trail** (6.4 mi/10.3 km round-trip, hikers only) traverses a southern slope before swinging north. It then makes four switchbacks up a west slope to crest a long ridge for a scenic walk that finishes with a 360-degree circle to Mount Washburn Lookout. In upper elevation cliffs and meadows, look for bighorn sheep.

The steeper **Chittenden Trail** (5.4 mi/8.7 km round-trip, bicycles allowed) ascends just below a ridge with a few switchbacks thrown in to work up the slope north of the lookout. On the final ridge, the trail swings east and then switchbacks west for the last steps to the summit of Mount Washburn.

At the summit, **Mount Washburn Lookout** is an ugly three-story cement block covered in radio equipment. Visitors can access only two levels: An

Yellowstone's Volcano: Waiting for the Big One?

It's always interesting to watch visitors' expressions when you tell them that in Yellowstone National Park they are standing atop one of the world's largest active volcanoes . . . and that it is overdue for an apocalyptic eruption. While those two facts are true, the reality is much less threatening. Indeed, there have been three super eruptions—Mike Poland, the scientist-in-charge at the Yellowstone Observatory, explains there is no such thing as a super volcano, only super eruptions—over the course of the last two million years, and the patterns do indicate that the volcano is overdue to erupt. But scientists agree that the chances of a massive eruption in the next 1,000 or even 10,000 years are very slight.

An Explosive History

The first super eruption 2.1 million years ago was 6,000 times more powerful than the 1980 eruption of Mount St. Helens, spouting rock and ash from Texas to Canada, Missouri to California. The eruption emptied the magma chamber located just underneath the park and caused a massive sinking of the earth, known as a caldera.

The second major eruption occurred 1.3 million years ago and created the Henry's Fork Caldera. The most recent massive eruption took place roughly 640,000 years ago and created the Yellowstone Caldera, which is 30 by 45 mi (48 by 72 km) in size. The perimeter of the Yellowstone Caldera is still visible in places throughout the park: from Mount Washburn; at Gibbon Falls, Lewis Falls, and Lake Butte; and at Mount Everts, near Mammoth, where you can see layers of ash from the various eruptions.

Today's Earthquakes are Hints

But volcanic activity is not a thing of the past in Yellowstone. The magma, which some scientists think is just 5 mi (8 km) beneath the surface of the park in places as opposed to the typical 40 mi (64 km), has created two enormous bulges, known as resurgent domes, near Sour Creek and Mallard Lake that are growing at an impressive rate of 1.5 in (3.8 cm) per year, causing Yellowstone Lake to tip southward, leaving docks on the north side completely out of the water and flooding the forested shore of the south side. In addition, there are roughly 1,500 earthquakes every year centered in Yellowstone, most of which cannot be felt, but that shift geothermal activity and keep the natural plumbing system that feeds the geyser basins flowing. They also suggest volcanic activity. In 2023 there were 24 earthquake swarms, one of which included 138 quakes. But the total number of quakes in the park was down by 806 from the 2022 total number of earthquakes.

Don't Worry!

Still, the scientists at the Yellowstone Volcano Observatory have no reason to suspect that an eruption, or even a lava flow, is imminent. For more than three decades, scientists have been monitoring the region for precursors to volcanic eruptions—earthquake swarms, rapid ground deformation, gas releases, and lava flows—and although there is activity, none of it suggests anything immediate or foreboding. Current real-time monitoring data are available online at http://volcanoes.usgs.gov. The bottom line is that the volcano is real and active, but certainly not a threat in the immediate future, and not a reason to stay away from this awe-inspiring place.

Mount Washburn

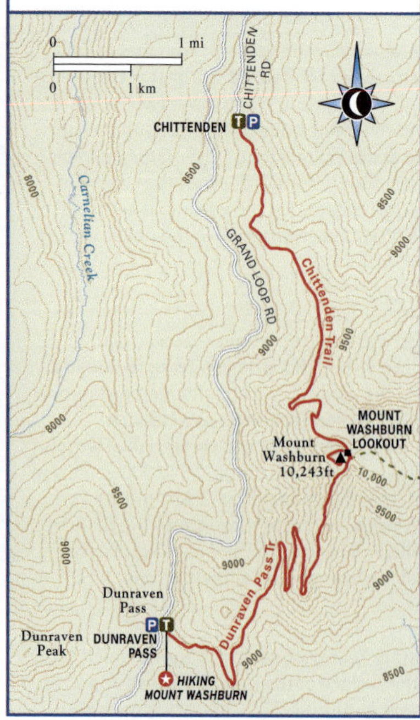

observation room with windows on three sides has interpretive displays and a viewing scope, and a windy deck offers views. Restrooms are available.

Slopes may be **snow-covered in June** but burst with alpine wildflowers by July. Due to afternoon thunderstorms, plan to **descend before early afternoon.** Even though the treeless trail looks hot, **bring warm clothing;** the alpine tundra summit is often windy and cold. Due to the trail's popularity, you'll have company at the lookout.

North Rim of Grand Canyon of the Yellowstone

Distance: 3.8-6.6 mi (6.1-10.6 km) one-way
Duration: 3-4 hours
Elevation gain: 250-1,500 ft (75-460 m)
Effort: Easy to strenuous
Trail surface: Pavement, dirt, rocks
Trailhead: Wapiti Lake Trailhead on South Rim Drive, on the west side of the bridge over the Yellowstone River. Park at Wapiti Picnic Area on the east side of South Rim Drive. Walk back across the Chittenden Bridge over the Yellowstone River to find the trailhead heading north.

This trail is not about backcountry solitude, but rather tremendous views of the Grand Canyon of the Yellowstone. Paved and dirt trails link together multiple overlooks; some include steel stairways and boardwalks down to overlook platforms. You can start at either the north or south end to hike the entire trail, or shorten the distance by driving some segments. (In several places, the trail pops out to cross parking lots on North Rim Drive.) Spur trails also drop down switchbacks and steep stairways to viewing platforms; all require climbing back up. Completing all the spurs adds a climb of nearly 1,500 ft (460 m) in elevation and an additional 2.8 mi (4.5 km).

To start at the **south end** of the North Rim Trail, cross Chittenden Bridge to follow the Yellowstone River downstream (heading north). In 0.4 mi (0.6 km), the trail reaches the first viewpoint at **Brink of the Upper Falls.** A spur trail drops 42 ft (13 m) to an overlook of the 109-ft (33-m) falls. Continue north, passing the parking lot for Brink of the Upper Falls, to the 130-ft (40-m) **Crystal Falls** as it spews from a slot in the North Rim cliffs. Next, the 308-ft (94-m) **Lower Falls** comes into view; follow the trail to a junction where a spur plummets 600 ft (185 m) down switchbacks and stairs to the **Brink of the Lower Falls.** Climb back up and continue east to the **Lookout Point Trailhead,** where a short trail goes up 25 ft (8 m) to **Lookout Point.** Just west, a longer trail plunges 500 ft (150 m) in 0.4 mi (0.6 km) down switchbacks and steep stairs to **Red Rock Point.** Returning to the North Rim Trail, continue north to **Grand View Point,** where a short, paved trail drops about 150 ft (45 m) to the viewpoint. Past Grand View Point, the trail curls northeast about 1.3 mi (2.1 km) to

Grand Canyon of the Yellowstone Trails

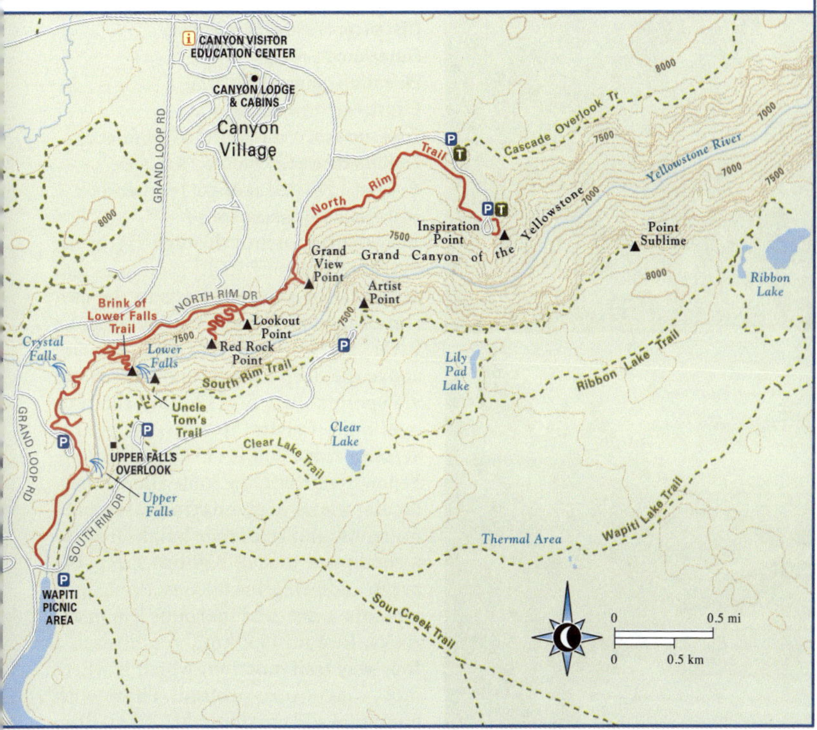

the **Inspiration Point** parking lot, where you can take in canyon views from four viewpoints.

To hike the trail in reverse, start at the **north end** by parking at Inspiration Point parking lot. For the 3.8-mi (6.1-km) one-way hike, leave a car shuttle at either the Inspiration Point or Wapiti Picnic Area parking lot. Or return the way you came for a 7.6-mi (12.2-km) out-and-back hike.

Hellroaring Trail

Distance: 6.2 mi (10 km) round-trip
Duration: 2-3 hours
Elevation gain: 600 ft (182 m)
Effort: Moderate to strenuous
Trail surface: Dirt, sagebrush
Trailhead: 3.5 mi (5.6 km) west of Tower Junction

A choose-your-own-length hike in the vicinity of Tower Junction is along the Hellroaring Trail, a beautiful but strenuous hike through wide-open sagebrush and along fishable water. The trailhead is 3.5 mi (5.6 km) west of Tower Junction and starts with a steep descent to a suspension bridge over the Yellowstone River. Day hikers can enjoy a 6.2-mi (10-km) there-and-back hike through scenic sagebrush plateau to the confluence of Hellroaring Creek and the Yellowstone River. The trail also intersects with the **Buffalo Plateau Trail,** the **Coyote Creek Trail,** and the **Garnet Hill Loop.** This is Yellowstone, so come prepared: Bring bear spray, sunscreen, water, and a fly rod!

Lamar Valley and the Northeast Corner

Narrows of the Yellowstone River

Distance: 4 mi (6.4 km) round-trip
Duration: 2.5 hours
Elevation gain: 393 ft (120 m)
Effort: Easy to moderate
Trail surface: Uneven dirt, rocky, loose rocks
Trailhead: Yellowstone River Picnic Area Trailhead, 1.2 mi (1.9 km) east of Tower Junction on the Northeast Entrance Road

A steep grunt uphill through sagebrush meadows with pink sticky geraniums and arrowleaf balsamroot leads to the east rim of the Narrows of the Yellowstone River. The trail saunters along the rim above the deep canyon and has several viewpoints. In 1 mi (1.6 km), the trail overlooks **Calcite Springs.** As it traverses a ridge 500 ft (152 m) above the Yellowstone River, the route affords spectacular views of the narrows, sculpted minarets, and columnar basalt. It's also a good place to spot bighorn sheep, ospreys, and peregrine falcons. Pronghorn cross the ridge, and marmots live in the rocks. In 2 mi (3.2 km), you'll reach a **four-way trail junction,** which is where most hikers turn around. Those with gumption add on a 0.8-mi (1.3-km) drop to the Yellowstone River and back on the spur trail that plunges steeply 0.4 mi (0.6 km) to the historic **Bannock Ford,** which was used by several Indigenous west-side groups that traveled east to hunt bison.

Specimen Ridge

Distance: 3 mi (4.8 km) round-trip
Duration: 3-4 hours
Elevation gain: 1,024 ft (312 m)
Effort: Strenuous
Trail surface: Uneven dirt, rocky, loose scree
Trailhead: Look for a hiker symbol at a pullout 4.5 mi (7 km) east of Tower Junction on the Northeast Entrance Road just before the Lamar River Bridge.

The route up Specimen Ridge goes to a

Top to bottom: bison in Lamar Valley; Trout Lake; view of Lower Falls from Artist Point

fossil zone, where you can see many petrified redwood trees. Most of the fossils date back some 50 million years; some are species that no longer grow in the park. One toppled petrified tree stretches 20 ft (6 m) long and 8 ft (2 m) in diameter. Do not confuse this unmaintained route with the Specimen Ridge Trail from Yellowstone River Picnic Area, which does not go to the fossils.

Starting on an **old faint road** and veering off to the right, the route tromps through sage meadows, disappearing frequently in wet seeps. Aim for the trail grunting straight uphill. It will cross multiple wildlife paths before reaching a small forest. The trail switchbacks through the trees to reach an **open ridge.** A rock outcropping marks the **petrified redwood tree trunks** area, and sweeping views span the bison herds in Lamar Valley and the Absaroka Mountains.

Trout Lake Trail

Distance: 1.2 mi (1.9 km) round-trip
Duration: 1 hour
Elevation gain: 220 ft (67 m)
Effort: Easy to moderate
Trail surface: Uneven dirt, rocky, roots
Trailhead: A small pullout with limited parking on the Northeast Entrance Road, 3 mi (4.8 km) north of Soda Butte Trailhead and 1.5 mi (2.4 km) south of Pebble Creek Campground

An idyllic little lake sitting at about 7,000 ft (2,100 m) in elevation, **Trout Lake** is the largest of three small lakes tucked near the Northeast Entrance Road in the **Absaroka Mountains.** From the trailhead, the path catapults vertically through a Douglas fir forest to the lake. About 0.3 mi (0.5 km) up the trail, the **route splits** to circle the lake. Go either way. The trail circles the shoreline, which is semi-forested on the east shore and open meadows on the west shore. In early summer, phlox blankets the hillsides, cutthroat trout spawn in the inlet stream, and ospreys hang around to fish. Short unmaintained trails connect with Shrimp and Buck Lakes.

The Southern Loop

Lone Star Geyser

Distance: 5.3 mi (8.5 km) round-trip
Duration: 2 hours
Elevation gain: 127 ft (39 m)
Effort: Easy
Trail surface: Pavement, gravel
Trailhead: Upper Geyser Basin

Among the geysers in the Upper Geyser Basin is Lone Star Geyser, named for its lonely location about 5 mi (8 km) from Old Faithful. An old once-paved road leads to the geyser and makes a nice level hike or bike trip. There is parking at the trailhead on the south side of the road, 3.5 mi (5.6 km) east of the Old Faithful interchange. Lucky viewers will get to see a 30-50-ft (9-15-m) eruption, which happens every 3 hours or so and can last up to 30 minutes.

Hiking the trail from **Old Faithful Lodge** almost doubles the mileage. From the southeast corner of the Old Faithful cabin complex, hop onto the **Mallard Lake Trail.** After crossing the Firehole River, turn right to follow the signage to **Kepler Cascades.** The trail climbs through forest and meadows until it parallels Grand Loop Road, then crosses to the Kepler Cascades parking lot. Locate the Lone Star Geyser Trailhead just south of the cascades. For an alternative return, take the Howard Eaton Trail 2.9 mi (4.7 km) north back to Old Faithful.

Natural Bridge

Distance: 2.6 mi (4.2 km) round-trip
Duration: 2 hours
Elevation gain: 181 ft (55 m)
Effort: Easy
Trail surface: Uneven dirt, roots, rocks
Trailhead: Bridge Bay Marina parking lot near the entrance to the campground

This scenic loop tours Natural Bridge, a 51-ft-high (16-m-high) sculpture of rhyolite rock that has been eroded through by Bridge Creek. The bridge is impressive, although much smaller than Utah's famed arches. Note that this trail is **closed late spring to early summer** due

Lone Star Geyser

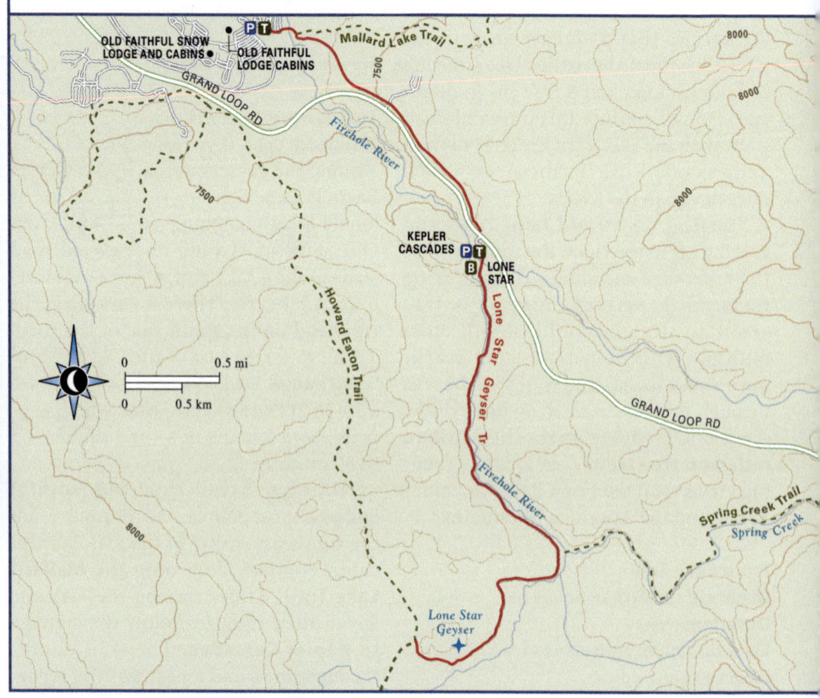

to grizzlies feeding on spawning trout in Bridge Creek. A bicycle route also begins south of the bridge from a separate trailhead.

From the parking lot, the trail cuts west through the forest for 0.7 mi (1.1 km) before joining an old **paved road.** The route continues working westward for 0.4 mi (0.6 km), turning right at all junctions to reach an **interpretive exhibit** at the base of the loop trail. From the exhibit, a short, steep path switchbacks 0.2 mi (0.3 km) up to the top of **Natural Bridge;** cross the creek behind the bridge to loop back down the other side. The top of the bridge is closed in order to protect the fragile rock, but you'll see marmots run across it.

Yellowstone Lake Overlook

Distance: 2 mi (3.2 km) round-trip
Duration: 1.5 hours
Elevation gain: 194 ft (59 m)
Effort: Easy
Trail surface: Uneven dirt, rocks
Trailhead: West side of the West Thumb Geyser Basin parking lot

The Lake Overlook Trail climbs from the start, beginning in a meadow and entering a forest. In 0.3 mi (0.5 km), the trail crosses the **South Entrance Road** and reaches a **fork.** Turn left and continue hiking south up to a meadow with red paintbrush and yellow buckwheat in early summer; the panoramic views of Yellowstone Lake and the Absaroka Mountains unfold. Sit on the **bench** to enjoy the view, and climb a **short spur** behind the bench about 30 ft (9 m) for a peekaboo view of the Tetons. Complete the loop to return to the parking lot.

Yellowstone Lake Overlook

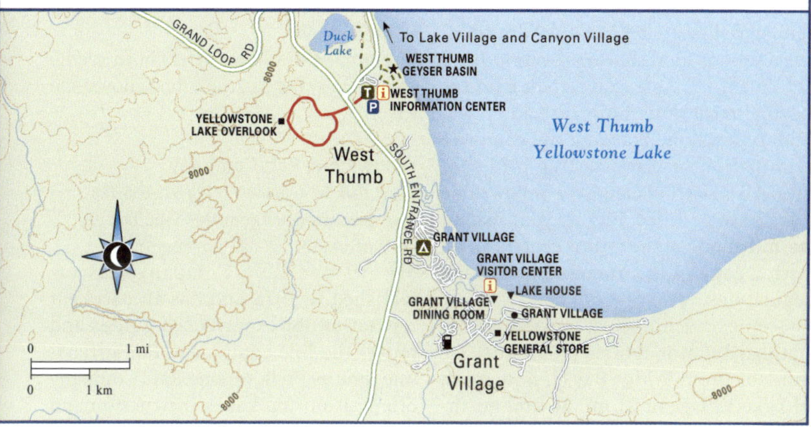

Elephant Back Mountain

Distance: 3.6 mi (5.8 km) round-trip
Duration: 2 hours
Elevation gain: 793 ft (242 m)
Effort: Moderate
Trail surface: Uneven dirt, rocks
Trailhead: Elephant Back Mountain Trailhead

This lollipop loop leaves from the Elephant Back Mountain trailhead at a pullout 1 mi (1.6 km) south of Fishing Bridge Junction and just north of the turnoff to Lake Village Road. The trail leads through a dense lodgepole forest—do not forget your bear spray or your wits—to a stunning overlook of Yellowstone Lake.

Alum Creek Trail

Distance: 8.3 mi (13.4 km) round-trip
Duration: 4 hours
Elevation gain: 292 ft (89 m)
Effort: Moderate
Trailhead: North end of the Hayden Valley

The Alum Creek Trail, 4.4 mi (7.1 km) south of Canyon at the north end of the Hayden Valley, is a good hike that incorporates some of the Mary Mountain Trail as well as the Nez Perce Trail, which go deep into the Hayden Valley. Wide open and relatively flat, the trail offers an out-and-back trip through prime bison and grizzly habitat. There are also some thermal features along Alum Creek.

Boating and Fishing

Anglers do not need state fishing licenses in Yellowstone, but a Yellowstone fishing permit—available at any of the visitor centers in the park—is required.

The Southern Loop

Some 50,000 anglers are lured to Yellowstone each year by the promise of elusive trout, and they are seldom disappointed by the offerings at **Yellowstone Lake.** In addition to the prized native cutthroat, the lake is home to a population of nonnative lake trout that is devastating the cutthroat trout population and threatening all the animals that eat the cutthroat trout. Introduced in 1890 into Lewis and Shoshone Lakes by the US Fish Commission, the lake trout were first documented in Yellowstone Lake in the mid-1990s; scientists believe they were illegally introduced from a nearby lake in the 1980s. The average lake trout lives and spawns in deep waters, feeding on as many as 40 cutthroat each year. By comparison, cutthroat trout spawn in the shallow tributaries of the lake, making them an important food source for a variety of creatures that include eagles and bears. Since the lake trout have no predators in the deep waters of Yellowstone Lake, they are creating a serious food shortage by devouring the cutthroat. As a result, the eagles are having to eat other birds instead of fish, and Yellowstone is facing the complete elimination of some nesting bird species. All lake trout caught in Yellowstone Lake must be killed. Pick up your **fishing permit** at one of the visitor centers along with a copy of the Yellowstone fishing regulations.

Scenic or fishing boat tours as well as outboard motor rentals ($68/hour) are available from **Bridge Bay Marina,** south of Lake Village or 21 mi (34 km) northeast of West Thumb.

Xanterra

307/344-7311 or 866/439-7375; www.yellowstonenationalparklodges.com

Reservations can be made through Xanterra for hour-long guided cruises of Yellowstone Lake aboard the *Lake Queen* ($21.25), which departs regularly from the marina mid-June to mid-September and cruises around Stevenson Island.

Gardiner

The Yellowstone is the longest free-flowing river in the Lower 48, and as such it offers excellent boating and fishing opportunities. With the river plunging through town on its way to Yankee Jim Canyon, Gardiner is home to several outfitters that can whet your appetite for adventure, trout, or both.

Flying Pig Adventure Company

511 Scott St.; 888/792-9193; www.flyingpigrafting.com; May-Sept.; 2-hour scenic or whitewater trips from $74, full-day trips from $148

The Flying Pig Adventure Company is a full-service outfitter offering guided white-water rafting, horseback rides, wildlife safaris, and cowboy cookouts.

Montana Whitewater

603 Scott St.; 406/763-4465 or 406/848-7398; www.montanawhitewater.com; half day from $74, full day from $140

Montana Whitewater offers both scenic and white-water floats on the Yellowstone River.

Yellowstone Raft Company

212 W. Park St.; 406/848-7777 or 800/858-7781; www.yellowstoneraft.com; May-Sept.; half-day raft trip from $74, full-day trips from $129

Yellowstone Raft Company was established in 1978 and has an excellent reputation for experienced guides and top-of-the-line equipment. For adrenaline junkies, Yellowstone Raft Company offers sit-on-top kayak instruction and adventures.

Parks' Fly Shop

202 2nd St. S.; 406/848-7314; www.parksflyshop.com; 8am-6pm daily summer, 9am-5pm Mon.-Sat., 10am-4pm Sun. fall-spring; walk/wade trips for 2 anglers $578-683, float trips $600-710

For anglers eager to wet a line in or out of the park in search of native cutthroats or brown trout, Parks' Fly Shop is the best place to start. This is an old-school shop with a 1920s cash register—nothing fancy here. It offers half-day and full-day walk and wade or float trips. Anglers can pick up their licenses and any supplies in the retail shop, which stays open year-round. And since Parks' has been serving the area since 1953, its guides are keenly aware of the spots where the fish greatly outnumber the anglers. After Thanksgiving, half of the shop becomes a **cross-country ski and snowshoe rental** shop.

Cooke City

One short but worthwhile hike can be found 2 mi (3 km) west of the Pebble Creek Campground at **Trout Lake.** The hike itself is short and steep, just 1.2 mi (1.9 km) round-trip, and leaves from the Trout Lake Trailhead on the north side of the road. Anglers can bring a rod

Be Safe and Smart in the Backcountry

Hiking and camping in the Yellowstone backcountry is undoubtedly the best way to understand and appreciate this magnificently wild place. But with this opportunity comes the responsibility to keep yourself safe, protect the animals from human-caused altercations, and preserve this pristine environment.

When hiking, **prevent erosion and trail degradation** by hiking single file and always staying on the trail. Don't take shortcuts or cut corners on switchbacks. If you do have to leave the trail, disperse your group so that you don't trample the vegetation.

Wildlife Safety

Chances are good that you will encounter some kind of wildlife in the backcountry, so you need to be prepared. **Never approach an animal:** Always stay at least 25 yards/meters away from all wildlife, and at least 100 yards/meters away from predators, including bears. Make noise as you hike to give animals the opportunity to depart before an encounter. Do not hike at the edges of day—dawn or dusk—or at night, as these are the most active times for bears and other predators. Always be aware of your surroundings and pay attention to wind direction. Look for overturned rocks and logs, dug-out areas, and, of course, carcasses, all of which suggest bear activity.

If you do **encounter a bear,** know what to do. If there is some distance between you and the bear, give the bear an opportunity to leave, or redirect your own party. If you run into a bear at close range, be as nonthreatening as possible. Talk calmly and back away. Never turn your back, and never run. Make sure you have your bear spray accessible. If the bear charges, stand your ground. Bears will often bluff charge to determine whether you will run and are thus prey. If the bear does attack, keep your pack on, fall to the ground on your belly, protect your head and neck with your arms, and play dead. When the bear leaves, get up and retreat. In the very uncommon circumstance that a bear provokes an attack or enters a tent, fight the bear with every resource you have.

Go to great lengths to **avoid attracting bears** by hanging all food, cooking utensils, and scented items (toothpaste, deodorant, other toiletries, menstrual supplies, and trash) in a bear bag in a tree or atop a bear pole. Designate a separate cooking and eating area away from the sleeping tents. Dispose of your trash and personal waste properly.

Permits

You need to plan your trip carefully and secure all permits (required year-round) and **backcountry campsites** online in advance or in person in the walk-up period at any one of nine backcountry permit offices: Bechler Ranger Station, Canyon Visitor Center, Grant Village Visitor Center, Bridge Bay Ranger Station, Mammoth Visitor Center, Old Faithful Ranger Station, South Entrance Ranger Station, Tower Ranger Station, or the West Yellowstone Visitor Information Center (307/344-2160; www.nps.gov/yell; permits available 8am-4:30pm daily June-Aug.; $50 annual backcountry pass, $5 pp over nine years old per night, plus a $10 reservation fee). Some of Yellowstone's 293 backcountry campsites can be reserved in advance (www.recreation.gov) during the Early Access Lottery (Mar. 1-20) or General On-Sale period (beginning late Apr.).

Walk-up backcountry permits are available on a first-come, first-served basis at one of the backcountry permit offices no more than 48 hours before your trip. A park booklet titled ***Beyond Road's End*** is available online and will help familiarize you with the backcountry regulations and restrictions.

after July 15 when it opens to catch-and-release fishing for native cutthroats. In late spring and early summer, trout can be seen spawning in the inches-deep inlet, a fairly miraculous sight. There is an excellent trail around the 12-acre (5-ha) lake and shallow inlet and a decent chance of spotting playful otters, but hikers should take great care not to disturb the fish, especially during spawning. Bear awareness and a can of bear spray are necessary, as the bruins like fish too.

Another great place to combine fishing, hiking, and wildlife-watching is along the trail at **Slough Creek.** East of Tower Junction 6 mi (9 km) or west of the northeast entrance is an unpaved road on the north side of the road leading to Slough Creek Campground. The trailhead is 1.5 mi (2.4 km) down the road on the right side, just before the campground. The trail itself is a double-rutted wagon trail that leads to Silver Tip Ranch, a legendary private ranch just outside the park. The trail is maintained for 11 mi (17.7 km) one-way and only gains 400 ft (122 m) in elevation. All along the trail there is world-class fishing in slow-moving Slough Creek, home to a healthy population of native cutthroat trout. You may meet elk, bison, wolves, and even grizzlies along the trail, so be prepared and be safe.

West Yellowstone

The fishing around West Yellowstone tends to be as plentiful as it is phenomenal. In addition to the big-name rivers like the **Madison, Firehole, Yellowstone,** and the nearby **Henry's Fork** across the border in Idaho, there are all sorts of small streams and beautiful lakes of all sizes. **Hebgen Lake** and **Quake Lake** are two favorites for year-round fishing.

Big Sky Anglers

39 Madison Ave.; 406/646-7801; www.bigskyanglers.com; 7am-10pm daily during the season, 9am-5pm daily off-season; full-day walk/wade or float trip for 2 anglers from $699, walk/wade clinic for 1-2 anglers $375

You won't have any difficulty finding guides and gear in the town of West Yellowstone. Among the best is Big Sky Anglers, which has been outfitting anglers for 60 years. They also offer guided interpretive tours in the park.

Jacklin's Outfitters

105 Yellowstone Ave.; 406/646-7336; www.jacklinsflyshop.qwestoffice; 7am-10pm daily summer, 8am-6pm daily off-season; full-day guided float for 1-2 people $450, half-day guided walk/wade for 1-2 people $450

A pretty famous name among anglers is Bob Jacklin of Jacklin's Fly Shop. Bob is happy to give private casting lessons for beginning anglers; call for rates.

Skiing and Mountain Sports

Cooke City

With an average of 194 in (493 cm) of snowfall each year, mountainous terrain with elevation that ranges 7,000-10,000 ft (2,134-3,048 m), and a nearly interminable winter, Cooke City is a winter mecca with 60 mi (97 km) of groomed snowmobile trails and endless acres of ungroomed terrain for skiing and snowmobiling. Some favorite trails are **Daisy Pass, Lulu Pass,** and **Round Lake Trail.** A number of places in town rent snowmobiles and all the necessary gear. Most important, you'll need to talk with experts about local conditions, trail closures, and avalanche dangers.

Cooke City Motorsports

203 Eaton St.; 406/838-2231; www.cookecitymotorsports.com; snowmobiles from $345

Cooke City Motorsports offers snowmobile and UTV rentals for all skill levels. Guided tours start at $750, which does not include rentals.

Biking Through the Park

Car-Free Days

For a few magical weeks between the end of the snowmobile season and the onset of the summer car traffic, and from the park's closure to the first big snowfall, Yellowstone's roads are open exclusively to nonmotorized users. This means that bicyclists, walkers, runners, in-line skaters, and roller skiers can cruise through the park in near silence with eyes focused on bison traffic as opposed to Winnebagos.

The following timeframes suggest when the roads are typically closed to autos but open to everyone else. Bear in mind that the dates change yearly and are always weather-dependent, so check the live road status map (www.nops.gov/yell/planyourvisit/parkroads.htm) or call 307/344-2117. Also, be aware that the roads between Madison Junction and Old Faithful and Tower to Canyon are closed in spring for human safety and bear management. And the roads from Norris Junction to Canyon, and West Thumb to Canyon and Old Faithful, are not open to bikes in fall or spring.

Where and When to Bike

- **West Entrance and Mammoth Hot Springs:** Open to bikes when closed to vehicles, usually first three weeks in April, and early November to early December.
- **East Entrance to the east end of Sylvan Pass:** Open to bikes when closed to vehicles, usually early May and early November.
- **Madison to Old Faithful:** Early November to early December.
- **South Entrance to West Thumb:** Early November to early December.

Rules for the Road

There is something truly spellbinding about being on the open road in the park, the wind whistling through your helmet. The relative silence allows some unrivaled wildlife-viewing and necessitates great care. As nerve-racking as it can be to get engulfed by a herd of bison while driving in your car, coming across them on your bike is an entirely different scenario. Still, if you are cautious and respectful, being on your bike can allow you to feel somewhat less like an intruder and more like a resident. You can fall into sync with the flow of the rivers, the movement of the breeze, and the calls of the animals. It is an unforgettable way to experience the park.

With that said: Respect, restraint, and absolute caution are important for your safety and the well-being of wildlife. Keep a good distance from all wildlife—25 yards/meters from ungulates and 100 yards/meters from predators. Remember that bison can run at speeds topping 30 mph (48 kph), and they can jump a 6-ft (2-m) fence. Harbor no illusions about your immunity from an attack. The fact that you have approached silently allows for more of a startle factor and increases the likelihood of a conflict. Wear a helmet, and dress in layers: Yellowstone can go from blue skies to blizzard conditions in a staggeringly short period of time. Be prepared for anything, and understand that there are no services in the park at these off-season times. For information about road conditions, call 307/344-2109 (8am-4:30pm Mon.-Fri.).

Cooke City Exxon

204 Main St.; 406/838-2244; www.cookecityexxon.com; side-by-side rentals from $245 for 2 hours, full-day snowmobile rentals from $375

Cooke City Exxon rents snowmobiles and side-by-sides in the appropriate seasons as well as the necessary gear.

Bearclaw Bob's Sales and Service

309 E. Main St.; 406/838-2040; www.bearclawsalesandservice.com

When the snow melts, you can rent ATVs and side-by-sides ($305-360/day) from Bearclaw Bob's Sales and Service as another way to get out and cover a lot of ground. They also rent sleds ($285-450/day) when snow is on the ground. They rent all the equipment needed in any season, and you can—and should!—buy or rent bear spray.

West Yellowstone

Sandwiched between Yellowstone and the Gallatin National Forest on a high plateau, West Yellowstone offers excellent terrain for mountain biking. Because of its high altitude and location at the top of a reasonably flat plateau, West Yellowstone is also known for its cross-country ski trails.

Rendezvous Ski Trails

Look for the archway at the south end of Geyser St.; 406/646-7701; www.skirunbikemt.com; passes required Dec.-Mar., day pass $15, 3-day pass $30

The town's excellent Rendezvous Ski Trails offer roughly 22 mi (35 km) of rolling terrain, groomed for both skate and classic skiers, which easily converts to a single-track for mountain bikers and trail runners when the snow melts. Athletes from around the world come to train in West thanks in large part to this trail system. And it should be noted that the proximity to Yellowstone opens up a whole new world of opportunity for skiers.

Freeheel & Wheel

33 Yellowstone Ave.; 406/646-7744; www.freeheelandwheel.com; 9am-7pm Mon.-Sat., 9am-6pm Sun. summer, 9am-5pm daily fall-spring

The best bike and ski shop in town—which also has surprisingly stylish clothes, great gear, and killer coffee—is the Freeheel & Wheel. It rents, sells, and services bikes and skis and can offer advice on the region's best rides and trails. Front suspension kid and adult mountain bikes and road bikes can be rented ($50/day) and come with a helmet and water bottle. Skate skis, classic skis, and backcountry touring skis are all rentable for $35/day. Touring ski packages (for machine-groomed or skier-groomed trails) and snowshoes are available for $30/day. Pull sleds can be rented for $25/day. Any of this gear can be delivered to your hotel for $5/package.

High Mark Rentals

633 Madison Ave.; 406/646-7855; www.highmarkrentals.com; 8am-5pm Tues.-Sat. summer, 8am-5pm daily winter; trail and crossover sleds $200-230, mountain sleds $270-300, high-performance sleds for experts only $350-425

High Mark Rentals offers snowmobile, ATV, electric bike, and bike rentals. They rent Polaris, Ski-Doo, and Arctic Cat machines, and are the only place in town to rent SLP Stage 2 snowmobiles for experienced riders who want extra power for climbing and speed. Importantly, they also rent avalanche packs, beacons, and radios, plus all the winter gear you'll need to stay warm on your snowmobile adventure.

Two Top Snowmobile Rentals

645 Gibbon Ave.; 800/522-7802 or 406/646-7802; www.yellowstonevacations.com; 7:30am-5pm daily

There are numerous places in town to rent a snowmobile, and since the park mandates that all snowmobilers within park boundaries use a guide, several outfits offer guiding services both in and out of the park. Two Top Snowmobile Rentals has rentals for self-guided tours outside the park starting at $180-225 for single-riding machines and $240 for double-riding machines. Guided tours around Old Faithful or the Grand Canyon start at $340 for a single-riding machine and $370 for a double-riding machine. They have licensed guides, Yellowstone-mandated four-stroke engines, and other rental equipment, including clothing. Drivers must be 16+ with a valid driver's license.

Yellowstone Dog Sled Adventures

406/223-5134; www.yellowstonedogsledadventures.com

For those who want to explore the backcountry outside Yellowstone National Park in a quieter way, dogsledding might be the perfect choice. Yellowstone Dog Sled Adventures offers half-day "Learn to Mush" tours ($295 pp) where guests get to drive their own sled. Other offerings allow guests to dive deep into the world of sled dogs and huskies (from $95/hour), snowshoe with huskies ($95 pp for 45 minutes-1.5 hour), or try an overnight campout in a wood-heated tent ($500 pp). Gear is provided.

Yellowstone National Park Lodges

307/344-7311; www.yellowstonenationalparklodges.com

Another amazing way to see the park is on a guided snow coach tour. Transportation between Old Faithful and Mammoth ($168.40), and an array of guided tours, can be arranged through Yellowstone National Park Lodges. Day tours of the Grand Canyon (from $334) include the Hoodoos, Swan Lake Flats, Obsidian Cliff, and Roaring Mountain; night tours focus on steam, stars, and winter soundscapes (from $80). Other tours whisk visitors through a winter wonderland to destinations like West Thumb Geyser Basin (from $108) and the Firehole Basin (from $100). Shuttles for skiers and snowshoers can also be arranged.

Food

As the southern loop is generally the most heavily traveled section of the park, there are plenty of dining opportunities. In the park restaurants, breakfast and lunch are on a first-come, first-served basis, but reservations are strongly recommended for dinner, particularly if 5pm or 9pm is not your ideal dining hour. In almost all the venues, you will find some good vegetarian options and many items made with sustainable or organic ingredients; these are identified on each menu. If you are planning a day activity away from the center of things, many restaurants or cafeterias offer box lunches. Place your order the night before, and it will be ready in the morning. The Yellowstone General Stores at Grant Village, Lake Village, and Old Faithful also have fast-food service, groceries, and snacks.

Inside the Park

The Northern Loop

★ Old West Dinner Cookout

100 Roosevelt Lodge Rd.; 307/344-7311; www.yellowstonenationalparklodges.com; early June-mid-Sept.; $89-123

By far the most unusual meal option in the park is the Old West Dinner Cookout, which operates daily early June to mid-September from the Roosevelt Lodge and is served in Yellowstone's wilderness. The hearty steak-and-potatoes dinner with all the cowboy trimmings can be attended on horseback (1-hour rides from $123) or via covered wagon (from $89).

Roosevelt Lodge Dining Room

101 Roosevelt Lodge Rd.; 307/344-7311; www.yellowstonenationalparklodges.com; 7am-10am, 11:30am-3:30pm, and 4:30pm-9:30pm daily early June-early Sept.; $8-28

Breakfast, lunch, and dinner are served daily throughout the season in the Roosevelt Lodge Dining Room. The offerings tend to be heartier, with options like beef and bison burgers, pulled pork, and pork carnitas. Guests are seated first-come, first-served in the charming rustic lodge atmosphere.

Canyon Lodge Eatery

83 B Lupine Court; 307/344-7311; www.yellowstonenationalparklodges.com; 6:30am-10am, 11:30am-3pm, and 5pm-9:30pm daily mid-May-mid-Oct., reduced hours and limited menu mid-Oct.-late Oct.; $9-22

Touted as the "ultimate food hall," Canyon Lodge Eatery is a fun 1950s-inspired café that serves "slow food fast," from shredded barbecue pork and bison pastrami sandwiches for lunch to rotisserie chicken, beef short rib, and roasted trout for dinner. There's also a wok station serving made-to-order rice bowls and a counter for grab-and-go items.

Canyon Lodge Falls Café

83 B Lupine Court; 307/344-7311; www.yellowstonenationalparklodges.com; 6am-10am and 11am-8pm, beer and wine 11am-3pm daily late May-early Sept.; $4-13

Serving espresso drinks, bagel breakfast sandwiches, and plenty of grab-and-go options for breakfast, lunch, and dinner, plus made-to-order flatbreads, Canyon Lodge Falls Café sources local, sustainable, and organic ingredients.

Mammoth Hotel Dining Room

305 A Albright Ave.; 307/344-7311; www.yellowstonenationalparklodges.com; 6:30am-10am, 11:30am-2:30pm, and 5pm-9pm daily late Apr.-mid-Oct. and mid-Dec.-early Mar., extended dinner hours 4:30pm-10pm mid-May-mid-Oct.; $10-31

The elegant Mammoth Hotel Dining Room is the first four-star Certified Green Restaurant in the park, the first in the state of Wyoming, and one of only 25 in the country. The menu includes a hearty breakfast buffet plus à la carte items like a vegan breakfast bowl and seven-grain buttermilk pancakes. Lunch options include fish tacos, tofu banh mi, and burgers with local beef. Upscale dinner options range from Maine lobster and corn chowder to various steaks, fish, and chicken. Reservations are required for dinner. Don't miss the Basque cake with brandied Flathead cherries if it's on the menu.

Mammoth Terrace Grill

305 A Albright Ave.; 307/344-7311; www.yellowstonenationalparklodges.com; 7am-10:30am daily early June-early Sept., 10:30am-8pm daily late Apr.-early June, 10:30am-9pm daily early June-early Sept., 11am-7pm daily early Sept.-mid-Oct.; $7-12

Mammoth Terrace Grill is a great option for a quick meal between adventures. Closed in winter, the grill offers standard fare and three meals a day.

The Southern Loop

Grant Village Dining Room

550 Sculpin Ln.; 307/344-7311 or 866/439-7375; www.yellowstonenationalparklodges.com; 6:30am-10am, 11:30am-2:30pm, and 5pm-10pm daily late May-early Oct.; $16-33

The Grant Village Dining Room offers a view of the lake, good service, and a nice variety of American cuisine. In addition to the à la carte menu for breakfast, a buffet is available. The restaurant calls itself a fish house and serves everything from clam chowder and calamari to mussels, salmon, fish-and-chips, and, of course, trout. There is also a raw bar serving oysters. Other entrées include Wagyu burgers, chicken curry, and corn ravioli. Reservations are required for dinner. For cocktails, the **Seven Stool Lounge** is open daily 5pm-10pm.

Lake House

1095 Grant Marina Rd.; 307/344-7311 or 866/439-7375; www.yellowstonenationalparklodges.com; 5pm-10pm (hours can change without notice) daily late May-Sept.; $5-18

Just a short walk (or drive) through the woods from the Grant Village Lodge buildings, Lake House sits right on the lake, with great views and a casual ambience. Diners in this repurposed marina are seated first-come, first-served, and the restaurant serves street-style tacos with pork, chicken, fish, beef, or veggies, along with classic Mexican desserts including tres leches cake and churros.

★ Lake Yellowstone Hotel Dining Room

235 Yellowstone Lake Rd.; 307/344-7311 or 866/439-7375; www.yellowstonenationalparklodges.com; 6:30am-10am, 11:30am-2:30pm, and 4:30pm-10pm daily mid-May-early Sept.; $17-40

The Lake Yellowstone Hotel Dining Room is the most elegant dining room in the park, with a gorgeous view of the lake. The restaurant is committed to creating dishes with fresh, local, organic, and sustainable ingredients. Lunch is a good way to sample some of the gourmet fare without putting too large a dent in your pocketbook. Try the bison burger au poivre or the coq au vin sandwich. Dinner (reservations required) at the hotel is sure to be a memorable experience, with options like olive oil-poached halibut and cassoulet with pork, rabbit, antelope, and duck. The **Sun Room** serves appetizers and dessert with plenty of adult drink options.

Directly inside the hotel is the **Lake Hotel Deli** (check website for hours, generally open daily mid-May-early Sept., shortened hours early/late seasons; $5-14), which serves a nice selection of soups, salads, and sandwiches. **Wylie's Canteen at Lake Lodge** (check website for hours, generally open daily for breakfast, lunch, and dinner early June-late Sept., shortened hours early/late seasons; $7-34) is a casual place for a quick bite. It serves basic breakfast standards, plenty of kids' favorites, and dishes such as burgers and hot dogs with all the toppings, pot roast, and salmon.

Old Faithful Inn Dining Room

3200 Old Faithful Inn Rd.; 307/344-7311 or 866/439-7375; www.yellowstonenationalparklodges.com; 6:30am-10am, 11:30am-2:30pm, and 4:30pm-10pm daily early May-mid-Oct.; $14-33

Five eateries are located in the Old Faithful complex, but by far the most desirable is the Old Faithful Inn Dining Room, which offers a buffet for each of the main meals daily as well as an à la carte menu. Lunch is a "Western buffet" with items such as battered walleye, pulled pork, and bison bratwurst. If you don't opt for the dinner buffet (featuring prime rib and smoked trout), you could try pork osso buco, fried chicken, or New York strip steak. Reservations are required for dinner.

Bear Paw Deli

3200 Old Faithful Inn Rd.; 307/344-7311 or 866/439-7375; www.yellowstonenationalparklodges.com; 6:30am-10am and 10:30am-9pm daily late May-early Sept., closes at 1:30pm in May and early Sept.-mid-Oct.; $4-14

The Bear Paw Deli, also inside the inn, is perfect for on-the-go meals. It offers a continental breakfast, including bagel sandwiches, and sandwich and salad deli fare for lunch, as well as several flavors of ice cream. There is also a cafeteria and bakeshop in the lodge and a dining room and grill in the Old Faithful Snow Lodge.

Outside the Park

Gardiner

★ The Corral

711 Scott St. W., across from the Super 8 Motel; 406/848-7627; www.corralvillas.com/restaurant; 7am-10pm daily summer, noon-8pm Thurs.-Tues. winter, hours subject to change; $13-18

Known since 1960 for its "Hateful Hamburgers" and the huge personality of its owner, Helen, this fabulous burger joint is now known as The Corral. Even without Helen, this is still the kind of place you might easily drive 100 mi (161 km) to for the burgers, shakes, and old-school ambience. The limited seating is mostly outside, and there is often a line of people waiting to order. But none of that will matter when you take your first bite of a bison bacon cheeseburger or a grilled elk burger. They source their meat and produce locally whenever possible. The Corral even managed to improve on Helen's by expanding the menu and cleaning the place up a bit. This is still a little slice of hamburger paradise—if you like that sort of thing.

Yellowstone Grill

404 Scott St. W.; 406/848-9433; 7am-11:30am Tues.-Sun. summer, 7am-11:30am Wed.-Sun. winter; $8-15

For a good, hearty breakfast, excellent pastries, smoothies, fresh Mexican food, and more, the Yellowstone Grill is sure to please. Remember though, this is small-town Montana. Sometimes the place closes when short-staffed. Or when the owners' youngest son has a Legion baseball game. Be glad for that; the important stuff still matters here.

Tumbleweed Bookstore & Café

501 Scott St. W.; 406/848-2225; www.tumbleweedbooksandcafe.weebly.com; 7am-3pm daily summer; $5-12

A great place for a grab-and-go meal, with fantastic book browsing while you wait, is Tumbleweed Bookstore & Café. They have excellent breakfast burritos, grilled sandwiches, wraps, soups, salads, and baked goodies. Vegetarians, vegans, and gluten-free people will be delighted with the broad offerings.

Wonderland Café & Lodge

206 Main St.; 406/223-1914; www.wonderlandcafeandlodge.com; 7am-8:30pm daily summer; $13-45

Wonderland Café & Lodge serves coffee and baked goods all day, plus excellent lunch and dinner items including elk chili, trout, rib eye, pasta, and burgers. They also have free Wi-Fi and charging stations.

Yellowstone Pizza Company

210 E. Park; 406/848-9991; www.yellowstonepizzaga.wixsite.com; noon-9pm daily May-Oct.; $19-27

If pizza is what you're craving, head to Yellowstone Pizza Company, which serves 13-inch thin-crust pizzas, plus pastas, salads, and appetizers.

Cooke City

There are a million ways to work up an appetite in and around Cooke City. Be assured you won't go hungry (or thirsty, for that matter).

★ Beartooth Café

211 Main St.; 406/838-2475; www.beartoothcafe.com; 11am-4:30pm and 5pm-9pm daily late May-late Sept.; $13-30

Beartooth Café offers excellent mountain fare—think steak, barbecue, and trout—in a cozy setting. The front-porch outdoor dining is a treat.

Prospector Restaurant

210 US 212; 406/838-2251; www.cookecity.com; 8am-10:30am and 11am-4:30pm daily, 5pm-8:30pm Sun.-Thurs., 5pm-9:30pm Fri.-Sat., saloon 11am-9pm Sun.-Thurs., 11am-10pm Fri.-Sat.; $15-29

The Prospector Restaurant, inside the Soda Butte Lodge, is open year-round and particularly known for steak and prime rib—not a stretch in these parts. The Soda Butte Saloon in the lodge serves standard bar snacks.

Cooke City Store

101 Main St.; 406/838-2234 or 406/698-8353; www.cookecitystore.com; 8am-7pm daily mid-May-Sept., hours subject to change

For those wanting to pick up some supplies, the bright red Cooke City Store is as much a local museum and community center as it is a place to grab some bread and a bottle of sunscreen. At the fly shop inside, **Trout Rider Fly Shop,** you can get fishing licenses for Montana, Wyoming, and Yellowstone National Park as well as flies and other supplies.

West Yellowstone

Ernie's Bakery & Deli

406 Hwy. 20; 406/646-9467; www.erniesbakery.com; 7am-3pm daily summer, 7am-2pm daily winter; $10-16

A great spot for a full breakfast, hot lunch, or terrific boxed lunches is the long-standing Ernie's Bakery & Deli. Boxed lunch orders will not be filled on the day of; they must be ordered the day before in person during business hours or online before 7pm.

Timberline Café

135 Yellowstone Ave.; 406/646-9349; www.timberlinecafe.net; 6:30am-9pm daily mid-May-early Oct.; $18-40

For the best soup, salad, and potato bar in town, try the Timberline Café, an old-school establishment that has been feeding Yellowstone visitors and locals during the summer season since the early 1900s. Don't miss the homemade pie.

Firehole Bar-B-Que Company

120 Firehole Ave.; 406/641-0020; www.fireholebbqco.com; 4pm-sold out May-Oct.; $11-32

Firehole Bar-B-Que Company smokes their meats daily, and the flavor comes out in this Central Texas-style barbecue joint. From pulled pork and brisket to ribs and buffalo sausage, these folks serve up the real deal. They're open summer and fall, but only until they sell out the day's meat, which can often be well before sunset.

★ Taqueria Las Palmitas

21 N. Canyon St.; 208/760-8174; 11am-10pm daily early Apr.-mid-Oct.; $6-15

If you like Mexican street food, the best place within a day's drive from Yellowstone is, without a doubt, Taqueria Las Palmitas, known locally as "The Taco Bus." We're talking soft tacos, beans, and more, piled onto paper plates and served

Top to bottom: Mammoth Terrace Grill; Cooke City Store; Timberline Café

in an old-school bus. It couldn't be less fancy or more satisfying.

Embers at Bar N Ranch

890 Buttermilk Creek Rd.; 406/646-0300; www.bar-n-ranch.com; 7am-10am and 5pm-10pm daily mid-May-mid-Oct.; $18-26

About 6 mi (10 km) outside of town is the Bar N Ranch, a wonderful place for a meal. With beautiful views all around from the Embers dining room, you can indulge in terrific Western gourmet cuisine including game burgers, bison stir-fry, steaks, and pasta. One favorite is the camp-out chicken sandwich with spicy slaw, huckleberry barbecue sauce, pickled onions, and cheddar on a brioche bun. Gourmet picnic lunches are available, too.

Accommodations

Inside the Park

Reservations for all hotels inside the park should be made through **Xanterra/Yellowstone National Park Lodges** (307/344-7311 or 866/439-7375; www.yellowstonenationalparklodges.com). Note that there are no televisions, radios, telephones, or air-conditioning provided in the accommodations.

The Northern Loop

Mammoth Hot Springs Hotel and Cabins

2 Mammoth Hotel Ave.; late Apr.-early Oct. and mid-Dec.-early Mar.; $124-345

Mammoth Hot Springs Hotel and Cabins has 79 rooms, each with private bath, and another 116 cabins, four with hot tubs. Suites start at $664. Set amid historic Fort Yellowstone, Mammoth provides convenient access to restaurants, gift shops, a gas station, and the visitor center, so guests may forget they're somewhat out in the wild. Despite human and car traffic in Mammoth, wolves have been known to sneak onto the green watered lawns at night to take down an unsuspecting well-grazed elk. You can imagine the surprise when early risers spotted the carcass on their way to get a breakfast burrito.

★ Roosevelt Lodge Cabins

100 Roosevelt Lodge Rd.; early June-early Sept.; $114-182

Named for Yellowstone champion Theodore Roosevelt, the Roosevelt Lodge Cabins offer a timeless rustic setting reminiscent of a great old dude ranch in a quieter corner of the park. The Roughrider Cabins offer double beds and a wood-burning stove. What they lack in amenities they make up for with charming authenticity. Toilets and communal showers are available nearby. The Frontier Cabins are slightly larger and include a private bathroom with a shower, toilet, and sink.

Canyon Lodge & Cabins

41 Clover Lane; early June-late Sept.; $242-500

Set adjacent to the spectacular Grand Canyon of the Yellowstone, Canyon

Lodge & Cabins is the largest lodging property in the park. The facilities were built in the 1950s and 1960s, then added on to and renovated significantly in 2016 to bring the total to 590 rooms and cabins. Options include standard rooms, deluxe rooms, and Western cabins, which are basic motel-style units with private full bathrooms. Suites start at $940.

The Southern Loop

★ Lake Yellowstone Hotel

235 Yellowstone Lake Rd.; mid-May-early Oct.; $285-822

Lake Yellowstone Hotel is both grand and picturesque, perched on the shores of Yellowstone Lake. Originally built in 1891 and completely renovated in 2014 to celebrate its Colonial Revival influences, the hotel houses the nicest rooms in the park. As is true everywhere in the park, though, the appeal comes from the location and the views. If you are staying in the hotel, request a room with a view of the lake. Suites start at $1,114.

The Sandpiper Lodge

235 Yellowstone Lake Rd.; early May-early Oct.; from $350

In an adjacent building to the Lake Yellowstone Hotel, the Sandpiper Lodge also offers recently renovated rooms. Individual cabins, called Lake Cottages, are behind the hotel but part of the Lake Lodge operation. These duplexes were remodeled in 2004 and are simple and modest.

Lake Lodge Cabins

235 Yellowstone Lake Rd.; early May-early Oct.; $178-276

There are 186 Lake Lodge Cabins, which are clean and simple; many were renovated in 2018. Located just off the lake, the cabins are clustered around the main lodge, which is an inviting common area for guests to gather. It has a large porch that beckons guests to take a seat in one of the rocking chairs and soak in the view, as well as two fireplaces, a gift shop, and a cozy lounge. The Western cabins

Lake Yellowstone Hotel

are a bit more spacious, with two queen beds and a shower-tub in each bathroom. The Pioneer cabins are older and more spartan, with shower-only bathrooms and 1-2 double beds. The setting is tranquil and quiet, and early risers may spot a herd of bison wandering through the property.

★ Old Faithful Inn

3200 Old Faithful Inn Rd.; early May-early Oct.; $193-506

The Old Faithful Inn is the most popular lodging inside the park, and for good reason. The original part of the lodge, known as the Old House, was built in 1903-1904 by acclaimed architect Robert Reamer. Situated close to the Old Faithful geyser, the lodge epitomizes rustic beauty, originality, and strength. It has a large front lobby that houses a massive stone fireplace. The larger rooms are in the wings of the inn, built in the 1910s and 1920s, while the more modest rooms are in the Old House. The inn has a wide assortment of guest rooms and rates, ranging from two-room suites with sitting rooms and fridges (from $942) to simple rooms without individual baths. Since this is the most sought-after lodging in the park, make reservations well in advance.

Old Faithful Lodge Cabins

725 Old Faithful Lodge Rd.; mid-May-late Sept.; $116-192

Close to the inn are the Old Faithful Lodge Cabins, offering simple and rustic lodging. If you are looking for budget-friendly accommodations that put you in the center of park activity, these are a good option. The cabins are small motel-style units that vary in condition. Many of them were renovated in 2016. The lower-priced cabins do not come with baths, but there are communal showers nearby. The cabins are scattered around a main log cabin-style lodge. Built in the 1920s, the main lodge has a large cafeteria, bakery, and fully stocked gift shop, making it popular with park visitors throughout the day.

Old Faithful Snow Lodge and Cabins

2051 Snow Lodge Ave.; late Apr.-mid-Oct. and mid-Dec.-late Feb.; $146-365

The Old Faithful Snow Lodge and Cabins are among the newest accommodations in the park. The original lodge was torn down and a new structure was built in 1999. Its architecture is intended to complement, though not duplicate, the Old Faithful Inn, and the lodge won a Cody Award for Western Design. It offers comfortable, modern rooms decorated with Western flair. It also has a few motel-style cabins, built in 1989. The Western cabins are a good value for the money; they're large rooms with two queen beds and a full bath. This is one of only two lodges (the other is Mammoth Hot Springs Hotel) open during the winter season in Yellowstone.

Grant Village

24 Rainbow Loop; late May-early Oct.; from $306

Grant Village is about 20 mi (32 km) southeast of Old Faithful on the West Thumb of Yellowstone Lake. Although the accommodations do not have the same rustic feel or character of the other lodges, they do offer a comfortable and modern place to stay away from the crowds. The complex is made up of six small condo-like buildings. Each building has 50 nicely furnished hotel rooms that come with full baths and either two double beds or one queen.

Outside the Park

Gardiner

Gardiner is built to accommodate the overflow from the park, but in reality, many of the little motels have more charm and much better value, particularly in non-summer months, than those inside the park. For the most part, it's hard to go wrong in Gardiner. There are plenty of small cabins and larger vacation rentals in the area.

★ Gardiner Guest House

112 Main St. E.; 406/848-9414; $150-200 summer, $100-150 winter

The Folk Victorian Gardiner Guest House welcomes both children and pets and offers two modest but comfortable guest suites. Owners Richard and Nancy Parks (known lovingly as "Miss Nance") are longtime residents and an outstanding source of information on the area. Their guests, many of them from Europe, come back year after year for the wonderful hospitality, delicious breakfasts, and proximity to the park.

Yellowstone Park Riverfront Cabins

550 Old Yellowstone Trail S.; 406/570-4500; www.cabinsontheyellowstone.com; $375

Yellowstone Park Riverfront Cabins offers comfortable cabins that can accommodate up to six people in a quiet location above the river. There is a three-night minimum.

Hillcrest Cottages

400 Scott St.; 406/848-7353 or 800/970-7353; www.hillcrestcottages.com; early May-mid-Oct.; $190-270

Another option for small, basic, and reasonably priced cottages right in town is Hillcrest Cottages. The cottages come in various sizes that can sleep 1-5 people.

Flying Pig Adventure Company

511 Scott St. W.; 866/264-8448; www.flyingpigrafting.com

The Flying Pig Adventure Company offers a host of higher-end vacation rentals ranging from cozy canvas wall tents on a nearby ranch (from $200) and cabins ($275-400) to in-town houses ($175-185) and a private lodge (from $599) that can sleep up to 15. Minimum nights and cleaning fees apply.

Absaroka Lodge

310 Scott St.; 406/848-7414; www.yellowstonemotel.com; $125-260

For a more standard hotel experience, the riverfront Absaroka Lodge offers rooms with balconies looking into the park.

Cooke City

For a town with a population that hasn't made it to the triple digits yet, Cooke City has an impressive number of places to hang your hat. Lodging runs the gamut from cabins and vacation rentals to roadside motels, chain hotels, and small resorts, although not all of them are open year-round. Most of the photo galleries on the accommodations' websites are images of moose and bears or snowmobiles buried in powder rather than pictures of beds and baths. Clearly, Cooke City has morphed from a mining town into a tourist destination.

Big Moose Resort

715 US 212; 406/838-2393; www.bigmooseresort.com; $110-165

Big Moose Resort is 3 mi (5 km) east of town and a great place to set up base camp if you want to explore the region's trails and rivers. Open year-round, the lodge has a collection of eight old and new cabins, all of which are comfortable and can accommodate up to four people. There are no phones (and no cell service), but free Wi-Fi is provided, and you can schedule a Swedish massage on-site. There are four RV sites, the only full hookup sites in town.

Soda Butte Lodge

210 E. Main St.; 406/838-2251; www.cookecity.com; $89-189

In the heart of bustling Cooke City is the Soda Butte Lodge, a full-service hotel with 32 guest rooms, a saloon, and a restaurant. The guest rooms are basic, but you didn't come to Cooke City to hang out in your hotel room.

★ Silver Gate Lodging

109 US 212; 406/838-2371; www.silvergatelodging.com; $150-505

In nearby Silver Gate, Silver Gate Lodging offers 29 cabins, plus motel

Grizzly and Wolf Discovery Center

Grizzly and Wolf Discovery Center

If you have your heart set on seeing a grizzly or a wolf in Yellowstone, here's my advice: Get it out of the way before you even go into the park, like getting a first kiss on a first date out of the way before you order dinner. The **Grizzly and Wolf Discovery Center** (201 S. Canyon St.; 406/646-7001 or 800/257-2570; www.grizzlyctr.givecloud.co; 8:30am-5:30pm daily summer, 9am-3:30pm daily winter, hours can change; $16.50, admission valid for two consecutive days) is a nonprofit organization that acts something like an orphanage, giving homes to problem, injured, or abandoned animals. Although there is something melancholy about watching these incredible beasts confined to any sort of enclosure, particularly on the perimeter of a chunk of wilderness as massive as Yellowstone, there is also something remarkable about seeing them close enough to count their whiskers. Watching a wolf pack interact from a comfy bench behind floor-to-ceiling windows in the warming hut is a worthwhile way to spend an afternoon.

One opportunity for curious children ages 5-12 is the **Keeper Kids** program, which is offered twice daily during the summer season and once daily fall-spring. For roughly 30 minutes, the kids learn about grizzly eating habits and behavior. Then they get to go into the grizzly enclosure (the bears are locked away) and hide buckets of food for the bears. When the kids exit and the bears come racing out to search for their treats—overturning massive logs and boulders in the process—the kids (and their parents!) are mesmerized. Enrollment is first-come, first-served, and sign-up happens at the admissions counter at least 15 minutes ahead of the program.

Since these bears do not hibernate, this is a stop absolutely worth making any time of the year. Ultimately, this is a really nice place to learn a lot about bears, wolves, and raptors before heading into the park to look for them in the wild.

rooms and a big lodge that can accommodate up to 10 people. Some of the accommodations are pet-friendly, but be sure to ask ahead. The setting is both quiet and communal, with barbecue grills, horseshoe pits, and a playground. And because this is Yellowstone, you can also rent scopes, which will come in plenty handy. The staff know the park backward and forward, so don't hesitate to ask about their favorite places.

West Yellowstone

In the summer months there are more than 2,000 hotel rooms to be found in West, and about 1,300 when the snow covers the ground. Guest ranches, bed-and-breakfasts, and cabin rentals are also available. **See Yellowstone** (800/221-1151; www.seeyellowstone.com) is a full-service travel agency in West Yellowstone that can book everything from accommodations and private tours to complete packages. The **West Yellowstone Chamber of Commerce** (406/646-7701; www.destinationyellowstone.com) also has an excellent website that shows all lodging availability.

Three Bear Lodge

217 Yellowstone Ave.; 406/646-7353 or 800/646-7353; www.threebearlodge.com; $69-329

Open year-round, the Three Bear Lodge offers 44 guest rooms in its recently remodeled pet-friendly motel unit and 26 in the lodge, where no two rooms are alike. All guest rooms have a refrigerator, microwave, TV, handmade furniture, and fluffy duvets. They also offer log cabins in their guest ranch setting at Parade Rest Guest Ranch (800/753-5934; www.paraderestranch.com; from $2,000 pp doubles for 5-night stay) just 15 minutes from West Yellowstone.

Alpine Motel

120 Madison Ave.; 406/646-7544; www.alpinemotelwestyellowstone.com; May-Oct.; $100-240

The Alpine Motel is a budget-friendly choice with a variety of units, some including kitchens, just two blocks from the park entrance. The service by owners Brian and Patty is noticeably good.

Brandin' Iron Inn

201 Canyon; 406/646-9411 or 800/217-4613; www.brandiniron.com; $79-319

A couple of blocks farther from the entrance, but a long-standing and reliable choice in town, is the 79-room, pet-friendly Brandin' Iron Inn, which is very comfortable and open year-round.

Camping

Outside the Park

Gardiner

The difference between camping outside the park and inside Yellowstone is simply that you need to focus on reservations and availability instead of permits and regulations. There are six campgrounds in Gardiner—four national forest campgrounds and two private ones.

Yellowstone RV Park & Campground

121 US 89 S.; 406/848-7496; www.rvparkyellowstone.com; May-Oct.; tent sites from $54, RV sites from $100

The private Yellowstone RV Park & Campground is ideally situated on the Yellowstone River just 1.3 mi (2.1 km) north of the park entrance. They offer 46 pull-through and tent sites, including full-service riverfront sites, plus a wash house for campers.

Bear Creek Campground

Forest Rd. 493, 10.5 mi/16.9 km northeast of Gardiner; 406/848-7375; early June-late Oct. depending on weather; free

Those in search of a more rustic experience might enjoy checking out a national forest campground. The pack-in, pack-out Bear Creek Campground has four sites with no services and no turnaround room for long or towed vehicles. Reservations are not necessary.

Eagle Creek Campground

2 mi/3 km northeast of Gardiner on Hwy. 89 S.; www.recreation.gov; open year-round; $15-30

A 20-site Forest Service campground near Gardiner is Eagle Creek Campground, for which reservations can be made. There are no hookups available. The campground is set at 6,100 ft (1,860 m) overlooking the Gallatin Range. A small creek runs alongside the site and aspens provide shade. There are often elk in and around the camp.

Cooke City

Soda Butte

1 mi/1.6 km east of Cooke City on US 212; 406/848-7375; www.fs.usda.gov; July 1-early Sept. depending on weather; $20/vehicle

Soda Butte has 27 sites, restrooms, food boxes, and drinking water, and fishing is available nearby. Please note that due to bear activity, this is a hard-sided campground only, and advance reservations are not accepted.

Camping in Yellowstone

As accommodations cannot meet the demand of Yellowstone's nearly 5 million visitors each year, camping is an excellent option. More than 2,000 campsites spread over 12 campgrounds are located in the park.

The five largest—Bridge Bay, Canyon, Fishing Bridge RV Park, Grant Village, and Madison—are run by Yellowstone National Park Lodges; all inquiries and reservations should be made by calling YNPL (same-day reservations 307/344-7901, advance reservations 307/344-7311); these campgrounds have additional sales and utility tax fees. Mammoth Campground is the only one that offers first-come, first-served sites from mid-October to April 1. All other sites can be reserved in advance on www.recreation.gov.

Yellowstone also has more than 300 backcountry campsites, which require permits. Camping fees are discounted for bicyclists and hikers.

Campground	Number of Sites	Dates (Approx.)	Fees	Reservations
Bridge Bay	431	mid-May-Sept. 1	$33 + taxes	www.yellowstonenationalparklodges.com
Canyon	272	late May-mid-Sept.	$39 + taxes	www.yellowstonenationalparklodges.com
Fishing Bridge RV Park	310	early May-early Oct.	From $89 + taxes	www.yellowstonenationalparklodges.com
Grant Village	429	early June-early Sept.	$39 + taxes	www.yellowstonenationalparklodges.com
Indian Creek	70	mid-June-early Sept.	$20	www.recreation.gov
Lewis Lake	84	mid-June-mid-Oct.	$20	www.recreation.gov
Madison	276	early May-mid-Oct.	$33 + taxes	www.yellowstonenationalparklodges.com
Mammoth	82	year-round	$25	www.recreation.gov; walk-up available mid-Oct.-mid-Apr.
Norris	111	late May-late Sept.	$25	www.recreation.gov
Pebble Creek	27	mid-June-late Sept.	$20	www.recreation.gov
Slough Creek	16	mid-June-mid-Oct.	$20	www.recreation.gov
Tower Fall	31	late May-late Sept.	$20	www.recreation.gov

Colter Campground

2 mi/3.2 km east of Cooke City; 406/848-7375; www.fs.usda.gov; June-Labor Day depending on weather; $20/vehicle

Strictly a hard-sided campground, Colter Campground gives campers access to 18 sites, restrooms, food boxes, picnic tables, drinking water, and nearby fishing and hiking trails. Reservations are not accepted, so arrive early and have a backup plan in place.

Fox Creek Campground

6.7 mi/10.8 km east of Cooke City on Beartooth Hwy.; 307/527-6921; www.fs.usda.gov; July 15-Sept. 7 depending on weather; $30-90

Fox Creek Campground is a larger 33-site campground with awesome views of Pilot and Index Peaks. Water is available, as are vault toilets, but cell service is not. Maximum spur length is 32 ft (9.8 m). Reservations are not accepted.

West Yellowstone

With nearly two dozen private and public campgrounds in the vicinity of West, campers have plenty of choices, although most are geared to RV campers.

Baker's Hole Campground

250 Parkline Trail, 3 mi/4.8 km northwest of West Yellowstone on US 191; 406/823-6961; www.recreation.gov; May 15-Sept. 30 depending on weather; $26 for 2 vehicles, $9 for each additional vehicle, $35 for electrical sites

The nearest US Forest Service campground is Baker's Hole Campground, with 73 sites (33 with electricity) set on a scenic oxbow of the Madison River. Basic services such as water and trash pickup are provided, there is firewood for sale ($10), and the fishing is excellent.

Wagon Wheel RV Campground & Cabins

408 Gibbon Ave.; 626/848-3080; www.westyellowstonerv.com; mid-May-mid-Oct.; $74-84 full-hookup pull-through sites

Right in town, just six blocks from the park's west entrance, is Wagon Wheel RV Campground & Cabins, offering a forested and quiet setting for RV camping only. Free Wi-Fi is available in some public areas.

Under Canvas Yellowstone

890 Buttermilk Creek Rd.; 406/219-0441; www.undercanvas.com; late May-early Sept.; tents from $249

For a truly unique experience outside of town, Under Canvas Yellowstone offers "glamping" (glamour-camping) options ($249-1,484) ranging from classic safari tents to luxury safari suite tents with king-size beds, private baths with freestanding tubs, and woodstoves. The Madison River Suite pairs three tents and an expansive private deck to sleep up to seven. A variety of options are available, from shared bathrooms (the hot water showers are provided by a generator that runs 6am-11pm and is not quiet) to private but separate baths, influencing the price. But all of these tents are set in a mountain-ringed meadow with a creek running through. The guests are largely international, and it can be a treat to listen to campfire or next-tent pillow talk in several different languages. The only downside is that snoring is universally annoying, and with all but the most expensive tents situated so close together, light sleepers are bound to hear plenty of snorers. Still, this is fun, comfortable camping without the work.

Red Lodge

At the edge of the massive Beartooth Plateau, Red Lodge (pop. 2,331, elev. 5,568 ft/1,697 m) is a mountain town with the Great Plains spread out at its feet. There are a couple of great places to stay and some world-class skiing just beyond town, but downtown Red Lodge is a worthwhile destination on its own. Cute shops and wonderful restaurants line Broadway, and the spectacle of nature—the rush of Rock Creek and the drama of the Beartooths—is evident from every part of the street. The town's Western hospitality combined with historic zeal for a good time make Red Lodge a fantastic getaway or a fun launching point to the wildness of the Beartooth Plateau and Yellowstone National Park.

Getting to Red Lodge

From **Cooke City,** Red Lodge is 65 mi (105 km) east on US 212, which takes a minimum of 2.5 hours to drive.

The two major airports closest to Red Lodge are **Billings Logan International Airport** (BIL; 406/657-8495; www.flybillings.com) and **Bozeman Yellowstone International Airport** (BZN; 406/388-8321; www.bozemanairport.com). One of the best options for getting to Red Lodge is by car; both airports have a selection of car-rental companies.

From the Billings airport, **Phidippides Shuttle Service** (307/527-6789; www.codyshuttle.com) transports visitors to Red Lodge.

Sights

Beartooth Scenic Highway and Pass

Start: Red Lodge
End: Cooke City
Distance: 65 mi (105 km)
Duration: 3 hours

Considered one of the most beautiful roadways in the country, the Beartooth Scenic Highway begins in Cooke City, climbs and twists its way through 60-million-year-old mountains, and ends 65 mi (105 km) later in Red Lodge. Numerous switchbacks and steep grades demonstrate why it is closed during winter. As you ascend, you come upon vistas of the Beartooth Plateau, Glacier Lake, and the canyons forged by the Clark Fork River. After about 33 mi (53 km), you reach the mountain summit at 10,947 ft (3,337 m). Here, the aptly named **Top of the World** rest area provides the only services on the route. Keep an eye out for a herd of mountain goats that frequents the area.

If you plan to drive this byway, keep in mind that it is not about getting from A to B—the drive itself is the destination, and should be undertaken with plenty of time, about 3 hours without stops. You will encounter an array of wildlife, including black bears, bighorn sheep, and mountain goats, as well as vibrant wildflowers, depending on the season and moisture levels. Take time to stop and enjoy the vistas or explore the hiking trails and lakes. With snow falling almost year-round, skiing is popular in the area in June and July. The highway is only open May to October, weather permitting. Contact the **Montana Department of Transportation** (406/444-6200) or the **Red Lodge Visitors Center** (406/446-1718) for opening and closing dates.

Beartooth Plateau

High atop these massive mountains is the vast and rugged grandeur of the Beartooth Plateau. It's a nature lover's paradise with spectacular scenery,

unrivaled vistas, abundant wildlife, and a tangle of trails and lakes to get out and enjoy. The **Beartooth Scenic Highway** makes this remarkable place a Sunday drive destination. But if you have the time, this is a wonderland that begs to be discovered. Take a hike, wet a line—heck, throw on your skis in midsummer; just get out and enjoy this magnificent place.

The truth of the matter is, you're already pretty much on top of the world here, so you don't need to aspire much when planning a hike. The plateau is crisscrossed with trails, and as long as you are amply prepared, you can't choose a bad one. The **Clay Butte Fire Lookout Tower** is only 1 mi (1.6 km) from the highway and can be accessed by a trail that takes hikers up and above 11,000 ft (3,350 m). The views are incredible, and an interpretive display gives great perspective on the 1988 Yellowstone fires and how they impacted the entire region. **Crazy Creek Cascade** is another short hike, and the **Clark Fork Trailhead,** just 3 mi (4.8 km) from Cooke City, offers an abundance of longer trails. Near the summit, an 8-mi (12.9-km) loop around **Beartooth Lake** offers easy terrain and lovely scenery. For trail maps, stop by the **US Forest Service ranger station** (6811 US 212, Red Lodge; 406/446-2103).

Biking the Beartooth Plateau is not for the faint of heart. Never mind the insane elevation climbs and descents, the vast grizzly habitat, and the possibility of a blizzard on virtually any day of the year; the real danger is the automobiles, which are plentiful, often wide, and driven by people who can't help but ogle the mountain vistas instead of the bike traffic. You can eliminate that danger by getting off the road and onto a network of trails.

Top of the World Resort

2823 US 212; 307/587-5368; www.topoftheworldresort.com

In order to fish any of the mountain lakes on the Beartooth Plateau, many of which have been stocked with trout, you'll need

Beartooth Scenic Highway and Pass

a Wyoming fishing license, which can be purchased at the Top of the World Resort or in Red Lodge or Cooke City. Rental gear is also available seasonally at the Top of the World Resort.

Yellowstone Wildlife Sanctuary

615 2nd St. E.; 406/446-1133; www.yellowstonewildlifesanctuary.com; 10am-4pm Wed.-Mon. May-Oct., 10am-4pm Fri.-Sun. Nov.-Dec. and Apr.; $12, tours from $55

This wildlife refuge is the only one of its kind in Montana. It houses indigenous animals that cannot be released back into the wild due to an injury or unfortunate dependency on humans. The Yellowstone Wildlife Sanctuary cares for some 60 animals that include bears, Canada lynx, bison, mountain lions, coyotes, red foxes, raptors, and many more.

Adventure and Recreation

Skiing

Red Lodge Mountain

305 Ski Run Rd.; 406/446-2610 or 800/444-8977; www.redlodgemountain.com

Situated in a glacial valley surrounded by the Beartooth Mountains, Red Lodge offers superb downhill and cross-country skiing. Red Lodge Mountain is just 6 mi (10 km) from downtown Red Lodge and boasts a mountain free of crowds and with reasonable lift ticket prices ($57-112, discounts for advance online purchase and multiday passes) as well as ski runs for beginners to experts. The mountain offers a higher base elevation (7,433 ft/2,266 m) than any other ski hill in the state, a spine-chilling 2,400-ft (730-m) vertical drop, 70 runs, and six **chairlifts** to keep you up to your elbows in the white stuff. The diverse terrain is groomed regularly, and the runs' features are frequently upgraded or even changed. Red Lodge offers a full-service lodge, with ski lessons, ski rentals, childcare, a restaurant, two bars, and two cafeterias, all on the hill. The resort also has two cross-country trails that offer about 11 mi (18 km) of skiing. On top of the outstanding terrain and the jaw-dropping views, one of the things that makes this hill so special is the small-town friendliness of just about everyone here, from the lift operators to the people sharing a chair with you. This feels like what skiing in Montana should be.

Red Lodge Nordic Center

2 mi (3 km) west of downtown off Hwy. 78; 406/446-1771; www.beartoothtrails.org; 8:30am-4:30pm daily in season; $10/day payable at the trailhead

Probably the best-known place for cross-country skiing in Red Lodge is the Red Lodge Nordic Center, 2 mi (3 km) west of downtown off Highway 78. The center is operated by the nonprofit Beartooth Trails Association (which also maintains several excellent trails for hiking when snow isn't covering the ground) and offers more than 9 mi (15 km) of groomed classic and skate trails rated from easy to most difficult. Rentals and lessons can be arranged prior to your arrival via online booking. Other than a Porta Potty, there are no services at the Nordic Center, so plan ahead.

Entertainment and Events

Festival of Nations

224 N. Broadway; 406/446-1718; late June; free

Since 1950, the Festival of Nations has been a Red Lodge tradition celebrating the wide diversity of ethnic groups that first came to the town during the late-1800s mining boom. The cultural groups honored include both southern and northern Europeans—German, Irish, Finnish, Italian, Norwegian, Scottish, Greek—and a variety of others. The festival was discontinued for several years but was reinstated in 2025. The celebration takes place in late June over two and a half days, with cultural exhibits, dancing, ethnic food, music, and children's activities. Contact the Carbon County Historical Society and Museum (406/446-3667) for information.

Red Lodge Winter Fest and Carnival

305 Ski Run Rd. and various locations downtown; 406/446-2610 or 800/444-8977; mid-Mar.; ticket prices vary by event

The Winter Fest and Carnival takes place at the Red Lodge Mountain Resort and in town and includes tried-and-true events. The Cardboard Classic race tests the skills of its participants as they guide their original crafts—made only from cardboard, duct tape, and glue—in a competitive downhill race. Other popular activities include parades, food contests, a film festival, skijoring, and fireworks.

Home of Champions Rodeo and Parade

101 Rodeo Dr.; 406/446-2422; www.redlodgerodeo.com; July 1-4; $20-35

The Home of Champions Rodeo and Parade takes place each year with daily parades in downtown Red Lodge. Rodeo competition in the area dates back to the 1890s, when cowboys used to get together on Sunday to ride broncos at the local stockyards. Formed in 1930, the Red Lodge Rodeo Association has been hosting this annual celebration ever since. The rodeo is part of the Professional Rodeo Cowboys Association circuit, so you will see many of the nation's top champions compete in events including bareback, bull riding, calf roping, and barrel racing.

Tippet Rise Art Center

96 S. Grove Creek Rd., Fishtail; www.tippetrise.org; concert season mid-Aug.-mid-Sept.; concert tickets $10

Lovers of classical music and fine art are in for a wildly unexpected treat at Tippet Rise Art Center, which brings together nature, art, and music in magnificent ways. Set on an 11,500-acre (4,650-ha) working ranch, in the shadow of the Beartooths, Tippet Rise brings world-class musicians to the area for intimate performances throughout summer at a variety of indoor and outdoor venues, all of them small and visually spectacular. Tickets for concerts and films are limited to just 100 seats at most—and are available online only for as little as $10, and free for ages 21 and younger—but sell out months in advance. Tickets to the art center are available online for free, but also in very limited quantities. From late June to early October, visitors can make reservations for free hiking, biking, and van tours of the property on Friday, Saturday, and Sunday only.

Shopping

Shopping in Red Lodge is a leisurely stroll through the historic downtown district. Broadway has managed to retain the charm and vibrancy of the coal-mining days with a diverse assortment of stores.

Sylvan Peak Mountain Shop

9 N. Broadway Ave.; 406/446-1770; 9am-6pm daily

Sylvan Peak Mountain Shop is a perfect starting point for anyone in need of adventure-related gear. The store carries its own line of clothing as well as more familiar brands such as Marmot, Mountain Hardwear, and Osprey. An outlet store on the main floor and the Mountain Shoppe downstairs not only sell equipment but also rent cross-country skis, telemark skis, and snowshoes. From climbing gear to boating gear, fleeces or bear spray, you will find it—plus the best insider's advice anywhere and a true commitment to protecting the great outdoors—at Sylvan Peak.

Back Alley Metals

116 Broadway Ave. N.; 406/425-1533; www.backalleymetals.com; 10am-4pm Mon.-Fri.

For a unique, handmade gift, visit Back Alley Metals, where artists can realize any metal dream you may have, from personalized signs and art to custom metalwork like railings and gates to furniture.

Carbon County Arts Guild & Depot Gallery

11 8th St. W.; 406/446-1370; www.carboncountydepotgallery.org; 10am-5pm Thurs.-Sat., noon-4pm Sun.-Mon.

Another favorite spot for local art is Carbon County Arts Guild & Depot Gallery set in the historic railway depot, which has new exhibitions by regional artists every month and works for sale by more than 150 artists.

Food

The Wild Table

113 Broadway Ave. N.; 406/446-0226; www.thewildtable.com; 8am-2pm Mon.-Sat. summer, 8am-2pm Mon.-Thurs. winter; $5-16

An excellent spot for a quick breakfast (served all day) or lunch is the Wild Table, which serves from a new menu every week. Staples include breakfast burritos and sandwiches, shakshuka (poached eggs in spicy tomato sauce), English breakfasts, French toast, sandwiches, and hot lunch entrées. They serve espresso too, and their treats (huckleberry pie! meringues! triple chocolate brownies!) are beyond compare. They do have gluten-free options.

★ Café Regis

501 Word Ave. S.; 406/446-1941; www.caferegis.com; 7am-2pm Thurs.-Mon.; $7-14

Attached to the Regis Grocery and known for outstanding breakfasts and organic, whole foods, Café Regis is an excellent spot for a hearty, healthy, and very reasonably priced meal. The service is quick and friendly, and every delicious item on the menu—from omelets and breakfast burritos to soup, sandwiches, salads, and mouthwatering daily blue plate specials—is available to go. Grab a ready-to-go picnic lunch or find all the gourmet fixings for whatever adventure you have planned. Breakfast is served all day. The Regis Grocery has a huge selection of organic, gluten-free, and other specialty products.

Piccola Cucina at Ox Pasture

7 Broadway N.; 406/446-1212; www.oxpasture.com; 11:30am-10pm Tues.-Sun. summer, 11:30am-8:30pm Tues.-Sun. winter; $16-40

At the heart of Red Lodge's burgeoning food scene is Piccola Cucina at Ox Pasture. The small menu changes frequently to make the most of seasonal produce. From Sicilian specialties like arancini (rice balls) and paccheri alla carbonara (pasta with eggs, Italian bacon, and cheese) to grilled sea bass, rib eye, and handmade pastas, this foodie heaven puts together phenomenal flavors. They also have a great wine list. Check the website or call ahead to make a reservation and ask about the well-known chefs from around the world who show up from time to time.

Accommodations

★ Yodeler Motel

601 S. Broadway Ave.; 406/446-1435; www.yodelermotel.com; $125-185

If you want to stay close to downtown Red Lodge without breaking the bank, try the pet-friendly Yodeler Motel. This historic, Swiss-themed chalet, owned by delightful former guides Mac and Tulsa Dean, is only three blocks from downtown. Remodeled guest rooms offer nice amenities that include cable TV, free Wi-Fi, jetted tubs, steam showers, and even a wax room to work on your skis. The rooms on the lower level are more budget-friendly and do not have balconies like the upper level, but every room is clean, comfortable, and well maintained. Plus Mac and Tulsa will give you the best advice for your Red Lodge or Yellowstone adventure.

★ The Pollard Hotel

2 N. Broadway Ave.; 406/446-0001; www.thepollard.com; $210-275

In historic downtown Red Lodge, the Pollard Hotel should not be overlooked. The hotel was the first brick building constructed in Red Lodge and dates to 1893. It has played host to some of the West's most famous legends, including Calamity Jane, Buffalo Bill Cody, and famed orator William Jennings Bryan. The 39 guest rooms and suites are individually decorated, more traditional than modern, and can come with mountain views, jetted tubs, and balconies.

Rock Creek Resort

6380 US 212 S.; 800/667-1119; www.rockcreekresort.com; $284-374

Rock Creek Resort is about 5 mi (8 km) south of Red Lodge in a gorgeous canyon at the base of the Beartooth Mountains. The resort has 87 rooms sprawled over a 30-acre (12-ha) site and offers many outdoor activities. The facility has a heated indoor pool, tennis courts, a soccer field, a fully stocked fish pond, and numerous trails for hiking and biking (along with bikes for rent). Accommodations range from hotel rooms and condos to cabins and larger homes. Most have impressive views of the mountains.

Camping

Thirteen campgrounds along US 212 offer 226 sites between Red Lodge and Cooke City. Because of the elevation and volume of snow, many do not open until late June or July. Campsites along the Beartooth Highway are managed by the **Custer National Forest** (406/446-2103; www.fs.usda.gov/custergallatin) and range in price from free to $20 per night, depending on the site.

Beartooth Lake Campground

US 212, 23 mi/37 km east of Cooke City and 40 mi/64 km west of Red Lodge; July-mid-Sept.; $25

This first-come, first-served campground has a stunning setting with 21 sites near several lakes. Food storage is required for bears, and there is no cell service.

Island Lake Campground

US 212, 25 mi/34 km east of Cooke City and 38 mi/61 km west of Red Lodge; July-mid-Sept.; $20

Another high-elevation campground with 21 sites on a gorgeous waterside setting, Island Lake Campground offers picnic tables and vault toilets and is first-come, first-served.

Information and Services

Visitor Information

The **Red Lodge Chamber of Commerce** (701 N. Broadway Ave.; 406/446-1718 or 888/281-0625; www.redlodgechamber.org; 9am-5pm Mon.-Fri., 10am-4pm Sat.-Sun. summer, 9am-5pm Mon.-Fri., 10am-2pm Sat. winter) is at the intersection of US 212 and Highway 78. It has a 24-hour brochure room that offers local information. Inside the center you will find knowledgeable staff and plenty of state publications, visitor guides, and maps.

US 212 climbs another 5,000 ft (over 1,500 m) past Red Lodge. If you want to know the road conditions for the Beartooth Highway, you can stop by the chamber of commerce or check with the state of Montana **Traveler Road Information** (800/226-7623, TTY 800/335-7592; www.511mt.net).

Services

Access the internet at **Red Lodge Carnegie Library** (3 8th St. W.; 406/446-1905; 10am-5pm Mon.-Tues. and Thurs.-Fri., 10am-7pm Wed., plus noon-6pm Sat. in summer). The library has several internet-connected computers available to the public. You can also stop by the **Coffee Factory Roasters** (22 S. Broadway Ave.; 406/446-3200; www.coffeefactoryroasters.com; 6:30am-6pm daily), where the Wi-Fi is free.

Emergency Services

The **Beartooth Billings Clinic** (2525 N. Broadway Ave.; 406/446-2345; 7:30am-6pm walk-in care) offers 24-hour emergency care.

Big Sky

In the shadow of Lone Peak, tucked in the winding and rugged beauty of Gallatin Canyon, the resort town of Big Sky (pop. 2,919, elev. 7,218 ft/2,200 m) actually has *four* resorts: Big Sky, Moonlight Basin, Spanish Peaks, and the entirely private Yellowstone Club. Although there are not any sights per se, the town and resorts are geographically blessed with mountains for skiing, hiking, climbing, and biking; rivers for fishing and floating; and trails aplenty for horses, hiking, cross-country skiing, and mountain biking. Visitors can take solace in the fact that mountains make up for museums, and the area can be used as a launching point for Yellowstone National Park (51 mi/82 km south) or Bozeman (50 mi/80 km north). Big Sky feels more like a collection of enclaves, resorts, and villages dotting the mountainside than a town, but the area is growing.

Getting to Big Sky

From **West Yellowstone,** Big Sky is 51 mi (82 km) north on US 191, a 1-hour drive.

From **Gardiner** in winter, it's 120 mi (193 km) north on US 89, west on I-90, then south on US 191, a 2.5-hour drive. In the summer and fall, when park roads are open, it's 105 mi (169 km), on the park loop road to US 191, about a 2.5-hour drive.

The closest airport is **Bozeman Yellowstone International Airport** (BZN; 406/388-8321; www.bozemanairport.com) in Belgrade, about 50 mi (80 km) north.

A variety of shuttle services run from the airport. **Karst Stage** (406/556-3540 or 800/845-2778; www.karststage.com) has a counter next to National Rent-a-Car and provides shuttles ($95 pp one-way or $165 pp round-trip) to Big Sky. **Shuttle to Big Sky & Taxi** (406/995-4895 or 888/454-5667; www.bigskytaxi.com) provides private van and SUV transportation to, from, and around Big Sky, as does **Big Sky Bound** (406/539-3828; www.bigskyboundshuttleandtransportation.com; $250/ride one-way between Big Sky and the airport 8am-8pm).

Getting Around

Once in Big Sky, take advantage of the free bus service, **Skyline** (406/995-6287; www.skylinebus.com). In addition to covering the Big Sky area, buses also run between Bozeman and Big Sky. Hours vary by season.

Shuttle to Big Sky & Taxi (406/995-4895 or 888/454-5667; www.shuttletobigsky.com) offers taxi service around Big Sky. **Lone Peak Taxi** (406/640-2865; www.lonepeak.taxi; 8am-11pm) offers rides in Subarus rather than SUVs, which is kind of refreshing in this land of limousines.

Dollar Rent-a-Car (1 mi/1.6 km from the airport, Belgrade) will deliver a vehicle to any Big Sky location.

Adventure and Recreation

Skiing

Big Sky Resort

50 Big Sky Resort Rd.; reservations 800/548-4486, snow sports school 406/995-5743; www.bigskyresort.com; single-day pass $56-267, discounts for advance purchase and multiday tickets

One thing that distinguishes Big Sky from other ski destinations in the Rockies is the plentiful elbow room—there are fewer skiers per skiable acre than in most places. Big Sky Resort calls itself a ski resort without limits. It has 5,800 skiable acres (2,300 ha) and 4,350 vertical ft (1,326 m), and the area averages over 400 in (over 1,000 cm) of the fluffy stuff annually. The ski season generally lasts from Thanksgiving to mid-April. With short lift lines (except during holidays), this is an ideal place for ambitious skiers and families.

The resort's **Lone Peak Tram** takes daring skiers 16 ft (5 m) shy of the mountain's summit and offers 300 degrees of skiing from the top of Lone Peak.

Manicured terrain parks with many groomed features are available for snowboarders. Even with some of the steepest terrain in the country, Big Sky offers plenty of groomers for beginning and intermediate skiers and snowboarders.

In addition to the Mountain Sports School, which offers a wide range of ski and snowboard lessons and programs in winter, Big Sky Resort has the **Basecamp** (406/995-5769), an activity center offering two zip line courses, a high ropes course, a bungee trampoline, a climbing wall, and snowshoeing.

Lone Mountain Ranch

750 Lone Mountain Rd.; 406/995-4644 or 800/514-4644; www.lonemountainranch.com; $40

Down the mountain is Lone Mountain Ranch, a cross-country skier's paradise with 53 mi (85 km) of groomed and forested trails on 5,000 skiable acres (2,020 ha) with 2,200 vertical ft (671 m). Snowshoeing is another option, as are guided naturalist tours, lessons, and clinics. Rental equipment (skis and snowshoes) and lessons are available, and with so much terrain, this is one of the biggest bargains around.

Fishing and Floating

The **Gallatin River** runs through the canyon beneath Big Sky and offers a plethora of recreational opportunities. Since US 191 runs parallel to the river for 40 mi (64 km), fishing access is easy. The road is not meant for casual driving—no stopping and looking here—but there are several pullouts that double as parking lots. Float fishing is prohibited, but the wade fishing is enticing, if somewhat tricky given the size and number of rapids created as the water tumbles down the canyon over beautiful car-size boulders. Fishing licenses are required outside of Yellowstone and can be purchased online at www.fwp.mt.gov or at many fly shops and gas stations. Nonresident licenses start at $31.50 for a day; Montana residents can get an annual license for $21.

Rainbows, browns, and cutthroats can all be found in these chilly waters, and the fish have to be lean and mean to battle the currents. They tend to be slightly less selective than downriver in Bozeman, where the decline slows and the water flattens out. There are caddis hatches practically all summer, and a salmonfly hatch in mid-June to early July. Late in the season, terrestrials are the way to go.

Wild Trout Outfitters

47520 Gallatin Rd.; 406/995-2975 or 800/423-4742; www.wildtroutoutftters.com; 7:30am-7:30pm daily; half-day Gallatin River wade trip $400 for 1 angler, $450 for 2 anglers, all-day Gallatin River wade trip $550 for 1 angler, $600 for 2 anglers

Wild Trout Outfitters can offer professionally guided trips—wading or floating—including into Yellowstone National Park.

East Slope Outdoors

44 Town Center Ave.; 406/995-4369 or 888/359-3974; www.eastslopeoutdoors.com; 8am-7pm daily summer, 10am-6pm daily fall-spring, half-day Gallatin River wade trip $425 for 1 angler, $475 for 2 anglers, all-day Gallatin River wade trip $625 for 1 angler, $675 for 2 anglers

East Slope Outdoors offers equipment, rental gear, and guided fly-fishing trips, both wade and float trips.

Montana Whitewater

63960 Gallatin Rd.; 800/799-4465; www.montanawhitewater.com; half-day from $89, full day from $180

If the tranquility of fishing appeals less than the mayhem of white water, rafting on the Gallatin River is a good option. Montana Whitewater offers a range of trips to suit any adrenaline level, including half-day scenic floats, full-day white-water trips, and paddle-and-saddle overnighters. Plus, from the Gallatin Canyon base camp—which is like a small outdoors-loving city—you can mix and match adventures for every age and ability level, including rafting, zip-lining, fly-fishing, and horseback riding. The on-site **Blazin' Paddles Café** is a convenient food truck.

Hiking and Mountain Biking

The hiking opportunities are endless around Big Sky, with three mountain ranges, the Gallatin National Forest, the Lee Metcalf Wilderness Area, and Yellowstone National Park all nearby. Big Sky is becoming known for its mountain biking culture, and there is no shortage of challenging and scenic trails.

Big Sky Scenic Lift

406/995-5769; $37-48

In summer, the mountain at Big Sky unfolds into a network of mountain-bike and hiking trails. The Big Sky Scenic Lift gives riders and hikers a lift up (and down, if they choose) and a chance to tackle terrain for every skill level.

Different Strokes Bike Shop

Snowcrest Building at 54 Big Sky Resort Rd.; 406/995-5840; www.bigskyresort.com; 9:30am-5pm daily early June-mid-Sept.

All variety of bikes, helmets, and other gear can be rented at Different Strokes Bike Shop, after which bikers can enjoy 20 mi (32 km) of lift-serviced mountain biking.

Ousel Falls

Distance: 1.8 mi (2.9 km) round-trip
Duration: 1 hour
Elevation gain: 242 ft (74 m)
Effort: Easy
Trailhead: Ousel Falls Rd.

Some favorite local hiking trails include Ousel Falls, an easy up-and-down stroll to a waterfall. (Find the parking lot and trailhead on Ousel Falls Rd., 2 mi/3.2 km beyond the intersection of Ousel Falls Rd. and Spur Rd.) Picnic benches along the well-traveled way make the path good for small children. Do watch for bears and other wildlife, as they are frequently seen in the area.

Beehive Basin Trail #40

Distance: 6.9 mi (11.1 km) round-trip
Duration: 4 hours
Elevation gain: 1,630 ft (497 m)
Effort: Moderate to strenuous
Trailhead: Beehive Basin

For more ambitious hikers, Beehive Basin offers a variety of options. (Find the parking lot and trailhead by following the Beehive Basin turnoff—1.3 mi/2.1 km beyond Big Sky Mountain Village and 30 yards/meters before the entrance gate to Moonlight Basin—for 2.8 mi/4.5 km.) The #40 trail, which leads to a lovely lake, is sky-high at 9,200 ft (2,804 m) and offers 360-degree views. As with all of Montana, the weather can change quickly—snow can fall in July—and hikers need to be fully prepared for whatever Mother Nature sends their way, including bears. Carry spray! There is not much shade on the trail, so pack sun protection and water accordingly.

Lava Lake

Distance: 6 mi (9.7 km) round-trip
Duration: 4 hours
Elevation gain: 1,653 ft (504 m)
Effort: Moderate
Trailhead: Lava Lake off US 191

Farther north in Gallatin Canyon is Lava Lake, a well-traveled trail that leads to an icy-cold mountain lake. Only the hardiest will swim it. (From Big Sky, the trailhead is 13.5 mi/21.7 km north on US 191, just north of the Gallatin River Bridge, but since left turns cannot be made from there, you will need to turn around at the first turnout and approach the gravel turnoff from the north.) The out-and-back trail is almost entirely shaded.

Golf

Big Sky Golf Course

2100 Black Otter Rd.; 406/995-5780; www.bigskyresort.com; mid-May-late Sept.; $89-169, $59 twilight play after 3pm

For those who choose to hoof it around the links instead of a mountain trail, the 18-hole Arnold Palmer-designed Big Sky

Golf Course is open to nonguests and is well worth playing. Abundant wildlife often shares the par-72 course. A driving range, bar and grill, and full pro shop are available.

Entertainment and Events

Although it is set up as a winter resort, Big Sky does an excellent job of capitalizing on the relatively short summer with events that draw crowds from near and far.

Music in the Mountains

Center Stage at Town Park; 406/995-2742; www.bigskyarts.org; 6pm Thurs. June-Sept.; free

There are few better venues in the state for live music: Concerts are held in a glorious meadow surrounded by rocky peaks at the free Music in the Mountains series. Past headliners in Big Sky have included Lukas Nelson, the Wailin' Jennies, and Jason Isbell.

Montana Chamber Music Summer Festival

www.montanachambermusic.org; $35

Held over the course of a week at locales across the state—including one night in Big Sky—this annual chamber music festival attracts some of the finest classical musicians in the country.

Big Sky Farmers Market

Firepit Park, Big Sky Town Center; 406/570-6579; www.bigskytowncenter.com; 5pm-8pm Wed. June-Sept.

The weekly Big Sky Farmers Market features local vendors in addition to prepared food, a great kids' area, musical entertainment, and personal enrichment that includes yoga and massage.

Food

Something about the high mountain air produces serious appetites, and Big Sky has a substantial selection of eateries for

Top to bottom: Big Sky Mountain Village and Lone Peak; Ousel Falls; Beehive Basin Trail

every taste. From the top of the mountain to the bottom, you're never more than a quick jog from your next meal.

Blue Moon Bakery Pizzeria & Café

120 Big Pine Dr.; 406/995-2305; www.bigskybluemoonbakery.com; 8am-9pm daily; $10-32

Blue Moon Bakery Pizzeria & Café is a good bet for everything from breakfast sandwiches and baked goods to salads and gourmet pizza pies.

The Riverhouse

45130 Gallatin Rd.; 406/995-7427; www.riverhousebbq.com; 3pm-10pm daily; $16-42

The Riverhouse is known for its excellent smoked barbecue with a view. From their fried pickles, okra, and sweet corn nuggets to beef brisket, baby back ribs, and pulled pork, owners Kyle and Greg don't let anyone leave hungry. As if the sound of the rushing Gallatin weren't enough, this riverfront venue hosts plenty of live music.

The Corral

42895 Gallatin Rd., 5 mi/8 km south of Big Sky; 406/995-4249; www.corralbar.com; 8am-10pm Wed.-Sun.; $14-50

The Corral offers up an excellent old-school take on the Montana menu. From wild game Bolognese and elk tenderloin to rib eye, chicken-fried steak, and good ol' hamburgers, the Corral's food is consistently good, with plenty of chicken, seafood, and pasta options. You can't go wrong with the smoked trout appetizer.

Olive B's Big Sky Bistro

151 Center Ln.; 406/995-3355; www.olivebsbigsky.com; 11am-2pm and 5pm-9pm Mon.-Fri.; $32-48

For an elegant meal, Olive B's Big Sky Bistro is a great choice. Owned by a couple from the East Coast, the restaurant offers good seafood including lobster mac and cheese, duckling, and shrimp and grits. But the spot also serves up the best of the West: Rocky Mountain elk with huckleberry demi-glace, pork prime rib, wild game Bolognese, and beef tenderloin.

★ Horn & Cantle at Lone Mountain Ranch

750 Lone Mountain Rd.; 406/995-4644 or 800/514-4644; www.lonemountainranch.com; 7am-10am, 11am-2pm, and 5pm-9pm daily, saloon noon-close; $24-175

A good place for an upscale meal any time of day is Horn & Cantle, which serves up gourmet local fare ranging from elk meatballs and lamb leg ragù to rib eye and more, all prepared in inventive ways and presented with flair. The three squares a day (breakfast buffet $27, lunch $19-37, dinner $24-175) are excellent, and reservations can be made up to 30 days in advance.

Winter Dinner Experiences

For a truly unique meal during the ski season, try a sleigh-ride or yurt dinner. Both experiences offer hearty meals and unparalleled ambience, and both sell out well in advance—so book ahead.

Sleigh Ride Dinner

750 Lone Mountain Rd.; 406/995-2782; www.lonemountainranch.com; $145-229 pp

The sleigh-ride dinner at Lone Mountain Ranch whisks diners up a snowy trail to a candlelit cabin in the woods for a steak and potato dinner. There are two departures a day, in season, at 4:30pm and 7:30pm.

Yurt Dinner

50 Big Sky Resort Rd.; 406/995-3880; www.bigskyyurt.com; from $189 pp

The dinner in a yurt (via snowcat instead of horse-pulled sleigh) high atop Lone Mountain also includes time for sledding.

Accommodations

Big Sky was built as a resort, and it caters to visitors and vacationers. A wide range of accommodations, from ski-in/ski-out mountainside lodging to rustic roadside motels, inviting guest ranches, luxe resorts, and condo or cabin rentals, can address your specific needs—staying put or traveling around, skiing or golfing, walking or driving to dinner. But be warned, prices reflect the chichi resort culture here.

The Summit Hotel at Big Sky

Mountain Village Center; 800/548-4486; www.bigskyresort.com; studio rooms from $449

On top of the mountain is the Summit at Big Sky, a deluxe slope-side facility with the convenience of a hotel and the amenities of a condo. It offers both residences and temporary lodging, all in a comfortable and sophisticated atmosphere. There are indoor and outdoor pools, hot tubs, a sauna and fitness facility, and fireplaces in most accommodations. The entire hotel has been remade for their 2025 vision. Lodging packages can include lift tickets. **Big Sky Resort** (800/548-4486) can arrange a variety of lodging, from hotels including Summit and Huntley Lodge to slope-side rooms and condos to ski-in/ski-out cabins and homes for rent.

Wilson Hotel

145 Town Center Ave.; 406/995-9000; www.thewilsonhotel.com; from $430-789

Among the newest hotels in the Big Sky area is the Wilson Hotel, a Residence Inn by Marriott, which opened in 2019 in the heart of town center and offers simple, nice rooms with lots of options for suites.

Montage Big Sky

995 Settlement Trail; 406/993-8142; www.montagehotels.com; from $610 in low season to $2,275 in high season

The largest private building in the state, Montage Big Sky is as glamorous as it gets in Montana, with several on-site restaurants, a spa, and most rooms costing several thousand dollars per night.

Information and Services

Big Sky Medical Center

334 Town Center Ave.; 406/995-6995; www.bozemanhealth.org

Big Sky Medical Center has a 24-hour emergency room.

The B2 Urgent Care

83 Beaverhead Trail; 406/995-6650; 9am-5pm daily during ski season, closed summer and shoulder seasons

The B2 Urgent Care is at the base of Lone Peak in the ski patrol building.

Grand Teton
National
Park

Highlights

★ **Cruise to Elk Island:** Lure yourself out of bed and into this wonderland with an early morning cruise (page 106).

★ **Signal Mountain:** Follow this exciting 5-mi (8-km) drive with expansive views of the entire valley (page 108).

★ **Laurance S. Rockefeller Preserve:** The longtime summer home of the Rockefeller family, this lovely preserve exemplifies the family's commitment to stewardship (page 110).

★ **Jenny Lake:** Resting like a mirror at the base of the Tetons, this alpine lake is a gem for hikers, boaters, and picnickers (page 112).

★ **Hidden Falls and Inspiration Point:** The glorious views along this popular hike are worth every step (page 115).

★ **Jackson Town Square:** Surrounded by archways constructed entirely from elk antlers, this is the heart of the community for shoppers, art lovers, and diners (page 130).

★ **National Museum of Wildlife Art:** This collection is dedicated to all things wild, spanning George Catlin's bison to incredible works by Georgia O'Keeffe, Charlie Russell, and marvelous contemporary artists (page 130).

★ **Rafting on the Snake River:** The Snake winds through the valley, giving floaters unparalleled access to the area's most stunning views (page 133).

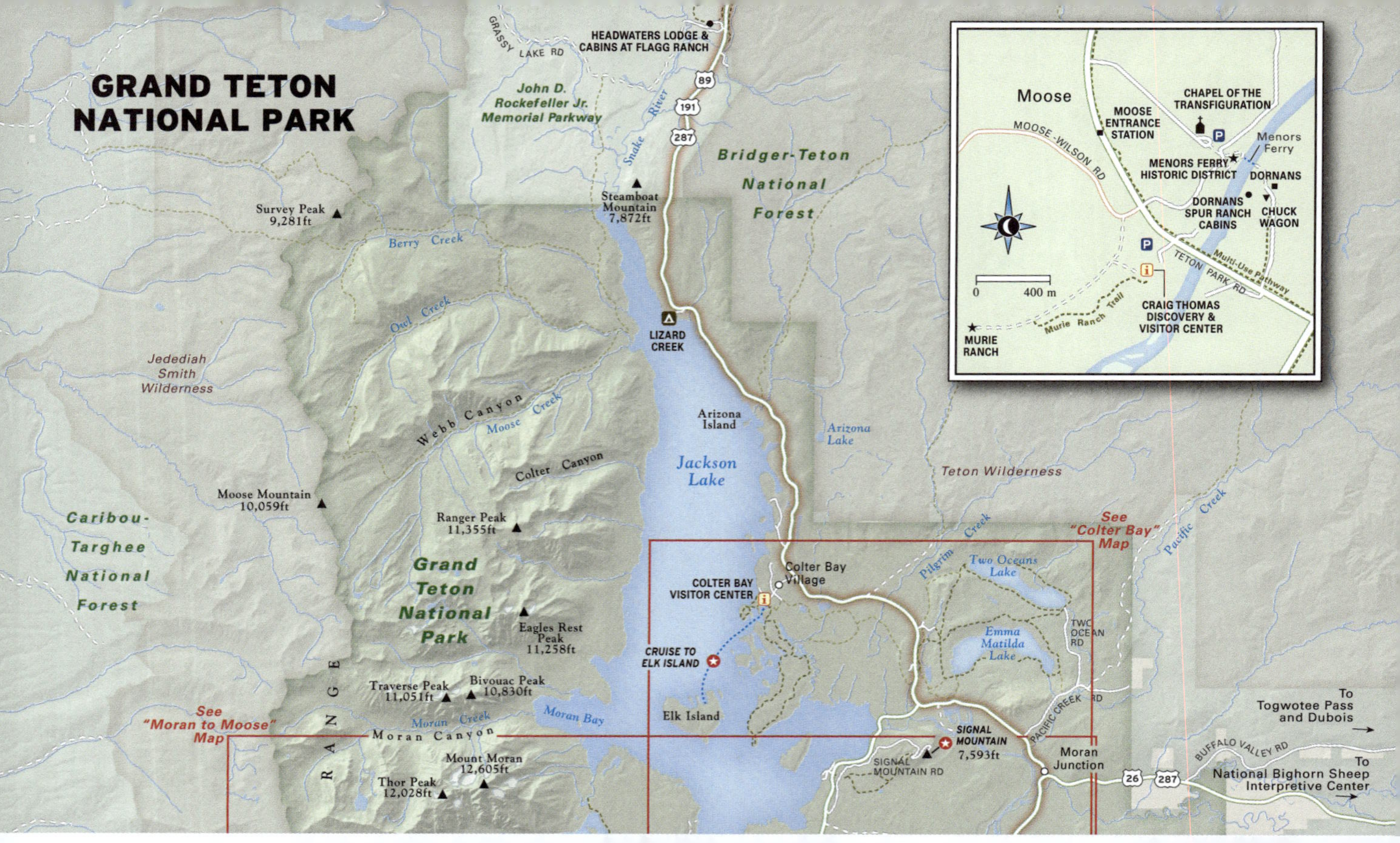

GRAND TETON NATIONAL PARK
HEADWATERS LODGE & CABINS AT FLAGG RANCH
GRASSY LAKE RD
John D. Rockefeller Jr. Memorial Parkway
89
191
287
Snake River
Bridger-Teton National Forest
Steamboat Mountain 7,872ft
Survey Peak 9,281ft
Berry Creek
Owl Creek
LIZARD CREEK
Jedediah Smith Wilderness
Webb Canyon
Moose Creek
Arizona Island
Arizona Lake
Jackson Lake
Teton Wilderness
Colter Canyon
Moose Mountain 10,059ft
Ranger Peak 11,355ft
Caribou-Targhee National Forest
Grand Teton National Park
See "Colter Bay" Map
Pilgrim Creek
Pacific Creek
Two Oceans Lake
Colter Bay Village
COLTER BAY VISITOR CENTER
Eagles Rest Peak 11,258ft
TWO OCEAN RD
Emma Matilda Lake
CRUISE TO ELK ISLAND
Traverse Peak 11,051ft
Bivouac Peak 10,830ft
Moran Bay
Elk Island
PACIFIC CREEK RD
See "Moran to Moose" Map
Moran Creek
Moran Canyon
RANGE
SIGNAL MOUNTAIN 7,593ft
SIGNAL MOUNTAIN RD
Moran Junction
Mount Moran 12,605ft
Thor Peak 12,028ft
26
To Togwotee Pass and Dubois
BUFFALO VALLEY RD
To National Bighorn Sheep Interpretive Center
Moose
MOOSE-WILSON RD
MOOSE ENTRANCE STATION
CHAPEL OF THE TRANSFIGURATION
Menors Ferry
MENORS FERRY HISTORIC DISTRICT
DORNANS
DORNANS SPUR RANCH CABINS
CHUCK WAGON
TETON PARK RD
Multi-Use Pathway
0 400 m
Murie Ranch Trail
CRAIG THOMAS DISCOVERY & VISITOR CENTER
MURIE RANCH

Bridger-Teton National Forest
Caribou-Targhee National Forest
Jedediah Smith Wilderness
Gros Ventre Wilderness
National Elk Refuge
Jackson Hole
TETON
Leigh Canyon
Leigh Lake
Paintbrush Divide
Mount St. John 11,430ft
String Lake
HIDDEN FALLS & INSPIRATION POINT
JENNY LAKE
Cascade Creek
Mount Owen 12,928ft
Teewinot Mountain 12,325ft
Grand Teton 13,770ft
Teton Glacier
Middle Teton 12,804ft
South Teton 12,514ft
Bradley Lake
Taggart Lake
Alaska Basin
Buck Mountain 11,938ft
Static Peak 11,308ft
Death Canyon
Prospectors Mountain 11,246ft
Phelps Lake
Mount Hunt 10,788ft
Granite Canyon
Rendezvous Mountain 10,450ft
JACKSON HOLE MOUNTAIN RESORT
Teton Village
Aerial Tram
Rendezvous Peak 10,932ft
Teton Crest Trail
Teton Creek
Darby Creek
Fox Creek
Moose Creek
To Driggs
Spalding Bay
TETON PARK RD
The Potholes
RIVER ROAD
River
RAFTING ON THE SNAKE RIVER
Snake
OUTSIDE RD
Antelope Flats
Shadow Mountain
SHADOW MTN RD
Ditch Creek
ANTELOPE FLATS RD
See Detail
Moose
Moose Junction
MORMON ROW RD
GROS VENTRE RD
Lower Slide Lake
Kelly
LAURANCE S. ROCKEFELLER PRESERVE
Blacktail Butte 7,688ft
Multi-Use Pathway
GROS VENTRE RIVER RD
Gros Ventre River
JACKSON HOLE AIRPORT
Snake River
Moose-Wilson Bike Route
MOOSE-WILSON RD
26
89
191
TETON PINES COUNTRY CLUB
To Phillips Pass
NATIONAL MUSEUM OF WILDLIFE ART
To Jackson and JACKSON TOWN SQUARE
To Curtis Canyon Campground
0 3 mi
0 3 km
Road Trip Route

Just south of Yellowstone, Grand Teton National Park is even more dazzling in alpine splendor than its more prominent neighbor. The Tetons soar skyward, three in a sea of 12 peaks topping 12,000 ft (3,658 m).

The mountains are young—still growing, in fact—and utterly spectacular, perhaps the most dramatic anywhere in the Lower 48. The park itself contains approximately 310,000 acres (125,500 ha; roughly 15 percent the size of Yellowstone), 100 mi (160 km) of paved road, and, much to the delight of hikers, some 200 mi (320 km) of trails.

Like Yellowstone, Grand Teton is home to healthy populations of wildlife—this is among the best places in the West to see a moose—but the rugged terrain and limited number of roads afford the animals better places to hide. Still, you always need to be prepared for bear encounters in the park. Beyond the fascinating natural and geological history of the region, Grand Teton offers some interesting human-built attractions—including the historic and elegant Jenny Lake Lodge, the Chapel of the Transfiguration, and the Laurance S. Rockefeller Preserve—that are well worth seeing. At the end of the day, though, Grand Teton is a place for nature lovers and outdoors enthusiasts. The vistas are unparalleled, as are the recreational opportunities.

Getting to Grand Teton National Park

Grand Teton National Park is fairly small in terms of road miles, especially compared to Yellowstone. From the north boundary of the park at the top of Jackson Lake to the south entrance at Moose is 36 mi (58 km) on US 89/191 and the Teton Park Road, about a 1-hour drive.

While distances through the park may seem short in actual mileage, your drive time is often extended by lower speed limits, traffic congestion, and animal jams. In addition, most of the park roads are **closed in winter.**

Driving from Yellowstone

70-106 mi (113-171 km); 2-3 hours

From the north entrance of Yellowstone at **Gardiner,** the northern boundary of Grand Teton National Park, just south of the **Flagg Ranch Information Station,** is 100 mi (161 km) south on US 89 and US 191, a 3-hour drive that goes through the western side of Yellowstone (this route passes Old Faithful).

If you're coming from Gardiner but driving along the eastern part of Yellowstone (through Tower Junction and Canyon Village), the drive to Flagg Ranch is 106 mi (171 km), and will take about 3 hours.

From **West Yellowstone,** Flagg Ranch is 70 mi (113 km) west and south on US 191, about a 2-hour drive (this route passes Old Faithful).

Driving from Jackson, Wyoming

13 mi (21 km); 30 minutes

From Jackson, Grand Teton's south entrance at **Moose** is 13 mi (21 km) north on US 191/89, about a 30-minute drive.

Driving from Cody, Wyoming

122 mi (196 km); 3 hours

To get from Cody to the Headwaters Lodge & Cabins at Flagg Ranch, it's 122 mi (196 km) west on US 14/16/20, then south on US 89/191. The drive, which takes travelers from the east side of Yellowstone to its southern entrance, takes about 3 hours.

Bus and Shuttle

Mountain States Express (307/733-1719 or 800/652-9510; www.mountainstatesexpress.com), which is operated by **Alltrans** (www.jacksonholealltrans.com), offers a daily **shuttle** (starting at $79) from Salt Lake City, Utah, to Jackson. The ride to Jackson is 5.5 hours.

Greyhound (www.greyhound.com)

One Day in Grand Teton

Morning

Wherever you wake up in Jackson, head straight to breakfast at **Persephone Bakery.** A cappuccino and some quiche Lorraine will get you far in these parts. While you're there, pick up a picnic lunch.

From town, head north into the park to the **Craig Thomas Discovery & Visitor Center.** In addition to the exhibits, check out the schedule of **ranger programs** for the day. You could take a hike, tour the Murie Home, or listen to a talk about bears. Continue on to **Jenny Lake,** where you can find a quiet spot for a picnic and maybe a swim.

Afternoon

After lunch, hit the trailhead for **Hidden Falls and Inspiration Point.** If you aren't eager to climb, you can choose a lovely, flat walk—though still lengthy—to **Leigh Lake.** After your hike, head north again to **Signal Mountain** and drive to the top for a spectacular view. When you come back down, drive northeast to look for moose or other wildlife at the scenic **Oxbow Bend.**

Evening

For dinner, make your way to Colter Bay for a **scenic dinner cruise** to **Elk Island.** If there's time, stop in to see the David T. Vernon Indian Artifacts Collection at the **Colter Bay Visitor Center.** Bed down at the beautiful **Jackson Lake Lodge.**

stops at the Albertsons (105 Buffalo Way) in Jackson.

Air

The only airport in the country within a national park, **Jackson Hole Airport** (JAC; 1250 E. Airport Rd., Jackson; 307/733-7682; www.jacksonholeairport.com) is served by American, Delta, United, and Frontier. The schedules change seasonally but include regular flights from Salt Lake City, Denver, Seattle, Chicago, Minneapolis, Dallas, Houston, Phoenix, San Francisco, and Los Angeles.

Visiting Grand Teton National Park

Planning Your Time

Grand Teton National Park is smaller, and in some ways more manageable, than its northerly neighbor. There are only 100 mi (161 km) of paved road, all of which can be driven easily in less than a day's time. With fewer accommodations than Yellowstone, Grand Teton lends itself to easy day trips from various locations in Wyoming, such as **Jackson Hole** or **Dubois,** 65 mi (105 km) from the east entrance. **Cody** is about a 3-hour drive from the park, via Yellowstone, so overnighting there is an option when rooms cannot be found any closer. A destination in its own right, Grand Teton is a paradise for outdoors enthusiasts. Hikers, bikers, boaters, and, in winter, cross-country skiers will have no problem coming up with marvelous weeklong itineraries. Still, for those on a time budget, you can get an excellent sampling of the park in two days, but even if you are just driving through, there are a few places that should not be missed.

While summer is by far the busiest time in the park, spring and fall can be magnificent with wildflowers, golden aspens, and more active wildlife. **Hiking** and **climbing** in the Tetons is best done in summer and early fall, after the winter snow has melted and before it starts flying again. Still, snow squalls and bad weather can surprise hikers at any time

Best Restaurants

★ **Dornans Moose Chuck Wagon, Moose:** Eating cowboy cuisine with a view of the Tetons is just plain fun, not to mention the fact that everything tastes better outside (page 123).

★ **Persephone Bakery, Jackson:** When it comes to buttery French pastries and daily staples, there is no better place than this bakery (page 140).

★ **The Bunnery, Jackson:** A longtime Jackson favorite for a casual breakfast or lunch, the Bunnery has outstanding bread and pastries, plus hearty and fresh sandwiches, burgers, salads, and more (page 140).

★ **Wild Sage, Jackson:** As gourmet as it gets in Jackson, dining at Wild Sage is a culinary adventure (page 140).

★ **Pica's Mexican Taqueria, Jackson:** In a town with lots of great Mexican food, Pica's stands out for its tortillas made on-site daily and its authentic specialties like caramelized al pastor tacos and traditional tortas on talera bread (page 140).

★ **The Kitchen, Jackson:** Grab a table outside at this modern, Asian-influenced restaurant and settle in for an outstanding, fresh meal (page 141).

of year, so come prepared. Park rangers offer educational programs throughout the year that are an excellent way to make the most of the time you have. In the fall, for example, drivers can join ranger-led **wildlife caravans** from the Craig Thomas Discovery and Visitor Center that guide visitors to the best places to see wildlife that day. **Ranger-led hikes and eco-talks** are geared to the seasons and offer visitors an insiders' look at the park.

The National Park Service offers an excellent **trip-planning tool online** (www.nps.gov), or you can order a booklet by mail by calling 307/739-3600.

Entrances

Grand Teton National Park has two official entrance stations but can be accessed from the south (Jackson), the east (Dubois), and the north (Yellowstone). Although you will be in Grand Teton National Park starting just 5 mi (8 km) north of Jackson, the southernmost **Moose Entrance Station** is about 20 mi (32 km) north of town. The eastern entrance at **Moran Junction** is 30 mi (48 km) north of Jackson and 55 mi (89 km) west of Dubois, Wyoming, over the Togwotee Pass, which is closed in winter. From the north, visitors enter Grand Teton National Park from Yellowstone; the $35 admission (for private passenger vehicles) is valid for seven days. Visitors coming in from Yellowstone can stop for information at **Flagg Ranch Information Station** or the **Colter Bay Visitor Center** 18 mi (29 km) south of Yellowstone.

Park Fees and Passes

Single-entry entrance fees are $35 per vehicle, $20 per person for hikers or bicyclists, and $30 per motorcycle for seven days in both Grand Teton National Park and Yellowstone National Park. Entrance permits are also required for the Multi-Use Pathway and are available for purchase at an automated fee station next to the Moose Entrance Station. Annual passes are $80 (free for military and 4th graders, $20 for seniors).

With more than 200 mi (320 km) of maintained trails in the park, backpacking and backcountry camping provide a

Best Accommodations

★ **Triangle X Ranch, Moran to Moose:** The premier guest ranch inside Grand Teton National Park, this fifth-generation family ranch offers warm hospitality and arguably the world's best setting for active vacationers (page 125).

★ **Anvil Motel, Jackson:** Just off Town Square, with comfortable rooms and prices that won't break the bank, this classic spot is a hip, mountain-rustic getaway (page 142).

★ **Rustic Inn Creekside Resort & Spa, Jackson:** Set on 12 lush acres (5 ha) just out of town and next to a nature preserve, this resort offers lodge rooms, cabins, and spa suites with high-end amenities and world-class service (page 142).

★ **Hotel Terra, Teton Village:** Right at the base of the mountain, this hip boutique hotel offers eco-friendly luxury, terrific on-site dining, a spa, and easy access to everything from the heart of Teton Village (page 142).

unique way to explore the area. **Permits** ($20/permit and $7/person/night) are required and can be obtained in advance online (www.recreation.gov) or in person on a first-come, first-served basis no more than one day before the start of a trip at the Craig Thomas Discovery and Visitor Center, Colter Bay Visitor Center, or Jenny Lake Ranger Station. Roughly one-third of **backcountry campsites** in heavily used areas can be reserved in advance online January 1-May 15 (307/739-3309; www.recreation.gov) and must be picked up in person. After May 15, all permits must be obtained in person. All campers are required to use bear-proof canisters below 10,000 ft (3,048 m) and at sites without bear boxes. Free canisters are provided when registering for a permit.

Visitor Centers

There are four main visitor centers in the park.

Craig Thomas Discovery and Visitor Center

307/739-3399; 8am-5pm daily early June-Sept., 9am-5pm daily May and Oct.

The Craig Thomas Discovery and Visitor Center is 12 mi (19 km) north of Jackson and 0.5 mi (0.8 km) west of Moose Junction. Exhibits include a relief map of the park, a 24-minute high-def movie, and natural history displays.

Jenny Lake Visitor Center

307/739-3392; 9am-5pm daily mid-May-late Sept.

Housed in the historic Crandall Studio, Jenny Lake Visitor Center is 8 mi (13 km) north of Moose Junction on Teton Park Road. Visitor services include guided walks and talks, and exhibits focus on park geology. The nearby Jenny Lake Ranger Station offers backcountry permits.

Colter Bay Visitor Center

307/739-3594; 8am-5pm daily early June-early Oct., 9am-5pm daily early May-early June

Half a mile (0.8 km) west of Colter Bay Junction is the Colter Bay Visitor Center, which is home to the Indigenous Arts and Cultural Demonstration Program, where visitors can see exhibits of Indigenous art and meet the artists. There are daily ranger-led programs and a park film showing in the auditorium throughout the day.

Laurance S. Rockefeller Preserve Center

307/739-3654; 9am-5pm daily early June-late Sept.

Four mi (6 km) south of Moose on the Moose-Wilson Road (closed to RVs and trailers), the Laurance S. Rockefeller Preserve Center offers 8 mi (13 km) of hiking trails, fishing and swimming opportunities in Phelps Lake, and unique sensory exhibits. There are daily ranger programs including a hike to Phelps Lake.

Services

The main concessionaire in the park is the **Grand Teton Lodge Company** (307/543-3100 for reservations, 307/543-2811 for operator; www.gtlc.com), which operates lodging, restaurants, tours, and activities. Its website can aid in planning your visit. The Grand Teton Lodge Company is responsible for the lodging, restaurants, tours, and activities at Jackson Lake Lodge, Jenny Lake Lodge, Colter Bay Village, Headwaters Lodge & Cabins at Flagg Ranch, and six campgrounds throughout the park. Reservations are available on a 12-month rolling basis.

For **medical emergencies** within the park, dial 911.

St. John's Health

625 E. Broadway, Jackson; 307/733-3636

St. John's Health is open 24 hours a day, year-round.

Grand Teton Medical Clinic

100 Jackson Lake Lodge Rd.; 307/543-2514 during business hours or 307/733-8002 after hours; 9am-5pm daily mid-May-mid-Oct.

The Grand Teton Medical Clinic is open daily and located in the Jackson Lake Lodge.

Getting Around

There are no shuttle services in Grand Teton National Park, so visitors will either need to have access to a private vehicle or book a tour. Guests at any of the Grand Teton Lodging Company properties have access to the free GTLC guest shuttle, which stops in Jackson as well as Jackson Lake Lodge, Colter Bay Village, and the South Jenny Lake Visitor Center.

Private Vehicles

If you are driving through the park, keep an eye on your fuel gauge. The only gas station open year-round is at **Dornans** (10 Moose Rd.; gas pumps available 24 hours if paying with a credit card) in Moose. Other gas stations open May-October are at Signal Mountain, Jackson Lodge, and Colter Bay.

For up-to-date road information and closures in the park, call 307/739-3682 or 307/344-2117 for Yellowstone road reports. For Wyoming road information, contact the **Wyoming Department of Transportation** (888/996-7623; www.wyoroad.info), or use the Wyoming 511 app.

Tours

Grand Teton Lodge Company

307/543-3100; www.gtlc.com; late May-early Oct.; bus tours $85-130 pp, private tours $850 for 1-5 guests

The Grand Teton Lodge Company offers tours throughout the park, including 4-hour tours departing from Jackson Lake Lodge during summer.

Teton Science Schools

700 Coyote Canyon Rd.; 307/734-3707; www.tetonscience.org; summer wildlife tours $179-399 pp, 4-12 hours early May-early Nov., winter wildlife tours $189-635 pp, 4-12 hours mid-Dec.-mid-Mar.

A great educational opportunity is provided by the Teton Science Schools, based in Jackson. The organization is committed to creating a deeper appreciation and understanding of the wilderness and natural ecosystems found in the Greater Yellowstone area. Experts provide classes and programs to engage students from small children to adults. Courses focus on everything from ecology and geology to unique plant and animal life. Even if you only plan to be in the park for a day or two, visit the website to see what is being offered. Regular programs can include hikes, campfires, canoe tours, and wildlife-viewing. The school also offers

Bear No. 399 and the Grizzlies of Grand Teton

In July 1975, grizzly bears were listed as **"threatened"** under the Endangered Species Act. At that time, and for several years afterward, not a single grizzly was known to wander the wilds of Grand Teton National Park. The animal's listing and passionate involvement by good people have changed that. In 2024, the number of grizzlies in the Greater Yellowstone Ecosystem—which includes Yellowstone and Grand Teton National Parks and their surrounds—hovered somewhere around 1,002 bears.

Bear No. 399

Because it's true that we protect what we love, and love what we know, perhaps no bear has done as much for **grizzly protection** as No. 399. Born in 1996 and collared in 2001, this bear has become the most famous grizzly in the world. She has had 18 cubs and several grandcubs and has been watched along roadsides by thousands upon thousands of park visitors.

By her willingness to live so much of her life in sight of humans, Bear No. 399 has demonstrated the challenges bears face to simply survive. Nearly **75 percent of her descendants died** as a result of **human encounters**—struck by cars, killed illegally by big-game hunters, euthanized for preying on cattle or for coming too close to human development. She lost other cubs to starvation or encounters with dominant males.

Grizzly Bears Today

Even with postcard bears like No. 399 and citizen advocates, the **fight to protect bears** is far from won. After the success of the bears' recovery over the last 40 years, the US Fish and Wildlife Service proposed in 2016 that grizzly bears be removed from the federal List of Endangered and Threatened Wildlife, opening grizzlies to hunting. As the status of grizzly bears is questioned—and tied up in court—their value in our wild world should not be. While scientists call the grizzly an "indicator" species—meaning that when the grizzlies thrive, so too do the other plants and animals that inhabit their world—naturalist and writer Doug Peacock, who has dedicated his life to grizzlies, goes further in asserting the importance of their survival. "Really, we are as much endangered as the grizzly bears. The **fate of humans and grizzlies** is a single, collective one," he said.

Twenty-eight years old in 2024 when she emerged from hibernation with her 18th cub, born in 2023 and named Spirit, No. 399 was killed by a car in late October. While her life ended tragically, let us hope and work for better as we navigate the place for grizzly bears in our wild world.

renowned **Wildlife Expeditions** (877/404-6626). These can be 4-12 hours or multiday guided tours with professional wildlife biologists.

EcoTour Adventures

307/690-9533; www.jhecotouradventures.com; summer or winter half-day from $189 pp, summer or winter full-day from $349 pp

Another tour company that focuses on getting visitors to see wildlife from comfy 4WD vehicles is EcoTour Adventures. Guided half-day tours, often at sunrise or sunset, run roughly 4 hours. Full-day trips—which can include snowshoeing and wildlife adventures, geology explorations, birding, and more—last 8-12 hours and can take visitors into Grand Teton and Yellowstone. These tours include lunch at one of the park lodges.

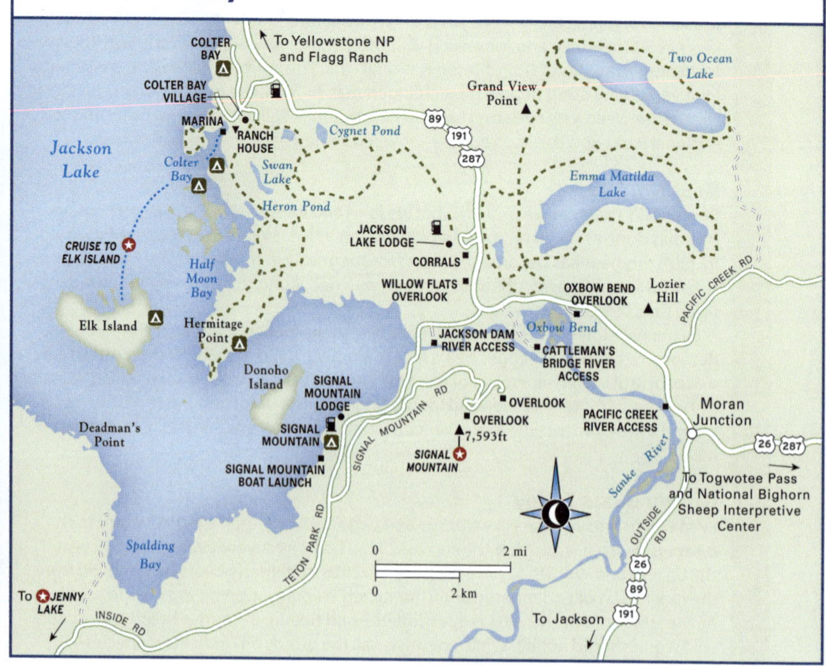

Sights

Flagg Ranch and Colter Bay

Just south of the Yellowstone border, Flagg Ranch was a US Cavalry outpost, converted to a guest ranch in 1910 and now known as Headwaters Lodge & Cabins at Flagg Ranch. It is ideally situated for visitors to explore both Yellowstone and Grand Teton National Parks from one location. In addition to full resort lodging, Flagg Ranch offers a gas station, grocery store, deli, and coffee shop for those just passing through.

One of the busiest spots in the park, with a marina, lodging, a campground, a visitor center, and a museum on the shores of Jackson Lake, Colter Bay Village is a practical, if not exactly quiescent, place to stay, and it is a worthwhile region to explore.

Colter Bay Visitor Center

640 Cottonwood Way, Moran; 307/739-3594; 8am-5pm daily early June-early Oct., 9am-5pm daily early May-early June; free

Set on Jackson Lake, the unassuming Colter Bay Visitor Center offers the same useful information as all of the visitor centers in the park, including a park film shown throughout the day in the auditorium. The structure itself is a surviving Mission 66 visitor center, built in the 1950s as part of a 10-year plan to dramatically increase visitor services in national parks. Colter Bay is also the home of the **Indigenous Arts and Cultural Demonstration,** where visitors can see various exhibits and meet the artists.

★ Cruise to Elk Island

307/543-3100; www.gtlc.com; schedules vary; $48-88

Since nothing builds an appetite like time

spent on an alpine lake, there are 3-hour breakfast, lunch, and dinner cruises departing from the marina that whisk guests across the lake to Elk Island, in the shadow of Mount Moran. The **breakfast cruise** serves hearty fare with eggs and trout, pancakes, pastries, fresh fruit, and the all-important cowboy coffee. Typically, it departs at 7:15am from June to August and at 8am late August to early September. The **lunch cruise** includes a sack lunch and time to explore the island. The **dinner cruise** serves such delectable mountain fare as steak and trout, baked beans, corn on the cob, roasted potatoes, and fruit cobbler. Scenic **lake cruises** (from $36) last about 90 minutes and are geared to different aspects of the park (with one cruise designed especially for kids). Schedules vary seasonally and annually, so call ahead or check the website for days and times.

Jackson Lake Lodge and Signal Mountain

Its breathtaking setting, coupled with access to hiking and sightseeing in the park's northeastern corner, makes Jackson Lake Lodge a vacation destination all its own. Though the lodge is not adjacent to Jackson Lake in the way that the Colter Bay Village is, the views over the lake to the Tetons are magnificent. Nearby, the rustic Signal Mountain Lodge is situated on the water, offering unlimited opportunities for enjoying Jackson Lake and its proximity to hiking and adventuring.

Oxbow Bend

Just southeast of Jackson Lake Lodge on the main road, US 89/191, is Oxbow Bend, a picturesque river area created when the Snake River carved a more southerly route. One of the most photographed areas in the park, the slow-moving water reflects towering Mount

Top to bottom: Signal Mountain; Oxbow Bend; trail with views of the Tetons and Jackson Lake

Moran. The serenity of the area attracts wildlife including moose, beavers, and otters along with a vast number of birds. White pelicans can occasionally be spotted passing through, as can sandhill cranes, trumpeter swans, nesting great blue herons, and bald eagles. Avid boaters like to paddle the area in their canoes and kayaks. Don't forget your binoculars and your camera.

★ Signal Mountain

Just 1 mi (1.6 km) south of Signal Mountain Lodge is the turnoff to Signal Mountain Road and one of the greatest viewpoints in the park. The winding 5-mi (8-km) road is completely **unsuitable for RVs and trailers.** Along the way are ample spots for wildlife-viewing—look for moose in the pond on the right as you start up the road; the pond lilies bloom in June. Two small parking lots are near the summit. The first offers the best view of the Tetons: Sunsets are sensational. From the second, a short walk takes you down to an overlook with a view of Oxbow Bend.

The story of Signal Mountain's name is rather tragic. Around the turn of the 20th century, a local rancher named Roy Hamilton got lost while hunting. Rescuers agreed to light a fire on the mountain as soon as anyone found Hamilton. After nine days, a fire was lit atop the mountain, signaling the end of rescue efforts. Tragically, Hamilton's body was found in the Snake River, and some speculated his business partner had suggested he cross the river in a particularly dangerous spot.

Moran to Moose

The stretch of US 191/26 between Moran Junction and the southernmost entrance to the park at Moose is scenic and full of interesting sights, both natural and human-made. From the crossing at **Menors Ferry** to the architecturally inspired **Craig Thomas Discovery and Visitor Center** and the wildlife-rich **Antelope Flats,** this part of the park is heavily traveled for a good reason: There is so much to see and many services including gas, food, and lodging at Dornans resort.

Cunningham Cabin

A relic of hardscrabble ranching days before the turn of the 20th century—and the murder site of two alleged horse thieves—Cunningham Cabin is 6 mi (10 km) south of Moran Junction. Pierce Cunningham built this sod-roofed "dogtrot" home on Flat Creek in 1888. A neighbor introduced Cunningham to two strangers, George Spenser and Mike Burnett, asking if they could buy hay for their horses. Cunningham sold them 15 tons of hay and arranged for them to winter in his cabin near Spread Creek. The rumor among locals was that the men were horse thieves.

In April 1893, 16 men on horseback rode up to the cabin and waited in silence for dawn. Spenser and Burnett's dog barked in the early morning hours, perhaps warning the men of ambush. Spenser armed himself and walked out the door. When the posse called for him to hold his hands up, Spenser fired his revolver and was immediately shot. He propped himself up on one elbow and continued to fire until he collapsed. Burnett came out next, armed with a revolver and a rifle. The men shot at him, but Burnett managed to shoot the hat off one of the posse members and "crease his scalp." Burnett was shot and killed moments later. The two men were buried in unmarked graves a few hundred yards southeast of the cabin on the south side of a draw. Their bones were eventually excavated by badgers.

Mormon Row and Antelope Flats

Interesting both for its wildlife and its human history, Mormon Row is instantly recognizable from some of the region's most popular postcards, featuring a weathered barn leaning into the

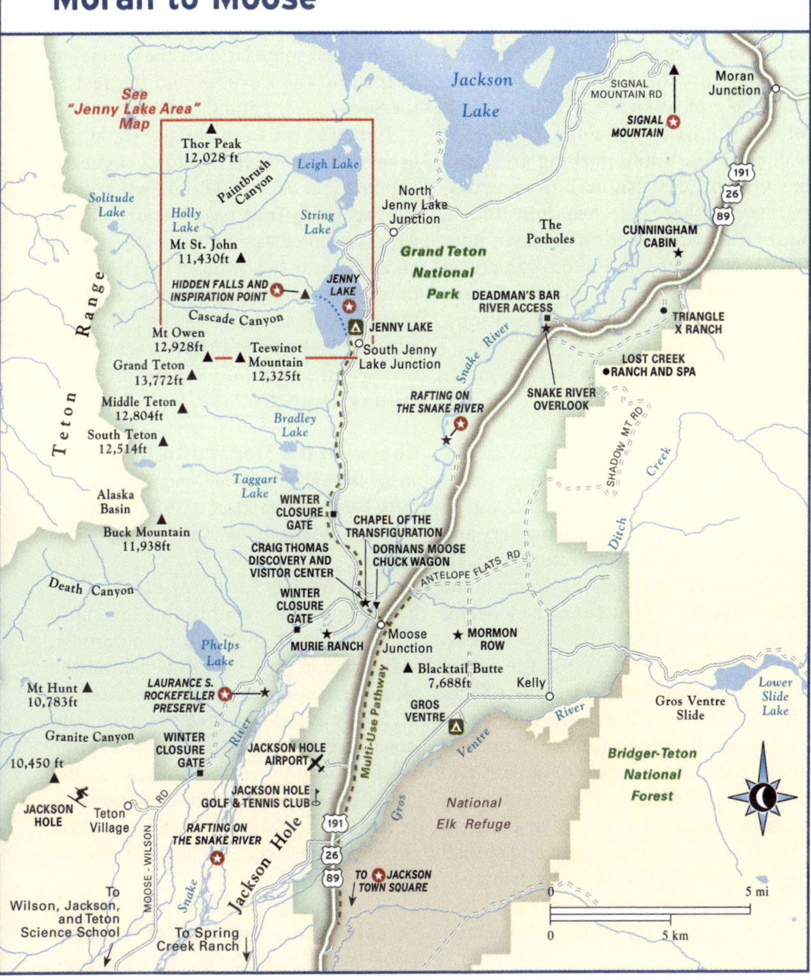

jagged mountains behind it. Listed on the National Register of Historic Places, Mormon Row is a collection of six dilapidated homesteads that can be explored on a **self-guided tour** (brochures are available near the pink house). The area was settled at the turn of the 20th century by Mormon families who built homes, a church, a school, and a swimming hole. The settlement was abandoned when the Rockefellers bought up much of the land and transferred it to the National Park Service. In the 1990s the historical and cultural value of the site was recognized and steps were taken to preserve the structures. From Jackson, drive north on US 191 past Moose Junction onto Gros Ventre Road to Antelope Flats Road. Continue 1.5 mi (2.4 km) on Antelope Flats Road until you see a north-south-running dust road. The parking area is next to the pink stucco house.

The Antelope Flats area—excellent for walking or biking on a flat, unpaved road—offers prime habitat for pronghorn, bison, moose, coyotes, ground squirrels, northern harriers, kestrels, and sage grouse. In the winter, the first mile (1.6 km) of Antelope Flats Road is plowed to a small parking area, giving visitors easy snowshoe or cross-country ski access to Moulton Ranch, one of the homesteads on Mormon Row. On the NPS website, visitors can access **audio tours** (www.nps.gov/grte/learn/photosmultimedia/audio-descriptions.htm) of Mormon Row.

Craig Thomas Discovery and Visitor Center

1 Teton Park Rd.; 307/739-3399; 9am-5pm daily May and Oct., 8am-5pm daily June-Sept.

Twelve mi (19 km) north of Jackson in Moose, the Craig Thomas Discovery and Visitor Center is an architectural masterpiece, mimicking the alpine drama of the Teton Range. The structure is a model for other national parks—in that more than half the funds used to build the center were private donations. The state-of-the-art facility, including video rivers that flow beneath your feet, places emphasis on the connection between humans and the natural world. Interpretive displays include a large relief model of the park that shows glacial movement and animal migration, and a photographic tribute to local mountaineering. Ranger-led hikes and tours depart from the visitor center.

Menors Ferry Historic District

In 1894, William D. Menor built a homestead along the Snake River. He built a ferryboat on cables to carry settlers and miners across the river, which was otherwise impassable during spring. Entire wagon teams crossed on the ferry, paying $0.50 per trip, while a horse and rider paid $0.25. In 1918, Menor sold the operation to Maud Noble, who doubled the fares ($1 for automobiles with local plates, $2 for out-of-staters) in the hope of attracting more tourists to the region. When a bridge was built in 1927, the ferry became obsolete, and in 1929, after having donated some land for the Chapel of Transfiguration, Noble sold the rest to the Snake River Land Company.

Today, a replica of the ferryboat has been built on-site, and visitors can meander down the 0.5-mi (0.8-km) self-guided **Menors Ferry Trail** past Menor's cabin, which doubled as a country store. Find an **audio tour** (www.nps.gov/grte/learn/photosmultimedia/audio-descriptions.htm) of Menors Ferry on the NPS website. From the park's south entrance at Moose, turn right into the Menors Ferry Historic District.

Chapel of the Transfiguration

1.1 mi/1.8 km north of Moose Junction on Chapel of the Transfiguration Rd.; 307/733-2603; Holy Communion 8am and 10am Sun. Memorial Day-Sept.

Built in 1925, Chapel of the Transfiguration is a humble log cabin with the most spectacular mountain view framed in the window behind the altar. An Episcopal church, operated by St. John's in Jackson, it was built on land donated by Maud Noble and is a favorite spot for summer weddings. A candlelight Christmas night service and sunrise Easter service are particularly wonderful ways to experience this historic place of worship.

★ Laurance S. Rockefeller Preserve

Moose-Wilson Rd.; 307/739-3399 or 307/739-3654; 9am-5pm daily early June-late Sept.

Four mi (6 km) south of Moose on the Moose-Wilson Road, the former JY Ranch and longtime summer home of the Rockefeller family, known as the Laurance S. Rockefeller Preserve, offers 8 mi (13 km) of trails through forest, wetlands, and meadows on reclaimed property along Phelps Lake and Lake Creek. The preserve is 1,106 acres (448 ha) and was donated to the Park Service in 2007 by the Rockefeller family.

The Laurance S. Rockefeller Preserve Center is the first platinum-level LEED-certified building constructed in a national park and was constructed to give visitors a sensory experience of the natural elements found on the preserve. A poem by beloved writer Terry Tempest Williams features prominently, and visitors can learn about the preserve and Rockefeller's beliefs about land stewardship. Several ranger programs, including sunrise hikes and children's programs, are available from the center daily throughout summer.

Murie Ranch

1 Murie Ranch Rd., Moose; 307/732-7752 or 307/739-3399; www.tetonscience.org; 9am-5pm Mon.-Fri. mid-Mar.-mid-Oct., tours 11:30am weekdays June-Sept.; free

The onetime STS Ranch and former residence of wilderness champions Olaus and Mardy Murie, Murie Ranch is dedicated to connecting people and wilderness. It is where the Wilderness Act was authored in the 1950s and early 1960s. The ranch is a National Historic Landmark and the site of ongoing conservation seminars and educational workshops. On-site accommodations are available to participants, and the entire facility can be rented for conservation education programs. An excellent library and bookstore is on-site, and rangers host naturalist programs throughout the summer. Free tours of the Murie home, Olaus Murie's studio, and the homestead cabin are given in summer.

Jenny Lake and Vicinity

Carved some 12,000 years ago by the same glaciers that dug out Cascade Canyon, Jenny Lake is perhaps the most picturesque and popular spot in the park. The hiking—to places like Hidden Falls, Inspiration Point, and the even more beautiful Leigh Lake—is sublime, and

Top to bottom: Mormon Row; Antelope Flats; Jenny Lake

Jenny Lake Area

the water activities—cruising, canoeing, kayaking, swimming, and fishing—are plentiful. The park's fanciest and most expensive lodging and dining are at the historic Jenny Lake Lodge.

In the same way that Old Faithful embodies the Yellowstone experience for many visitors, so too does Jenny Lake conjure up all that is wonderful about Grand Teton. A scenic drive from North Jenny Lake to South Jenny Lake skirts the water and affords breathtaking views of the Grand Teton, Teewinot, and Mount Owen. Those who are more interested in solitude should get off the main drag here, away from the crowds and into the wilderness.

★ Jenny Lake

In 1872 an English-born mountain man, known as "Beaver Dick" Leigh for his enormous front teeth and penchant for the animal, guided Ferdinand Hayden around the Tetons. Hayden named the alpine lake for Dick's wife, Jenny, a member of the Shoshone tribe. In the fall of 1876, pregnant Jenny took care of an ailing woman, not knowing the woman had smallpox. Jenny and all four of her children became ill. Her baby was born just before Christmas and, along with Jenny and the other four children, died within a week. Beaver Dick buried his family in Jackson Hole.

Despite its tragic namesake, Jenny Lake is among the most beautiful and visited spots in the park. From cruising across the lake to hiking its shores, there are endless ways to enjoy this idyllic spot. Set between two parking areas with easy walking access to the lake, trails, and campground, Jenny Lake Visitor Center is 8 mi (13 km) north of Moose at South Jenny Lake.

Leigh Lake

Named for mountain man "Beaver Dick" Leigh, Leigh Lake is much quieter and maybe even more beautiful than Jenny Lake. The lake offers unrivaled views of Mount Moran, Mount Woodring, and Rockchuck Peak, and is dotted with sandy beaches. A 5.4-mi (8.7-km) round-trip (out-and-back) trail on its east shore is flat and weaves in and out of the forest with a constant water view. The Leigh Lake Trailhead is at the northwest corner of the String Lake Picnic Area. The trail can be hiked as early as May or June, depending on snowmelt, and is typically passable well into September. Although popular, Leigh Lake does not attract the huge crowds of Jenny Lake.

Adventure and Recreation

Hiking

Flagg Ranch and Colter Bay

Lakeshore Trail

Distance: 2.2 mi (3.5 km) round-trip
Duration: 1 hour
Elevation gain: 100 ft (30 m)
Effort: Easy
Trail surface: Asphalt, dirt, gravel
Trailhead: Lakeshore Trail at Colter Bay behind the Colter Bay Visitor Center

The easy Lakeshore Trail circumnavigates Colter Bay with stunning views in every direction.

Hermitage Point Trail

Distance: 9.5 mi (15.3 km) round-trip
Duration: 4 hours
Elevation gain: 930 ft (283 m)
Effort: Moderate to strenuous
Trail surface: Dirt, some rocky sections
Trailhead: Hermitage Point Trail at Colter Bay

The hike to Hermitage Point is one of the most significant hikes in the area given its length. The elevation gain is minimal, and the trail, which starts immediately across from the boat launch at the southern end of the parking lot, meanders through forest, meadow, and alongside ponds and streams.

Jackson Lake Lodge and Signal Mountain

Christian Pond Loop

Distance: 3.5 mi (5.6 km) round-trip
Duration: 2 hours
Elevation gain: 490 ft (149 m)
Effort: Easy
Trail surface: Dirt
Trailhead: Christian Pond Loop from Jackson Lake Lodge

The Christian Pond Loop is a relatively flat and easy hike through prime waterfowl habitat. The trailhead is east of the parking lot adjacent to the Jackson Lake Lodge corrals. It starts off steep but quickly levels out.

Two Ocean Lake

Distance: 6.4 mi (10.3 km) round-trip
Duration: 4 hours
Elevation gain: 700 ft (210 m)
Effort: Moderate
Trailhead: Two Ocean Lake Trailhead off of Pacific Creek Road

Two Ocean Lake offers a hike around

Grand View Trails

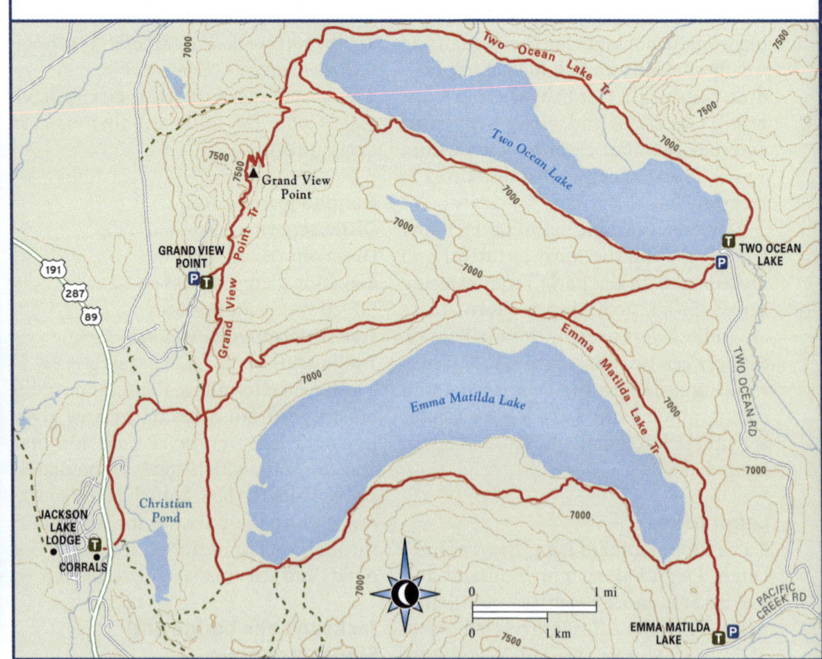

the lake though forest and meadow. The views of the lake are nonstop, as are the views of the Tetons.

Emma Matilda Lake Loop Trail

Distance: 10.7 mi (17.2 km) round-trip
Duration: 6 hours
Elevation gain: 1,430 ft (500 m)
Effort: Strenuous
Trail surface: Dirt, some wet areas
Trailhead: Park at Two Ocean Lake Trailhead parking lot off Pacific Creek Rd. and follow signs to the Emma Matilda Loop Trail

Emma Matilda Lake offers an even longer hike with fabulous Teton views from the north shore ridge. Since it's right next to the lake, the trail can get a little marshy in places.

Moran to Moose

Taggart Lake-Bradley Lake Loop

Distance: 5.6 mi (9 km) round-trip
Duration: 2-3 hours
Elevation gain: 890 ft (262 m)
Effort: Moderate
Trailhead: Taggart Lake Trailhead, 2.3 mi (3.7 km) northwest of the Moose Entrance Station

The Taggart Lake-Bradley Lake Loop Trail leads up through an aspen-covered moraine, first to Bradley Lake and then up to Taggart. Along the way are stunning views of the Tetons. You can return to the trailhead via the Beaver Creek Trail to make the hike 0.5 mi (0.8 km) longer.

Phelps Lake, Lake Creek, and Woodland Loop

Distance: 7 mi (11.3 km) round-trip
Duration: 3 hours
Elevation gain: 725 ft (221 m)
Effort: Moderate
Trail surface: Dirt, some gravel
Trailhead: Phelps Lake Loop Trailhead, Laurance S. Rockefeller Preserve

Signal Mountain

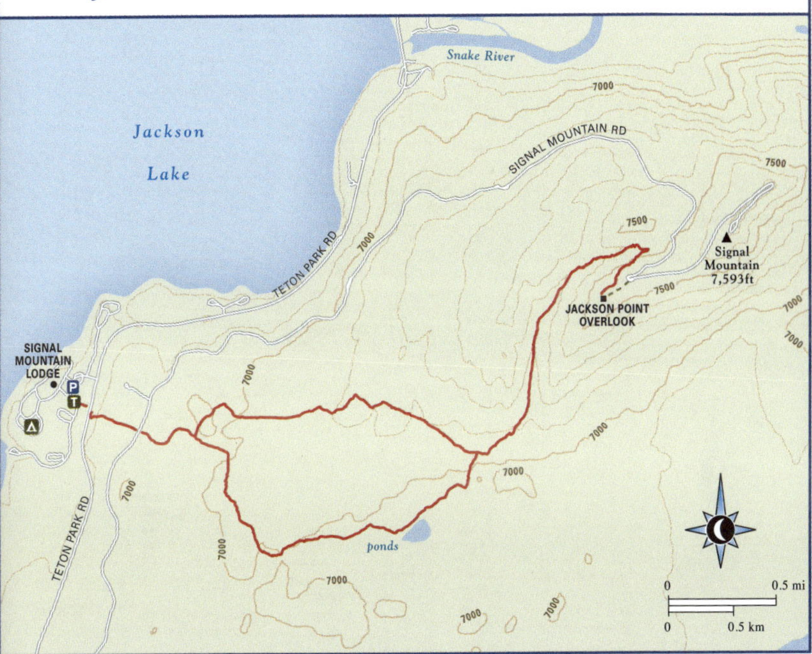

Leaving from Laurance S. Rockefeller Preserve, Phelps Lake trail winds through the forest and along Lake Creek to Phelps Lake. At the lake, hikers get a great view into **Death Canyon,** which offers many backcountry trail options into the high country. Woodland Trail takes you back via a loop to the preserve.

Jenny Lake and Vicinity

★ Jenny Lake Trail to Hidden Falls and Inspiration Point

Distance: 6 mi (9.6 km) round-trip
Duration: 2-3 hours
Elevation gain: 870 ft (270 m)
Effort: Moderate
Trail surface: Dirt with exposed rock and roots
Trailhead: Jenny Lake Trailhead

One of the area's most popular hikes leads to the spectacular Hidden Falls and Inspiration Point. From Jenny Lake's south shore, the hike follows a moderate 2.5-mi (4-km) trail (one-way) with 550 ft (168 m) of elevation gain to the 100-ft (30-m) cascade. It's another steep 0.5 mi (0.8 km) to Inspiration Point, with views over the lake and valley, plus Cascade Canyon and the Cathedral Group of mountains that give the spot its name.

Visitors who want to put fewer miles on their feet can take the **Jenny Lake Shuttle** (307/734-9227; www.jennylakeboating.com; every 10-15 minutes 10am-4pm mid-May-early June, 7am-7pm daily early June-early Sept.; round-trip $20, one-way $12), which runs throughout the day to shorten the hike to Hidden Falls to 1 mi (1.6 km) with 250 ft (46 m) of elevation gain.

Jenny Lake Loop Trail

Distance: 7.1 mi (11.4 km) round-trip
Duration: 4 hours
Elevation gain: 1,040 ft (317 m)

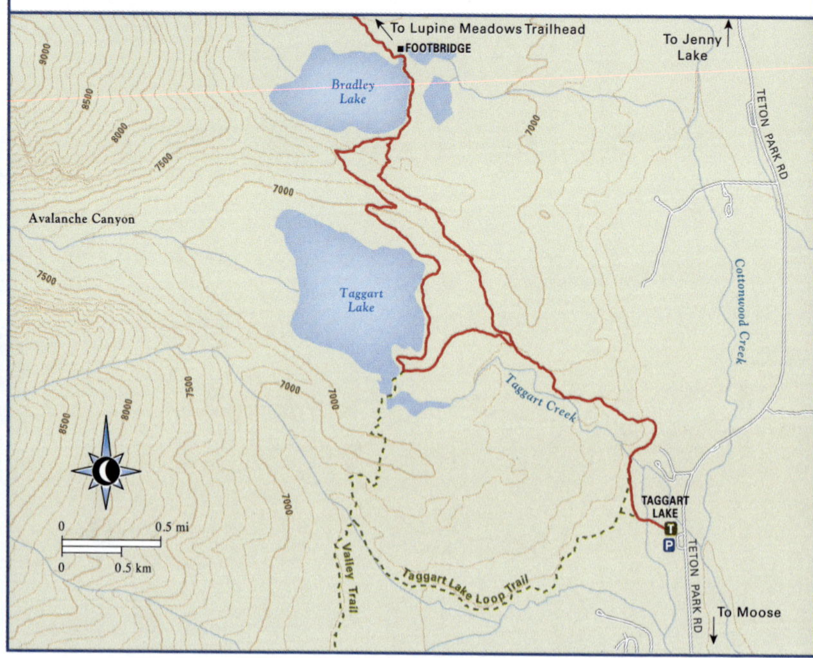

Effort: Moderate
Trail surface: Dirt with exposed rock and roots
Trailhead: Jenny Lake Trailhead, South Jenny Lake

The Jenny Lake Loop Trail circumnavigates the lake. Along the way are several other trails that lead to Hidden Falls, Inspiration Point, and Cascade Canyon. Moose Ponds are at the southern shore of Jenny Lake, which is a good place to look for, well, moose.

Leigh Lake Trail

Distance: 1.8 mi (2.9 km) round-trip
Duration: 45 minutes
Elevation gain: 110 ft (34 m)
Effort: Easy
Trail surface: Dirt with exposed rock and roots
Trailhead: String Lake Trail or Leigh Lake Trailhead, northwest corner of the String Lake Picnic Area

Unlike Jenny Lake, there is no road to Leigh Lake, making traffic just a bit lighter. The relatively flat trail winds through trees and along String Lake to Leigh Lake. From there, a longer 5.4-mi (8.7-km) round-trip out-and-back trail follows the east shore of the lake to Bearpaw and Trapper Lakes. The trail can be hiked as early as May or June, depending on snowmelt, and is typically passable well into September.

Lupine Meadows Trail to Amphitheater Lake

Distance: 10.1 mi (16.3 km) round-trip
Duration: 6-7 hours
Elevation gain: 3,000 ft (914 m)
Effort: Strenuous
Trail surface: Asphalt, dirt, rock
Trailhead: Lupine Meadows Trailhead, Lupine Meadows Rd. off Teton Park Rd., just south of Jenny Lake

The Lupine Meadows Trailhead offers

Phelps Lake and Death Canyon

hikers a number of ways to get up into the Teton Range, but most of them come after the first 3 mi (4.8 km) through conifers to shrub-covered slopes. Amphitheater Lake is a glacial lake surrounded by meadows at the base of Disappointment Peak.

Biking

Some of the best biking in the park is on the paved **Multi-Use Pathway** that heads north from Jackson and parallels US 89/191 to Antelope Flats Road, where secondary paved roads meander through sagebrush flats. From Moose Junction, the path follows the Teton Park Road to **South Jenny Lake.** A 7-mi (11.3-km) scenic loop starts at South Jenny Lake, follows the Teton Park Road for 3 mi (5 km), and then turns left at North Jenny Lake Junction and left again on the one-way return to South Jenny Lake.

North of Colter Bay, near the Flagg Ranch, is **Grassy Lake Road,** a 52-mi (84-km) dirt road—great for mountain biking—that follows an ancient Indigenous thoroughfare all the way to Ashton, Idaho. Along the way are hiking trails, streams, ponds, and splendid scenery.

A nice area for visitors who travel with their bicycles is in the vicinity of **Two Ocean Road,** southeast of Jackson Lake Lodge and northeast of Signal Mountain Lodge. The road itself is just 3 mi (5 km) long, but the scenery is sublime for a short, sweet ride. **River Road** is 15 mi (24 km) of gravel running along the west side of the Snake River between Signal Mountain and Cottonwood Creek. Do remember that this is bear country, and every precaution—including bear spray—should be taken.

There are plenty of biking opportunities on the paved and unpaved roads in the region, including **Antelope Flats**

Finding a Guide

Setting off into the wilds of Grand Teton National Park can be slightly intimidating, making guided tours a good option. The Park Service maintains a list of licensed, permitted, and park-approved guides.

Rock Climbing

- **Exum Mountain Guides** (South Jenny Lake in summer; 307/733-2297 for summer activities and 307/732-0606 for winter; www.exumguides.com) has been offering instruction and guided mountain climbing since 1931, making it the oldest guide service in North America and certainly one of the most prestigious. Exum offers numerous programs, from easy day climbing for families with kids to guided expeditions up the 13,770-ft (4,197-m) Grand Teton. They also offer guided **backcountry skiing and snowboarding** in the Tetons.

Hiking

- **The Hole Hiking Experience** (307/690-4453; www.holehike.com) offers a range of **guided hikes** and **snowshoe or ski tours** (half-day from $520 for 1-3 people) in and around the park for all interests and ability levels, from sunrise or sunset discovery tours to all-day wildlife-watching hikes (mixed groups on Tues. and Thurs. from $180 pp, private 4-hour tours from $600 for 1-3 people, 6 hours from $900 for 1-2 people). Kids will love the family day hikes with fun survival-like activities that include eating "lemon drop" ants and using butterfly nets. Winter cross-country ski and snowshoe tours are guided by naturalists and show off the best winter has to offer.

Horseback Riding

- The **Grand Teton Lodge Company** (307/543-3100 or 307/543-2811; www.gtlc.com) can arrange everything from a 1-2-hour ($68-100) horseback ride to breakfast wagon rides (call for updated pricing and schedule) and dinner rides (call for updated pricing and schedule) to 10-minute pony rides for the little ones. All riders in the park must be at least eight years old and under 225 lbs (102 kg).

Road all the way to Kelly, the **Shadow Mountain Road,** and the **Moose-Wilson Road** linking Moose and the Laurance S. Rockefeller Preserve. The **Multi-Use Pathway** from Moose or the Taggart Lake Trailhead to South Jenny Lake is popular for good reason.

Dornans

12170 Dornan Rd., Moose; 307/733-3307; www.dornans.com; 9am-6am daily

Bicycles can be rented from Dornans. In addition to a range of adult bikes (call for availability and current rates), Dornans rents kids' bikes, Trail-a-Bikes, bike racks, and Burley carriers for toddlers.

Boating and Fishing

With so much beautiful water in the park, boating is a fantastic way to explore. Rafting on the **Snake River,** canoeing or kayaking on any number of lakes, or cruising across **Jackson Lake**—there are

Fishing

- **Grand Teton Lodge Company** (307/543-3100; www.gtlc.com; $180/hour, $825/day) can arrange trips from any of the accommodations inside the park.
- Fishing trips on the Snake River or Jackson Lake can also be arranged through the lakefront **Signal Mountain Lodge** (877/841-1076 or 307/543-2831; www.signalmountainlodge.com; $169/hour, $529/day).
- **Grand Teton Fly Fishing** (307/690-0910; www.grandtetonflyfishing.com; $720-800) offers both float and wade trips on a variety of rivers and lakes in the region.

Rafting

- Leaving from Jackson Lake Lodge, **Grand Teton Lodge Company** (307/543-3100; www.gtlc.com) offers 3-5-hour scenic floats ($70-120) on the Snake with the option for a cookout lunch.
- **Barker-Ewing** (307/733-1800 or 800/365-1800; www.barker-ewing.com) is another option for 10-mi (16-km) scenic floats on the Snake ($100).
- **Solitude Float Trips** (307/733-2871; www.grand-teton-scenic-floats.com) puts in on the Snake at Deadman's Bar, just below the Snake River Overlook, and offers guests a leisurely 2-hour scenic float ($105) and private trips (from $1,140) for up to 12 guests.
- **Signal Mountain Lodge** (877/841-1076 or 307/543-2831; www.signalmountainlodge.com) offers 2-hour scenic float trips (from $99) along a 10-mi (16-km) stretch of the Snake River from mid-May to late September.

Naturalist-Guided Tours

Park Service rangers offer excellent tours throughout the year. Late December-March, depending on conditions, you can make a reservation for a guided **snowshoe hike** (307/739-3399; reservations required; $5 snowshoe rental fee). During the summer months, the range of offerings is vast—from 30-minute map chats and campfire programs to 3-hour hikes, evening astronomy programs, and tipi demos. For more information on ranger programs, pick up the park newspaper at any of the entrance stations, call 307/739-3300, or check out the visitor centers in Moose, Jenny Lake, Colter Bay, and the Laurance S. Rockefeller Preserve.

options for adrenaline junkies and diehard landlubbers alike.

Human-powered boats like kayaks and canoes are permitted on Emma Matilda Lake and Two Ocean Lake, east of Jackson Lake Lodge. Jackson Lake is open to motorboats, human-powered boats, sailboats, waterskiing, and windsurfers. Permits are required for motorized boats ($56) and nonmotorized crafts ($17), including stand-up paddleboards, and can be purchased at the visitor centers in Moose, Jenny Lake (cash only), or Colter Bay.

A Wyoming fishing license is required for all fishing in the park and can be purchased at **Snake River Angler at Dornans** (12170 Dornan Rd.; 307/733-3699; www.snakeriverangler.com), **Signal Mountain Marina** (307/543-2831; www.signalmountainlodge.com), and **Colter Bay Marina** (307/543-3100; www.gtlc.com). Pick up a fishing brochure from any of the visitor centers to learn about all park regulations.

Colter Bay Village Marina

10 mi/16 km north of Moran Junction; 307/543-2811, ext. 1097, or 307/543-2811; www.gtlc.com

Scenic cruises ($36-88 pp) lasting 1.5-2.5 hours depart throughout the day mid-June-mid-September from Colter Village Bay Marina. Kayaks ($35-45), canoes ($30), and motorboat ($120-300) rentals (2-hour minimums apply for all rentals) can be rented from the marina on a first-come, first-served basis. Guided fly-fishing tours can be arranged through the marina as well (prices and trips vary). Guided Jackson Lake **fishing** (307/543-2811) can be arranged from Colter Bay Marina starting at $180 per hour for 1-2 adults with a 2-hour minimum and $35 per hour per additional person; day trips start at $825 for two people. Free tours of the historical Colter Bay cabins are offered, along with a number of guided hikes and ranger programs.

Grand Teton Lodge Company

307/543-2811 and ask for the marina; www.gtlc.com

Anglers will be pleased with the varied offerings in this stretch of the park, from the lunkers in Jackson Lake, which can be fished on shore or by boat, to the healthy but discerning trout in the Snake River. **Guided trips** can be arranged through Grand Teton Lodge Company, from $180 per hour or $825 per day. The Grand Teton Lodge Company can also arrange various **boat rentals** (motorboats $60/hour, canoes $30/hour, single kayak $35/hour, double kayak $45/hour) throughout the park. Note that all the boat rentals have a 2-hour minimum. Scenic 3-5-hour floats ($70-120) can be arranged on the Snake River with the option of a cookout lunch.

Signal Mountain Lodge

307/543-2831; www.signalmountainlodge.com

From Signal Mountain Lodge, anglers can go out with experienced guides (late May-mid-Sept.) in pursuit of Jackson Lake's cutthroat, brown, and lake trout for $169 per hour or $529 per day. Scenic 10-mi (16-km) floats down the Snake can be arranged through Signal Mountain Lodge for $99. Boats can be rented, including pontoon boats ($130/hour, $599/day for up to 10 people), runabouts ($71/hour, $349/day for up to 5 people), fishing boats ($55/hour, $275/day for up to 5 people), and sea kayaks ($29/hour, $110/day single, or $39/hour, $125/day double).

Grand Teton Fly Fishing

307/690-0910 or 307/690-4347; www.grandtetonflyfishing.com; $720-800

Both float and wade trips can be arranged through Grand Teton Fly Fishing. Bruce has been guiding people in the park for almost 50 years, and knows where the fish are likely to hide.

Solitude Float Trips

307/733-2871; www.grand-teton-scenic-floats.com; 2-hour scenic float $105, private boat $1,140

Solitude Float Trips puts in on the Snake at Deadman's Bar, just below the Snake River Overlook, for scenic 2-hour floats, or private trips for up to 12 guests.

Jenny Lake Boating

Visitor Center at Jenny Lake; 307/734-9227; www.jennylakeboating.com; mid-May-late Sept., hours vary annually; $30

Scenic 1-hour **cruises** are guided by experts on flora, fauna, history, and geology. Departures vary throughout the season, so call ahead or check online. Hiker **shuttles** are available to the Cascade Canyon hiking trails (round-trip $20, one-way $12, departing every 10-15 minutes). Canoe and kayak **rentals** ($35/hour, $140/day) can also be arranged through Jenny Lake Boating.

Horseback Riding

There are several options for guided horseback riding trips, May-September, from a number of lodges in the park, including Colter Bay Village, Flagg Ranch, and Jackson Lake Lodge.

Grand Teton Lodge Company

307/543-3100 or 307/543-2811; www.gtlc.com; $68-100

The Grand Teton Lodge Company can arrange 1-2-hour horseback tours, breakfast wagon rides, dinner rides, and 10-minute pony rides for little ones. Additional options from Jackson Lake Lodge include trips to Emma Matilda Lake and an overlook of Oxbow Bend. All riders must be at least eight years old and under 225 lbs (102 kg).

Winter Sports

In the winter, when snow blankets the park, most park roads are closed to vehicles. The 14-mi (22.5-km) unplowed section of **Teton Park Road,** from the Taggart Lake Trailhead parking area to Signal Mountain Lodge, is groomed and open to **cross-country skiing** and **snowshoeing.** Dogs are permitted on leash. Accessible trailheads from the groomed section of the road include **Jenny Lake Trail** (8 mi/13 km round-trip; 200 ft/61 m elevation gain; easy) and the **Taggart Lake-Beaver Creek Loop** (4 mi/6.4 km round-trip; 500 ft/152 m elevation gain; moderate-difficult).

Some popular destinations for cross-country skiing and snowshoeing expeditions include the **Phelps Lake Overlook** (5.2 mi/8.4 km round-trip; 730 ft/223 m elevation gain; moderate), **Phelps Lake** (4 mi/6.4 km round-trip; 300 ft/91 m elevation gain; moderate), and the **Moose-Wilson Road** (5.8 mi/9.3 km round-trip; 500 ft/152 m elevation gain; easy). All three trailheads can be accessed from parking areas on the Moose-Wilson Road, including the Granite Canyon Trailhead (from Teton Village) and the gate at the Death Canyon road (coming from Moose).

Top to bottom: Jenny Lake from Inspiration Point; hiking to Taggart and Bradley Lakes; horseback riding out of Colter Bay Village

None of the park trails are marked or flagged, so planning and caution are important. Skiers and snowshoers should always carry water, high-energy snacks, and additional weather-appropriate clothing. For those who want to cover ground with a ranger, **guided snowshoe hikes** (307/739-3399; Tues., Thurs., and Sat. late Dec.-mid-Mar.; free) are offered three times a week from late December through mid-March. Call for more details or to make reservations.

Skinny Skis

65 W. Deloney Ave.; 307/733-6094; www.skinnyskis.com; 9am-6pm Mon.-Sat., 10am-5pm Sun.

In Jackson, all manner of winter gear can be purchased or rented from Skinny Skis.

Teton Mountaineering

170 N. Cache St.; 307/733-3595; www.tetonmtn.com; 9am-7pm daily

Teton Mountaineering sells and rents alpine and telemark ski packages along with snowshoe and cross-country ski packages.

Food

Flagg Ranch and Colter Bay

Headwaters Lodge & Cabins at Flagg Ranch

Sheffields Restaurant & Bar

100 Grass Lakes Rd.; 307/543-2861; www.gtlc.com; 7am-10am, 11:30am-2pm, and 5:30pm-9:30pm daily June-late Sept.; $16-40

Sheffields Restaurant & Bar, in the main lodge of Headwaters Lodge & Cabins, serves local cuisine—including bison burger, elk medallions, and grilled local trout—in a family-friendly setting. Reservations are required for dinner. The Bistro & Saloon (7am-close; $8-12) is open all day and serves grab-and-go meals and snacks.

Colter Bay Village

Café Court Pizzeria

100 Colter Bay Village Rd.; 307/543-2811; 11am-10pm daily late May-late Sept.; $9-31

The Café Court Pizzeria in Colter Bay Village serves up specialty salads, toasted subs, and pizza, both by the slice and whole pies.

Ranch House Restaurant

100 Colter Bay Village Rd.; 307/543-3335; 6:30am-10:30am, 11:30am-1:30pm, and 5:30pm-9pm daily late May-late Sept.; $14-39

Also at Colter Bay is the Ranch House Restaurant. The restaurant offers family-style meals with an emphasis on American comfort food. The full breakfast buffet ($22) can include eggs, French toast, hot specials, and organic oatmeal; or, if you want to order à la carte ($11-18), you can easily fill up on pancakes, huevos rancheros, or biscuits and gravy. Lunch ($10-22) consists of a good selection of salads, burgers, and sandwiches, while dinner offers hearty steaks, chops, and seafood dishes, plus lots of burgers and sandwiches. The bar is open 11:30am-10:30pm daily and has a small food menu as well.

Jackson Lake Lodge and Signal Mountain

Jackson Lake Lodge

Mural Room

101 Jackson Lake Lodge Rd.; 307/543-3463; 7am-9:30am, 11am-1:30pm, and 5pm-9pm daily mid-May-early Oct.; $29-52

The Mural Room has unmatched ambience with its windowed wall looking out onto the lake, Mount Moran, and the Teton Range along with the colorful murals by artist Carl Routers. The food is upscale and innovative, and when coupled with the view, it makes this one of the most pleasurable dining experiences in the park. Dinner reservations are recommended and can be secured on OpenTable.

Pioneer Grill

101 Jackson Lake Lodge Rd.; 307/543-2811; 6am-10pm daily late May-early Oct.; $10-39

Also in the lodge is the more casual and less pricey Pioneer Grill, a true-to-style 1950s diner. A fun place for a meal, the counter snakes 200 ft (60 m) through the room and encourages guests to interact with other diners. The Pioneer Grill offers American cuisine and has a takeout service if you decide you'd rather watch the sunset while munching on your burger. You should not leave without ordering a huckleberry shake.

Blue Heron Lounge

101 Jackson Lake Lodge Rd.; 307/543-2811; 11am-11pm daily late May-early Oct., food served until sunset; $13-23

The Blue Heron Lounge is another casual dining experience in Jackson Lake Lodge. It has a bar menu with a selection of appetizers and creative sandwiches and offers sustainable draft beer from local breweries. Enjoy an elk burger on the deck with a huckleberry mojito and a panoramic view of the mountains.

Poolside Cantina

Food service 11am-4pm daily, beverage service 11am-8pm daily early June-late Aug. depending on weather; $7-16

If you are at the Jackson Lake Lodge pool or with your kids at the playground, you may want to fill up on the Mexican food at the outdoor Poolside Cantina, which also serves salads, burgers, and hot dogs for the kids.

Signal Mountain Lodge

The Trapper Grill

1 Inner Park Rd.; 7am-10pm daily early May-early Oct.; $14-35

Serving three meals a day, the Trapper Grill sticks to American fare with some Tex-Mex thrown in. The lunch and dinner menu is filled with specialty sandwiches, salads, and burgers, but the restaurant prides itself on its homemade desserts. Save room for the Colter's Run chocolate pecan pie or the mountain cookie for two.

Deadman's Bar

1 Inner Park Rd.; 307/543-2831; noon-midnight daily early May-early Oct., kitchen closes at 10pm in high season and 9pm after mid-Sept.; $14-29

For a drink, snack, and a glimpse of television, stop at Deadman's Bar, which serves the largest plate of fully loaded nachos you've ever seen. They pair perfectly with a blackberry margarita and a Wyoming sunset.

Leek's Pizzeria

Leek's Marina Rd.; 307/543-2494; noon-9pm daily late May-early Aug., noon-8:30pm daily mid-Aug.-early Sept.; $14-29

Leek's Pizzeria is 10 mi (16 km) north of Signal Mountain Lodge at the marina on Jackson Lake. It serves specialty pizzas and calzones, sandwiches, salads, and microbrews in a fantastic outdoor setting.

Moran to Moose

You'll find most of your food options in this area at Dornans, a family resort on the banks of the Snake River.

★ Dornans Moose Chuck Wagon

12170 Dornans Rd.; 307/733-2415, ext. 300; breakfast, lunch, and dinner daily mid-June-Labor Day, weather dependent

Dornans Moose Chuck Wagon serves up hearty "cowboy cuisine" during the summer with beef from its own butcher shop and Dutch ovens heated over wood fires. Breakfast ($5-15) offers sourdough pancakes. Lunch and dinner (noon-7:30pm daily, $11-23) feature sandwiches, burgers, and barbecue. Monday night is the hootenanny starting at 6pm, an evening of acoustic delight. There's often live music Tuesday-Saturday between 5:30pm and 8:30pm. It's a good idea to call ahead for evening reservations and check that it's not privately booked for the evening.

Dornans Pizza and Pasta Company

12170 Dornans Rd.; 307/733-2415, ext. 204; 11:30am-9pm daily in season with reduced hours in spring and fall; $12-21

Dornans Pizza and Pasta Company is located in the **Spur Bar** and offers a variety of salads, hot sandwiches, gourmet pizzas, pasta dishes, and calzones.

Dornans Trading Post & Deli

12170 Dornans Rd.; 307/733-2415, ext. 201; 8am-8pm daily

To pick up something for your hike, stop at Dornans Trading Post & Deli for everything from freeze-dried meals and cold drinks to gourmet groceries and any camping equipment you might need. The deli is open May-September.

Dornans Wine Shoppe

12170 Dornans Rd.; 307/733-2415, ext. 202; 11am-8pm daily summer, reduced hours off-season

If you have the time, visit Dornans Wine Shoppe, a find for wine connoisseurs and novices alike with around 1,500 varieties of wines and 150 types of cheese. *Food & Wine* magazine named it one of the 50 most amazing wine experiences in the country, and *Wine Spectator* has bestowed its Wine Award on the shop several times.

Jenny Lake and Vicinity

Jenny Lake Lodge Dining Room

Jenny Lake Rd.; 307/543-3100 or 307/543-3351; www.gtlc.com; 7:30am-9:30am, 11:30am-1pm, and 5:30pm-8:30pm daily June-early Oct.; $125 five-course dinner

Jenny Lake Lodge Dining Room offers a fine-dining experience in an original log cabin. Reservations are required for dinner and recommended for breakfast and lunch and can be made on OpenTable. Men are requested to wear dinner jackets. The food is creative and incorporates local flavors. Ham steak Benedict and s'mores pancakes appear on the breakfast menu ($12-21), and lunch ($15-30) consists mostly of upscale sandwiches and salads. The main event at the restaurant is the prix fixe five-course dinner ($125 not including gratuity or alcohol). Options for each course rotate nightly, from Wagyu rib eye and filet of Idaho trout to lobster tagliatelle or bison filet; no matter what's on the menu, it's sure to be a memorable meal.

Accommodations

Flagg Ranch and Colter Bay

Headwaters Lodge & Cabins at Flagg Ranch

100 Grassy Lakes Rd.; 800/443-2311 or 307/543-3100; www.gtlc.com; June-Sept.; $348-449

The Headwaters Lodge & Cabins at Flagg Ranch is touted as the oldest continuously operating resort in upper Jackson Hole. It is ideally situated to take advantage of both Yellowstone and Grand Teton National Parks. Options include standard, deluxe, or premium log cabins. Log cabins have two queens or one king bed, coffeemakers, private baths, and patios with rocking chairs. There is no cell service or Wi-Fi in the area.

Colter Bay Village

307/543-3100; www.gtlc.com; late May-early Oct.; cabins from $294

Colter Bay Village on the northern shore of Jackson Lake offers some of the park's most affordable lodging, which isn't saying much anymore. The village has rustic cabins (from $294), an **RV park** (www.recreation.gov; from $117) with 102 full-hookup pull-through sites and 12 full-hookup back-in sites, and a tent village (late May-early Sept.; $104 tent cabins). The original homestead cabins, purchased by the Rockefellers and moved to the area, have been refurbished but still offer a glimpse into the past. Each cabin displays a description of its own history. While most of the one-room cabins sleep two, one can sleep up to six people, and the two-room cabin can sleep up to 10 with rollaway beds. Prices vary depending on the number of occupants in the room and the arrangement of beds.

Jackson Lake Lodge and Signal Mountain

Jackson Lake Lodge

101 Jackson Lake Lodge Rd.; 307/543-3100; www.gtlc.com; mid-May-early Oct.; lodge rooms and cottages from $459

The Jackson Lake Lodge is one of the largest resorts in the park and commands an unparalleled view of Jackson Lake and the Teton Range from the lobby's panoramic 60-ft-high (18-m-high) windows. There are 385 guest rooms in the main lodge and surrounding cottages, and the grounds also house a playground and swimming pool. The cottages are in clusters and come in a range of styles. Classic cottages have two queen beds and sleep up to four. Mountain-view cottages can sleep up to five and include a mini fridge and a patio or balcony. There are also suites available.

Signal Mountain Lodge

1 Inner Park Rd.; 877/841-1076 or 307/543-2831; www.signalmountainlodge.com; early May-mid-Oct.; cabins from $312

Signal Mountain Lodge sits on the banks of Jackson Lake with a view of the Tetons. It has a variety of options for lodging, ranging from rustic log cabins (one-room cabin $312-337, two-room $367-372) and premier Western rooms ($519) to one- or two-room bungalows ($374-574) on the beach. The country rooms ($373) are motel-style accommodations, and the deluxe country rooms ($414) have one king bed and fireplaces. The two-room lakefront retreats ($518-574) are ideal for families and have kitchenettes. There is one three-bedroom cabin aptly named Home Away from Home ($659); if you are lucky enough to get it, you'll have a bedroom, dining area, living room with a gas fireplace, kitchen, and small laundry room all to yourself; the only drawback is that there is no view.

Moran to Moose

★ Triangle X Ranch

2 Triangle X Ranch Rd.; 307/733-2183; www.trianglex.com; late May-mid-Oct. and Dec. 26-mid-Mar.; $2,118-2,936 pp/week summer, $303-339 pp/night spring and fall, from $180 pp/night winter

In operation since 1926, 26 mi (42 km) north of Jackson and 32 mi (52 km) south of Yellowstone, Triangle X Ranch is the only authorized guest ranch concessionaire in the entire National Park System and sits right inside Grand Teton National Park. Not surprisingly, the setting is gorgeous, and you can see the entire mountain range from this secluded getaway.

The lodge is the original house used by two generations of the Turner family. The 20 log cabins are also originals that once housed families in different parts of Jackson Hole. The cabins come with 1-3 bedrooms; all have modern amenities and are decorated with cozy Western charm.

The ranch is also the only concession in the park that is open during winter. During peak season (early-June-late Aug.), the minimum stay is one week (Sun.-Sun.). During spring and fall, the ranch requires a minimum four-night stay but offers reduced rates; and during winter, visitors can book per night. Meals are served family-style in the main lodge and included in the price, as are horseback rides, cookouts, square dancing, and special programs for children. Winter activities include cross-country skiing, snowshoeing, and snowmobiling.

Dornans Spur Ranch Cabins

12250 Dornans Rd., Moose; 307/733-2522; www.dornans.com; open year-round; one-bedroom $140-395, two-bedroom $190-495

Dornans Spur Ranch Cabins sits on the Snake River in the middle of a wildflower meadow and gives alpine views in all directions. This is a small, family-owned business that provides quality service with personal touches, and the location affords easy access to fly-fishing and floating adventures. There are eight one-bedroom cabins and four two-bedroom duplexes on the premises. The cabins were built in the early 1990s and are bright and airy. They each have queen beds, kitchens, living-dining areas, and covered porches with a barbecue grill nearby. Also on these 10 acres (4 ha) of property are a grocery and camping store, two restaurants, and an award-winning wine shop. Visitors can rent mountain bikes, canoes, and kayaks during the summer and cross-country skis and snowshoes in the winter.

Jenny Lake and Vicinity

Jenny Lake Lodge

Jenny Lake Rd.; 307/543-3100; www.gtlc.com; mid-May-early Oct.; cabins from $806/night for 2 people

A former dude ranch for sophisticated Easterners, Jenny Lake Lodge is the finest lodging in the park and the only four-diamond eco-resort. The cabins have log walls, renovated baths, and handmade bed quilts adding to the charm of each room. Situated among the three lakes, the lodge is secluded and offers beautiful vistas. The rooms are pricey, but guests get a lot for their dime. A gourmet breakfast, five-course dinner, horseback riding, and access to bicycles are all included. Each week, different activities are available and include options such as live raptor displays on the patio, stargazing, interpretive programs, live music, and games like bocce ball and croquet. If you are looking for a romantic getaway, consider booking one of the suites, which come with wood-burning stoves.

Grand Teton Climbers Ranch

314 Climbers Ranch Rd.; 307/733-7271 or 303/384-0110 off-season; www.americanalpineclub.org; early June-early Sept.; $25/bunk for AAC members, $35/bunk for nonmembers

A much more affordable, and truly rustic, option is the Grand Teton Climbers Ranch, owned by the American Alpine Club and located just 3 mi (5 km) south of Jenny Lake. The ranch has small log cabins that serve as dormitories for 4-8 people. Guests must bring their own sleeping bags and pads, towels, cooking equipment, and food. Cooking and dishwashing facilities, toilets, and showers with hot water are available; showers are also available for $6 per person for nonguests. No camping is allowed. A general store on the grounds allows you to stock up on groceries as well as hiking and camping supplies. The ranch often offers a work week in early June that allows volunteers to stay at the ranch for free.

Camping

All Grand Teton National Park campgrounds moved to a reservation-only system in 2022. Reservations can be booked online six months in advance through www.recreation.gov.

Flagg Ranch and Colter Bay

Colter Bay Campground

www.recreation.gov; late May-late Sept.; from $59/vehicle, $13 pp for hikers or bicyclists, $80 electric-only sites

The Colter Bay Campground has 330 sites.

Lizard Creek Campground

307/543-2831; mid-June-early Sept.; $49

Located 30 mi (48 km) north of Moose between Flagg Ranch and Colter Bay Village, the Lizard Creek Campground has 60 individual sites with no hookups.

Jackson Lake Lodge and Signal Mountain

Signal Mountain Campground

1 Inner Park Rd.; 307/543-2831; www.recreation.gov; early May-mid-Oct.; $55 vehicle standard site, $79 standard electric site, $100 RV electric

Set on the southeast shore of Jackson Lake, the Signal Mountain Campground is nestled among spruce and fir trees with views of the mountains, lakes, and hillside. It is also wildly popular. Reservations can be booked on a rolling basis up to six months in advance through www.recreation.gov. There are 80 smallish sites, each with a picnic table and fire ring, and RVs up to 30 ft (9 m) in length are permitted. There are 24 sites with hookups. There is potable water, flush toilets, camp sinks, and hot water in the campground. Shower and laundry facilities are available by token at the Signal Mountain Lodge.

Moran to Moose

Gros Ventre

100 Gros Ventre Campground Rd., Kelly; 307/543-3100; www.gtlc.com; late Apr.-mid-Oct.; $57 tent and dry RV sites, $77 electric sites

Gros Ventre is the closest park campground to Jackson and the largest campground in the park, 11.5 mi (18.5 km) southeast of Moose. Booked through www.recreation.gov up to six months in advance, each of 316 sites offers a fire pit and picnic table, and can accommodate

Gros Ventre Campground

two tents, two vehicles, and up to six people. The campground isn't far from the river, and there are sites to be had in the cottonwoods and open sage. Nearby bathrooms include flush toilets, but no showers. A grocery store and service station are within 2 mi (3 km) of the campground.

Jenny Lake and Vicinity

Jenny Lake Campground

South Jenny Lake, next to Jenny Lake Visitor Center; 307/543-3100 or 307/543-2811; www.recreation.gov; early May-early Sept.; $56/vehicle, $13 hikers and bicyclists

The Jenny Lake Campground is the smallest in the park with 61 sites, and like the others, can be reserved up to six months in advance on www.recreation.gov. Most sites can accommodate one vehicle, two tents, and up to six campers. Additional sites are set aside for hikers or bicyclists. There are no large group sites, nor are trailers, campers, or generators allowed in the area. Because of its size and popularity, the maximum stay is seven days (at the other campgrounds it is 14 days). Flush toilets and cold running water are available, but there are no shower facilities.

Jackson Hole

Visitors love Jackson (pop. 10,698, elev. 5,672 ft/1,729 m) because it encompasses the best of the West in a charming town and spectacular setting. Western indeed, Jackson boasts a classic boardwalk around town, saloons with swinging doors and saddles for barstools, and architecture built on elk antlers. At the same time, Jackson is clearly mountain chic, with high-end boutiques and art galleries, gourmet dining, and ritzy accommodations.

The valley itself, known as Jackson Hole because it is surrounded by mountains, is 48 mi (77 km) long and up to 8 mi (13 km) wide in places. With the Tetons the most significant landmark, the region gives rise to the headwaters of the Snake River, fed abundantly by numerous mountain streams. Jackson Hole is a natural playground with offerings for just about anyone. In winter, outdoors enthusiasts can ski downhill at two well-known ski areas, Snow King and Jackson Hole Mountain Resort, or go the cross-country route just about anywhere, including nearby Grand Teton National Park. For those less interested in working up a sweat, a sleigh ride in the National Elk Refuge is a memorable experience. When the snow melts, there is no end to the adventurous options this valley offers, with fly-fishing and wildlife-watching among the less exhausting. From hiking and mountain biking to rafting and rock climbing, Jacksonians do it all.

Getting to Jackson Hole

The major routes into Jackson Hole—including US 89/191/287 from Yellowstone and Grand Teton National Parks, US 26/287 from the east, Highway 22 from the west over Teton Pass, and US 189/191/89 from the south—can all experience weather closures in the winter, particularly over Teton Pass. There is no car traffic in the southern portion of Yellowstone during the winter. For Wyoming **road reports,** call 800/996-7623 (www.wyoroad.info).

Jackson is roughly 240 mi (385 km) south of Bozeman, 177 mi (280 km) southwest of Cody through Yellowstone National Park, and 275 mi (445 km) northeast of Salt Lake City. Keep in mind that while distances through the national parks may be shorter in actual mileage, the time is often extended by lower speed limits, traffic congestion, and animal jams. In addition, most of the park roads are closed in winter, and car travel is not possible between Bozeman and Jackson or between Cody and Jackson. Driving distances around the parks increase significantly.

Jackson

Driving from Yellowstone

130-150 mi (209-242 km); 2.5-4 hours

To get from the north entrance of Yellowstone at **Gardiner** to Jackson, it's 150 mi (242 km) south on US 89/191, a route that takes you through both national parks. This drive takes about 4 hours.

From **West Yellowstone** to Jackson is 165 mi (265 km) west and south on US 191, a 4-hour drive that takes you through both parks. To avoid driving through the parks, you can take US 20 from West Yellowstone to Ashton, then ID-32 to ID-33 East for a 130-mi (209-km), 2.5-hour drive to Jackson.

Air

Jackson Hole Airport (JAC; 1250 E. Airport Rd., Jackson; 307/733-7682; www.jacksonholeairport.com) is served by American, Delta, United, and Frontier. The schedules change seasonally but include regular flights from Salt Lake City,

Denver, Seattle, Chicago, Minneapolis, Dallas, Houston, Phoenix, San Francisco, and Los Angeles.

Getting Around

The airport has on-site car rentals from **Enterprise** (307/733-7066), **Avis/Budget** (307/733-3422), **Hertz** (307/733-2272), and **National** (307/733-0671). **Alamo** (307/733-0671), **Dollar** (307/733-9224), **Thrifty** (307/734-8312), and **Leisure Sports** (307/733-3040) are available off-site with complimentary shuttles.

In order to try to control traffic to and from this hopping airport, the Jackson Hole Airport created **Taxi Pool** (at the Information Desk across from baggage carousel 2), which gives travelers $10 off local fares for shared rides. Other private taxis include **Broncs Car Service** (307/413-9863; www.jackson-hole-taxi.com) and **Airport Taxi** (307/699-7221; www.airporttaxijacksonhole.com). Transportation to Jackson from the airport runs roughly $45-50 for 1-2 people. A taxi to Teton Village averages $75-80. A complete list of taxi services can be found under the Transportation heading on the airport website.

Planning Your Time

Jackson Hole boasts easy (but pricey) air access. It could easily occupy visitors for **2-3 days,** and is an excellent launching pad for day trips into Yellowstone and Grand Teton National Parks. The dude ranches outside Jackson offer tremendous opportunities to experience the state's vast open spaces close to the hustle and bustle of town. For many people, this is the ideal way to spend a week enjoying the best of Wyoming's offerings.

Sights

★ Town Square

10 E. Broadway

Almost European in its layout with a central square, Jackson's Town Square is distinguished by four archways constructed in 1932 entirely from naturally shed and sun-bleached elk antlers. It is the focal point of town and a good meeting spot. In the summer, late May-early September, Town Square is the site of the free **Jackson Hole Shootout** (6pm-7pm Mon.-Sat. Memorial Day-Labor Day), a spirited reenactment of frontier justice. In winter, the arches are illuminated by strings of lights, creating a magical setting.

Within easy walking distance of the square are more than 70 eateries—from pizza joints with ski-bum prices to the very tony—and fine-art galleries and shops that sell everything from high-end furs to T-shirts and knickknacks. There are also plentiful espresso and ice-cream shops for those in need of instant energy.

History Jackson Hole

175 E. Broadway; 307/733-2414; www.jacksonholehistory.org; 10am-6pm Tues.-Sat.; $12

Just down Broadway from Town Square, History Jackson Hole is dedicated to the connection of people and place, with emphasis on the history of homesteading and dude ranches in the area, and Indian history of the Tetons. The collections include historical photos, Indian artifacts, fur trade-era tools, and firearms. The society offers adult and youth education programs, including scholarly lectures, a Beers & Banter series, and walking tours (10:30am Wed. and Fri. May-Sept.) that explore landmarks and historic buildings and include stories of unforgettable local characters. Call for dates, time, prices, and custom tours.

★ National Museum of Wildlife Art

2820 Rungius Rd.; 307/733-5771; www.wildlifeart.org; 10am-5pm daily May-Oct., 10am-5pm Tues.-Sun. Nov.-Apr.; $18

Just 3 mi (5 km) north of Town Square overlooking the National Elk Refuge, the National Museum of Wildlife Art is a find. The museum's 14 galleries represent the lifetime study and collection of wildlife art by Bill and Joffa Kerr. More than 5,000 objects reside in the permanent collection, primarily paintings and sculptures by artists that range from early Native American artists to masters including Pablo Picasso, Carl Rungius, John James Audubon, Robert Bateman, and Kent Ullberg. An 0.8-mi (1.3-km) sculpture trail is free and open to the public. The trail combines marvelous art with the stunning landscape, and often plays host to live music, theater, yoga, and other programs. Audio guides to the museum are included with paid admission, and coupons for discounts on admission are offered on the museum's website. The museum itself is a work of art: Inspired by the ruins of a Scottish castle, the red Arizona sandstone building emerges from the hillside like a natural outcropping of rock and reminds visitors of Ancestral Puebloan ruins.

National Elk Refuge

532 N. Cache St.; 307/733-9212; www.fws.gov/refuge/national-elk; free

During the winter months, more than 5,000 elk—often as many as 8,000—descend from their mountain habitat to the nearly 25,000-acre (10,000-ha) National Elk Refuge in Jackson Hole. The large number of elk make the refuge a popular wintertime attraction (in the summer, birds and other wildlife populate the range). Forty-seven different mammal species and nearly 175 species of birds have been observed on the refuge.

Refuge Road Scenic Drive

The elk are accustomed to the vehicles, allowing visitors to travel easily through the herds on the Refuge Road scenic drive. In winter, only 3.5 mi (5.6 km) of the scenic drive is accessible by car. In summer there are 8.4 mi (13.5 km) of road providing access to the national forest via Flat Creek and Curtis Canyon roads. The refuge is open year-round from sunrise to sunset, and there

Top to bottom: Jackson Town Square; National Museum of Wildlife Art; National Elk Refuge

are **online narrated tours** available on Spotify (search National Elk Refuge Tours) for walking tours from the visitor center, as well as for summer and winter driving tours. From Jackson, drive east on Broadway Avenue until you see the National Elk Refuge sign, which is the entrance to the refuge.

Sleigh Rides

307/733-0277 or 800/772-5386; www.nersleighrides.com; 10am-4pm daily mid-Dec.-early Apr.; $40

Horse-drawn sleigh rides through the refuge are offered mid-December through the first Saturday in April. Reservations are strongly suggested and can be made by phone; tickets are also available to purchase on-site from the **Jackson Hole and Greater Yellowstone Visitor Center,** and a free shuttle will take visitors 3 mi (5 km) north of Jackson to the departure point. Blankets are neither provided nor sold, but you are welcome to bring your own. Tours run 10am-4pm daily and last about an hour (from check-in to drop-off is roughly 90 minutes). Dress warmly, as the wind can be quite biting during the tour.

Jackson Hole and Greater Yellowstone Visitor Center

532 N. Cache St.; 307/733-3316; 8am-7pm daily Memorial Day-Sept., 9am-5pm daily Oct.-Memorial Day

A terrific place to start any type of exploration of the area, including the National Elk Refuge, which operates out of the same building, the Jackson Hole and Greater Yellowstone Visitor Center is a phenomenal resource with seven agencies represented, including the local chamber of commerce, the National Park Service, and the Bridger-Teton National Forest. Visitors can obtain annual park passes and hunting and fishing licenses as well as get trip-planning assistance, directions, and maps—talk about convenient one-stop shopping. The wildlife exhibits inside are matched by wildlife observation decks outside that overlook the National Elk Refuge. The real treasure here, though, is the staff, all of whom are friendly, knowledgeable, and more than willing to roll up their sleeves for whatever help you need. Short interpretive talks are offered throughout the season, and naturalists are often on hand at the upper viewing deck with spotting scopes, binoculars, and field guides.

Teton Village

Twelve mi (19 km) northwest of Jackson is Teton Village, an Alps-like enclave nestled around the state's largest and most popular ski hill. The area pulses with energy and activity as soon as the snow flies, and although it quiets down in the shoulder seasons, it is a popular destination in summer as well. Even so, these days it's a bit quieter than the center of Jackson. In addition to lodging, shopping, and dining options, the area is a hub for outdoor activities such as hot-air ballooning, paragliding, horseback riding, and, of course, mountain-oriented sports. Plenty of concerts and special events are also held year-round.

National Bighorn Sheep Interpretive Center

10 Bighorn Ln. off US 26; 307/455-3429; www.bighorn.org; 9am-6pm daily summer, 10am-4pm Mon.-Sat. Labor Day-Memorial Day; $6

Set in Dubois, 85 mi (137 km) east of Jackson on US 287/26, the National Bighorn Sheep Interpretive Center is dedicated to educating the public about these majestic creatures and their habitats. Visitors are welcomed by a stunning bronze of a ram and led inside to several hands-on exhibits that will delight little ones and fascinate animal lovers. There are 16 mounts of wild sheep from around the world and a great little gift shop with everything from T-shirts to children's toys and wares by local artists. November-March, the center offers tours to the winter range of the **Whiskey Mountain Habitat Area,** providing an excellent opportunity to see the bighorn sheep in their natural, windswept environment. Reservations for the tours (3-4 hours, $250 for 2 people, $125 for each additional person) should be made in advance by calling the center.

Adventure and Recreation

TOP EXPERIENCE

★ Rafting on the Snake River

One of the greatest attractions for summertime visitors to Jackson is rafting the Snake River. There are close to two dozen rafting companies to choose from in the area, and most are open mid-May through September. Here are a few options for those who are interested in experiencing the river, whether it be a tranquil day float through Grand Teton National Park or white-water adventure a little farther south in the canyon. Most adult fares average $100-110 for an 8-10-mi (13-16-km) trip. Increasingly popular are combination trips, which include a scenic float or white-water raft trip with other activities ranging from wildlife tours to horseback rides to gourmet Dutch-oven meals.

Barker-Ewing

945 W. Broadway; 307/733-1800 or 800/365-1800; www.barkerewing.com; $100

Barker-Ewing is a family-operated business that has been running small river trips for more than 50 years.

Dave Hansen Whitewater

225 W. Broadway; 307/733-6295; www.davehansenwhitewater.com; $110-125

Dave Hansen Whitewater has been in the business since the late 1960s. Dave actually named two of the largest waves on the river, Lunch Box and Big Kahuna.

Mad River Boat Trips

1255 S. Hwy. 89; 307/734-8898; www.mad-river.com; $90-110

Another option with a variety of daily trips down the Snake River is Mad River Boat Trips, which uses both small boats and classic boats, all expertly guided and each with an option to paddle or not.

Rent-a-Raft

10925 US 89, Hoback Jct., 13 mi/21 km south of Jackson; 307/733-2728; www.rentaraftjackson.com; rafts $185-255, kayaks $66-110, tubes $45

For experienced floaters who want to tackle the Snake unguided, Rent-a-Raft offers 12-foot, 13-foot, 14-foot, and 16-foot rafts, as well as sit-on-top kayaks, one- and two-person duck kayaks, float tubes, and shuttle service from its headquarters.

Hiking

Snow King Mountain

Distance: 3.6 mi (5.8 km) round-trip
Duration: 3-4 hours
Elevation gain: 1,571 ft (479 m)
Effort: Strenuous
Trail surface: Uneven dirt, roots, rocky
Trailhead: At the corner of Snow King Ave. and Cache St.

Locals hike up Snow King Mountain in Bridger-Teton National Forest for exercise, but it's also a worthy climb for scenery. The huge view from the top takes in the Tetons, National Elk Refuge, Gros Ventre Mountains, and the town of Jackson. Prepare for a grunt, and carry water, because the route climbs 1,571 vertical ft (479 m). To avoid the knee-pounding descent, take the gondola (10am-10pm daily summer, shorter hours spring and fall; $20) down from Snow King Mountain (402 E. Snow King Ave.; 307/201-5464; www.snowkingmountain.com).

From the base area, the **Snow King Summit Trail** is a combination of trail and service roads. Climb up three switchbacks, passing the Sink or Swim Trail, to a signed junction with a mountain road. Turn west and traverse steeply up the slope to the end of a long switchback. Climb up three shorter switchbacks on the dirt road. The route crests out on the ridge, where a dirt road reaches the summit and the top of the gondola. Alternative trails also go to the summit.

Cache Creek Canyon Loop

Distance: 4 mi (6.4 km)
Duration: 1.5 hours
Elevation gain: 350 ft (107 m)
Effort: Easy
Trailhead: Cache Creek Canyon Trailhead

One trail with immediate proximity to town that skirts the Gros Ventre Wilderness Area is the Cache Creek Canyon Loop, which is part of the Greater Snow King Trail Network. It is popular with hikers, mountain bikers, and cross-country skiers. To get to the trailhead, drive east on Broadway to Redmond Street, across from the hospital; turn right and go 0.4 mi (0.6 km) to Cache Creek Road. Turn left and continue just over 1 mi (1.6 km) to the parking lot at road's end. Hikers can amble along both sides of the creek and connecting trails lead to Game Creek and Granite Falls, or back to Snow King in Jackson.

Phillips Pass

Distance: 8 mi (13 km)
Duration: 3-4 hours
Elevation gain: 1,824 ft (556 m)
Effort: Strenuous
Trailhead: Phillips Pass Trailhead from Phillips Canyon Rd.

Ten mi (16 km) west of town near Teton Pass is Phillips Pass, an incredible and somewhat strenuous day hike at the edge of the Tetons and the Jedediah Smith Wilderness Area. The trail is open to hikers and mountain bikers. To get to the trailhead, head west to Teton Pass on Highway 22. Two mi (3 km) east of the summit is Phillips Canyon Road (Forest Rd. 30972). There is no parking at the trailhead, which is 0.5 mi (0.8 km) down this road, so park safely across the highway in a small pullout or on Phillips Canyon Road close to the highway. The 8-mi (13-km) out-and-back trail starts at 8,000 ft (2,438 m) in elevation and is spectacularly beautiful, particularly in late summer, as it winds through flower-drenched meadows and forest to the alpine country above the tree line. As always in this part of the country, be prepared for significant weather changes and encounters with wild animals.

The Hole Hiking Experience

307/690-4453 or 866/733-4453; www.holehike.com; mixed tours from $380 for 1-2 people, private tours from $540 for 1-3 people

For excellent guided hiking in the Tetons and around the valley, contact The Hole Hiking Experience, which offers a wide variety of trips from half-day naturalist-guided trips geared to families to strenuous all-day hikes and even yoga-hiking combinations. They offer hiking and fly-fishing combos, hiking and hot springs, and many others. Evening picnics can be added for $25. In winter they offer guided snowshoe and cross-country skiing treks that can be combined with wildlife tours, sleigh rides, and more.

Mountain Biking

Teton Mountain Bike Tours

545 N. Cache St.; 307/733-0712; www.tetonmtbike.com; half-day tours from $100 pp, full-day tours from $135-185 pp plus $15 for boxed lunch

For guided mountain bike trips for the whole family (including kids on Trail-a-Bikes and in trailers) or more extreme riders, contact Teton Mountain Bike Tours for half-day, full-day, multiday, and specialty trip offerings. In winter, they offer fat bike rentals and guided tours. Bikes and accessories can be rented year-round, and trips can go as far afield as Old Faithful in Yellowstone National Park.

Hoback Sports

520 W. Broadway Ave.; 307/733-5335; www.hobacksports.com; 10am-6pm daily; bike rentals from $58-109

Hoback Sports has all kinds of rental bikes for adults and kids, from road bikes and e-bikes to full-suspension mountain bikes, and can point bikers in the direction of any kind of ride they seek. Rentals are available on a 3-hour or full-day basis and must be made at least one day in advance. They also rent car racks.

TOP EXPERIENCE

Horseback Riding

Another popular way to experience the great outdoors in Jackson is on horseback. Several options, including hourly rentals, half-day trail rides, and overnight pack trips, are available from the many local outfitters in and around town.

Jackson Hole Outfitters

Mile marker 14 Greys River Rd., Alpine; 307/699-3541; www.jacksonholetrailrides.com; early June-early Sept.; half-day rides from $245 pp, full-day rides from $375 pp

Located 35 mi (56 km) south of Jackson, Jackson Hole Outfitters starts its private trail rides in the secluded Greys River camp and follows trails through the Bridger-Teton National Forest. Choose from half-day rides, full-day rides, and 5.5-hour extreme rides and cattle drives (from $425 pp). You can upgrade to include overnight stays in comfortable canvas tents and real beds with dinner and breakfast included (from $195 pp).

Spring Creek Ranch

1600 N. East Butte Rd.; 307/733-8833 or 800/443-6139; www.springcreekranch.com; mid-May-mid-Oct.; 1-hour rides from $71 pp, 2-hour rides from $101 pp

Spring Creek Ranch offers 1- and 2-hour rides, as well as custom rides. They also offer wagon rides to a chuck wagon dinner (call for updated prices and schedule). Age restrictions vary for the different rides.

Mill Iron Ranch

3495 Horse Creek Rd.; 307/773-6390; www.millironranch.net; mid-May-late Sept.; 2-hour rides from $165 pp, 4-hour rides from $310 pp

Mill Iron Ranch, 10 mi (17 km) south of Jackson on US 89/191, offers 2-hour, 4-hour, or full-day trips that can be upgraded with breakfast, lunch, fishing, or a steak dinner. Private rides can be arranged.

Golf

Jackson Hole Golf & Tennis Club

5000 Spring Gulch Rd.; 307/733-3111; www.jhgtc.com; 18 holes w/ cart from $300

Golf is becoming increasingly popular in Jackson Hole (maybe because the ball seems to fly so much farther at altitude), and there are a couple of world-class public courses. The Jackson Hole Golf & Tennis Club offers an award-winning 18-hole course designed by Bob Baldock and renovated twice by Robert Trent Jones II. Local conservation hero Laurance S. Rockefeller once owned the course, which says a lot about its natural beauty.

Teton Pines Country Club

3450 Clubhouse Dr.; 307/733-1005 or 800/238-2223; www.tetonpines.com; 18 holes from $295

The 18-hole 72-par course at Teton Pines Country Club in Teton Village was designed by Arnold Palmer and has been highly ranked by *Condé Nast Traveler*, *Audubon International*, and *Golf Digest*, among others.

Skiing and Mountain Sports

Jackson's reputation among the West's premier ski towns is not hard to explain. There are three developed downhill ski resorts, the closest one being right in town.

For avid Nordic skiers, the blanket of snow transforms many favorite local hiking trails into first-rate ski trails. From hitting the groomers at local golf courses to hoofing into the backcountry of Grand Teton National Park, there is terrain for everyone.

Snow King Mountain

400 E. Snow King Ave.; 307/201-5464; www.snowkingmountain.com; full day $95, discounts for multiday passes

Snow King Mountain soars skyward just six blocks from Town Square, so Jackson is a ski town in the most literal sense. The mountain was developed for skiing in 1939, making it the first in the Jackson area and one of the first in the country. The area boasts 1,571 ft (479 m) of vertical drop over 500 acres (200 ha) with three chairlifts, a rope tow, a gondola, and the ever-popular **Snow Tubing Park** ($35/hour) and **Cowboy Coaster** ($40/hour). The area is open for day and night skiing. Discounts are available for lodging guests. Visitors who want to try every activity on the hill can get a day pass ($165). Nonskiers can pay to ride the lift ($30) just to enjoy the views from the summit. In summer, trails and lifts are open for hiking, mountain biking, and paragliding, plus the Cowboy Coaster, an alpine slide, a maze, a bungee trampoline, mini-golf, bouldering, and a treetop ropes course.

Jackson Hole Mountain Resort

3395 Cody Ln., Teton Village; 307/733-2292 or 888/333-7766; www.jacksonhole.com; $121-256, discounts online and for advance purchase

In nearby Teton Village, Jackson Hole Mountain Resort is in fact two mountains: Apres Vous and Rendezvous, which together offer 2,500 skiable acres (1,011 ha) and access to 3,000 acres (1,214 ha) of backcountry terrain. Daily lift ticket sales are capped, making advance purchase strongly recommended. Fifty percent of the 131 trails is geared to experts, 40 percent for intermediate skiers, and 10 percent for beginners. The ski hill average 458 in (1,163 cm) of snow annually.

The **aerial tram** (3275 West Village Dr., Teton Village; 307/733-2292; 9am-5pm late May-early Oct.; from $44), known as Big Red or the Red Heli, takes hikers, bikers, paragliders, backcountry

Top to bottom: rafting the Snake River; skiing at Jackson Hole Mountain Resort; horseback riding near Jackson Hole skiers, and lookie-loos up to the summit of Rendezvous Peak in 12 minutes. At the top, **Corbet's Cabin** (307/739-2688; 9am-4:30pm daily in season; from $8), a fabulous little waffle hut, makes you wish you had hiked the whole way.

Summer is busy with mountain bike adventure tours (mid-June-Sept.; electric or non-electric; from $425 for 1-2 riders) and Via Ferrata alpine journeys (half-day from $446 for 1-2 people, full-day $698 for 1-2 people), which is climbing using ropes, iron rungs, ladders, and hanging bridges. There are also paragliding adventures, guided rock climbing, a ropes course, and much more for all age, ability, and adrenaline levels.

Grand Targhee Resort

3300 Ski Hill Rd., Alta; 307/353-2300; www.grandtarghee.com; full-day $135-165

Although you need to go through Idaho to get there, Grand Targhee Resort in Alta, Wyoming, is a destination in itself. The skiing is out of this world, with huge dumps of powder and expansive terrain. The resort also offers Nordic skiing, tubing, guided snowcat tours, sleigh-ride dinners, snowmobile tours, and ice climbing. In summer, the mountain stays open for hiking, mountain biking, horseback riding, and a couple of renowned musical events, including the **Grand Targhee Bluegrass Festival** (early to mid-August). The resort is 45 mi (72 km) over the pass from Jackson.

Teton Pines Nordic Center

3450 N. Clubhouse Dr., Wilson; 307/733-1733; www.tetonpinesnordiccnter.com; $30, $40 with rentals

Teton Pines Nordic Center grooms 10 mi (16 km) of trail daily for both classic and skate skiers. The center is 4 mi (6 km) south of Jackson Hole Mountain Resort and offers chances to see wildlife including moose, fox, coyote, trumpeter swans, and more. This is skiing only—no dogs, walking, fat biking, or snowshoeing.

Jackson Hole Nordic Alliance

www.jhnordic.com

The Jackson Hole Nordic Alliance is the best resource for more than 100 cross-country and skate ski trails, as well as snowshoe and fat bike trails. It's a great site to find events, tours, rentals, lessons, and trail conditions.

Skinny Skis

65 W. Deloney Ave.; 307/733-6094; 9am-6pm Mon.-Sat., 10am-5pm Sun.; www.skinnyskis.com

In town, alpine, cross-country, skate, or snowshoeing gear can be purchased or rented from Skinny Skis. This specialty shop has been serving skiers and trail runners, hikers, backpackers, and climbers for 50 years, and they know their stuff. They don't release annual rental rates for touring and skate ski packages, snowshoes, and telemark skis until the snow flies, so be sure to check the website.

Teton Mountaineering

170 N. Cache St.; 307/733-3595; www.tetonmtn.com; 9am-7pm daily; snowshoe or cross-country touring packages $25/day or $125/week, telemark packages $45/day or $225/week

Teton Mountaineering has been an anchor in the Jackson outdoor scene since 1971. The shop sells and rents alpine and telemark ski packages, along with cross-country ski packages.

Entertainment and Events

Theater

Jackson Hole Center for the Arts

240 S. Glenwood St.; 307/734-8956 or box office 307/733-4900; www.jhcenterforthearts.org

Jackson Hole Center for the Arts is an inspired art campus in the heart of downtown offering educational programs and facilities along with professional theater, dance, and music. Check out the schedule online—there is always something happening. Of note is the **Off Square Theatre Company** (307/733-3021; www.offsquare.org), which produces excellent and wildly diverse shows ranging from family-favorite American musicals (*A Chorus Line*) and dramatic masterpieces (*Macbeth*) to side-splitting improv by Laff Staff.

Art Galleries

With more than 60 galleries in town, the art scene in Jackson is both rarefied and approachable, and an increasingly important part of both the community and the local economy. For more information on all the galleries in Jackson, visit the **Jackson Hole Gallery Association** (www.jacksonholegalleryassociation.com).

Trailside Galleries

130 E. Broadway; 307/733-3186; www.trailsidegalleries.com; 10am-5pm Mon.-Sat.

A local favorite, Trailside Galleries shows American representational art with an impressive roster of the country's leading Western, wildlife, figurative, Impressionist, and landscape artists.

Altamira Fine Art

172 Center St.; 307/739-4700; www.altamiraart.com; 10am-6pm Mon.-Sat. or by appointment

Altamira Fine Art has a more loftlike urban feel and represents groundbreaking contemporary artists, including Rocky Hawkins, Duke Beardsley, Ed Mell, Mary Roberson, and John Nieto.

Maya Frodeman Gallery

66 S. Glenwood St.; 307/733-0555; www.mayafrodemangallery.com; 11am-6pm Mon.-Sat.

The Maya Frodeman Gallery is cutting-edge cool with both big-name artists in a variety of media, past and present, including Stephen Talasnik, James Castle, and Donald Judd.

Festivals and Events

Jackson Rodeo

447 W. Snow King Ave.; 307/733-7927; www.jhrodeo.com; 8pm Wed. and Fri.-Sat.; $38-50

Weekly events in Jackson during the summer season (Memorial Day-Labor Day) include the Jackson Rodeo, a fun family event with bull riding, team roping, barrel racing, bareback broncs, and plenty of other action. Food and refreshments are sold at the chuck wagon.

Town Square Shootout

Jackson Town Square; 6pm-7pm Mon.-Sat. Memorial Day-Labor Day; free

For one of Jackson's favorite regular events, check out the Town Square Shootout on the Town Square. Since 1957, actors have been playing out the story of Clover the Killer versus the Cache Creek Posse. No one knows for sure how the story or the shootout got started, but it's been delighting summer visitors for more than 65 years.

Teton County Fair

Teton County Fairgrounds, 305 West Snow King Ave.; 307/733-5289; www.tetoncountyfair.com; late July-early Aug.; call for ticket prices

The nearly weeklong Teton County Fair includes family-friendly events like pig wrestling, rodeo, demolition derby, concerts, a carnival, and plenty of agricultural and animal exhibits.

Fall Arts Festival

307/733-3316; www.jacksonholechamber.com; mid-Sept.; prices vary for more than 50 scheduled events

The equivalent of Cody's Rendezvous Royale, Jackson's Fall Arts Festival is a 10-day event in mid-September that attracts a crowd of art lovers with a phenomenal range of art-related events, including the prestigious **Jackson Hole Art Auction** (www.jacksonholeartauction.com) and **Western Design Conference** (www.westerndesignconference.com), gallery walks, open-air art fairs, historic ranch tours, and culinary coups.

Grand Teton Music Festival

McCollister Dr., Teton Village; 307/733-1128; www.gtmf.org; July-Aug.; call for ticket prices

Grand Teton Music Festival is held annually in the all-wooden Walk Festival Hall. Known as one of the top classical music festivals in the country since 1962, it showcases an impressive list of musicians and singers. Past performers include Sarah Chang, Itzhak Perlman, Yo-Yo Ma, the New York Philharmonic, and the Mormon Tabernacle Choir. In addition to the summer festival, the organization hosts concerts during winter. Family concerts are free, and open rehearsals (Friday mornings at 10am) can be attended for reduced prices.

Jackson Wild

307/200-3286; www.jacksonwild.org; late Sept. or early Oct.; go online for event schedules and pricing

Jackson Wild, formerly the Jackson Hole Wildlife Film Festival, is dedicated to inspiring deeper connections to the natural world. Through an annual summit, forums, film showcases, and media awards, Jackson Wild attracts leaders in science, conservation, and media. The summit has traditionally been held at the Jackson Lake Lodge. Winners in 2024 included *Turtle Walker, Wilding, Poacher,* and *Lions of the Skeleton Coast.*

Winter Fest

www.jhfoodandwine.com/winter-fest; Mar.; whiskey tasting from $295, Big Wines & Small Plates from $450, grand tasting from $250

Winter Fest gives residents and visitors alike one more reason to celebrate the snow. Happening in Teton Village over a weekend in March, the 21+ celebration includes events that showcase Jackson Hole's status as a food and wine destination.

Shopping

For those with time and money, shopping can be an athletic pursuit in Jackson, particularly in the streets and alleyways around **Town Square.** In "olden times," Jackson was populated with outlet stores, but today all of those have been pushed out by more sophisticated boutiques. There are fascinating little shops to pop into, from high-end art galleries to the few remaining tacky but fun T-shirt and tchotchke shops.

Valley Bookstore

140 E. Broadway St.; 307/733-4533; www.valleybookstore.com; 9am-9pm daily June-Aug., 9am-6pm Sun. Sept.-May

Valley Bookstore has been providing local readers with fabulous books and stellar recommendations since 1949. The owners grew up in Jackson and have a superb local and regional section.

MADE

Gaslight Alley, 125 N. Cache St.; 307/690-7957; www.madejacksonhole.com; 10am-6pm daily

For an excellent selection of gifts, cards, stationery, candles, jewelry, clothing, and more, visit MADE, which features work made by local and regional artists. There's also a sister candy shop next door, **Mirsell's Sweet Shop.**

Terra on Town Square

160 E. Broadway; 307/734-0067; www.terr-jackson-hole.myshopify.com; 11am-5pm Mon.-Sat., 11am-4pm Sun.

For top-of-the-line women's and children's clothes in a spacious, Zen-like setting, visit Terra on Town Square, which would not be out of place in Manhattan or San Francisco.

Headwall Recycle Sports

520 S. Hwy. 89; 307/734-8022; www.headwallsports.com; 9am-7pm Mon.-Sat.

While most of the shops in Jackson cater to the second- and third-home crowd, Headwall Recycle Sports is geared more to the ski bums of yore with an excellent selection of well-vetted gear for folks who find the idea of a $500 jacket offensive. They carry loads of gear for camping, biking, fishing, hunting, climbing, skiing, and more.

Food

For every opportunity this region provides to exert energy by skiing, hiking, biking, or other pursuits, Jackson offers many more ways to replenish that supply. The number of outstanding restaurants in this town puts just about every other town in Wyoming—and many Western states—to shame.

Bakeries and Cafés

★ Persephone Bakery

145 E. Broadway; 307/200-6708; www.persephonebakery.com; 7am-6pm Mon.-Sat., 7am-5pm Sun., kitchen closes at 3pm, hours can vary seasonally; $7-16

Just off the square, and often with a line out front, Persephone Bakery is an artisanal bakery and café known for French-style rustic, elegant breads and pastries, and excellent salads and sandwiches for lunch. It also offers a nice wine list and cocktail menu. How's that for a Jackson Hole bakery? It's popular in Jackson, they opened a second location in Wilson at 3445 North Pines Way, which is open daily 7am-3pm.

★ The Bunnery

130 N. Cache St.; 307/733-5474; www.bunnery.com; 7am-3pm daily summer, 7:30am-2pm daily winter; $10-17

As a rule, every day in Jackson should start with a trip to The Bunnery. The food is entirely made from scratch and utterly scrumptious. The baked goods—including its trademark OSM bread (oats, sunflower, millet) and homemade granola—are beyond compare, and the enormous and diverse menu offers plenty of healthy options as well as a few decadent ones. The "Get Your Buns in Here" bumper stickers are also good for a laugh. Be prepared to wait, however; The Bunnery is beloved by visitors and locals alike.

Fine Dining

Million Dollar Cowboy Steakhouse

25 N. Cache St.; 307/733-1270; www.milliondollarcowboybar.com; 5pm-9:30pm daily, plus 10am-2pm Sun.; $25-89

Downstairs from the famous bar in a swanky dining room, Million Dollar Cowboy Steakhouse features specialties like bison carpaccio, cowboy lobster bisque, grilled elk tenderloin, seared duck breast, and any kind of steak you can imagine. Reservations are recommended.

★ Wild Sage

175 N. Jackson St.; 307/733-2000; www.rustyparrot.com; 5pm-9pm daily; $42-72

An elegant option for an unforgettable meal is at the Rusty Parrot's Wild Sage. From Long Island duck and swordfish to Idaho trout saltimbocca and braised lamb, Wild Sage has made quite a name for itself in the Intermountain West culinary scene. Reservations are strongly recommended and can be made on OpenTable.

Snake River Grill

84 E. Broadway; 307/733-0557; www.snakerivergrill.com; 5:30pm-9:30pm daily summer, from 6pm daily winter, closed late Oct.-early Dec.; $28-215

Right on the Town Square is one of Jackson's most celebrated eating establishments, the Snake River Grill. A visual feast in addition to being a gastronomical delight, the Snake River Grill has largely defined Jackson Hole cuisine with offerings like steak tartare pizza, bison New York steak, bison rib eye, Ora King salmon, and roasted duck breast. The menu is diverse, constantly changing, and completely mouthwatering. It's worth noting that although children are welcome in the restaurant, no highchairs or children's menus are available.

Mexican

★ Pica's Mexican Taqueria

1160 Alpine Ln.; 307/734-4457; www.picastaqueria.com; 11am-9pm daily; $11-21

Pica's Mexican Taqueria offers a fresh take on tacos, burritos, great salads, and authentic Mexican dishes including mole, chilaquiles, wet burritos, and conchinita pibil, the Yucatan's most famous dish. Their margaritas are outstanding, too.

The Merry Piglets

160 N. Cache St.; 307/733-2966; www.merrypiglets.com; 11:30am-10pm daily; $16-34

Another terrific Mexican restaurant right in town is the Merry Piglets, which serves classic Tex-Mex taco, burrito, chimichanga, and enchilada plates with fresh salsas, sauces, and tortilla chips, all made in-house daily. The fish is wild, the meat is pasture-raised, and no partially hydrogenated oils are used. The portions are big, and the flavors are very satisfying.

Casual Dining

Café Genevieve

135 E. Broadway; 307/732-1910; www.genevievejh.com; 8am-3pm daily; $14-20

Set in a 1910 log cabin, one of the oldest residential structures in town, Café Genevieve serves inspired home cooking for brunch and lunch daily. They serve a killer breakfast until 3pm with specialties like grits and eggs, sweet and spicy candied bacon (known as pig candy), corned beef hash, Cajun eggs Benedict, and fried chicken and waffles. And for lunch their burgers, sandwiches, and salads are sure to satisfy. Fido will appreciate the pet-friendly deck.

Yeah Buddy Pizza

20 W. Broadway; 307/201-1472; www.pizzeriacaldera.com; 11am-9:30pm Sun.-Thurs., 11am-1am Fri.-Sat.; $12-23

Every ski town worth its salt needs a good hometown pizza joint. Yeah Buddy Pizza serves up thin-crust Napoletana-style pizza baked over stone-hearth fires. Options range from classic Italian margherita to pure Jackson Hole, like the Bisonte, with bison sausage and fresh sage. There is also a great beer and wine list, plus yummy salads, pastas, and tapas. Folks who can't get enough thrill to find out that the restaurant ships pizza nationwide.

★ The Kitchen

155 Glenwood St.; 307/734-1633; www.thekitchenjacksonhole.com; 5:30pm-9:30pm Tues.-Sat.; $23-47

The Kitchen is a modern eatery that embraces an Asian influence and serves the freshest fish, meats, and seasonal vegetables. It's an interesting space architecturally, with the curvature of a modern diner, and the outside patio in summer is a wonderful place to eat an uncomplicated and delicious meal. There's a gorgeous raw bar and cooked dishes including Korean short rib skewers, grilled pork chop, wild mushroom ramen, and even a burger with garlic aioli and smoked bacon.

Accommodations

While there are plenty of places to hang your hat in Jackson, during the prime seasons those places will not come cheap. The best time to get a good deal on a great room is April or November, when the ski hill is closed but the days aren't summery yet or anymore. Keep in mind, though, that many hotels in the area shut down during the shoulder seasons.

Independent hotels and inns tend to reflect more of Jackson's charm, but there are plenty of nice chain hotels, some of which can offer good deals, particularly in the off-season.

Mountain Modern Motel

380 W. Broadway; 307/733-4340; www.mountainmodernmotel.com; $159-494

A boutique hotel in the heart of Jackson just two blocks from Town Square, Mountain Modern touts itself as functional and fun, with none of the fluff and all of the good stuff. The vibe is hip and young; the rooms are comfortable and make a lot of sense. There is plenty of space for gear storage, and some rooms have kitchens. The bunk rooms are a big hit too. The motel is impeccably clean and modern, and there are multiple dining options on-site. There's also a pool and a hot tub for the bunk-room crowd.

★ Anvil Motel

215 N. Cache St.; 307/733-3668; www.anvilmotel.com; $130-549

In summer, there really is no such thing as a good deal. Just off Town Square, the Anvil Motel might be as close as you can get, and only in the off-season. The rooms are mountain-rustic with thoughtful details and custom furnishings, and some have air-conditioning. In addition to standard kings and queens, there is a great family bunk suite.

★ Rustic Inn Creekside Resort & Spa

475 N. Cache St.; 800/323-9279 or 307/733-2357; www.rusticinnatjh.com; rooms and cabins $159-729

Just four blocks from Town Square, Rustic Inn Creekside Resort & Spa is an oasis of calm. The creekside cabins are farther from the road and quieter, but the whole property is lovely on 12 acres (5 ha) of beautiful landscaping. The log cabins are cozy and elegantly appointed. The spa is excellent, as are the on-site dining options.

The Wort Hotel

50 N. Glenwood St.; 307/733-2190 or 800/322-2727; www.worthotel.com; $285-778

Almost as close to Town Square but a bit higher on the luxury scale is the Wort Hotel, built in 1941 and a landmark in town, complete with the legendary Silver Dollar Bar & Grill, which has more than 2,000 inlaid silver dollars as time capsule-type decorations. The 55 rooms (some of which are pet-friendly, for dogs under 40 pounds, for a $45 nightly fee) and five suites are plush, and the location is great.

Spring Creek Ranch

1800 Spirit Dance Rd.; 307/733-8833 or 800/443-6139; www.springcreekranch.com; rooms from $261

Away from the hustle and bustle of town, perched on a ridge overlooking the entire valley, is the Spring Creek Ranch, which boasts a variety of accommodations, including hotel rooms, cabins, condos, and exclusive mountain villas. The property is entirely self-contained with two restaurants on-site, a spa, and a slew of activities. The views from here beat just about everything else in the region, and the quiet gives Spring Creek Ranch tremendous appeal.

★ Hotel Terra

3335 W. Village Dr.; 307/201-6065 or 800/318-8707; www.hotelterrajacksonhole.com; from $395

At Teton Village, Hotel Terra is a hip choice, at once luxurious and sustainable. The ecofriendly rooms have clean lines, retro-funky appointments, and lots of gadgets for techies. The 132 guest rooms and suites range in size and style from urban studios and Terra guest rooms to 1-3-bedroom suites. There are two restaurants on-site, a lively bar, a rooftop swimming pool and hot tub, a day spa, and a fitness center, plus a menu of activities.

Guest Ranches

For many visitors, the best way to enjoy Jackson Hole is to while away the days at a scenery-soaked dude ranch somewhere in the valley. After all, it was the dude ranches that jump-started Jackson's economy in the 1920s and 1930s. There are options for every preference: proximity to town, emphasis on riding, this century or last, weekend or weeklong stays, and more. For a comprehensive listing of the dude ranches in the vicinity of Jackson Hole, contact the **Dude Ranchers' Association** (866/399-2339 or 307/587-2339; www.duderanch.org).

Flat Creek Ranch

1 Upper Flat Creek Rd.; 307/733-0603; www.flatcreekranch.com; $1,475/night year-round for double occupancy, $475 for each additional person

Fifteen bumpy miles (24 km) from Jackson is the historic and rustic Flat

Creek Ranch, in the heart of national forest and heavy on isolated splendor. The waterfront setting and lovely renovated cabins make for a special stay. The food too is top-notch, and there is no shortage of activities, from riding and fishing to hiking and wildlife-watching. Don't miss the wood-fired sauna and hot tub.

Lost Creek Ranch & Spa

17820 Old Ranch Rd., Moose, 30 minutes north of Jackson; 307/733-3435; www.lostcreek.com; cabins from $11,000 for 2 people, $22,000 for 4-7 people

Historic and splendidly set, Lost Creek Ranch & Spa has been around for more than 100 years, and the view of the Tetons never gets old. This is an all-inclusive six-day stay where guests can choose how to spend every moment, from horseback riding to lounging poolside. There are 540 mi (869 km) of trails, 80 horses, and 10 guest cabins.

Heart Six Guest Ranch

16985 Buffalo Valley Rd., 35 mi/56 km north of Jackson in Moran; 307/543-2477; www.heartsix.com; rooms from $100-349 night

Heart Six Guest Ranch is just outside Grand Teton National Park and offers family-friendly ranch vacations à la carte. Guests can stay for a single night if they want (they won't!) and can arrange any manner of activity from horseback riding to fishing to wildlife safaris in Yellowstone and Grand Teton.

Camping

Camping is by far the most economical way to stay in and around Jackson, and there are 14 campgrounds within a 15-mi (24-km) radius of downtown.

For more information on specific public campgrounds, contact the **Bridger-Teton National Forest** (340 N. Cache St., Jackson; 307/739-5500; www.fs.usda.gov).

Curtis Canyon Campground

Flat Creek Rd., 8 mi/13 km northeast of Jackson; 307/739-5400; www.fs.usda.gov/btnf; mid-May-early Sept.; $20/night for 1 vehicle, $7 for 2nd vehicle

Among the closest to town is Curtis Canyon Campground, offering Teton views from its 11 sites, immediate access to the National Elk Refuge, and terrific mountain hiking trails. Vault toilets and drinking water are available. There are two spots that can accommodate RVs up to 24 ft (7 m). There are no reservations available.

Virginian Lodge

750 W. Broadway; 307/733-2792 or 800/262-4999; www.virginianlodge.com; May 1-Oct. 15; motel rooms $177-545, RV sites from $109/night

For RV parks in Jackson, try the large and conveniently located Virginian Lodge, which has both motel rooms and 103 RV sites in addition to amenities including a laundry, pool, hot tub, salon, restaurant, and saloon.

Information and Services

Jackson Hole and Greater Yellowstone Visitor Center

532 N. Cache St.; 307/733-3316; www.fws.gov; 8am-7pm daily Memorial Day-Sept., 9am-5pm daily Labor Day-Memorial Day

The most comprehensive spot to get information on the area is the Jackson Hole and Greater Yellowstone Visitor Center, which houses representatives from the Jackson Hole Chamber of Commerce (307/733-3316), the National Park Service, the Bridger-Teton National Forest, and four other agencies all under the same sod roof.

Rocky
Mountain
Front

Highlights

★ **Chico Hot Springs Resort:** Chico has all the trappings of a resort—hiking, riding, pool, day spa, and sumptuous cuisine—with none of the attitude (page 156).

★ **Last Chance Gulch and Reeder's Alley:** One of the few pedestrian malls in Montana is both the historic and modern heart of Helena (page 160).

★ **C. M. Russell Museum:** The most beloved and impressive art museum in the state is an extraordinary tribute to the life and work of the consummate Western artist (page 166).

★ **Lewis and Clark National Historic Trail Interpretive Center:** This compelling museum enables visitors to learn about the extraordinary challenges faced by Lewis and Clark and to appreciate the parallels between what they found and what exists today (page 166).

★ **First Peoples Buffalo Jump State Park:** One of only three protected buffalo jumps in the state, this mile-long cliff is considered the largest buffalo jump in North America, if not the world (page 167).

★ **Fishing on the Missouri River:** America's longest river attracts anglers from all over the world. The tailwater stretch between Holter Dam and Cascade serves up thousands of trout per mile (page 168).

★ **Blackfeet Tours:** Let Blackfeet culture and history come alive on this fascinating tour of the Badger Two Medicine region—hiking or on horseback—with Native first-voice interpretive guides (page 173).

Rocky Mountain Front

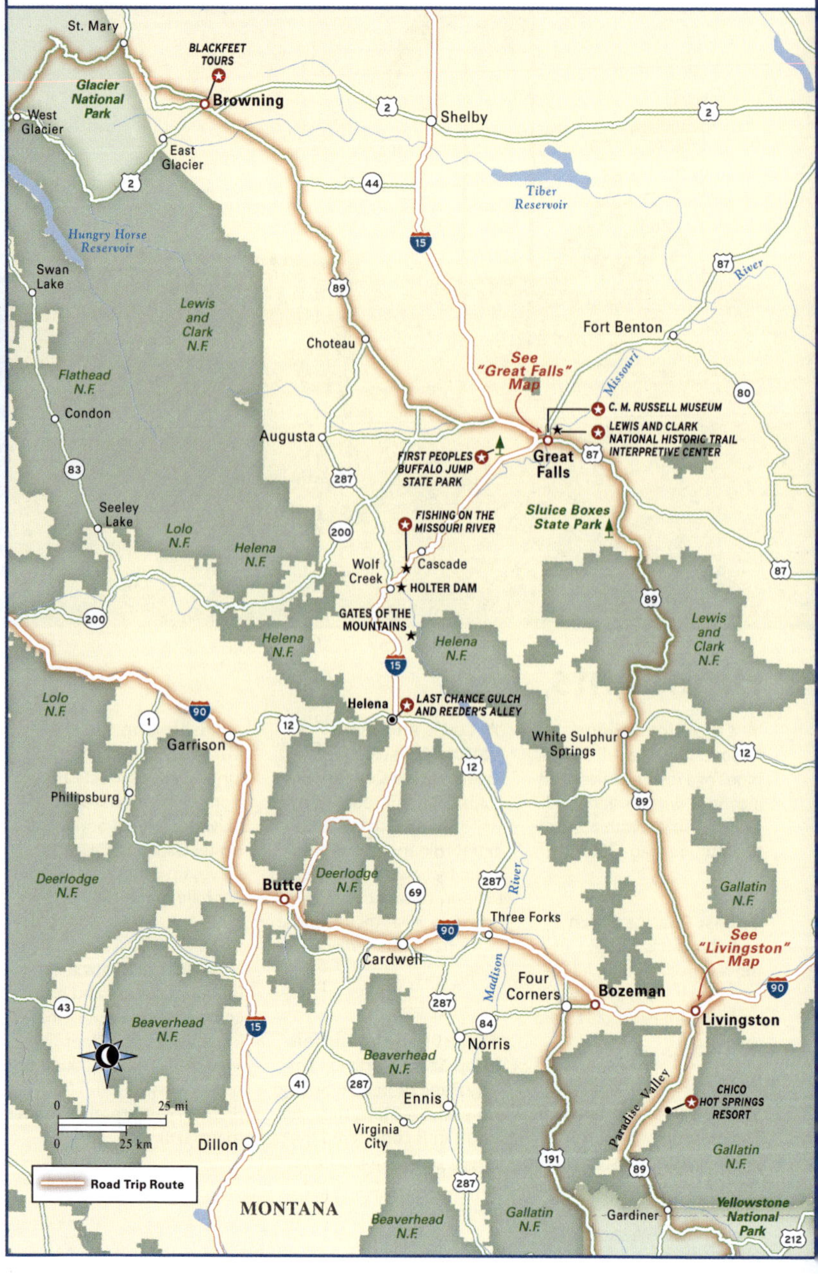

Best Stops Along the Rocky Mountain Front

Although people often race to get from one national park to the next, taking time to explore the cities, towns, and landscapes along the way is time well spent. For those who want to make it more of a day trip than a mad dash, here are some of the most worthwhile spots along the route from I-90 and I-15 to MT-2.

- Check out **Livingston,** where you can stroll Main Street, create your own dish at **Faye's Cafe,** and peek into the shops and galleries.
- Between Bozeman and Helena, visit **Madison Buffalo Jump State Park,** where you can hike up to the top of the cliff and see remnant tipi rings and eagle-catching pits.
- In **Helena,** wander down **Last Chance Gulch.** Grab a burger at **The Union** and then something sweet at **The Parrot Confectionery.** Art lovers will want to stop at the **Holter Museum of Art.**
- The **C. M. Russell Museum** and the **Lewis and Clark National Historic Trail Interpretive Center** in **Great Falls** give important context to Western travel.
- In **Browning,** visit the renowned **Museum of the Plains Indian** and take a fascinating hike or horseback tour with **Blackfeet Tours.**

One of the things that makes driving from Yellowstone to Glacier so memorable is that the landscapes and towns along the way are beautiful and interesting in their own right. There's no rush to get from one park to the next. Savor the journey by taking time to explore the back roads, and you'll have a much fuller experience.

There are a number of ways to travel between Yellowstone and Glacier, and not one of them is ugly. But there is something special about cruising along the Rocky Mountain Front, stopping in tiny towns that dot the map, moving back and forth between the mountains and the plains. Traveling between the high, heavily forested Yellowstone plateau and the jagged peaks of Glacier, this wide-open stretch of Montana feels like breathing room. Time moves slowly as you watch the sun drift across the sky and sink behind the spine of the continent. It's also a taste of real Montana—in communities like Livingston and Browning. There are excellent tours, fascinating museums, and some of the best small-town rodeos in the West.

There are bigger towns along the route, too—cities, even, including Helena and Great Falls—where you can find great meals, wonderful art museums, and a most unexpected tiki bar. Don't rush. Plan to spend your time outside, whether at mom-and-pop ski hills along the Rocky Mountain Front, or hiking some of the great trails that are outside every town. There's world-class fishing on the Yellowstone and Missouri Rivers, and plenty of unique and beautiful state parks along the way. Between parks, the point is to go slow. Take it in. Fill the day. Or, better yet, make it two.

Planning Your Time

Just above the northern entrance of Yellowstone is the aptly named **Paradise Valley.** The mountains surrounding the valley beg to be hiked. **Chico Hot Springs Resort** is the place to stay; it boasts some

Best Restaurants

★ **Pine Creek Lodge & Café, Paradise Valley:** This is comfort food through and through—burgers, smothered chicken, tacos, and panang coconut curry—all served in a cozy cabin (page 154).

★ **Campione, Livingston:** It doesn't get better than this tiny Roman café for brunch or dinner. Start with the meatballs and finish with the broken cheesecake; every bite in between will be remarkable (page 155).

★ **Chico Hot Springs Resort, Paradise Valley:** Known for exquisite food—often fresh from the on-site garden—and a romantic setting that's popular with Hollywood types, dinner at this resort will be a highlight of your trip (page 155).

★ **Benny's Bistro, Helena:** A small, farm-to-table restaurant in the heart of downtown Helena, Benny's serves a delicious meal you can feel good about, even if you didn't hike all day (page 163).

★ **Summit Mountain Lodge Steakhouse, East Glacier:** As if there were anything better than the heavenly alpine view from every seat in the house, try the view with wild Atlantic salmon on your fork, or one of their juicy spice-rubbed rib eyes and a slice of huckleberry cheesecake (page 175).

of the best dining in the state, plus a long list of activities.

Just north of Chico is the artsy town of **Livingston,** a small but vibrant community. You could happily spend a morning or afternoon browsing the shops and galleries and sampling its excellent restaurants. The town explodes with enthusiasm and visitors over the **Fourth of July,** and if you can secure a parking spot for the parade and a ticket to the **rodeo,** dealing with the crowds will be well worth the effort.

The state's capital, **Helena,** is a bustling city that has transitioned into modernity while preserving its past. **Reeder's Alley** and **Last Chance Gulch,** the city's wonderful pedestrian shopping destination, are, in some ways, where it all began with the glimmer of gold. Recreational opportunities just outside the city are plentiful.

There is as much to do in **Great Falls** as time will allow. Spend a day in the city to see some of the excellent **museums** and nearby natural attractions, including **First Peoples Buffalo Jump State Park.** Known for its consistent wind, this city is located on the **Missouri River** between the Rocky Mountains and Montana's Big Open. Any number of outdoor adventures can be dreamed up and launched from Great Falls.

Livingston and Paradise Valley

Rough-and-tumble Livingston (pop. 9,052, elev. 4,501 ft/1,372 m) has always been a crossroads of cultures. A railroad town, it was long the launching point for expeditions—both professional and leisurely—into Yellowstone National Park. Paradise Valley, the stunning agricultural and recreational corridor linking Livingston to the north entrance of Yellowstone National Park, was the stomping ground of the Apsáalooke people (also called the Crow), a prized region for fur trappers, and the end point of the great cattle drive from Texas. The town was surrounded by mines, which drew

Best Accommodations

★ **Chico Hot Springs Resort, Paradise Valley:** This resort offers a range of accommodations, from cozy lodge rooms to cabins and more. It also has the best swimming anywhere and an exquisite restaurant (page 156).

★ **Murray Hotel, Livingston:** Staying at this charming historic hotel right in the heart of downtown is like stepping back in time 100 years, only with pillow-top beds and Wi-Fi (page 157).

★ **O'Haire Motor Inn, Great Falls:** It's the tiki bar and the mermaid shows that make this motel a great place to stop for the night (page 172).

★ **Hotel Arvon, Great Falls:** Another historic gem with modern amenities, this 33-room boutique hotel features work by local artists and a great Irish pub (page 173).

a unique crowd, and today it probably has more literary figures and artists per capita than any other community in the state.

At one point in the early 1880s, there were 40 businesses in town, 30 of which were saloons. Such legendary characters as Calamity Jane and Madame Bulldog were residents. Evidence of those wild days is still visible in various establishments—for example, as bullet holes through the ceiling. The town still has a healthy number of bars, but in a nod to foodies, there are now an equal number of excellent restaurants.

Livingston's transformation into a haven for legendary artists, writers, and actors probably started in the 1960s. Iconic film director Sam Peckinpah took up residence in the town's Murray Hotel, and writers Tom McGuane, Doug Peacock, Tim Cahill, and Richard Brautigan all called Livingston home—and some still do. Actors including Peter Fonda, Jeff Bridges, Michael Keaton, and Dennis Quaid have made their homes on ranches outside of town.

Indeed, Livingston has a rich blended culture that is evident in everything from its sophisticated galleries and gourmet restaurants to its bawdy bars, rollicking rodeo, and fly-fishing paradise.

Getting to Livingston

Driving from Jackson, Wyoming

190-240 mi (305-385 km); 5-6.5 hours

From **Jackson Hole,** Livingston is 190 mi (305 km) away, traveling up the east side of Yellowstone National Park—past Lake, Canyon, and Tower Junction—a little over a 6-hour drive. Getting to Livingston from Jackson Hole via the west side of Yellowstone—past Old Faithful and Norris Geyser Basin—is 200 mi (320 km), a roughly 6.5-hour drive. When park roads are closed, the only route is via US 20 and US 191 North outside the western boundary of Yellowstone, a 240-mi (385-km), 5-hour drive.

Driving from Yellowstone

55 mi (89 km); 1 hour

From the north entrance of Yellowstone at **Gardiner,** Livingston is 55 mi (89 km) north on US 89, a 1-hour drive.

Sights

Depot Center

200 W. Park St.; 406/222-2300; www.livingstondepot.org; 10am-5pm Mon.-Sat. Memorial Day-Labor Day; donation

The town's Depot Center is a majestic building anchoring Livingston to its railroad heritage. In addition to being something of a community center where

Livingston

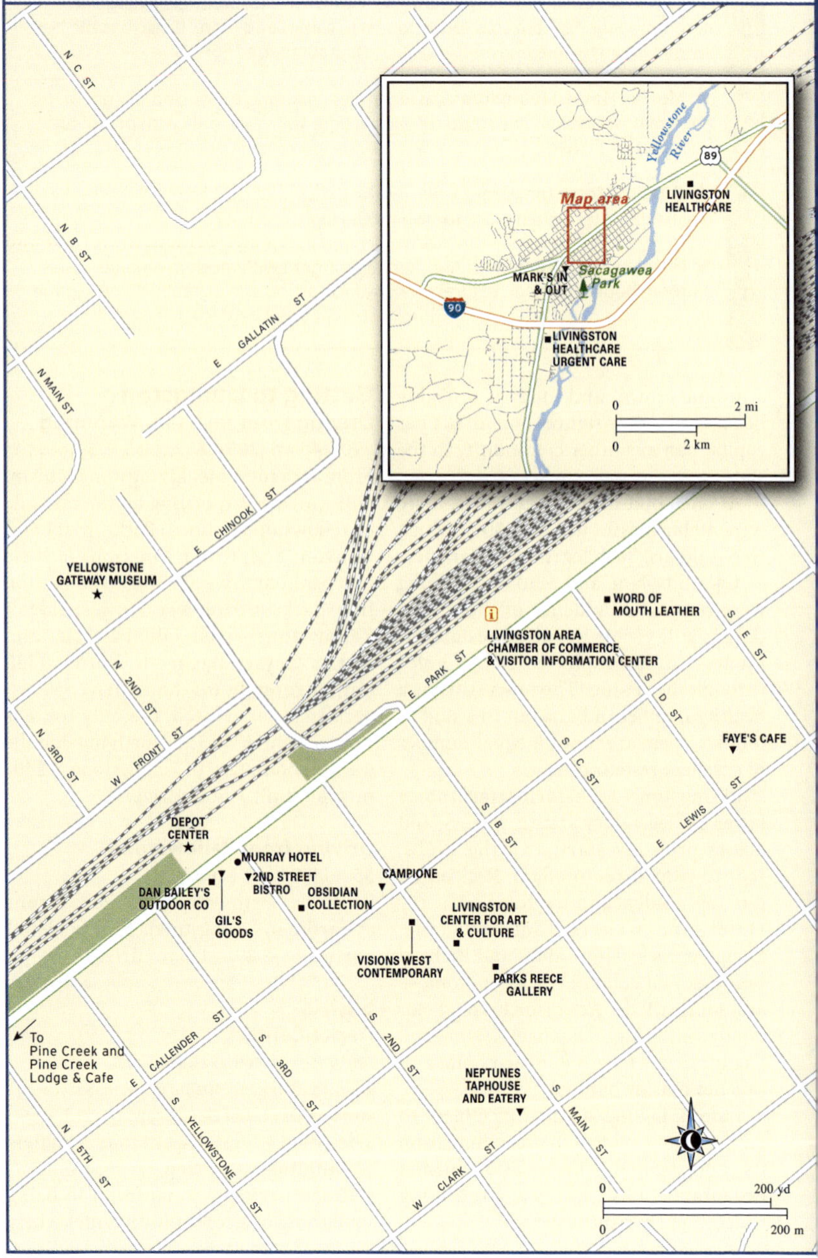

Yellowstone River
89
Map area
LIVINGSTON HEALTHCARE
Sacagawea Park
MARK'S IN & OUT
90
LIVINGSTON HEALTHCARE URGENT CARE
0 2 mi
0 2 km

N C ST
N B ST
E GALLATIN ST
N MAIN ST
E CHINOOK ST
YELLOWSTONE GATEWAY MUSEUM
N 2ND ST
N 3RD ST
W FRONT ST
E PARK ST
WORD OF MOUTH LEATHER
LIVINGSTON AREA CHAMBER OF COMMERCE & VISITOR INFORMATION CENTER
S E ST
S D ST
S C ST
FAYE'S CAFE
E LEWIS ST
S B ST
DEPOT CENTER
MURRAY HOTEL
2ND STREET BISTRO
CAMPIONE
DAN BAILEY'S OUTDOOR CO
GIL'S GOODS
OBSIDIAN COLLECTION
LIVINGSTON CENTER FOR ART & CULTURE
VISIONS WEST CONTEMPORARY
PARKS REECE GALLERY
To Pine Creek and Pine Creek Lodge & Cafe
E CALLENDER ST
S 3RD ST
S 2ND ST
NEPTUNES TAPHOUSE AND EATERY
S MAIN ST
N 5TH ST
S YELLOWSTONE ST
W CLARK ST
0 200 yd
0 200 m

the town gathers for concerts and special events, the depot houses a worthwhile museum featuring history, art, and culture of the region. Electric-train buffs should ask for a tour of the basement, where the region's train fanatics have built a wonderland.

Yellowstone Gateway Museum

118 W. Chinook St.; 406/222-4184; www.yellowstonegatewaymuseum.org; 10am-5pm daily Memorial Day-Sept., 10am-5pm Tues.-Sat. Oct.-Memorial Day; $5

On the other side of the tracks, the Yellowstone Gateway Museum, housed in a historic schoolhouse, holds the county's archives and presents some excellent local exhibits on railroad history, pioneer life, Native American cultures, and military history.

Adventure and Recreation

Fishing and Floating

If art defines Livingston, fishing feeds it. The **Yellowstone River** curves around the town and always makes its presence known. Paradise Valley lives up to its name in countless ways, fishing among them. **Nelson's, Armstrong's,** and **De Puy's Spring Creeks** are just minutes from town and offer some of the best and most consistent fishing in the state. Winter is an especially good time to fish the spring creeks because the springs flow constantly at a consistent temperature, the crowds are gone, and the rod fees go down significantly.

Angler's West Flyfishing

206 Railroad Ln., off US 89 S., Emigrant; 406/333-4401; www.montanaflyfishers.com; 7am-7pm daily summer, 8am-6pm daily spring and fall

Matson Rogers's Angler's West Flyfishing is a great resource, with both a fly shop and complete guiding service for the Yellowstone River and waters around the state.

Flying Pig Adventure Company

511 Scott St., Gardiner; 888/792-9193 or 406/848-7510; www.flyingpigrafting.com; May-Sept.; half-day white-water or scenic $84, full-day white-water $160, overnight rafting $415

To cover a lot of water in this country, with or without a rod, floating on a raft or drift boat can be a great option. Flying Pig Adventure Company offers raft trips, walk-and-wade fishing trips in the park (half-day $550 1-2 people, full-day $650 1-2 people), and combination float and fish trips ($550-650).

Montana Whitewater

603 Scott St., Gardiner; 406/763-4465; www.montanawhitewater.com; May-Sept.; half-day from $74, full-day from $140

Montana Whitewater focuses on rafting and offers scenic and white-water floats on the Yellowstone River. They also offer add-ons like zip-lining, horseback riding, and more.

Yellowstone Raft Company

212 W. Park St.; 406/848-7777 or 800/858-7781; www.yellowstoneraft.com; May-Sept.; half-day raft trip from $74, full-day trips from $129

Yellowstone Raft Company offers half-day and full-day scenic and white-water floats on the Yellowstone, with add-on options for kayaking and horseback riding.

Hiking

With mountains towering in every direction—the Absarokas and the Gallatins south of town, the Bridgers to the west, and the Crazies to the northeast—and a stiff wind usually blowing, heading out for a hike is never a bad idea in Livingston. Six mi (10 km) south of town on the east side of River Road in Paradise Valley, **Pine Creek** is a stunning and popular spot with camping (spots fill up early) and hiking options for every ability level.

Pine Creek Falls

Distance: 3.2 mi (5.1 km) round-trip
Duration: 1.5 hours
Elevation gain: 741 ft (226 m)
Effort: Moderate
Trailhead: Pine Creek Trail from the campground parking lot

A nice leisurely amble is the out-and-back forested trail to Pine Creek Falls. It's well-traveled by people and dogs, but bears frequent the area as well, so pack bear spray.

Pine Creek Lake

Distance: 9.5 mi (15.3 km) round-trip
Duration: 6.5 hours
Elevation gain: 3,654 ft (1,114 m)
Effort: Strenuous
Trailhead: Pine Creek Trail from the campground parking lot

Hard-core hikers can continue from Pine Creek Falls on the steep but mostly shaded trail to Pine Creek Lake. There are switchbacks and some very steep sections, but the trail follows the creek to a small meadow ringed by rock. Set amidst the cirque is the 32-acre (13-ha) Pine Creek Lake. There's another waterfall at the east end of the lake, which, along with the elevation and water depth, keeps the lake quite cold.

Dan Bailey's Outdoor Co.

209 W. Park St.; 406/222-1673; 8am-6pm Mon.-Sat., 8am-3pm Sun.

For hiking gear or just good ideas, talk to Dale at Dan Bailey's Outdoor Co., on the main thoroughfare into downtown Livingston.

Entertainment and Events

The Arts

Livingston is a railroad town, but to its core it is also an artists' town. There are more than a dozen galleries and many more artists, both brilliant amateurs and sophisticated professionals.

Top to bottom: section of the Yellowstone River near Gardiner; Livingston; Pine Creek Falls

Music Ranch Montana

4664 Old Yellowstone Trail N., 9 mi/14.5 km south of Livingston; 406/222-2255; www.musicranchmontana.net

One of the area's best-kept secrets is Music Ranch Montana, a unique music venue for indoor/outdoor concerts in summer. Founded by a well-known entrepreneur and his wife, Music Ranch has a large barn with both indoor and outdoor seating, including terraces built into the hillside.

Visions West Contemporary

108 S. Main St.; 406/222-0337; www.visionswestcontemporary.com; 10am-5:30pm Tues.-Sat.

Visions West Contemporary has three galleries—in Livingston, Bozeman, and Denver—and uses the space to push the boundaries of art in the West. The stunning and often surprising work is inspired by a passion for nature, animals, the environment, and the region.

Parks Reece Gallery

119 S. Main St.; 406/222-5724; www.parksreece.com; 10am-5pm Mon.-Fri., 11am-4pm Sat.

Local character and talented artist Parks Reece captures the beauty of the region with a delightful and often mischievous sense of humor.

Livingston Center for Art & Culture

119 S. Main; 406/222-5222; www.livingstoncenter.org; noon-5pm Tues.-Fri., 11am-4pm Sat.

The mission of the Livingston Center for Art & Culture is to "spark new ways of seeing and thinking through the experience of art and culture." To that end, they offer interesting exhibits—including by students at Montana State University—and classes for both kids and adults.

Festivals and Events

Livingston Roundup Rodeo

406/222-3199; www.livingstonroundup.com; $25-35

Since 1924, the annual Livingston Roundup Rodeo has enticed cowboys from across the country with its fat purse on the Fourth of July holiday. As crowds overtake the town's fairgrounds with rabid rodeo fever, regular events include barrel racing, bareback team roping, tie-down roping, saddle bronc, steer wrestling, and bull riding. The three-day event—held July 2-4—kicks off with a hometown parade and ends each evening with fireworks. This is without a doubt when Livingston most shines. General admission and reserved seating rodeo tickets are available online or by calling, but both sell out well before July.

Livingston Farmers Market

229 River Dr.; 406/222-0730; 4:30pm-7:30pm Wed. early June-mid-Sept.

The wonderful community-centered Livingston Farmers Market offers up the region's fresh local bounty in a friendly and festive environment. Live music is performed until 9pm.

Shopping

Downtown Livingston is a wonderful place to shop, with stores all within walking distance of one another offering a convenient escape from the town's ever-present wind along with an eclectic assortment of wares, from art and clothes to books and equipment. Most shops are closed on Sunday.

Word of Mouth Leather

403 E. Park St.; 406/222-7349; www.wom-leather.com; 10am-5:30pm Wed.-Fri., 10am-1pm Sat.

Word of Mouth Leather is the shop of Reid Flatten, who makes incredibly beautiful and fitted custom saddles and accessories, chaps and links, gun and knife leather, belts, cases, book covers, cuffs, and more. Crafting both modern and historical pieces, Flatten is the real deal.

The Obsidian Collection

108 N. 2nd St.; 406/222-2022; www.theobsidiancollection.com; 10am-6pm Mon.-Sat.

The Obsidian Collection offers an appealing selection of gifts, children's items, jewelry, cards, stationery, soaps, and lotions. Customers are loyal, often driving significant distances to see the latest and greatest collections. They also have a killer section of cheaters/readers for those who need a little help with menus and phones and whatnot.

Dan Bailey's Outdoor Co.

209 W. Park St.; 406/222-1673; www.danbaileys.com; 8am-6pm Mon.-Sat., 8am-3pm Sun.

For almost any kind of outdoor gear—including fly-fishing, cycling, hiking, and backpacking—visit the venerable Dan Bailey's Outdoor Co. Founded in 1938 by an NYC physics professor who left in order to open a fly shop in Montana, the shop has always committed to the community and worked to protect wild rivers and public land. Now owned and run by Dale Sexton, who founded Timber Trails in 1996, Dan Bailey's offers the best in all sorts of outdoor gear and athletic clothing. They rent bikes and fly-fishing gear, and are the best resource in town to guide you toward your next outdoor adventure.

Food

Mark's In & Out Drive-In

801 W. Park St., Livingston; 406/222-7744; www.marksbeefburgers.com; 11am-10pm daily late spring-early fall; $2-6

Not gourmet by any stretch of the imagination, Mark's In & Out Drive-In just might be the town favorite, and the most affordable. There is no seating at this seasonal walk-up or drive-up joint right out of the 1950s, but the burgers, fries, and shakes are so good that you won't mind. And there's a park across the street if you can't wait to dig in.

Faye's Cafe

415 E. Lewis St., room 104 inside the Shane Lalani Center; 406/223-7481 text only; www.sarahfayemontana.com; 7am-11am Mon.-Fri.; $16

For a delicious and truly creative breakfast, try Faye's Cafe, where diners are asked to look at a colorful chalkboard and name their favorite words—from Eggs Benny and Meaty + Cheesy to huckleberry, bacon, tacos, and amazeballs—which Faye will then turn into a delicious breakfast creation.

★ Pine Creek Lodge & Café

2496 E. River Rd., 10 mi/16 km south of Livingston; 406/222-3628; www.pinecreeklodgemontana.com; 5pm-9pm Wed.-Sun.; $11-21

Closer to town but still set in the grandeur of Paradise Valley, the Pine Creek Lodge & Café is a longtime favorite and an off-the-beaten-path gem. The menu is simple and features sandwiches, burgers, wings, and salads. Live music and outdoor barbecues take place in summer, readings by local authors in winter. Call for reservations as opening hours can change.

Gil's Goods

207 W. Park St.; 406/222-9463; www.gilsgoods.com; noon-8pm Thurs.-Mon. with extended hours in summer; $13-24

A favorite spot for locals and visitors

alike is Gil's Goods, which serves up excellent burgers, wood-fired pizza, salads, and starters. The restaurant is attached to the always-busy **Murray Bar,** so diners can have a drink with their meal.

Neptune's Taphouse & Eatery

232 S. Main St.; 406/333-2400; 11:30am-8pm Sun.-Thurs., 11:30am-8:30pm Fri.-Sat.; $15-30

For a casual bite in a festive setting, Neptune's Taphouse & Eatery serves a broad menu from bar food and burgers to sushi, seafood, and steak. They also serve a great selection of beers brewed down the street at Neptune's Brewery.

★ Campione

101 N. Main St.; 406/333-2427; www.eatcampione.com; 5pm-9pm Wed.-Mon., brunch 10am-1:45pm Sat.-Sun.; $26-32

Campione is one of the best places to enjoy a meal—if you can get a table, that is. The restaurant immediately gained a following—and accolades in *The New York Times*—since everything is made from scratch and utterly delicious. They have all sorts of traditional antipasti, both hot and cold; beautiful pastas; salads; and meat, fish, and veggie entrées. Whatever you do, save room for dessert. Reservations are strongly encouraged for this intimate eatery, or you can show up and wait for a seat at the bar, which they leave open nightly for walk-ins.

2nd Street Bistro

123 N. 2nd St.; 406/930-2356; www.secondstreetbistro.com; 5pm-9pm Tues.-Sat.; $24-36

Housed in the venerable Murray Hotel, 2nd Street Bistro serves simple but inspired French cuisine—both small and large plates. The elk short ribs are a favorite. All of the meat served is raised locally, and so is much of the produce.

★ Chico Hot Springs Resort

163 Chico Rd., off US 89 S., 23 mi/37 km south of Livingston; 406/333-4933; www.chicohotsprings.com; breakfast 7:30am-10:30am Mon.-Sat., 8am-11am Sun., dinner 5pm-9pm daily; $28-50

Pine Creek Lodge & Café

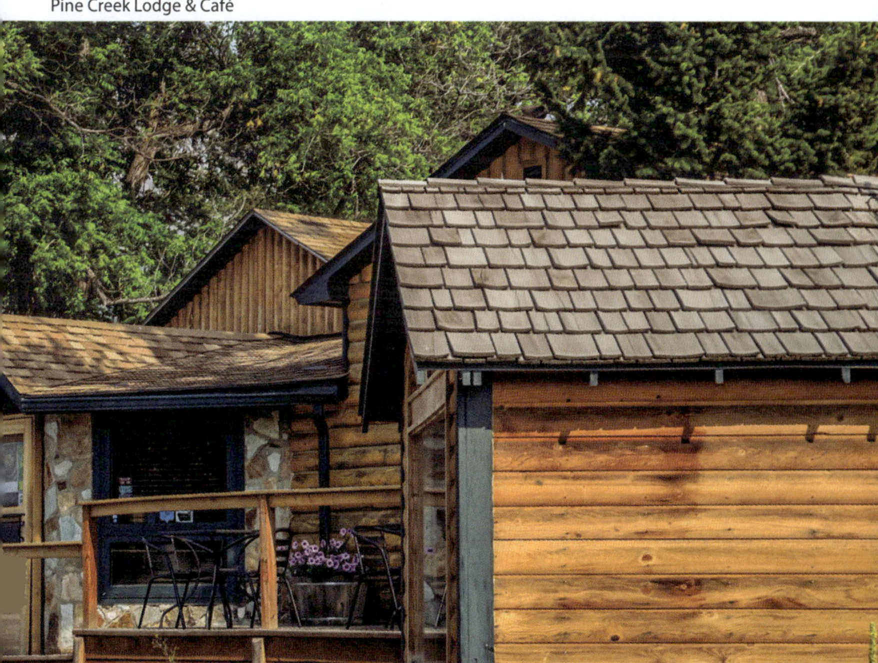

Back Roads Along the Rocky Mountain Front

Though just about any road in Montana or Wyoming can look and even feel like a back road, sometimes it's worth it to get even further off the beaten path to experience places that don't see as much traffic. The difference between choosing US 89 (225 mi/360 km) or the main route through Helena (260 mi/420 km) is only about 20 minutes of driving time. And the experience you'll have away from the madding crowd makes all the difference. The one-lane road between Livingston and Great Falls, US-89, winds through the Shields Valley and small towns like White Sulphur Springs and Belt.

From Livingston, head north on US 89 along the Shields River to the cowboy town of **White Sulphur Springs** (pop. 1,071, elev. 5,045 ft/1,542 m). Soak in the namesake **springs** (202 W. Main St.; 406/547-3366; www.spahotsprings.com; $14) if you are so inclined, pick up the sturdiest pair of women's work pants you'll ever own at **Red Ants Pants** (206 E. Main St.; 406/547-3781; www.redantspants.com), and grab lunch at **Bar 47** (24 E. Main St.; 406/547-2247; www.bar47montana.com; $11-22). Continue north for 65 mi (105 km), stopping at **Sluice Boxes State Park** (page 168) to stretch your legs.

Continue another 13 mi (21 km) to tiny Belt, Montana, where you can sip an excellent microbrew at **Harvest Moon Brewing Company** (7 5th St. N.; 406/277-3188; www.harvestmoonbrew.com). From there, drive just 22 mi (35 km) to **Great Falls,** grab dinner at **Howard's Pizza** (page 172), and see a mermaid show at the **Sip-N-Dip Lounge** (page 169) before you settle in for the night at the **O'Haire Motor Inn** (page 172).

If the pools bring people to Chico Hot Springs Resort, the food is what transforms them into regulars. From the first taste of burrata à la Chico with a balsamic vinegar reduction, to the house-smoked rainbow trout and the gorgonzola filet mignon, to the legendary flaming orange, Chico has gone a long way in defining Montana cuisine with fresh, local ingredients in simple, hearty, and outstanding dishes.

Accommodations

It's true that Livingston has quite a collection of funky roadside motels that have seen better days, but there are some treasures around town and down the valley.

TOP EXPERIENCE

★ Chico Hot Springs Resort

163 Chico Rd., 23 mi/37 km south of Livingston in Pray; 406/333-4933; www.chicohotsprings.com; from $114 lodge with shared bath, from $179 cabins

Built around a natural hot spring that was discovered in the late 1800s, the Chico Hot Springs Resort has become a Montana icon, as much for its sensational food and raucous saloon as for its heavenly year-round outdoor pools. The resort got its start when Bill and Percie Knowles offered weary miners a clean bed, a hot bath, and fresh strawberries with every meal. The resort has stayed true to its humble origins by offering simple, no-frills guest rooms with shared baths in the main lodge starting at $114. Modern accommodations are available in Warren's Wing and the Lower Lodge (from $249), and in pet-friendly rustic cabins (from $179). Cottages, houses, and chalets (call for rates and availability) can accommodate larger parties.

For travelers in search of more than a memorable meal and a luxurious soak, Chico offers a number of activities, all of which take advantage of its spectacular location just north of Yellowstone National Park in Paradise Valley. From horseback riding and dogsledding to hiking and cross-country skiing, Chico affords every visitor ample opportunity to earn their dinner.

★ Murray Hotel

201 W. Park St.; 406/222-1350; www.murrayhotel.com; from $109 winter, from $189 summer, pets welcome for $25

Right in town, the Murray Hotel is a Montana standard. It hasn't been glamorously overhauled, but the authenticity in each of the 25 unique rooms and suites works well, and the place is rich with history, including the story of Will Rogers and Walter Hill trying to bring a saddle horse to the 3rd floor in a 1905 hand-cranked elevator. Guest rooms are well appointed, with amenities like pillow-top beds and Wi-Fi.

Pine Creek Lodge

2496 E. River Rd.; 406/222-3628; www.pinecreeklodgemontana.com; from $119

Pine Creek Lodge offers unique accommodations in a beautiful setting. Cabin options include rustic-yet-modern overhauled shipping containers (from $149), cabins (from $259), glamping tents (from $119), and several tent sites (available on www.hipcamp.com; starting at $199). Bathhouses are modern and clean, available to both campers and cabin guests. Pets are welcome in the cabins for $25 (free for campers). The on-site restaurant is outstanding and fun, and there are often live music events throughout the summer.

Mountain Sky Guest Ranch

480 National Forest Development Rd. 132, Emigrant; 406/333-4911 or 800/548-3392; www.mountainsky.com; all rates weekly Sun.-Sun., $13,750 for up to 2 people in studio cabin, $16,800 for up to 2 people in 1-bedroom cabin

For travelers who long to stay in one place and experience life as a dude, Mountain Sky Guest Ranch sets the gold standard for summertime family ranch vacations. Set on 10,000 acres (4,047 ha) of mountains and forests, Mountain Sky offers impeccable service, gourmet dining, charming log cabins, and fantastic activity possibilities, including golf on a Johnny Miller course, a high-energy kids' program, endless alpine trails for horseback riding and hiking, swimming, and even a spa. With such superlative options for balancing family time and adult relaxation, it's small surprise that 87 percent of the guests return year after year, and that entire summers are often booked more than a year in advance.

Information and Services

Visitor Information

The **Livingston Chamber of Commerce** (303 E. Park St.; 406/222-0850; www.livingston-chamber.com; 9am-5pm Mon.-Fri., 9am-1pm Sat.-Sun. Memorial Day-Labor Day, 10am-5pm Mon.-Fri., 10am-4pm Sat. Labor Day-Memorial Day) is housed in the former crew quarters of the Burlington Northern Railroad.

Emergency Services

Livingston HealthCare (320 Alpenglow Ln.; 406/222-3541) has a 24-hour emergency room. For nonemergency medical care, visit **Urgent Care** (104 Centennial Dr.; 406/222-0030; 8am-7pm daily).

Services

The **Livingston-Park County Public Library** (228 W. Callender St.; 406/222-0862; www.livingstonparkcountylibrary.blogspot.com; 10am-8pm Mon.-Thurs., 10am-6pm Fri., 10am-5pm Sat.) offers cozy spaces to work or browse through your guidebook. It has a terrific collection of fly-fishing material and even offers a genealogy service for visitors in the summer. It also has **free internet access.** Computers are available for up to an hour at a time.

Detour: Helena

Montana's capital, Helena (pop. 34,464, elev. 4,090 ft/1,247 m) is the demure and pious little sister to Butte. Founded in 1864 with a gold strike at Last Chance Gulch, Helena had more millionaires per capita than any other US city when

Montana became a state in 1889. The city has done a particularly good job of preserving its history by maintaining architecture, including the Greek Renaissance-style Montana State Capitol building. With its soaring spires and stained glass, the St. Helena Cathedral would look at home in Europe, while humble miners' cabins line the streets in Last Chance Gulch.

Helena is becoming recognized as the arts capital of the state, with an edgy, contemporary fine arts scene in addition to extensive performing arts. Located in a wide-open valley surrounded by mountains, lakes, and rivers, Helena also offers endless opportunities to get out of the city and into nature.

Getting to Helena

Driving from Livingston

125 mi (201 km); 2 hours

From Livingston, Helena is a 125-mi (201-km), 2-hour drive west on I-90 and north on US 287.

Driving from Great Falls

90 mi (145 km); 1.5 hours

To get to Helena from Great Falls, it's a 90-mi (145-km) drive southwest via I-15, which will take about 1.5 hours.

Air

The **Helena Regional Airport** (HLN; 2850 Skyway Dr.; 406/442-2821; www.helenaairport.com) is just 2.5 mi (4 km) from the city center and is served by Delta, Alaska-Horizon, and United. The car-rental agencies at the airport are **Avis, Budget, Hertz, National,** and **Enterprise.**

Bus

Greyhound (1415 N. Montana Ave.; 406/447-8078) runs several bus routes to and from nearby cities, including Bozeman, Billings, and Butte.

Getting Around

Capital Transit (406/447-8080; www.helenamt.gov; $3-5) operates curb-to-curb service (6:30am-6pm Mon.-Fri.) around the city and East Valley. Call to pre-book.

Helena Taxi (406/407-2738; www.helenataxiservices.com) offers standard taxi service. **Helena Towncar** (406/437-8585; www.helenatowncar.com) is another option. **Uber** and **Lyft** also offer service in Helena.

Sights

Last Chance Tour Train

Montana Historical Society, 225 N. Roberts St. at E. 6th Ave.; 406/442-1023; www.lctours.com; Mon.-Sat. June-Sept. 15; $12

One of the best ways to get a historical overview of the city is by hopping on one of the Last Chance Tours (11am and 1pm early June and early Sept., 11am, 1pm, and 3pm mid-late-June, 9:30am, 11am, 1pm, and 3pm July-Aug.). The wheeled trains and trolley cruise around town with commentary on places like Reeder's Alley, the Old Fire Tower, Last Chance Gulch, and the city's Mansion District. Arrive 15 minutes before departure.

Montana State Capitol

1301 E. 6th Ave.; 406/444-2694 or 406/444-4789; www.leg.mt.gov; 7am-6pm Mon.-Fri., 9am-3pm Sat.-Sun.

Visible for miles around with its weathered copper dome, the Montana State Capitol unites Montana's past and present in an ornate and interesting way. The building is something of a Greek Renaissance masterpiece. Started in 1898, the main portion was completed in 1902, and the wings were unveiled 10 years later. The building is filled with dramatic art by some of Montana's most recognizable legends, among them Charles M. Russell and Edgar Paxson.

Guided tours (Mon.-Fri. June-early July, daily mid-July-mid-Sept., Sat. mid-Sept.-mid-May; free) are offered multiple times a day. The legislature is in session in odd-numbered years, when tours are offered 9am-2pm Monday-Saturday January-April. The capitol is always closed on state holidays and on Sunday when the legislature is in session.

Montana Historical Society and Heritage Center

225 N. Roberts St.; 406/444-2964; www.mhs.mt.gov, www.montanamuseum.org; 8am-5pm Mon.-Sat.; call for prices

With a phenomenal collection spanning 12,000 years of history, the Montana Historical Society and Heritage Center is the best historical resource in the state. Exhibits include an impressive art gallery, photo archives, a Native American collection, and decorative arts—more than 50,000 artifacts in all. A wonderful long-term exhibit explores what Montana must have been like at the time of Lewis and Clark. The institution was founded in 1865, making it among the oldest of its kind in the western United States. The museum has been closed for several years, undergoing a $108-million renovation, and will open in late 2025 with a 66,000-sq-ft (6,130-sq-m) addition for collection exhibition and a complete renovation of the 95,000-sq-ft (8,830-sq-m) historical building. Tours and entrance fees will be announced when the center reopens.

Holter Museum of Art

12 E. Lawrence St.; 406/442-6400; www.holtermuseum.org; 10am-5:30pm Tues.-Sat., noon-4pm Sun.; $10

In a town that has established a reputation for its art, Holter Museum of Art is a fascinating place to spend some time. The building was constructed in 1914 and expanded in 1999 to add 6,000 sq ft (560 sq m) of gallery space. The museum's contemporary collection includes art in a variety of media displayed in over 25 exhibitions annually, creating a unique voice in the Northwest art scene.

Top to bottom: St. Helena Cathedral; Montana State Capitol building; Archie Bray Foundation

Archie Bray Foundation

2915 Country Club Ave.; 406/443-3502; www.archiebray.org; 11am-5pm Tues.-Fri., noon-4pm Sat.; free

A cutting-edge artists' workshop and gallery, the Archie Bray Foundation is an international hotbed of ceramic art in what was once a brick factory. Hundreds of well-known artists have come to work and exhibit here. Their annual **Brickyard Bash** (late July) combines fabulous art with live music to raise money for the foundation. Classes and workshops are available for people of all ages and abilities, and some of the studio spaces are open to visitors. The grounds are open during daylight hours daily year-round.

★ Last Chance Gulch and Reeder's Alley

Rarely in the West have important gold or other mineral discovery sites gone on to become the center of big modern cities. Helena is an exception. Four prospectors, known as "the four Georgians," discovered gold in a small tributary of Ten Mile Creek. A mining camp quickly grew up around them, and the discovery site became the camp's main drag. Businesses sprouted up around the creek and never left. Both Last Chance Gulch and Reeder's Alley are worth spending an afternoon or evening, enjoying a meal and some shopping.

Last Chance Gulch

Between W. 6th Ave. and Pioneer Park

Nearly 160 years after that first discovery, Last Chance Gulch is still at the heart of the city. But rather than a dusty collection of saloons and brothels, the area has been transformed into a marvelous pedestrian mall that includes dozens of great eateries, a few museums and galleries, wonderful shopping, and one of the most popular candy shops in the state. If your time in Helena is limited, Last Chance Gulch should be your first stop.

Reeder's Alley

Between S. Park Ave. and S. Benton Ave., across from Pioneer Park; www.reedersalley.com

Near Last Chance Gulch, Reeder's Alley is a unique little corner of downtown that reflects its more humble origins. The area has remained authentic visually, while some of the small miners' shacks, tenements, stables, and other buildings have been transformed into upscale shops and eateries. The buildings have been designated a historic district on the National Register of Historic Places and are maintained by the Montana Heritage Commission.

Exploration Works

995 Carousel Way; 406/457-1800; www.explorationworks.org; usually 10am-5pm Tues.-Sun.; $11

This hands-on museum is an interactive science center with frequently changing exhibits like space exploration, waterworks, and amazing airways. After you've exhausted your brain in the museum,

head next door to the hand-built **Great Northern Carousel** (989 Carousel Way; 406/457-5353; www.gncarousel.com; 11am-6pm Wed.-Fri., 10am-7pm Sat., 11am-5pm Sun. summer, call for off-season hours; $3) for a leisurely ride and a fantastic ice cream cone.

Broadwater Hot Springs

4920 W. US 12; 406/443-5809; www.broadwatermt.com; 6am-10:30pm Mon.-Thurs., 6am-11:30pm Fri., 7:30am-11:30pm Sat., 7:30am-10:30pm Sun.; day use $17-22

The only hot springs in Helena, Broadwater is the perfect place to spend an afternoon. The freeform pools, heated from natural artesian wells, have bench seating, which makes them ideal for soaking. There are also cold-plunge pools and a rec pool for kids. On-site restaurant **The Springs Taproom & Grill** (11am-9pm daily; $10-17) serves standard pub fare like pizza, tacos, wings, sandwiches, and burgers in a very cool setting. If you have your heart set on a soak, this is the place.

Gates of the Mountains

Just outside Helena is one of the loveliest canyons in Montana. Named Gates of the Mountains by Lewis and Clark in 1805 because of the 1,200-ft (370-m) limestone cliffs that tower on either side of the Missouri River, it has become a favorite recreation area for Helena residents.

Gates of the Mountains Boat and Bat Tours

3131 Gates of the Mountains Rd., 20 mi/32 km north of Helena at I-15 exit 209; 406/458-5241; www.gatesofthemountains.com; 8am-8pm daily; $20-65

There are many ways to enjoy this scenic area on your own, but Gates of the Mountains Boat Tours has 120-minute cruises from the marina; schedules change daily, so call or go online for details. Abundant wildlife inhabit the area, including bighorn sheep, mountain goats, and more than 120 bird species. You can bring a picnic lunch and get off the boat at Meriwether Picnic Area, returning

Gates of the Mountains

later on another boat. It is also possible to hike from the Meriwether Picnic Area to **Mann Gulch,** where 13 firefighters were killed by a fast-moving wildfire in 1949. Also on offer is a unique **Bat Tour** (7:45pm-10:15pm, late Aug.; reservations required; $10 pp). The total of four evening tours each year sell out in minutes when they are released annually on May 1.

Festivals and Events

For a full listing of daily events in Helena, visit www.helenamt.com or www.helenaevents.com.

Weekly Summer Events

There's something going on in Helena just about every day when the summer sun is out. Mondays bring **Mondays at the Myrna** (15 N. Ewing St.; 406/443-0287; www.myrnaloycenter.com), featuring a broad lineup of live music, including funk, folk, and electro-pop. Every Wednesday a different block of Helena comes to life for **Alive at 5** (406/447-1535; www.aliveatfivehelena.com; 5pm-9pm Wed. June-Aug.), a fun and family-oriented event that combines live music, food, and drinks for a fantastic summer evening. And on Thursdays, crowds show up at the Great Northern Town Center amphitheater for **Out to Lunch** (40 W. 14th St.; 406/447-5542; www.greatnortherntowncenter.com; 11:30am-1:30pm Thurs. June-Aug.; free), with food vendors and live music. **First Friday Arts** (406/447-1535; www.downtownhelena.com; 5pm-9pm 1st Fri. of the month) invites visitors to explore downtown shops, galleries, and restaurants.

Symphony Under the Stars

406/442-1860; www.helenasymphony.org; 8:30pm, date varies mid-late July; free

Once each summer, the Helena Symphony joins Carroll College in presenting Symphony Under the Stars on the hillside at Carroll College (1601 N. Benton Ave.). Concerts feature classical, opera, or Broadway-oriented music, and end with a spectacular fireworks display.

Last Chance Stampede and Fair

98 W. Custer Ave.; 406/457-8516; www.lewisandclarkcountyfairgrounds.com; late July or early Aug.

Helena puts on the annual Last Chance Stampede and Fair at the fairgrounds, with big country-music concerts, a rodeo, a carnival, food, and a variety of entertainment.

Shopping

General Mercantile

413 N. Last Chance Gulch; 406/442-6078; www.generalmerc.com; 8am-5pm Mon.-Fri., 9am-5pm Sat., 11am-4pm Sun.

The General Mercantile is like a step back in time. The Merc serves every variety of coffee and tea, including espresso from vintage machines, and there are all sorts of cozy nooks to sip a latte while perusing a book. The store has gifts and cards galore, but it's the atmosphere in the Merc that makes it so welcoming.

Spokane Bar Sapphire Mine & Gold Fever Rock Shop

5360 Castles Rd.; 877/344-4367 or 406/227-8989; www.sapphiremine.com; 9am-5pm daily summer

For an experience you can't get many other places, visit Spokane Bar Sapphire Mine & Gold Fever Rock Shop, where you can dig for your own sapphires, garnets, rubies, jasper, agates, jade, and quartz. The shop will provide you with bags of gravel and a screen to help you sift, or you can take home a 30-lb (14-kg) bag of sapphire concentrate gravel ($95) and sift through it. Most of the gemstones are small, but occasionally people find big ones.

The Parrot Confectionery

42 N. Last Chance Gulch; 406/442-1470; www.parrotchocolate.com; 9am-6pm Mon.-Sat.

For a real taste of Montana, look no further than The Parrot Confectionery, an absolute Montana standard for candy shops and diners. The shop makes 130 different varieties of candy, and its reputation for hand-dipped chocolates has won over customers worldwide. Try a cherry phosphate from the original soda fountain, and sit up at the bar for a bowl of the secret-recipe chili. A local favorite since 1922, The Parrot should not be missed.

Food

Steve's Café

1225 E. Custer Ave., 406/444-5010; and 630 N. Montana Ave., 406/449-6666; www.stevescafe.com; 6:30am-2:30pm Wed.-Sun.; $6-15

For a quick bite between sights and breakfast all day, try Steve's Café for wonderful huckleberry pancakes, breakfast burritos, steak and eggs, burgers, sandwiches, and the like. A secret menu offers specialties like pork verde chilaquiles, Irish eggs Benedict, a BLT wrap, and more. Just ask!

Bad Betty's Barbecue

812 Front St.; 406/459-2303; www.badbettysbarbecue.com; 11am-3pm Tues.-Wed. and Sat., 11am-7pm Thurs.-Fri.; $7-18

Barbecue lovers will delight in the offerings at Bad Betty's Barbecue, which serves mouthwatering barbecue from brisket and pulled pork to chicken and ribs. They have daily specials that include street tacos, brisket burnt ends, and barbecue nachos.

The Union

361 N. Last Chance Gulch; 406/500-6328; www.oldsaltco-op.com; 8am-9pm daily; $19-33

One of the coolest new places in Montana, The Union is a wood-fired grill and butcher shop that specializes in—and in fact was created to support—locally sourced meat. The atmosphere is elegant and inviting, and the food, from shepherd's pie to nightly steak specials, is magnificent and farm-fresh. The Union is part of the Old Salt Co-op behind the **Old Salt Festival** (Mannix Family Ranch, Helmville; June), a celebration of food, music, makers, and land stewardship.

★ Benny's Bistro

108 E. 6th St.; 406/443-0105; www.bennyshelena.com; 11am-3pm Tues., 11am-3pm and 5pm-9pm Wed.-Sat.; $27-42

A nice spot just off Last Chance Gulch is Benny's Bistro. Set in a renovated historic building, Benny's does a phenomenal job of catering to the locavore movement by using as many fresh, locally grown ingredients as possible. Its list of Montana suppliers is vast. Taste the best of the state in Montana-raised beef stroganoff, ginger-rubbed Montana pork loin, a local cheese board, Flathead cherry salad, and scratch-made fettuccine with chicken from the Hutterite colony.

Wassweiler Dinner House and Pub

4528 US 12; 406/442-1442; www.wassweiler.com; 5pm-8:30pm Wed.-Thurs., 5pm-9pm Sat.-Sun.; $24-76

For a really fancy Montana dinner in a beautiful setting, Wassweiler Dinner House and Pub is a treat. Not far from Broadwater Hot Springs, the building was built in 1883 as an inn and bathhouse. Everything about the experience is elegant. With such entrées as duck breast, bison sirloin, cowboy cut rib eye, and seafood pasta, the dishes are as wonderful to look at as they are to eat. Save room for dessert.

Accommodations

While Helena is long on hotels, perhaps for all the legislators who come to govern for four months every other year, most fall into the category of chain hotels or bed-and-breakfasts. Chain hotels and motels line the major thoroughfares.

Delta Hotels Helena Colonial

2301 Colonial Dr.; 406/443-2100; www.marriott.com; $170-369

Close to the highway is the Delta Hotels Helena Colonial, a large, full-service, and comfortable hotel.

Lamplighter Cabins & Suites

1006 Madison Ave.; 406/442-9200; www.lamplighterhelena.com; $130-269

A far cry from a chain hotel but cozy, clean, and adorable, the Lamplighter Cabins & Suites has lots of character and local owners who can point you anywhere you want to go.

The Sanders, Helena's Bed and Breakfast

328 N. Ewing St.; 406/442-3309; www.sandersbb.com; $250-280

For a more historic option near downtown and the state capitol, The Sanders offers seven guest rooms in an 1875 Queen Anne mansion. Many furnishings are original to the home, and the owners, Rock and Bobbi, are gracious and welcoming. The breakfasts are healthy and delicious, with plenty of protein.

Information and Services

Visitor Information

A terrific website for planning a trip to Helena is www.helenamt.com. Plug in your dates of travel and the site shows you all the available hotels and their average nightly rates. Another good source of visitor information is the **Helena Chamber of Commerce** (225 Cruse Ave.; 406/442-4120; www.helenachamber.com; 8am-5pm Mon.-Thurs., 8am-4pm Fri.).

Health and Emergencies

St. Peter's Hospital (2475 E. Broadway; 406/457-4180; www.stpetes.org) has a 24-hour emergency room. The hospital also runs the **St. Peter's Urgent Care Clinic** (2475 Broadway; 406/457-4180; www.stpetes.org; 8am-7pm Mon.-Fri., 8am-5pm Sat.-Sun.) and **North Clinic** (3330 Ptarmigan Lane; 406/495-7901; www.stpetes.org; 7am-6pm Mon.-Fri., 7am-4pm Sat.-Sun.).

Great Falls

At the edge of the mountains and the plains, Great Falls (pop. 60,422, elev. 3,674 ft/1,120 m) has more romantic origins than its modern-day grittiness may suggest. A few days ahead of William Clark, Meriwether Lewis stumbled on the region in June 1805, calling the falls themselves "the grandest sight I ever beheld." Seventy-five years later, Fort Benton merchant Paris Gibson sought the same views that had captivated Lewis and later recollected,

> I had never seen a spot as attractive as this . . . I had looked upon this scene for a few moments only when I said to myself, here I would found a city.

Just three years later, in 1883, the city of Great Falls was named and platted.

With the falls long since dammed to create power—Great Falls is known as the "Electric City" for all its dams and power plants—the city has worked to capitalize on the beauty of the Missouri River with a scenic roadway (River Drive), trails, parks, and picnic areas along the waterway. The Lewis and Clark National Historic Trail Interpretive Center sits atop a bluff and affords visitors an unspoiled view of what the area might have looked like 200 years ago. Another kind of beauty celebrated by this city is art. There are a couple of excellent—and surprising—art museums to visit.

But Great Falls is still a rough-and-tumble Montana town. There is cowboy culture, military culture, and serious wind, all of which give the state's third-largest city a little bit of an edge. Its location between the mountains and plains and amid rivers is ideal for lovers of the outdoors, and Great Falls is an excellent launching point for adventures in any direction.

Great Falls

To Fort Benton and Havre
To River's Edge Trail
Giant Springs Heritage State Park
GIANT SPRINGS RD
RAINBOW FALLS AND DAM
River
Missouri
LEWIS AND CLARK NATIONAL HISTORIC TRAIL INTERPRETIVE CENTER
BLACK EAGLE FALLS AND DAM
0
1 mi
0
1 km
SMELTER AVE
3RD ST NW
14TH AVE NW
NW BYPASS
See Detail
8TH AVE N
MONTANA EXPO PARK
Riverside Park
C. M. RUSSELL MUSEUM
MONTANA COWBOYS ASSOCIATION MUSEUM & BAR
Gibson Park
2ND AVE N
26TH ST S
38TH ST S
CENTRAL AVE W
BUS.
15
1ST AVE N
CENTRAL AVE
To Choteau, Glacier Park, and Shelby
ELECTRIC CITY WATER PARK
56TH ST
6TH ST NW
RIVER DR
2ND ST S
3RD ST S
5TH ST S
6TH ST S
9TH ST S
14TH ST S
15TH ST S
To North 40 Outfitters, Benefis Health Systems, Lewistown, and Billings
10TH AVE S
Sun River
89
200
VISITOR CENTER
13TH AVE S
15TH ST S
WALK-IN CLINIC
26TH ST S
17TH AVE S
UPPER RIVER RD
FOX FARM RD
13TH ST S
21ST AVE S
To Helena and Butte
24TH AVE S
RIVER DR N
8TH AVE N
Riverside Park
CROOKED TREE COFFEE RESTAURANT
ROADHOUSE DINER
PARK DR N
GREAT HARVEST BREAD COMPANY
GREAT FALLS CHAMBER OF COMMERCE
C. M. RUSSELL MUSEUM
CIVIC CENTER/ GREAT FALLS FARMERS MARKET
PARIS GIBSON SQUARE MUSEUM OF ART
HOWARD'S PIZZA
2ND AVE N
5TH ST N
1ST AVE N
HOTEL ARVON
MONTANA MOSAIC
CENTRAL AVE
PLANET EARTH
THE FARMER'S DAUGHTER FIBERS
THE KITCHEN AT WILD HARE
O'HAIRE INN/ CLARK AND LEWIES/ SIP-N-DIP LOUNGE
ENBAR
MIGHTY MO BREWING CO
2ND ST S
6TH ST S
5TH AVE S
14TH ST S
15TH ST S

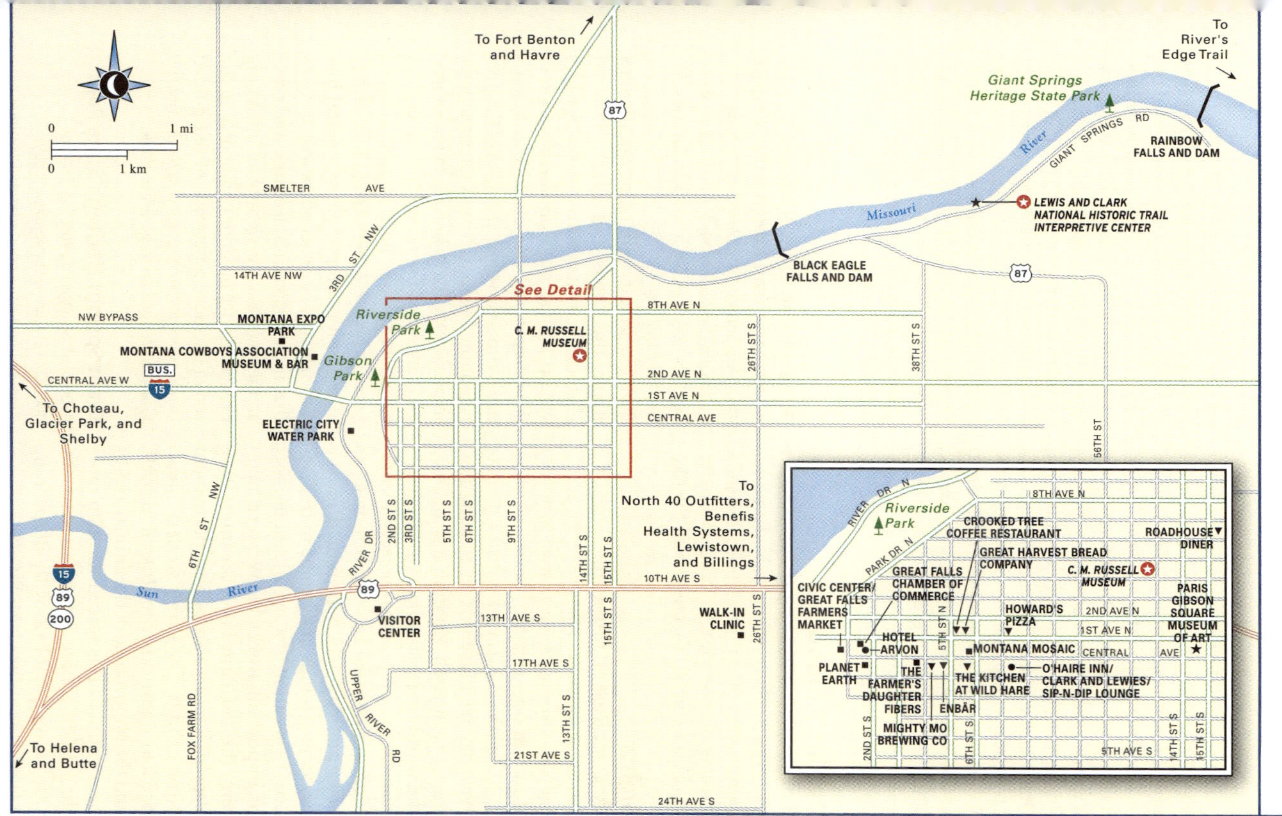

Getting to Great Falls

From **Helena,** Great Falls is 92 mi (147 km) north on I-15, about a 90-minute drive.

From **East Glacier,** Great Falls is 138 mi (222 km) southeast via US 2, US 89, and I-15, a little more than a 2-hour drive.

The **Great Falls International Airport** (GTF; 2800 Terminal Dr.; 406/727-3404; www.flygtf.com) is southwest of the city. It is served by Alaska Airlines, Allegiant, Delta, and United. The airport's on-site car-rental companies are **Alamo, Avis, Enterprise, Hertz, National,** and **Budget.**

Greyhound Bus Lines (326 1st Ave. S.; 800/231-2222; www.greyhound.com) offers service to other major towns and cities in Montana.

Getting Around

Blacked Out 406 Limo & Taxi Service (406/781-5218; www.blackedout406limo.com) is an option for airport transfers, regular taxi service, or crazy over-the-top limousine SUVs, buses, and the like.

Sights

★ C. M. Russell Museum

400 13th St. N.; 406/727-8787; www.cmrussell.org; 10am-5pm daily May-Sept., 10am-5pm Thurs.-Mon. Oct.-Apr.; $18

One of the best and most intimate Western art museums in the country, the C. M. Russell Museum has amassed the world's largest collection of Charlie Russell art and personal objects, including his illustrated letters. His home has been meticulously maintained on the museum grounds and can be toured online. In addition to a significant number of important works by Western masters, the museum takes an interesting approach to art through its permanent bison exhibit. The iconic western ungulate had significance to Russell himself, and the importance of the animal and its near extinction is traced through more than 1,000 Native American artifacts. Don't leave Great Falls without spending a few hours at the C. M. Russell.

Paris Gibson Square Museum of Art

1400 1st Ave. N.; 406/727-8255; www.the-square.org; 10am-5pm Wed.-Fri., 10am-9pm Tues., 10am-3pm Sat.; free

At the eastern end of downtown Great Falls, the Paris Gibson Square Museum of Art is known as "The Square" and occupies an entire city block. Built in 1896 as a school, the impressive structure was renovated, renamed after the city's founder, and reopened in 1977. The museum houses an impressive permanent collection of contemporary art as well as important traveling exhibitions. In addition to classes, lectures, tours, and performances, the museum has a café and gift shop. Don't miss a stroll through the sculpture garden out on the beautifully landscaped grounds.

★ Lewis and Clark National Historic Trail Interpretive Center

4201 Giant Springs Rd.; 406/453-6248; www.fs.usda.gov; 9am-5pm daily Memorial Day-Labor Day, 9am-5pm Tues.-Sat., noon-5pm Sun. Labor Day-Memorial Day; $8

Built into a bluff overlooking the Missouri River, the Lewis and Clark National Historic Trail Interpretive Center provides visitors with a hands-on interpretation of the intrepid explorers' cross-country journey. With a two-story diorama of the portage at the Missouri River's five great falls, impressive videos by Ken Burns and others, and ranger-led programs, the center does an excellent job of portraying the importance of Native Americans to the journey along with a comprehensive natural history exhibit. The center offers special events that include concerts, lectures, and reenactments (check the website for upcoming events). A nice outdoor component to the center includes a network of self-guided trails, one of which leads you to the nearby Giant Springs Heritage State Park.

Giant Springs Heritage State Park

4600 Giant Springs Rd.; 406/454-5840 or 406/727-1212; www.stateparks.mt.gov; sunrise-sunset daily; nonresidents $8/vehicle

Among the largest freshwater springs in the country, Giant Springs was discovered by Lewis and Clark in 1805. The spring, now in Giant Springs Heritage State Park, produces 156 million gallons (590 million liters) of crystal-clear water each day. The water stays at a constant 54°F (12°C) all year, making it an ideal spot for fishing. Attractions include a fish hatchery on-site, a **visitor center** (8am-5pm daily), a picnic area, and several trails that wind through the lush area. There are four Missouri River waterfalls within the park. For trivia buffs, the 201-ft-long (61-m-long) **Roe River,** the second shortest in the world, flows from the springs.

★ First Peoples Buffalo Jump State Park

342 Ulm-Vaughn Rd., Ulm; 406/866-2217; www.stateparks.mt.gov; park open daily in summer and Wed.-Sun. in winter, visitor center open 8am-6pm daily mid-Apr.-mid-Sept., 10am-4pm Wed.-Sat., noon-4pm Sun. mid-Sept.-Mar.; nonresidents $8/vehicle

Considered to be among the largest buffalo jumps in North America, and in use more than 1,000 years before Lewis and Clark explored the area, First Peoples Buffalo Jump State Park is exceptional in that it offers an extensive on-site education center that houses buffalo culture exhibits, a storytelling circle, a gallery, and an outdoor powwow area. The site itself is impressive, with a mile-long sandstone cliff from which the bison were chased to their deaths, but more than anything, this is the best place in the state to learn about buffalo jumps. Watch your step on or off the trails for both rattlesnakes and prickly pear cacti. An adjacent prairie dog town is home to protected black-tailed prairie dogs and worth the short detour. The park is 10 mi (16 km) south

Top to bottom: the Great Falls; First Peoples Buffalo Jump State Park; fly-fishing in the Missouri River

of Great Falls off I-15 at Ulm; follow signs for the state park 3.5 mi (5.6 km) northwest on a county road.

Sluice Boxes State Park

38 Evans Riceville Rd., Belt; 406/454-5840; www.stateparks.mt.gov; nonresidents $8

A rugged state park combining natural beauty, old mines, and a railroad, plus historic cabins and a limestone canyon, Sluice Boxes State Park is about a 35-mi (56-km), 45-minute drive southeast of Great Falls. Hikers can amble along the creek, admiring the soaring cliffs of Belt Creek Canyon, and peek into the old prospector cabins.

Adventure and Recreation

★ Fishing on the Missouri River

With no shortage of world-class waters in the region, including the Missouri and Sun Rivers, there are endless opportunities to wet a line in and around Great Falls. Among the fish in local waters are northern pike, walleye, perch, catfish, large- and smallmouth bass, plus the venerable trout. For trout fishing on the Missouri, the 30-mi (48-km) stretch of river running from **Holter Dam to Cascade** is the most productive (and the most heavily fished!) for both rainbows and browns. Average size for rainbows is 14-18 in (36-46 cm), and browns are generally a bit bigger. Blue-winged olive hatches start in late April and often last through June, and then hit again in the fall. The river's biggest hatch, the pale morning dun, can happen anytime from June well into August and gives skilled anglers a thrilling chance to catch very big fish on very small flies. Fish in these parts see a lot of flies and thus are wary of clumsy anglers.

North 40 Outfitters

1000 3rd St. NW, 406/453-0200; and 4400 10th Ave. S., 406/761-7441; www.north40.com; 7am-7pm Mon.-Sat., 9am-5pm Sun.

North 40 Outfitters is one of the West's best all-around ranch supply stores, selling everything from baby chicks and barbed wire to snakeskin cowboy boots, and also has a well-respected fly-fishing shop (only at their 3rd St. location on the west side of town) staffed by passionate local anglers.

Blackfeet Outfitters

Edkins St., East Glacier; 406/450-8420; www.blackfeetoutfitters.com; $575 for up to 2 people

A member of the Blackfeet tribe, Alger Swingley, owner of Blackfeet Outfitters, offers phenomenal guided fishing adventures on the Missouri and on alpine lakes in the Badger Two Medicine area south of Glacier National Park. Each trip is custom planned, and all gear can be provided. Alger also guides visitors on **day hikes** ($325), **day horseback trips** ($475 pp, must be over 12), **backcountry pack trips,** and **hunting** expeditions (prices vary by trip) for everything from upland birds to elk, deer, moose, bighorn sheep, and mountain goats. Certified interpretive guides will teach you the Native names of mountains and valleys, and about flora, fauna, and the relationship between the Blackfeet tribe and the Badger Two Medicine area. Tipis, bedding, fishing gear, and hearty meals are provided. Premium combination trips are available, too.

River's Edge Trail

The River's Edge Trail is the envy of nearly every town in Montana. With nearly 60 mi (97 km) of trail, some 20 mi (32 km) of which are paved for wheelchair access, the River's Edge Trail accommodates single-track and double-track mountain biking on 19 mi (31 km) of dirt, as well as walkers on graveled paths. Started in the 1990s, the trail winds along both sides of the Missouri River and past five waterfalls, including Black Eagle Falls, Rainbow Falls, Crooked Falls, and the renowned Great Falls of the Missouri below Ryan Dam.

Electric City Water Park

100 River Dr. S.; 406/454-9008; www.greatfallsmt.net; noon-6pm daily; $10

The Electric City Water Park, on the River's Edge Trail, is a favorite with kids and includes surfing features, giant slides, a lazy river, and a toddler-friendly water-play structure. The facility boasts the largest heated outdoor swimming pool in the state, **Mitchell Pool,** and concessions are available on-site.

Entertainment and Events

Nightlife

Sip-N-Dip Lounge

17 17th St. S.; 406/454-2141 or 800/332-9819; www.ohairemotorinn.com; 11am-12:30am Mon.-Thurs., 11am-2am Fri.-Sat., 11am-11pm Sun.

An authentic and unforgettable tiki bar in the heart of cowboy country, the Sip-N-Dip Lounge is housed in the O'Haire Motor Inn. You can sip exotic cocktails as you gaze out the glass window into the pool behind the bar, watch exhibitionist guests, or, most evenings depending on the season, see mermaid- and (occasionally) merman-costumed performers (check Facebook or Instagram for current schedule). Daryl Hannah, the quintessential mermaid, has even taken a dip here.

Montana Cowboys Association Museum & Bar

311 3rd St. NW; 406/453-0651; www.cowboysbarmca.com; 8am-2am daily

A one-in-a-million bar in Great Falls is the Montana Cowboys Association Museum & Bar. Whether this is a bar in a museum or a museum in a bar is open to debate, but either way there is no shortage of cool old stuff to look at while you sip something frosty. An authentic log cabin built in 1941, it boasts two fireplaces and hundreds of artifacts from the Old West, including a sizable gun collection, Charlie Russell's well-worn boots, a rare photo of Jeremiah "Liver-Eating" Johnson, and a handsome collection of saddles. An evening spent bellied up to the bar is bound to be unforgettable. Bring some friends; the bar closes earlier when the number of guests drops below five.

Festivals and Events

Western Art Week

Event venues vary; 406/761-5036; www.visitgreatfallsmontana.org; mid-Mar.

With major art-related events held across Great Falls in mid-March, around Charlie Russell's March 19 birthday, Western Art Week puts Great Falls on the map of top destinations for serious Western art collectors. Including **The Russell, Best of the West Art Show,** and **March in Montana,** there are several major auctions, exhibitions and sales of fine art and cowboy and Native American collectibles. Considered *the* social event of the year for lovers of Western art, the celebration takes over several hotels, where artists and art dealers set up mini galleries and provide a rare opportunity for collectors to mingle with the artists they collect. Lectures, tours, artist demonstrations, parties, and a quick-draw event are scheduled throughout the week.

Lewis and Clark Festival

Event venues vary, many held at Gibson Park on the River's Edge Trail; 406/899-7993; www.lewisandclarkfoundation.org; late June; free

Since 1989, Great Falls has been celebrating the Corps of Discovery's 1806 month-long stay in the city. The Lewis and Clark Festival takes place each year in late June. For a full weekend, history comes alive in various locations around the city. Highlighting events from Lewis and Clark's experience in Great Falls, the festival is as much about education as it is about fun. There are children's activities such as a discovery camp and storytelling, float trips, tours of Lewis and Clark sites, and presentations by Native American groups. Actors help re-create daily life from this period with dramatic readings and plays, and other

The History of Buffalo Jumps

Used by Native Americans for more than 5,000 years, buffalo jumps are typically rocky cliff formations that entire herds of bison were driven over. Throughout Montana, the jumps have become significant archaeological sites.

Using rock cairns, hunters carefully constructed drive lines to form an ever-narrowing pathway from the base of the jump up the gradual slope to the cliff's edge. Several warriors dressed in animal hides and interspersed among the herd would, at a specific moment, throw off their hides to startle the bison into a stampede toward the jump. Hundreds of bison could go over the cliff's edge in one event, providing a substantial harvest for the hunters.

First Peoples Buffalo Jump State Park

The animals were processed on-site, a painstaking process since every piece of the animal was used for meat, clothing, shelter, tools, and even toys. Archaeologists have uncovered significant prehistoric camps at the base of many jumps. Such sites were used by a variety of Native American tribes until the 19th century, when the Spanish brought horses to North America and Indians began hunting on horseback.

Where to See Them

- **First Peoples Buffalo Jump** (page 167): Thought to be used for 1,000 years prior to Lewis and Clark's visit through the region, this mile-long sandstone cliff is considered among the largest buffalo jump sites in the country. Visitors can guide themselves to see remnants of drive lines where hunters herded the animals to their deaths.
- **Madison Buffalo Jump State Park** (page 276): Though there are no tours available at this state park, a small interpretive pavilion guides visitors to their own exploration of the site. It's an ideal walking spot, both to the top of the jump and across the draw where remnants of tipi rings and eagle-catching pits can be seen.
- **Wahkpa Chu'gn** (1753 US 2, Havre, MT; 406/265-4000; $15): Located unfortunately behind the Holiday Village Mall in Havre, this 2,000-year-old site was used by peoples of the Besant, Avonlea, and Old Women's/Saddle Butte nations. Guided 1-hour tours show visitors a wooden bison corral, stone boiling and roasting pits, and areas where the layers of bones are up to 20 ft (6 m) deep.
- **Vore Buffalo Jump** (369 Old US 14, Sundance, WY; www.vorebuffalojump.org; tours $12): Located just off I-90 between Mount Rushmore and Devil's Tower in northeast Wyoming, the Vore Buffalo Jump is a 40-ft-deep (12-m-deep) sinkhole rather than a cliff. Only 10 percent of the site has been excavated, but tours are offered in summer, and the site is being developed as an archeological research center to study the remains of an estimated 20,000 bison and the human tools used to process the animals.

attractions include a traditional arts and crafts show, concerts, food, nature outings, and exhibits.

Montana State Fair

Montana ExpoPark, 400 3rd St. NW; 406/727-8900; www.goexpopark.com; July-Aug.; general admission $9

The Montana State Fair takes place in Great Falls at the end of July into August. It is one of Montana's largest parties and a true celebration of the state's unique history and culture. It includes a five-day rodeo (the largest in the state), horse racing, carnival rides, and big-name entertainment at the Montana ExpoPark. There are more than 250 vendor booths selling arts, crafts, clothes, music, and plenty of food as well as local, national, and international exhibits.

Great Falls Original Farmers' Market

Civic Center Park, 2 Park Dr. S.; www.farmersmarketgf.com; 8:30am-1pm Sat. June-Sept.

During summer, wander over to the Great Falls Original Farmers' Market, which was started in 1982 by some of the local Hutterite colonists. Claiming to be the largest farmers market in the state, more than 150 vendors gather to sell their goods, and you'll find the best home-grown fruits and vegetables, delicious jams, tasty baked goods, and handmade gifts and crafts. Pony rides are available for the little ones, and musicians wander among the stalls to keep you entertained. On Thursday nights, the Farmers' Market is held at the Scheels Aim High Big Sky Aquatic and Recreation Center (900 29th St. S.; 6pm-8pm Thurs. mid-July-late Aug.).

Shopping

Unique specialty stores line either side of Central Avenue in downtown Great Falls. You can start at the beginning of Central Avenue at Park Drive and stroll down the avenue.

Planet Earth

116 Central Ave.; 406/761-7000; 10am-5pm Tues.-Sat.

The fun and funky Planet Earth is full of eclectic gifts. Browse the assortment of cards, accessories, and jewelry. It also has a fragrance bar where you can create your own scent from essential oils and add it to specific bath or skin-care products.

The Farmer's Daughter Fibers

320 Central Ave.; 406/890-8809; www.thefarmersdaughterfibers.com; 9am-3pm Mon., 11am-5pm Tues., 10am-6:30pm Wed.,10am-5pm Thurs.-Fri., 10am-3pm Sat.

The Farmer's Daughter Fibers is a gorgeous yarn store and space for makers that will delight even those who don't know how to knit—yet! There are classes and workshops, and the owners started a nonprofit called Sisters United that aims to empower Indigenous women and girls.

Montana Mosaic

800 10th Ave. S., Ste. 2.; 406/761-3226; 9am-6pm Tues.-Sat., 11am-4pm Sun., 10am-5pm Mon.

Montana Mosaic is an art gallery and gift shop with a great selection of Montana-made gifts, keepsakes, and works in various media by more than 100 local artists.

Food

Great Harvest Bread Company

515 1st Ave. N.; 406/452-6941; www.greatharvestgreatfalls.com; 6am-5pm Mon.-Fri., 6am-3pm Sat.; $6-12

Another Montana success story, Great Harvest Bread Company is a national chain that started in Great Falls in 1976. Its motto starts, "Be loose and have fun," and the food follows suit with inventive offerings that change daily and range from molasses whole wheat to white chocolate cherry bread and the more savory Asiago sun-dried tomato sourdough bread. The menu revolves around freshly baked bread and is filled with delicious hot and cold breakfast and lunch options.

And the cinnamon rolls, muffins, and "toe-curling brownies" will leave you begging for mercy.

Roadhouse Diner

613 15th St. N.; 406/788-8839; www.roadhousegf.com; 11am-7pm Wed.-Sat.; $14-19

Roadhouse Diner is the real deal when it comes to burgers and fries. It has inventive, and strangely delicious, options like the Bacon Mac-N-Cheeseburger and PB&J Burger—which pairs bacon, cheddar, peanut butter, and grape jelly—but the basics are plenty good. A true mom-and-pop outfit, the Roadhouse gets as much of its ingredients as possible locally and makes most everything from scratch. It's no wonder they win best burger in just about every contest they enter.

Mighty Mo Brewing Company

412 Central Ave.; 406/952-0342; www.mightymobrewing.com; 11am-10pm Sun.-Thurs., 11am-11pm Fri.-Sat.; $11-26

Housed in a beautifully refurbished historical building, Mighty Mo Brewing Company serves microbrews with wings, pizza, nachos, breadsticks, pretzels, and the like. On Monday nights, 5pm-8pm, Mighty Mo donates $1 from every pint they sell to the featured nonprofit of the night.

Howard's Pizza

713 1st Ave. N.; 406/453-1212; www.howardspizzamt.com; 4pm-midnight daily; $14-26

One of Great Falls' most well-known restaurants is a local pizza joint, Howard's Pizza, started in 1959. Much beloved for its signature thin crust, famous sauce, and homemade ranch dressing, Howard's now has four locations citywide (4300 3rd Ave. S., 900 8th Ave. NW, and 750 6th St. SW) for dining in, takeout, or delivery.

The Kitchen at Wild Hare

518 Central Ave.; 406/770-0784; 11am-9pm Mon.-Fri., 10am-9pm Sat.; $15-27

This farm-to-table gem focuses on big flavors and local ingredients, with specialties including Philly cheesesteak tortellini and banh mi chicken, plus a good selection of flatbreads, burgers, and salads. The restaurant is part of a sports bar complex in a cool 1914 building.

Enbär

8 5th St. S.; 406/952-1520; 4pm-11pm Sun.-Thurs., 4pm-midnight Fri.-Sat.; $9-32

For small plates and craft cocktails, Enbär is the place. From the Juniper, with Montgomery Distillery gin, fresh blueberries, and house-made mint simple syrup and lime juice, to the Spotted Apple with Spotted Bear tequila, apple cider, lime, and huckleberry, their concoctions are elegant to say the least. They also serve steak, fish tacos, pasta, salmon, and a delicious assortment of tapas. Don't miss the double-fried Enbär fries with truffle and parmesan.

Crooked Tree Coffee and Cakes

501 1st Ave. N.; 406/315-1221; www.crookedtreecoffeeandcakes; 7am-4pm Mon.-Fri., 8am-2pm Sat.-Sun.; $4-10

The homey and gorgeous Crooked Tree Coffee and Cakes was started by two sisters who love coffee and all that goes with it, including simple breakfast sandwiches, soup, and an incredible assortment of beautiful treats.

Accommodations

★ O'Haire Motor Inn

17 7th St. S.; 406/454-2141; $130-175

If you are looking for a memorable motel stay in downtown Great Falls, look no further than the O'Haire Motor Inn, with 68 pet-friendly guest rooms, an indoor pool, indoor parking, and free Wi-Fi.

Its full-service restaurant, **Clark and Lewie's** (7am-9pm Mon.-Thurs., 7am-10pm Fri.-Sat., 7am-8pm Sun.; $12-25), offers up hearty meals—from burgers and barbecue to steak, Mexican, sandwiches, and pasta—and even room service. The biggest draw at the inn is its authentic and unforgettable tiki bar, the **Sip-N-Dip Lounge.**

★ Hotel Arvon

118 1st Ave. S.; 406/952-1101; www.hotelarvon.com; $155-170

The upscale Hotel Arvon is a 33-room boutique hotel with a coffee shop, wine bar, restaurant, and pub in the city's oldest commercial building. There are standard king and queen rooms, plus suites, gorgeous lofts, and even cooking suites.

Information and Services

Visitor Information

Most services are conveniently located in a walkable downtown area. The **Great Falls Chamber of Commerce** (9 3rd St. N., Ste. 101; 406/761-4434; www.greatfallschamber.org; 8am-5pm Mon.-Fri.) and **Great Falls Visitor Information Center** (15 Overlook Dr.; 406/761-4436; www.visitgreatfallsmontana.org; 9am-4pm Mon.-Fri., 10am-2pm Sat.-Sun. Oct.-Apr., 9am-6pm Mon.-Fri., 10am-4pm Sat.-Sun. May-Sept.), under the huge American flag in Overlook Park, both have city brochures, books, Made in Montana goods for sale, and friendly, knowledgeable volunteers.

Emergency Services

Benefis Health Systems (1102 26th St. S.; 406/455-5000; www.benefis.org) is a first-class hospital with a 24-hour emergency room as well as a **walk-in clinic** (1401 25th St. S.; 406/731-8300; 7am-8pm Mon.-Fri., 9am-6:30pm Sat.-Sun.) for immediate medical care.

Browning

Agency headquarters for the Blackfeet Indian Reservation, home to Montana's largest tribe, Browning (pop. 1,005, elev. 4,377 ft/1,334 m) has retained much of the culture of the Blackfeet people. The setting is spectacular, at the eastern edge of Glacier National Park, but the town doesn't offer anything in the way of striking architecture or high-end hotels. What it does offer, though, is an exceptional opportunity to learn about and experience Blackfeet culture. In addition to the significant Museum of the Plains Indian, there are annual events open to visitors, including North American Indian Days, as well as tours given by well-versed local guides.

Getting to Browning

From **Great Falls,** Browning is 126 mi (203 km) northwest on I-15 and US 89, a little less than a 2-hour drive. From Glacier National Park's eastern entrance at **St. Mary,** Browning is 30 mi (48 km) south on US 89, a 45-minute drive.

Sights

★ Blackfeet Tours

406/450-8420; www.blackfeettours.com; interpretive guide for 4 hours from $325

Owned by Blackfeet tribe member Alger Swingley, Blackfeet Tours offers authentic all-inclusive Native American culture tours—seeing the country around the reservation, learning the Native names for mountains and valleys, plus exploring flora and fauna—in a variety of ways. You could take a horseback tour ($475 pp), hike the Badger Two Medicine area with a certified interpretive guide ($325 pp), or do a 4-hour sightseeing tour on the reservation in a Jeep ($425 pp). Multiday backpacking and horseback trips are also possible.

Blackfeet Outfitters

222 Edkins St., East Glacier; 406/450-8420; www.blackfeetoutfitters.com

The sister company of Blackfeet Tours, also owned by Swingley, Blackfeet Outfitters offers **guided fishing** ($575 for up to 2 people) adventures on the Missouri and on a number of alpine lakes in the Badger Two Medicine area south of Glacier National Park. **Hunting** expeditions ($625-7,000) for everything from upland birds to elk and deer are also offered.

Powwow Etiquette

Attending a powwow on one of eight Indian reservations in Montana and Wyoming offers an extraordinary opportunity to learn about and appreciate Native culture and traditions. While most powwows are open to any visitors and spectators, there are some things to know to be properly respectful of the people and events.

- Tipis and wall tents are often used to house powwow participants and are referred to locally as "campgrounds." Calling a powwow a "fair" or the campground "fairgrounds" can be insulting.
- Many powwows have an "intertribal dance" where everyone can mingle and greet one another. The dancers wear regalia or traditional dress, not costumes. These clothes are painstakingly handmade using the finest materials and detail, and are often passed down through the generations.
- When the honor songs are being performed—such as the flag song during grand entry—men and women should stand and pay their respects to the flag as they would at any event in the United States or Canada, by removing their hats (except for the very elderly) and not talking. Photos should not be taken during honor or prayer songs.
- Dancing contests are meant to be healthy, fun, and inspiring. Visitors should enjoy the celebration; when in doubt, look around to see what other spectators are doing. When you see people standing or removing their hats, follow their lead.

Museum of the Plains Indian

19 Museum Loop; 406/338-2230; www.doi.gov; 9am-4:45pm Tues.-Sat. June-Sept., 10am-4pm Tues.-Fri. Oct.-May; $6

Just west of Browning at the junction of US 2 and US 89 is the Museum of the Plains Indian. The museum exhibits the arts and crafts of the Northern Plains Indians. The permanent collection highlights the diversity of tribal arts and displays artifacts from everyday life, including clothing, weapons, toys, and household implements. Two galleries are dedicated to showcasing contemporary Native American artists. During summer, painted tipis are assembled on the grounds.

Entertainment and Events

North American Indian Days

406/338-7521; Facebook @NDNDAYS; July

Held annually the second week in July for four days, North American Indian Days is an excellent powwow and signature celebration in Browning, giving insight into the Blackfeet culture and traditions. Events include contest dancing, games, sporting events, horse relay races, and drum contests, and there's plenty of food.

Heart Butte Indian Days

406/338-7521; Facebook @HBNDNDays; Aug.

Set in the shadow of Heart Butte, known among Blackfeet as Moskitsipahpi-istuki, Heart Butte Indian Days is held in one of the oldest traditional communities on the Blackfeet Indian Reservation. It's a four-day celebration, usually held in the middle of August, and features dancing and drumming contests, stick-game tournaments, parades, vendors, and plenty of food.

Food

Glacier Grind Coffee House

Inside Glacier Peaks Hotel & Casino, 46 Museum Loop; 406/338-4678; www.glacierpeakscasino.com; 7am-10pm Mon.-Fri., 8am-10pm Sat.-Sun.

For great coffee and quick bites, try Glacier Grind Coffee House.

Nation's Burger Station

205 Central Ave.; 406/338-2422; www.nationsburgerstation.com; 10:30am-9:30pm Mon.-Fri., 10:30am-10:30pm Sat.-Sun. May-mid-Aug., 11am-8pm Mon.-Thurs., 11am-9pm Fri. mid-Aug.-Apr.; $7-17

Serving everything from burgers to Indian tacos is Nation's Burger Station. They also serve salads and wraps, plus an impressive menu of frozen treats including root beer floats, slushies, and snow cones. On a hot day, this is the place.

Jackpot Restaurant

46 Museum Loop; 406/338-2274; www.glacierpeakscasino.com; 11am-10pm daily; $9-17

Also inside the Glacier Peaks Hotel & Casino, the Jackpot Restaurant serves three meals a day, including soups and salads, burgers, sandwiches, chicken-fried steak, Indian tacos, and more.

★ Summit Mountain Lodge Steakhouse

16900 US 2; 406/226-9319; www.summitmtnlodge.com; 5pm-9pm Tues.-Sun.; $19-38

Twenty-four mi (39 km) southwest of Browning, and getting rave reviews from locals and tourists alike, is Summit Mountain Lodge Steakhouse, housed in an old train station with a beautiful outside dining area. The food is marvelous and locally sourced whenever possible. There is a good wine list, and entrées include saltimbocca, grilled beef tenderloin, wild prawns piccata, and a variety of salads and pasta. You could eat dirt on a summer night, with a view like this, and be happy. But luckily, you don't have to.

Accommodations

Glacier Peaks Hotel & Casino

50 Museum Loop; 406/338-2400; www.glacierpeakscasino.com; $145-350

By far the largest and newest hotel in Browning is the Glacier Peaks Hotel & Casino, which has comfortable, well-appointed nonsmoking rooms with mini fridges, flat-screen TVs, microwaves, and free high-speed internet. Amenities include a complimentary hot breakfast buffet, a fitness area, a heated indoor pool, and a guest laundry area.

Summit Mountain Lodge

16900 US 2; 406/226-9319; www.summitmtnlodge.com; from $169

A few miles from town is Summit Mountain Lodge, which offers eight cabins with modern amenities. Single cabins (from $249) have one queen bed and a full kitchenette. Double units (from $199) have two queens and a living area. Family cabins (from $545) sleep six, eight, and ten. The setting and the views are world-class, and the on-site steakhouse, in an old train station, is a special place for a memorable meal.

Information

The **Blackfeet Country Visitor Information** (intersection of US 2 and US 89, Browning; 406/338-7406; www.blackfeetnation.com; 8am-4:30pm Mon.-Fri.) can offer local advice.

Getting to Glacier National Park

The drive from Browning to Glacier's east entrance at St. Mary is short, but scenic. Just 30 mi (48 km) west on Starr School Road and north on US 89, the drive takes just over half an hour. Even as you drive the open country and rolling hills, the relief of Glacier's jagged peaks is always in view, reminding you that you're pointed someplace beautiful, someplace wild. At this point, you'll want to get into the park, and the spectacular blue-green of St. Mary Lake is a wonderful place to do just that.

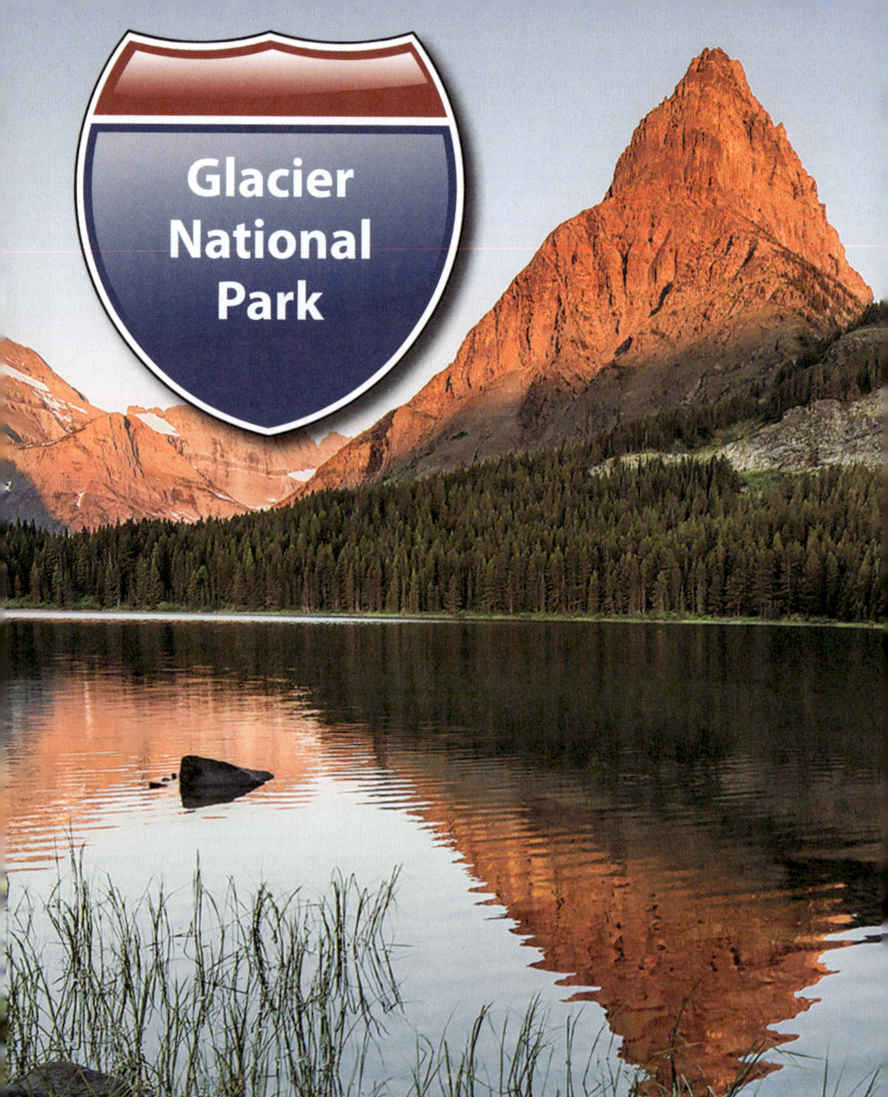
Glacier
National
Park

Highlights

★ **Many Glacier:** Prime hiking, boating, and horseback-riding country, this stunning area in the northeast section of the park is popular but can be less crowded than other parts (page 190).

★ **Grinnell Glacier:** Current data suggest that the glaciers in the park could disappear entirely by the end of the century, which means seeing Grinnell Glacier may be a once-in-a-lifetime opportunity. The ranger-led hike is especially worthwhile (pages 190 and 197).

★ **Going-to-the-Sun Road:** Stretching just over 50 mi (81 km), this phenomenal feat of engineering gives viewers an extraordinary overview of Glacier. Don't forget your reservations! (page 192).

★ **Lake McDonald:** The largest lake in the park and arguably one of the most beautiful, glacially carved Lake McDonald is easy to access. Pack a picnic for the rocky beach or cruise the waters on a boat tour (page 193).

★ **Hiking the Highline Trail to Granite Park Chalet:** Among the best-loved trails in the park is the Highline, which climbs to the historic Granite Park Chalet and then drops back to Going-to-the-Sun Road. The views are staggering, but the hike is not for the faint of heart (page 200).

★ **Skiing at Whitefish Mountain Resort:** This phenomenal ski area has a view over Whitefish Lake, the most haunting trees anywhere, and perhaps the best après-ski scene in the state (page 217).

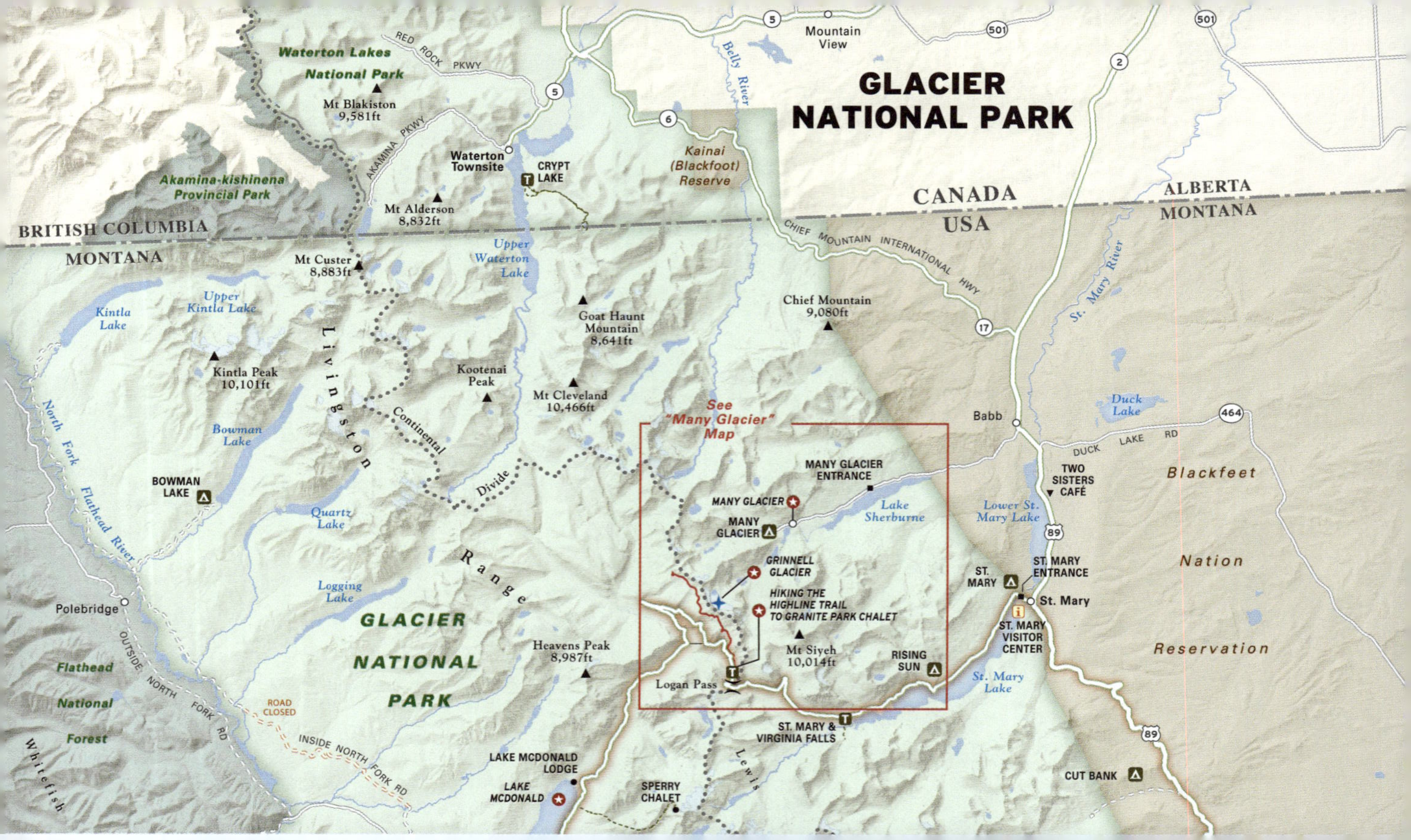
GLACIER NATIONAL PARK
CANADA
USA
ALBERTA
MONTANA
BRITISH COLUMBIA
MONTANA
Waterton Lakes National Park
Akamina-kishinena Provincial Park
Kainai (Blackfoot) Reserve
Mountain View
Belly River
RED ROCK PKWY
AKAMINA PKWY
Mt Blakiston 9,581ft
Waterton Townsite
CRYPT LAKE
Mt Alderson 8,832ft
Upper Waterton Lake
Mt Custer 8,883ft
Kintla Lake
Upper Kintla Lake
Kintla Peak 10,101ft
Livingston
Range
Continental
Divide
Goat Haunt Mountain 8,641ft
Kootenai Peak
Mt Cleveland 10,466ft
Chief Mountain 9,080ft
CHIEF MOUNTAIN INTERNATIONAL HWY
St. Mary River
Duck Lake
Babb
DUCK LAKE RD
Blackfeet
Nation
Reservation
TWO SISTERS CAFÉ
See "Many Glacier" Map
MANY GLACIER ENTRANCE
Lake Sherburne
MANY GLACIER
MANY GLACIER
Lower St. Mary Lake
ST. MARY
ST. MARY ENTRANCE
St. Mary
ST. MARY VISITOR CENTER
GRINNELL GLACIER
HIKING THE HIGHLINE TRAIL TO GRANITE PARK CHALET
Mt Siyeh 10,014ft
RISING SUN
St. Mary Lake
Logan Pass
ST. MARY & VIRGINIA FALLS
North Fork Flathead River
BOWMAN LAKE
Bowman Lake
Quartz Lake
Logging Lake
Polebridge
GLACIER NATIONAL PARK
Heavens Peak 8,987ft
Flathead National Forest
OUTSIDE NORTH FORK RD
ROAD CLOSED
INSIDE NORTH FORK RD
Whitefish
LAKE MCDONALD LODGE
LAKE MCDONALD
SPERRY CHALET
Lewis
CUT BANK
5
501
2
6
17
464
89

Kiowa
Triple Divide Peak 8,020ft
Stimson Peak 10,142ft
Range
ROCKY POINT
FISH CREEK
CAMAS RD
GOING-TO-THE-SUN ROAD
Apgar
APGAR VISITOR CENTER
West Glacier
BELTON CHALET
SKIING AT WHITEFISH MOUNTAIN RESORT
WHITEFISH MOUNTAIN
DANNY ON TRAIL NATIONAL SCENIC TRAIL
Range
Running Eagle Falls
TWO MEDICINE
Lower Two Medicine Lake
Two Medicine Lake
No Name Lake
Two Medicine Valley
TWO MEDICINE ENTRANCE
East Glacier
GLACIER PARK LODGE
Middle Fork
Flathead River
See "Whitefish" Map
Whitefish Lake
Whitefish
Coram
Hungry Horse
Columbia Falls
Whitefish River
Flathead River
Great Bear Wilderness
Flathead Range
Hungry Horse Reservoir
Flathead National Forest
Essex
IZAAK WALTON INN
Elk Mountain 7,835ft
Marias Pass
Helena-Lewis and Clark National Forest
Bob Marshall Wilderness Complex
See "Kalispell" Map
Kalispell
Somers
Flathead Lake
Swan Range
Road Trip Route
0
5 mi
0
5 km
2
49
40
206
35
93
83

Two Days in Glacier National Park

Day 1

Enter Glacier on the west side after fueling up with an early breakfast and a killer piece of pie at **Loula's Café** in Whitefish.

Stop at **Lake McDonald** to soak in the glorious views and even take a morning dip. Indulge in a huckleberry elk burger in the **Russell's Fireside Dining Room** at the historic **Lake McDonald Lodge.**

After a leisurely lunch, enjoy the scenery as you climb the **Going-to-the-Sun Road** and stop at the Logan Pass Visitor Center, behind which you'll find the **Hidden Lake Overlook** trailhead. Often covered with snow until late June or even July and frequented by both mountain goats and bighorn sheep, the trail climbs through wildflower meadows and beneath rocky peaks to the shores of Hidden Lake. Anglers can cast a line before heading back up the trail to the visitor center.

With tired legs, make your way down the east side of the Going-to-the-Sun Road and through St. Mary and Babb before heading back into the park for a cozy room and delicious meal at the **Many Glacier Hotel.**

Day 2

Plan to spend the day adventuring around **Many Glacier,** where canoeing, kayaking, and hiking are all options. You could combine a scenic cruise across both **Swiftcurrent Lake** and **Lake Josephine** with a short hike up to the famed Grinnell Glacier, or hike the longer version with a ranger departing from the Many Glacier dock. Be sure to bring a lunch, plenty of water, foul-weather gear, and bear spray.

From here you'll head back out of the park and fill up on roasted Mexican chicken or chili burgers or nachos at the fun **Two Sisters Café** in Babb, before traveling on to your next stop.

Known as the "Crown of the Continent," Glacier National Park is one of the largest intact ecosystems in the Lower 48, an amalgam of stunning landscapes that, for many visitors, defines the entire state of Montana.

The beauty of Glacier is rugged, raw, and dynamic. The mountains thrust skyward, and the gravity-defying roads are ribbons that snake toward the summits. The legendary Going-to-the-Sun Road is one of the West's most impressive engineering feats and one of the best scenic drives in the country. There are still 25 "active" glaciers (at least 25 acres/10 ha in area) to be found within the park, along with countless waterfalls and hundreds of crystalline lakes. In summer the landscape is heavy with huckleberries and dotted with fuzzy white bear grass. While wildlife-viewing from the road can be challenging in this mountainous terrain, the animals—grizzly and black bears, mountain goats, bighorn sheep, wolves, and more—are here in abundance. With 1,583 sq mi (4,100 sq km) of alpine majesty, the scenery, if not the altitude, will leave you breathless.

Glacier National Park is a haven for nature lovers, and visitors can enjoy the natural beauty in a number of ways—hiking, bicycling, boating, and cross-country skiing, to name a few. There are 746 mi (1,200 km) of trails throughout the park and a smattering of historic lodges and chalets for cozy accommodations. Yet despite its extensive offerings, Glacier still provides visitors a rare and precious sense of solitude. The crowds are gone as soon as your feet hit the trail, and there are miles of shoreline where the only other picnickers are four-legged. More than just the Crown of the Continent, Glacier is like no place on earth.

Getting to Glacier National Park

Driving from Yellowstone

St. Mary: 375-380 mi (605-610 km); 6-6.5 hours

The fastest route between the north entrance of Yellowstone at **Gardiner** and Glacier's east entrance at St. Mary is 380 mi (610 km) via US 89 through Livingston and Great Falls, about a 6.5-hour drive.

Just a few miles and minutes shorter, the northward route via US 287 and US 89 is 375 mi (605 km) and will take just over 6 hours, traveling along the Rocky Mountain Front through Bozeman, Helena, and Choteau.

West Glacier: 390-420 mi (630-675 km); 7-7.5 hours

From Gardiner to West Glacier, via I-90 West and US 93 North, the drive is roughly 420 mi (675 km) and will take approximately 7.5 hours without stops. This drive takes you through Bozeman, Missoula, and Kalispell.

The route from West Yellowstone to West Glacier, north through the Seeley-Swan Valley on MT-83, is 390 mi (630 km) and will take roughly 7 hours. This drive takes you through Big Sky, Bozeman, Helena, and Seeley Lake.

Driving from Great Falls

155 mi (250 km); 2.5 hours

From Great Falls, the east entrance of Glacier National Park at St. Mary is 155 mi (250 km) north on I-15 and US 89, just over a 2.5-hour drive.

Driving from Kalispell and Missoula

35-140 mi (56-225 km); 1-2.5 hours

From Kalispell, the west entrance of Glacier National Park is 35 mi (56 km) northeast on US 2, just under an hour's drive.

From Missoula, the shortest route to the park is 140 mi (225 km) north on US 93 and MT-35 to West Glacier and will take a little over 2.5 hours. Longer routes through the Seeley-Swan Valley via MT-83 (165 mi/265 km) or along the west side of Flathead Lake via MT-200 and MT-28 (175 mi/280 km) will take roughly 3 hours.

Driving from Calgary

180 mi (290 km); 3 hours

From Calgary, Alberta, the east entrance of Glacier National Park at St. Mary is 180 mi (290 km) south on AB-2, and takes roughly 3 hours without time allotted for crossing the border at Carway.

Air

The closest airport to Glacier is 30 mi (48 km) away in Kalispell. The **Glacier Park International Airport** (FCA; www.iflyglacier.com) is served by Delta, Alaska Airlines, American, and United. Seasonal and twice- or three-times-weekly flights can be found on Sun Country, Jet Blue, Frontier, and Allegiant. At the airport, **Avis, Budget, Hertz,** and **National/Alamo** have car-rental counters, and **Dollar, Thrifty,** and **Enterprise** have car-rental lots off-site but near the airport. Taxi and shuttle service is available from **Airport Shuttle Express** (403/509-4799; www.airportshuttleexpress.com), **Arrow Shuttle** (406/300-2301; www.arrowshuttletaxi.com), and **Mountain Shuttle** (406/493-2345; www.mountainshuttlemt.com).

Great Falls International Airport (GTF) is 130-165 mi (209-265 km) southeast of the park entrances at St. Mary, Two Medicine, and Many Glacier.

Missoula Montana Airport (MSO) is roughly 138 mi (222 km) south of the park entrance at West Glacier.

Calgary International Airport (YYC) is approximately 187 mi (301 km) north of the entrance at St. Mary and should take just over 3 hours to reach by car. Among the car-rental companies at the airport are **Avis, Budget, Hertz, Dollar, Thrifty, Enterprise, National,** and **Alamo.**

Best Restaurants

★ **Park Café, St. Mary:** An institution since 1952, this spot is known for breakfasts that'll stick to your ribs, hearty burgers and sandwiches, and excellent homemade pies (page 209).

★ **Two Sisters Café, Babb:** On a fairly lonesome highway, this unexpected restaurant boasts delicious handmade meals—from bison steaks to huckleberry pie—and a festive atmosphere (page 210).

★ **Belton Dining Room, West Glacier:** Set in a beautifully appointed 1910 railroad chalet, this upscale place serves innovative and gourmet cuisine including Montana Wagyu beef, lamb linguini, and wild salmon (page 210).

★ **Loula's Café, Whitefish:** Serving three meals a day, Loula's offers family-friendly comfort food—like chicken potpie and country-fried steak—using fresh local ingredients. But the pie is the thing here (page 220).

Train

Amtrak runs the **Empire Builder** from Chicago to Seattle, with daily stops in both directions in East Glacier (summer only), Essex, and West Glacier.

Visiting Glacier National Park

Planning Your Time

Depending on the amount of time you have to spend in Montana, Glacier National Park could easily absorb all of it, but often it is a spectacular route to get from one side of the Continental Divide to the other, in which case some sights take priority.

The 50-mi (80-km) **Going-to-the-Sun Road,** which now requires an advance reservation through www.recreation.gov, is one of the most scenic drives you will ever take and the best way to get an overview of the park if your time is limited. The alpine vistas provide a marvelous sense of the geography, and the park's history comes alive for those who stop to notice the architecture of the road itself. The drive will likely take at least 2 hours, not accounting for construction, traffic, or weather-related delays, but if time permits even just an extra hour, there are plenty of turnouts and hiking opportunities (if you can find parking) along the way. **Hidden Lake Overlook** is a wonderful 2.7-mi (4.3-km) round-trip hike from the **Logan Pass Visitor Center** that provides opportunities to view seasonal wildflowers and wildlife. Any time in Glacier's backcountry will be time well spent, but visitors should be prepared for changes in the weather (dress in layers and bring water) and wildlife encounters.

With more than a day, visitors can see some of the park's idyllic corners. **Many Glacier** is a launching spot for day hikes to numerous alpine lakes and glaciers. **Lake McDonald,** the park's largest, is a favorite place to spend the day. The southern section of the park, accessed from US 2, is especially popular in winter with cross-country skiers who make tracks from the **Izaak Walton Inn** in Essex.

Planning is critical in Glacier, as accommodations within and immediately surrounding the park fill up as much as a year in advance. The 1,009 campsites throughout the park, on the other hand, are filled primarily on a first-come, first-served basis (with a few notable exceptions: Fish Creek, Sprague Creek, and St. Mary can be reserved in advance, as

Best Accommodations

★ **Glacier Park Lodge, East Glacier Area:** Opened in 1913, the Glacier Park Lodge is still the grand dame of Glacier's historic hotels. Built just outside the park, the hotel offers a variety of accommodations with excellent ambience (page 211).

★ **Granite Park Chalet, East Glacier Area:** You have to hike to get here, and unless you consider alpine views and grizzly bear sightings amenities, it's not glamourous, but a night at Granite Park is unforgettable (page 212).

★ **Many Glacier Hotel, Many Glacier:** Set on the idyllic shores of Swiftcurrent Lake, this Swiss-style chalet puts guests in the heart of the Many Glacier region with old-world accommodations and loads of activities (page 214).

★ **Belton Chalet, West Glacier:** Small and rustic, the Belton Chalet was magnificently restored in 1999 and offers charming rooms and cottages with one of the best restaurants in the area (page 215).

can half the individual and group sites at Apgar and some of the campsites at Many Glacier). Still, last-minute travelers are not necessarily out of luck. For park brochures, which can be immensely helpful in planning your trip, visit www.nps.gov/glac. For those who are willing to stay outside of the park and launch day trips, the gateway towns of Whitefish and Kalispell have many more choices for accommodations.

Entrances

The two main entrances to Glacier National Park are at either end of Going-to-the-Sun Road. **West Glacier,** on the west side of the park, can be accessed from US 2, and **St. Mary,** on the park's east side, can be accessed from US 89. Entrance stations on the west side are at **Camas Creek** and the **Polebridge Ranger Station** off Outside North Fork Road, and on the east side at **Two Medicine** off Highway 49, **Many Glacier** off US 89, and at **Waterton Lakes National Park** accessible from Alberta Provincial Highways 5 and 6. Entrance fees must be paid even when entrance stations are closed. There is a self-registration area available at the entrance stations when the stations are not staffed. Alternatively, visitors can buy passes online in advance through www.recreation.gov.

Park Fees and Passes

Entrance to **Glacier National Park** (406/888-7800; www.nps.gov/glac) costs $35 per vehicle, $30 for motorcycles, and $20 for hikers and bikers for seven days May-October. From November 1-April 30, most roads and services are closed, though generally the road is plowed from West Glacier to Lake McDonald. Entrance fees then are $25 per vehicle, $20 for motorcycles, and $15 for hikers, bikers, and skiers, and are good for seven days. An annual Glacier park pass costs $70, and an annual America the Beautiful Pass is $80 ($20 for those over 62) and permits entrance into all national parks for one year.

In an effort to deal with crowds and the problem of more cars than parking spots, Glacier has implemented a pilot **vehicle reservation program** requiring reservations for some places and roads at specific date ranges and times of day. Though specific dates vary annually, from late May until early September reservations are required for the west side of the Going-to-the-Sun Road between 6am and 3pm. From early July through

Planning a Last-Minute Trip to Glacier

Rooms in Glacier's historic lodges and chalets can already be full up to a year ahead, but spontaneous travelers are not necessarily out of luck. Last-minute cancellations and room openings are possible and well worth a couple of phone calls.

Resources

- **Glacier Park Collections by Pursuit** (844/868-7474; www.glacierparkcollection.com) is the booking service for the Glacier Park Lodge, St. Mary Village, Apgar Village Lodge & Cabins, Motel Lake McDonald, West Glacier Basecamp Lodge, West Glacier Cabins, West Glacier RV Park, Paddle Ridge, Belton Chalet, and Prince of Wales Hotel. Call and ask specifically for cancellations. You may have better luck if you are open to whatever they have to offer; being flexible with your dates helps.

- **Glacier National Park Lodges/Xanterra** (855/733-4522; www.glaciernationalparklodges.com) is the booking service for Many Glacier Hotel, Swiftcurrent Motor Inn & Cabins, Rising Sun Motor Inn & Cabins, Lake McDonald Lodge, and Village Inn at Apgar. In this case, too, a phone call to ask about cancellations can lead to a windfall.

Backcountry Chalets

- For visitors willing to hike in to their accommodations, **Granite Park Chalet** (page 212) is a fantastic option and well worth a call to see if they have last-minute openings.

- The 17 rooms in **Sperry Chalet** (page 213) burned to the ground in a 2017 wildfire, but the historic property was ambitiously rebuilt and opened in 2020. There are also a handful of workshops put on at Sperry Chalet each summer on topics including glaciers, high alpine ecology, and Glacier Park history that include two nights in the chalet. Still rustic—there is no heat, electricity, or running water—and only accessible on foot, Sperry offers beds with bedding and three informal meals with each night's stay.

Campgrounds

- For true spontaneity, pitch a tent in one of Glacier's 1,000-plus campsites in 13 campgrounds, at least some of which are open May to mid-October. Just over 160 of the park's developed campsites are available on a first-come, first-served basis, including those at Bowman Lake (48 sites; $25), Cut Bank (14 sites; $20), Kintla Lake (13 sites; $25), Quartz Creek (7 sites; $15), and Rising Sun (84 sites; $30). An excellent page on the National Park Service website (www.nps.gov/glac) shows updated availability at campsites across the park, and even gives the time of day each campground was filled the day before. To check for cancellations at any of the advance reservations campgrounds, contact the **National Park Reservation System** (877/444-6777; www.recreation.gov).

Rentals

- In the spirit of spontaneity, almost anything you need for your recreational purposes can be rented from **Glacier Outfitters** (page 205), from bear spray to camping gear.

early September reservations are required for Many Glacier from 6am to 3pm. Reservations are available online 120 days in advance starting in January at 8am (MST) on a daily rolling basis. Starting just before Memorial Day, some next-day vehicle reservations will be available starting at 7pm (MST) on a daily rolling basis. Nonrefundable vehicle reservations cost $2 and must be booked on www.recreation.gov.

Visitor Centers

At the park entrance, visitors are given a copy of *Vacation Planner,* which provides important general information about the park. Once inside the park, visitor centers are the best sources of information. Hours of operation vary, but during the summer the centers are open every day. The park's visitor centers all have knowledgeable staff, guidebooks and maps, and basic amenities.

Visitor Information Headquarters Building

64 Grinnell Dr.; 406/888-7800; 8am-4:30pm Mon.-Fri. year-round, excluding holidays

The Visitor Information Headquarters Building is just inside the West Glacier park entrance before the actual entrance station; turn right after passing the Glacier National Park sign. They can issue a variety of passes and permits as well as answer most questions.

Apgar Visitor Center

Intersection of Camas Rd. and Going-to-the-Sun Rd., 2 mi/3 km north of west entrance; 406/888-7800; open daily mid-May-mid-Oct. and on Sat.-Sun. in fall, spring, and winter as staffing permits, hours vary

Near the town of West Glacier, Apgar Visitor Center is about 2 mi (3 km) north of the west entrance.

St. Mary Visitor Center

Going-to-the-Sun Rd. at St. Mary entrance; 406/888-7800; open daily late May-early Oct., hours vary

St. Mary Visitor Center, adjacent to the St. Mary entrance on the park's east side, is Glacier's largest visitor center and offers trip planning information, the *Land of Many Journeys* film on Glacier, a bookstore, wilderness permitting, shuttle service, and various ranger-led activities.

Logan Pass Visitor Center

Going-to-the-Sun Rd., 32 mi/52 km from west entrance and 18 mi/29 km from St. Mary entrance; 406/888-7800; open daily when road conditions permit, typically early July-early Oct., hours vary

Logan Pass Visitor Center is in the center of the park at the highest point of the Going-to-the-Sun Road, 32 mi (52 km) from the west entrance and 18 mi (29 km) from the entrance at St. Mary. It is often the most crowded location in the park, and parking can be impossible.

Ranger Stations

Starting in 2024, the status of the park's 22 historic ranger stations became fluid due to staffing and plans for construction. As such, if you plan to visit a ranger station or need to get a wilderness permit, it's best to visit www.nps.gov in advance of your trip, and to ask for ranger station status when you enter the park. The park no longer publicizes the ranger stations in any way and encourages travelers to instead visit the more reliable visitor centers.

Wilderness permits can be picked up at the Apgar Wilderness Permit Center and the St. Mary Visitor Center.

Services

Lodging in Glacier is available through separate providers. **Glacier National Park Lodges** (855/733-4522 or 303/265-7010 outside the US; www.glaciernationalparklodges.com) manages Many Glacier Hotel, Swiftcurrent Motor Inn & Cabins, Rising Sun Motor Inn & Cabins, Lake McDonald Lodge, and Village Inn at Apgar. **Glacier Park Collection by Pursuit** (844/868-7474; www.glacierparkcollection.com) operates Glacier Park Lodge, St. Mary Village, Belton Chalet,

Bear Safety

Glacier has significant concentrations of both grizzly and black bears, both of which can be threatening in any encounter. The keys to safe travel in the backcountry are acting to prevent bear encounters and knowing what to do in the event you do meet a bear. The following are simple guidelines for responsible behavior in bear country:

- **Don't surprise bears.** Make noise, even on well-traveled trails, to allow bears the opportunity to get away from you. Bells can be effective, as can singing, handclapping, and loud talking. Never assume that a bear has better senses than you and will see, hear, or smell you coming.
- **Don't approach bears.** Be aware of their feeding opportunities and behavior so that you can avoid potential feeding locations and times of day. Avoid hiking through berry patches, cow parsnip thickets, or fields of glacier lilies. Never approach a carcass, which could be under the surveillance of a bear. Try not to hike at sunrise or at dusk, both active times for bears. Always keep children in close proximity.
- **Minimize the possibility that a bear would be attracted to your belongings or campsite.** Abide by all the park regulations about hanging your food and garbage away from your sleeping area. Don't carry odiferous food, and never bring anything potentially edible, including medicines and toothpaste, into your tent. Take special care with used feminine hygiene products by sealing them in several zip-top bags with baking soda to absorb the odor.
- **Be prepared for an encounter.** Carry pepper spray that is not out of date and know how to use it. Do a test spray so you can be sure the device works properly and that you know how to use it. Pay attention to wind direction. Familiarize yourself with the behaviors most likely to ensure your safety in a bear encounter.

Apgar Village Lodge & Cabins, Motel Lake McDonald, West Glacier RV Park & Cabins, West Glacier Cabin Village, and Prince of Wales Hotel. Granite Park Chalet (www.graniteparkchalet.com) and Sperry Chalet (www.sperrychalet.com) are booked and managed by **Belton Chalets, Inc.** (888/345-2649).

If you arrive and discover you are missing recreational equipment—or more important, bear spray—almost anything you need can be rented from **Glacier Outfitters** (196 Apgar Loop; 406/219-7466; www.goglacieroutfitters.com). From camping gear and backpacks to bicycles, paddleboards, kayaks, canoes, fishing rods, GoPro cameras, and, yep, bear spray, this is the place to make sure you have what you need.

Pets

Although pets are allowed in drive-in campgrounds, picnic areas, and on roads open to cars, they are required to be on a leash no longer than 6 ft (1.8 m) at all times. They are not permitted on any trails in the park, and park officials strongly discourage the presence of pets in Glacier. Because of this policy, it's nearly impossible to find pet-friendly accommodations in the area. Well-socialized pups can enjoy a ritzy stay with open-plan sleeping and tons of outdoor space at **K9 Camp & Boarding Retreat** (Hwy. 35, Kalispell; 406/755-7487; www.k9campandboardingretreat.com) or at **Glacier Bark Kennels** (636 Kelley Road, Columbia Falls; 406/314-8106; www.glacierbarkkennels.com).

Bear Encounters

If you do surprise a bear, keep your wits about you. While there is no easy or universal answer about how to react—bears are as individual and unpredictable as humans—the following are accepted behaviors outlined on Glacier's website:

- **Talk quietly and calmly.** If you have surprised a bear, don't attempt to threaten it; if possible, back away or try to detour around it. A bear standing up is not threatening you but rather trying to get more information and determine if you are a threat. Bears will often bluff charge, even a couple of times, to see if you will run. Panicking will make the situation worse.
- **Never run.** Don't turn your back; instead, back away slowly, unless it agitates the bear. Running could trigger its predator instincts.
- **Use peripheral vision.** Bears may perceive direct eye contact as aggressive behavior on your part.
- **Drop something (not food) to distract the bear and keep your pack on for protection.** If you have bear spray, grab it and be prepared to use it.
- **Protect yourself if the bear attacks.** Protect your chest and abdomen by falling to the ground on your stomach or assuming the fetal position. Cover the back of your neck with your hands, and if the bear tries to roll you over, attempt to stay on your stomach. If the attack is defensive, the bear will leave once it has determined you are not a threat. If the attack is prolonged, fight back!

Getting Around

Private Vehicles

Vehicles and vehicle combinations longer than 21 ft (6.4 m), including bumpers, wider than 8 ft (2.4 m), including mirrors, or taller than 10 ft (3m) are not permitted on Going-to-the-Sun Road between Avalanche Campground and the Rising Sun Parking Area. Stock trucks and trailers can access Packers Roost on the west side and Siyeh Bend on the east side.

Shuttles

406/892-2525; 8am-7pm daily July-Labor Day

Operating on a first-come, first-served basis, Glacier's free shuttle system picks up and drops off at 14 different stops, including Apgar Visitor Center, Avalanche Creek, Logan Pass, St. Mary Visitor Center, and several trailheads. Shuttles depart every 15-30 minutes. The shuttle is an excellent option for hiking from the Logan Pass Visitor Center, which regularly has a full parking lot, or for doing trails that start at one trailhead and end at another. To travel the entire Going-to-the-Sun Road from the Apgar Visitor Center to the St. Mary Visitor Center and back, or vice versa, takes approximately 7 hours on the shuttle. The last service to Logan Pass with time to visit and return departs Apgar Visitor Center at 4:15pm and St. Mary Visitor Center at 5:30pm. Check daily schedules online at www.nps.gov for early morning express service from Apgar Visitor Center to Logan Pass. And since the number of stops along the route has decreased, be sure to confirm on the map that you can board and disembark where you planned. Reduced service is available for the first two weeks in September.

Hands-On Learning

Founded in 1983, the **Glacier Institute** (320 Nucleus Ave., Columbia Falls; 406/755-1211; www.glacierinstitute.org) is a private nonprofit offering hands-on educational experiences for all ages and levels of fitness using Glacier National Park and Flathead National Forest as its classrooms.

The 2-6-day youth camps (from $175) have a variety of focuses, including the first overnight camp experience for children away from their parents and a 6-day backpacking trip, with experienced guides and experts to foster each child's learning. Outdoor education courses are open to young and old. Enroll for a day hike ($150) with expert instructors on topics such as wolves of the North Fork Valley. Memberships to the institute cost $150 annually and allow you to take members-only day courses throughout the year for no extra charge.

Peruse the institute's extensive offerings on its website. If you see a course that's not offered when you plan to be here, the Glacier Institute creates custom programs and can plan a half-day to several-day course for your group (up to 40 people; from $750, $2,300 for a bus of 14).

A free **hiker-biker shuttle** allows recreational access for hikers and bikers beyond vehicle gate closures on Going-to-the-Sun Road prior to the season opening. Shuttles run 9am-4pm on weekends only during hiker-biker season, early May-June 30 or whenever the Going-to-the-Sun Road fully opens. Shuttles stop at Apgar Visitor Center, Lake McDonald Lodge, and Avalanche Creek every 15-30 minutes. Each vehicle carries 15 people and comes equipped with a bike trailer that fits tires narrower than 3 in (7.6 cm), and those without extended or full front fenders. Shuttles are available on a first-come, first-served basis only.

Red Bus Tours

855/733-4522 or 303/265-7010; www.glaciernationalparklodges.com; $60-128

Interpretive Red Bus Tours are another way to see the park. These snazzy vintage buses, known as "Jammers," were originally built by the White Motor Company from 1936 to 1939. The vehicles, which have been overhauled for safety, are 25 ft (8 m) long, seat 16 on benches, and have the added bonus of roll-back canvas tops, ideal for sunny summer days. Numerous tours take 2.5-9.5 hours, and informative guides entertain with facts and stories about Glacier. It's an excellent way to leave the driving and vehicle reservations to someone else.

Sun Tours

406/226-9220 or 800/786-9220; www.glaciersuntours.com; June-Sept. 1; $100-140

Slightly less flashy but more comfortable are the air-conditioned and large-windowed coaches of Sun Tours. Tours last 4, 6, or 8 hours and are guided from a Blackfeet perspective: for example, plants and roots used for Blackfeet medicine are pointed out, as are natural features that relate to the Blackfeet Nation. The coaches can accommodate 25 passengers and depart daily from East Glacier, Browning, St. Mary, and West Glacier. Park entrance passes and lunch are not included in the tour price. Sun Tours also offers a hiker shuttle service and private custom tours.

Sights

East Glacier Area

Located on the Blackfeet Indian Reservation at the southeast corner of the park, East Glacier (pop. 262, elev. 4,799 ft/1,463 m) has long been a primary entrance into Glacier National Park. Early visitors from the east often arrived by rail at East Glacier and spent the night in the grand Glacier Park Lodge before heading into the wilds of the park.

Today the town of East Glacier bustles year-round and is a hub of activity during the summer months as visitors stream in and out of the park. There are numerous accommodations, including the still-majestic Adirondack-style Glacier Park Lodge, several good restaurants, local outfitters, and a smattering of shops. There is also a tremendous amount of wilderness to be explored both inside the park and in immediate proximity to East Glacier. The stunning Two Medicine Valley is just a few miles away, and hiking, skiing, and even snowmobiling trails are within steps of the main drag.

Two Medicine Valley

Geographically, Two Medicine Valley is not at the heart of Glacier, but this remote southeastern corner is staggeringly beautiful and seemingly less known among the mass of summer visitors. The rocky peaks and glacially carved valleys meet in clear alpine lakes, and the area offers plenty of activity. There are boat tours that intersect with hiking trails, numerous waterfalls to ogle, fishing, and a lovely campground. The entrance at Two Medicine is 7 mi (11 km) north of East Glacier via MT 49/Looking Glass Road and Two Medicine Road.

St. Mary to Many Glacier

This place feels like it's at the edge of two worlds: mountains to the west, plains to the east. St. Mary is a small village nestled between St. Mary Lake and Lower St. Mary Lake that marks another entrance to the park and the start of Going-to-the-Sun Road. With all the splendor of the jagged peaks and the wide-open vistas created by sparse stands of aspen and sweeping prairie, the recreational opportunities are abundant and the scenery spectacular.

Top to bottom: Grinnell Glacier; a hiker in Two Medicine Valley; Lake McDonald

Farther north, Many Glacier is the ideal base camp for outdoors lovers, with extensive opportunities for hiking, canoeing, and horseback riding. The popular boat tours and Red Bus Tours are also accessible from Many Glacier. Grinnell Glacier is a dwindling but still phenomenal work of nature, and daily ranger-led hikes take visitors up to its toe. The Many Glacier Hotel is a 1915 Great Northern Railway Swiss chalet-style lodge that welcomes guests with a rambling veranda and cozy guest rooms.

From Browning, the St. Mary entrance is 30 mi (48 km) northwest on US 89. To get to the Many Glacier entrance from St. Mary, take US 89 9 mi (14 km) north to Babb, and then head west on Many Glacier Road for another 8 mi (13 km). From Browning, the Many Glacier entrance is 51 mi (83 km) northwest via Highway 464/Duck Lake Road and Route 3.

St. Mary Lake

One of the most photographed lakes in the park for its absurdly beautiful mountain backdrop, St. Mary Lake is among the best places in Glacier to watch the sun rise. The lake and its many hiking trails are accessible from Going-to-the-Sun Road. The **Sun Point Nature Trail** is 1.4 miles (2.3 km) round-trip, and the trailhead is 10 miles (15 km) west of the St. Mary Visitor Center. It is worth the short walk for views of Baring Falls and the lake itself. An even quicker stop is **Sunrift Gorge,** 0.6 mi (1 km) west of Sun Point, an incredible cascade slicing between two rock walls; it is just 200 ft (61 m) from the parking area. **Baring Falls** is another 0.3-mi (0.5-km) walk down the trail.

TOP EXPERIENCE

★ Many Glacier

The Many Glacier region is a palpable reminder of why Glacier has long been known as the Switzerland of America. Marked by grand accommodations and a landscape that was visibly scoured and carved by glaciers, from the U-shaped valleys and milky-blue glacial lakes to the rocky moraines and the last remaining glaciers themselves, this region is among the most dramatic and startlingly beautiful in the park.

This is not a place to be enjoyed from inside a car, although those on a tight schedule would still benefit from making the journey just to walk around the hotel to take in the stunning surroundings. **Vehicle reservations** are required 6am-6pm daily July-early September. Many Glacier is best suited for active travelers: The hiking and boating are exceptional, and it is one of the rare places in the Lower 48 where a day hike can lead you to an actual glacier. Come to Many Glacier to see the splendid scenery, but if possible, stay a few days to truly enjoy it. From St. Mary to the Many Glacier Hotel, it's a 20-mi (33-km) drive via US 89 North and Route 3/Many Glacier Road and will take roughly 30 minutes.

★ Grinnell Glacier

Named for conservationist and explorer George Bird Grinnell, Grinnell Glacier lies in the heart of Many Glacier and is a symbol both of the park's wilderness and of the dramatic climatic changes that are occurring. Because the glacier is accessible within a day's hike, its startling shrinkage—from 710 acres (287 ha) in 1850 to 220 acres (89 ha) in 1993 and 152 acres (62 ha) in 2005—has been captured on film.

The options for seeing the glacier up close are to hoof it from the **Many Glacier Hotel** (5.5 mi/8.9 km one-way; 1,600 ft/490 m elevation gain) or to take a boat across Lake Josephine with **Glacier Park Boat Company** (406/257-2426; www.glacierparkboats.com; $40) and hike the remainder of the trail from the head of Lake Josephine (3.8 mi/6.1 km one-way; 1,600 ft/490 m elevation gain). There is also an excellent ranger-guided hike to the glacier (8:30am daily from mid-July,

Many Glacier

weather permitting) that makes use of the boat, departing from the Many Glacier dock. The 8.5-mi (13.7-km) round-trip outing takes up to 9 hours. The trail twists and climbs above impossibly blue alpine lakes and within sight of Salamander Glacier. In summer, hikers get wet with runoff from the overhanging waterfalls along the trail. Come prepared! Though the trail is one of the most popular hikes in the park, and thus heavily trafficked, wildlife is plentiful in the area too, and grizzly bears are commonly spotted on or near the trail. The trail often does not open until late July and is seldom clear of snow until well into August.

Upper Waterton Lake and Goat Haunt

Canada's Waterton Lakes National Park is a fjord-like valley, reminiscent of Norway, especially when it is shrouded in fog and mist. Upper Waterton Lake runs north-south, straddling the border. Not only is the area stunningly beautiful, but because of its remoteness, it's also far less crowded than many other corners of the park and offers excellent hiking and wildlife-viewing at the lake's edge. Most people arrive at Goat Haunt by boat from the Waterton Marina on the Canadian side, but it's possible to hike into Goat Haunt from Canada (only US and Canadian citizens with proper ID can continue the hike deeper into Glacier). Non-landing cruises to the area do not require passports for US entry, but anyone who plans to stay at Goat Haunt for more than the 30 minutes provided by the landing cruises does need to have their passport and will have to clear US Customs ahead of time.

On the Canadian side, **Crypt Lake Trail** (10.8 mi/17.4 km round-trip) is an ambitious hike that includes a natural tunnel through a rock wall, stomach-dropping heights, waterfalls galore, and a dazzling hidden cirque. There are several hikes, ranging from mellow to death-defying, from the Goat Haunt ranger station. Check online or call ahead to see if there are ranger-led hikes from the ranger station. A few favorites are **Rainbow Falls** (2 mi/3.2 km round-trip; no elevation gain), **Kootenai Lakes** (5 mi/8 km round-trip; 200-ft/61-m elevation gain), **Lake Janet** (6.6 mi/10.6 km round-trip; 750-ft/229-m elevation gain), and **Lake Francis** (12.4 mi/20 km round-trip; 1,050-ft/320-m elevation gain). For those willing to huff and puff, but only briefly, **Goat Haunt Overlook** (2 mi/3.2 km round-trip; 800-ft/244-m elevation gain) offers a phenomenal view of the valley. The isolation and lack of roads tends to keep visitor numbers down around Upper Waterton Lake, but the mosquitoes are abundant; come prepared.

To get to Canada's fourth national park from Glacier, you'll need a passport and a car to take you the 27 mi (43 km) over the Chief Mountain Highway via US 89 and Highway 17 from St. Mary to Waterton Lakes National Park.

West Glacier Area

A bustling entrance to Glacier, West Glacier (pop. 174, elev. 3,220 ft/982 m) has the feeling of "last chance to get bug spray" and "first non-PB&J meal in a while." It is not a destination but a portal, and a good place to find lodging, dining, and supplies.

The town grew up around Belton Chalet, a lodge built by the Great Northern Railway in 1910, the same year Glacier became a national park. The Belton, an arts and crafts-style gem, was the first permanent lodging on the west side of Glacier, and thanks to a painstaking restoration in 2000 and a wonderful restaurant, it remains one of the best.

TOP EXPERIENCE

★ Going-to-the-Sun Road

Completed in 1932, Going-to-the-Sun Road is a marvel of modern engineering. Spanning 50 mi (80 km) from West Glacier to St. Mary, the road snakes up and around mountains that include its namesake, Going-to-the-Sun Mountain, giving viewers some of the most dramatic vistas in the country. The road crosses the Continental Divide and required more than two decades of planning and construction. It climbs more than 3,000 ft (900 m) with only a single switchback, known as **The Loop.** Going-to-the-Sun is an architectural accomplishment as well: All of the bridges, retaining walls, and guardrails are built of native materials, so the road blends into its majestic alpine setting.

In addition to being an experience on its own, Going-to-the-Sun is also the primary access road to the park and the only way to get to some of the park's best-known highlights: the visitor center at Logan Pass, the Highline Trail, Lake McDonald, and an array of hiking trails. For visitors who are not keen on driving the road themselves, there are a few options, including free shuttles, vintage tours, and Blackfeet tours, to see the road as a sightseer.

As of 2024, with visitor levels hitting

Ranger Programs

Some of the best resources on Glacier National Park are the Park Service rangers—encyclopedias in hiking boots. Their stations are conveniently located at major sites throughout the park, and the rangers host a number of outdoor educational events geared to the whole family. Though COVID-19 severely limited the number of hosted events, the ranger programs in Glacier normally begin in late spring and run throughout the summer, with most activities offered at St. Mary, Apgar, Logan Pass, Many Glacier, Goat Haunt, and Two Medicine. Rangers typically lead several guided hikes each day that allow visitors to learn about the park's geology, history, wildlife, flora, fauna, and more. The St. Mary Visitor Center, Fish Creek Amphitheater, Lake McDonald Lodge, and Many Glacier Hotel host slide lectures as part of the ranger program. Full-day hikes, boat tours, and Junior Ranger programs are also available.

One of the most noteworthy park programs is "Native America Speaks," where members from the Blackfeet, Salish, Kootenai, and Pend d'Oreille tribes provide campfire talks about their life, culture, and influence in Glacier. The speakers range from artists and musicians to historians who intersperse their talks with personal stories and Native American legends. These talks are given at the Apgar, Many Glacier, Two Medicine, and Rising Sun Campgrounds. July-August, the St. Mary Visitor Center also hosts weekly Native American dance troupes. For times, locations, and descriptions of the ranger programs offered, pick up the free "Ranger-led Activity Schedule" available at any of the park's visitor centers.

For information on ranger stations or programs and to download park brochures, contact **Park Service Headquarters** (406/888-7800; www.nps.gov/glac).

historic highs, the National Park Service is operating a pilot **vehicle reservation system** for Going-to-the-Sun Road via the west entrance, as well as Many Glacier and the North Fork area of the park from the Polebridge Entrance Station. Entry tickets (www.recreation.gov; $2) are required 6am-3pm daily late May-mid-September for the Going-to-the-Sun Road corridor, the North Fork area, and Many Glacier. A printed or digital copy of the ticket is valid for one day and will be scanned at the park entrance station.

★ Lake McDonald

The largest lake in the park at 9.4 miles (15.1 km) long and 464 ft (141 m) deep, Lake McDonald was gouged out by a glacier. Surrounded by jagged peaks on three sides, it is bordered by the Lewis Range to the east, which creates a rain block and makes the Lake McDonald Valley one of the mildest and lushest environments in the region. Not unlike the Pacific Northwest, the valley boasts dense forests of towering western red cedars and hemlocks.

Although the lake and surrounding forests are serene, the area is a hub of activity in summer for human visitors and the bear population alike. Modeled after a Swiss chalet and opened in 1914, the grand and slightly worse-for-wear **Lake McDonald Lodge** sprawls along the northeast shore and provides expensive lodging with unmatched views. The dining room, lounge, and pizzeria are open to nonguests. Stop in to warm yourself by the massive fireplace, check out the animal mounts that have decorated the place since its origins, or lounge lakeside on the veranda with a beverage.

There are great hiking trails around the lake, including those to Fish Lake, Mount Brown Lookout, and the mellow Johns Lake Loop. Plenty of fish populate the lake—17 varieties in all, mainly trout. Boat tours depart from the lodge,

Scenic Point

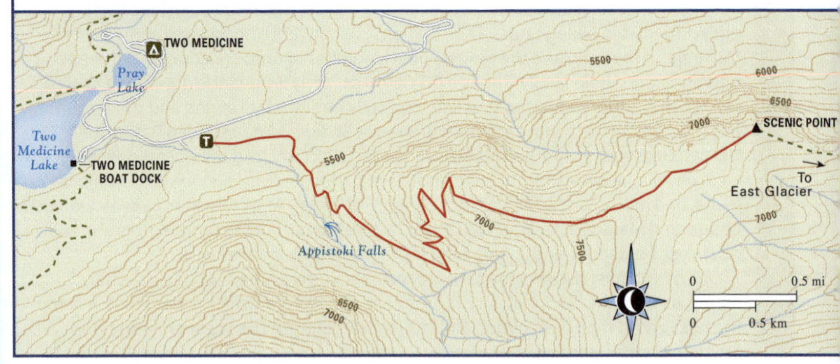

as well as Red Bus Tours and ranger-led activities.

Bowman Lake

Some 32 mi (52 km) north of the west entrance to Glacier in the North Fork area, and only 30 mi (48 km) south of Canada, is crystalline Bowman Lake, ringed by mountains and forest. A long, bumpy ride gets you here and keeps the crowds away. The density of mosquitoes also tends to discourage visitors. Boats are permitted on the 7-mi-long (11-km-long) lake with restrictions on engines. Kayaks and canoes are a wonderful way to explore this photogenic setting. The lake is filled with kokanee and cutthroat trout, and the fishing is legendary, particularly in late spring. There are plenty of hikes from the area, including the arduous 13-mi (21-km) round-trip **Quartz Lakes Loop,** but be warned that this is the heart of grizzly country, and visitors should come prepared with bear spray and a solid understanding of bear behavior and habitat. Camping is available on a first-come, first-served basis at primitive 48-site **Bowman Lake Campground.** Glacier's pilot **vehicle reservation program** requires an entry ticket (www.recreation.gov; $2) for the North Fork area 6am-6pm daily late May-mid-September.

Adventure and Recreation

Hiking

East Glacier Area

Scenic Point

Distance: 7.4 mi (11.9 km) round-trip
Duration: 4 hours
Elevation gain: 2,124 ft (647 m)
Effort: Moderate to strenuous
Trail surface: Narrow dirt path with roots and rocks
Trailhead: Milepost 6.9 up Two Medicine Road

Scenic Point is one short climb with big scenery. The trail launches up through a thick subalpine fir forest. A short side jaunt en route allows a peek at Appistoki Falls. As switchbacks line up like dominoes, stunted firs give way to silvery dead and twisted limber pines. Broaching the ridge, the trail enters seemingly barren alpine tundra. Only alpine bluebells and pink mats of several-hundred-year-old moss campion cower in crags.

On the ridge, the trail traverses a north-facing slope; avoid the early summer steep snowfield by climbing a worn path that goes above it before descending to Scenic Point. To reach the actual Scenic Point above the trail, cut off at the sign, stepping on rocks to avoid crushing fragile

Two Medicine Lake Trails

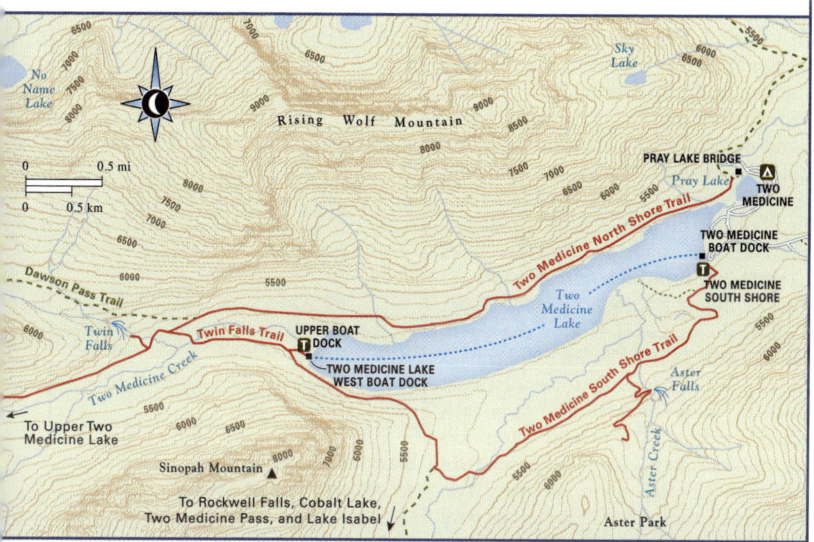

alpine plants. At the top, views plunge several thousand feet straight down to Lower Two Medicine Lake and across the plains. Return the way you came, or drop 7 mi (11 km) to East Glacier, passing outside the park boundary, where cow pies buzz with flies. The latter half of the Scenic Point-East Glacier Trail requires a Blackfeet recreation permit ($10), available at the Two Medicine Ranger Station or Bear Track Travel Center (Exxon gas station) in East Glacier.

Two Medicine Lake Loop, Twin Falls, and Upper Two Medicine Lake

Distance: 2-10.7 mi (3.2-17.2 km) round-trip
Duration: 1-5 hours
Elevation gain: none-424 ft (none-129 m)
Effort: Easy to moderate
Trail surface: Narrow dirt path with roots and rocks
Trailhead: North Shore Two Medicine Lake trailhead at Pray Lake Bridge in Two Medicine Campground, South Shore Two Medicine Lake trailhead near boat launch, or Two Medicine Lake west boat dock

Two Medicine and Upper Two Medicine Lake are a set of subalpine lakes formed by the immense Two Medicine Glacier. As an added treat for hikers, the trail also takes in Twin Falls, a double flume of cascades. The North Shore and South Shore Trails connect at the west end of Two Medicine Lake to form the loop, a route that cuts through forest, avalanche chutes, huckleberry bushes, and meadows. The South Shore Trail takes in beaver ponds, a swinging bridge over Paradise Creek, and the precipitous slopes of Mount Sinopah, while the North Shore Trail trots along the base of Rising Wolf, the biggest peak in the area, and captures views of Pumpelly Pillar. A spur trail at the west end of the lake leads to Twin Falls and Upper Two Medicine Lake below Lone Walker Mountain. In early summer, water floods the upper lake's beach, leaving only a brushy shoreline. For lunch, help maintain the safety of those sleeping in the backcountry campground by sitting in the cooking area to eat.

To hike the Two Medicine Lake Loop, Twin Falls, and Upper Two Medicine Lake (10.7 mi/17.2 km), go either direction starting at the North Shore trailhead or South Shore trailhead, connecting the two trailheads with 0.8 mi (1.3 km) of road walking. Other routes vary depending on starting trailheads, ending points, and whether or not you opt to use the Two Medicine Lake boat as a shuttle. Taking the boat round-trip across the lake makes for the shortest hikes (2 mi/3.2 km round-trip for Twin Falls and 4.2 mi/6.8 km round-trip for Upper Two Medicine Lake). Hiking the North Shore Trail, Twin Falls, and Upper Two Medicine Lake to end at the west boat dock for a one-way shuttle (pay cash when boarding, $7) across the lake makes for midsize hikes (4.6 mi/7.4 km for Twin Falls and 7.2 mi/11.6 km for Upper Two Medicine Lake). All trail junctions have signage, but maps help with clarifying routes.

No Name Lake

Distance: 9.7 mi (15.6 km) round-trip
Duration: 5 hours
Elevation gain: 1,305 ft (398 m)
Effort: Moderate to strenuous
Trail surface: Dirt with some exposed rock
Trailhead: North Shore Trailhead in the campground at Two Medicine Lake

Luckily, the name gives no indication of how beautiful this alpine lake at the base of Pumpelly Pillar is. Snow stays well into June up here, and the bugs seem to always be around, but so are the wildflowers. The hike is gentle for the first 3 mi (4.8 km) and then requires a steady 2-mi (3.2-km) climb with some exposed areas up to the lake. It can be muddy and slick after a rain, but the hike provides solitude and a stunning lake view. To shorten the hike, taking the historic wooden boat *Sinopah* (www.glacierparkboats.com; $20 round-trip) from the east side of Two Medicine Lake shaves off 2.8 mi (4.5 km).

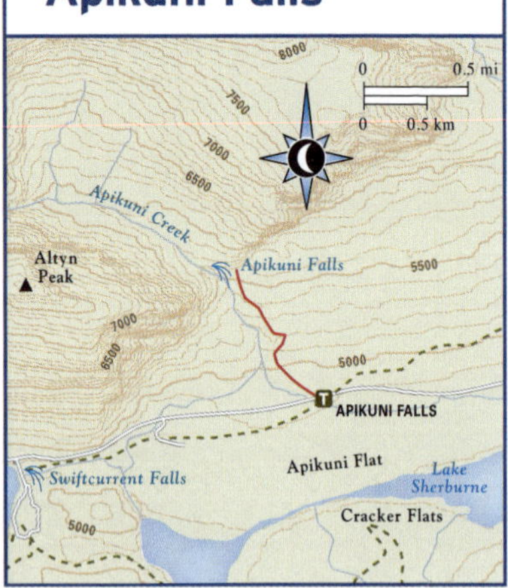

Blackfeet Tours

406/450-8420; www.blackfeettours.com; $325-625

Visitors who want to explore the Badger Two Medicine region with an expert local guide can contact Alger Swingley of Blackfeet Tours to plan a hike with a certified interpretive guide (6+ hours), a horseback day trip (6+ hours, no children under 16, minimum 2 participants), or an educational cultural Jeep tour (4 hours, no children under 2).

St. Mary to Many Glacier

Apikuni Falls

Distance: 1.6 mi (2.6 km) round-trip
Duration: 1 hour
Elevation gain: 570 ft (174 m)
Effort: Moderate
Trail surface: Dirt with some rocky sections
Trailhead: Grinnell Glacier interpretive site, 10 mi (16 km) west on Many Glacier Road

Apikuni Falls springs from a hanging valley, which you can see from the trailhead. The short walk starts out across a flat meadow where wildflowers bloom thickly in July: geraniums, arrowleaf balsamroot, paintbrush, lupine, and stonecrop. But soon, the path steepens to climb to the cliffs between Mount Altyn

Grinnell Glacier Trail

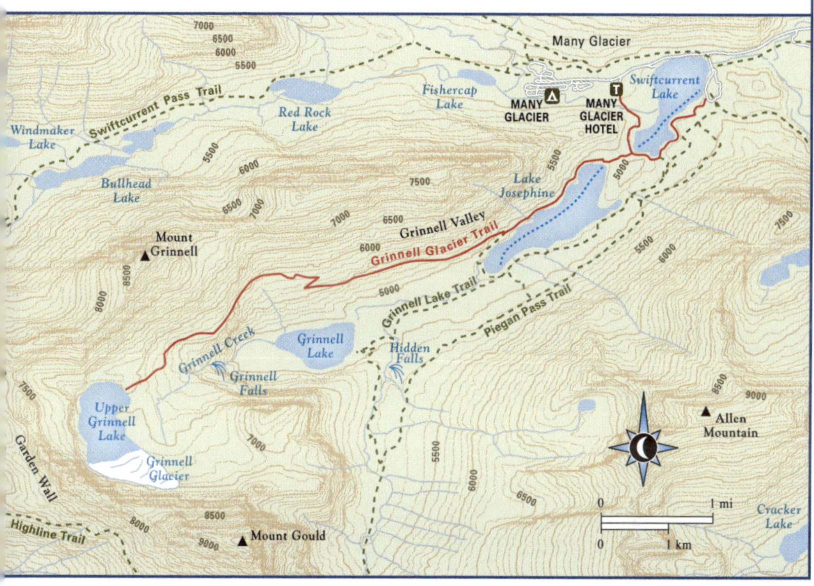

and Apikuni Mountain, where the falls drop out of the basin above. Those with scrambling skills can climb a rough trail into the upper hanging valley.

★ Grinnell Glacier

Distance: 11 mi (17.7 km) round-trip
Duration: 6 hours
Elevation gain: 1,619 ft (493 m)
Effort: Moderate to strenuous
Trail surface: Packed and loose gravel
Trailheads: On the south side of Many Glacier Hotel, at Swiftcurrent Picnic Area, or via the tour boat

In early summer, a large, steep snowdrift frequently bars the path into the upper basin until early July; check the trail status before hiking. The most accessible glacier in the park, Grinnell Glacier still requires stamina because most of its elevation gain packs within 2 mi (3 km). Many hikers take the boat shuttle, cutting the length to 7.8 mi (12.5 km) round-trip, or just trimming 2.5 mi (3.5 km) off the return. To hike the entire route from the picnic area, follow Swiftcurrent Lake's west shore to the boat dock. From Many Glacier Hotel, round the southern shore to meet up with the same dock. Bop over the short hill and hike around Lake Josephine's north shore.

Toward Josephine's west end, the Grinnell Glacier Trail diverges uphill. As the trail climbs through multicolored rock strata, Grinnell Lake's milky turquoise waters come into view below. Above, you'll spot Gem Glacier and Salamander Glacier, both shrunken to static snowfields, long before Grinnell Glacier appears. The trail ascends on a cliff stairway where a waterfall douses hikers before passing a rest stop with outhouses. A steep grunt up the moraine leads to a stunning view. Trot through the maze of paths crossing the bedrock to Upper Grinnell Lake's shore, but do not walk out on the glacier's ice, as it harbors deadly hidden crevasses.

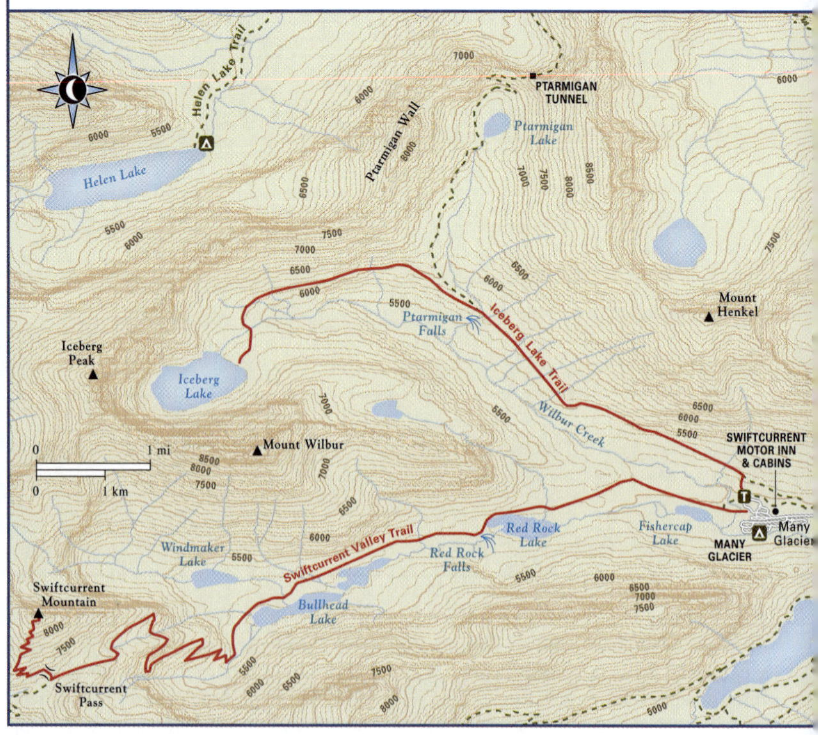

Swiftcurrent Valley and Lookout

Distance: 3.6-16.2 mi (5.8-26.1 km) round-trip
Duration: 2-8 hours
Elevation gain: 100-3,496 ft (30-1,066 m)
Effort: Easy to strenuous
Trail surface: Packed gravel, dirt, rocks
Trailhead: Swiftcurrent parking lot in Many Glacier

This popular trail leads to various destinations along a scenic path dotted with lakes, waterfalls, moose, glaciers, and wildflowers. The trail winds through pine trees and aspen groves as it rolls gently up to **Red Rock Lake and Falls** at 1.8 mi (2.9 km). At the top of the falls, a knoll provides a viewpoint to scan hillsides with binoculars for bears. The trail continues level through meadows rampant with Sitka valerian in July to Bullhead Lake at 3.9 mi (6.3 km). Scan scree slopes for bighorn sheep.

From the lake, the trail switchbacks uphill. It cuts around a cliff face before reaching **Swiftcurrent Pass** at 6.6 mi (10.6 km). From here, Granite Park Chalet is 0.9 mi (1.4 km) downhill. To reach the lookout, take the spur trail up another 1.4 mi (2.3 km) of switchbacks (you'll lose count of them). The lookout surveys almost the entire park: glaciers, peaks, wild panoramas, and the plains. Many Glacier Hotel looks minuscule. Enjoy the one-of-a-kind view from the outhouse. For a different descent, drop to The Loop to catch a shuttle.

Iceberg Lake

Distance: 9.6 mi (15.4 km) round-trip
Duration: 5 hours

St. Mary Lake Trails

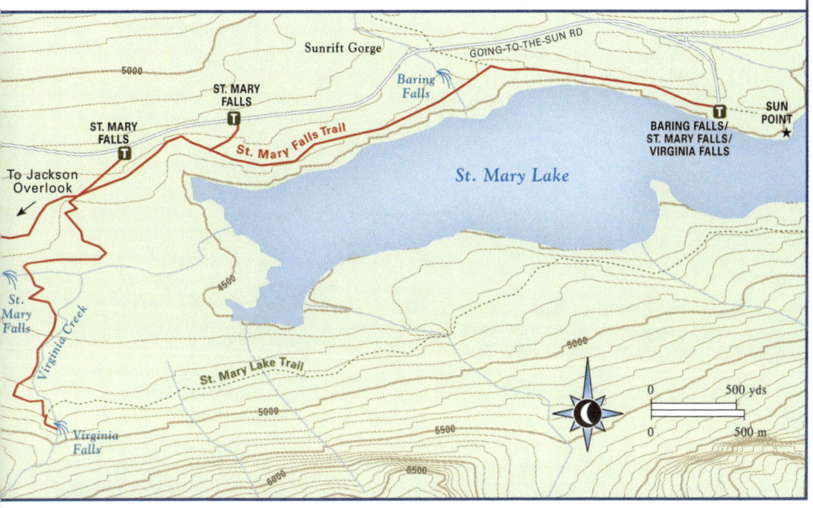

Elevation gain: 1,459 ft (445 m)
Effort: Strenuous
Trail surface: Packed dirt, possible snow
Trailhead: Iceberg Lake

For bear-savvy hikers with a penchant for floating ice, Iceberg Lake is an extraordinary day hike. The trail is well traveled by hikers of the two-legged variety, but it also has one of the densest concentrations of grizzly bears in the park thanks to an abundance of huckleberries. Bear encounters are common, and no overnight camping is allowed. The well-marked trailhead is at the end of Many Glacier Road, the only road in this section of the park.

The lake itself is a sublime glacial blue with chunks of ice floating in it, often as late as September. The elevation is gained slowly, except for a short steep stretch at the beginning, which is enough to turn some hikers around, and passes through meadows bursting with wildflowers. Mountain goats and bighorn sheep are often visible on the last stretch. Ptarmigan Falls is halfway to the lake. Most mornings in July-August, hikers can join a ranger-led hike to the lake, an especially good option for those concerned about bears.

St. Mary and Virginia Falls

Distance: 3.1 mi (5 km) round-trip
Duration: 1.5-2 hours
Elevation gain: 452 ft (138 m)
Effort: Easy to moderate
Trail surface: Dirt, loose gravel
Trailhead: St. Mary Falls

For a close-up look at a couple of stunning waterfalls in the St. Mary area, head to the St. Mary Falls trailhead, just west of Sunrift Gorge. It's a relatively gentle hike to St. Mary Falls and then Virginia Falls. There are plenty of places to take a dip along the way. Parking can be difficult and there are likely to be others on the trail.

West Glacier Area

Trail of the Cedars

Distance: 0.9 mi (1.4 km) round-trip
Duration: 30 minutes
Elevation gain: 49 ft (15 m)
Effort: Easy
Trail surface: Asphalt, boardwalk
Trailhead: Trail of the Cedars/Avalanche Lake

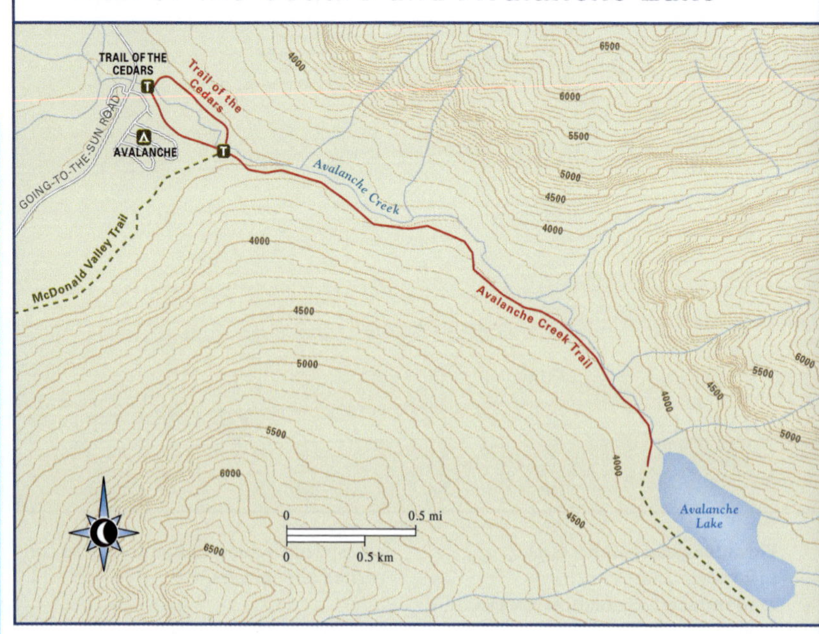

The popular Trail of the Cedars is an easy loop on a wheelchair-accessible boardwalk through spectacular forest, making for an ideal nature walk on a hot day. Leaving from Avalanche Campground, less than 5 mi (8 km) east of Lake McDonald Lodge, the trail crosses an impressive footbridge over Avalanche Gorge.

Avalanche Creek Trail

Distance: 5.9 mi (9.5 km) round-trip
Duration: 2.5-3 hours
Elevation gain: 757 ft (231 m)
Effort: Moderate
Trailhead: Trail of the Cedars/Avalanche Lake
Trail surface: Asphalt, boardwalk, packed dirt, gravel

Avalanche Creek Trail begins south of the Avalanche Gorge Footbridge on the Trail of the Cedars and takes hikers to the picturesque, mountain-ringed, and glacial blue Avalanche Lake. Parking at both trailheads tends to fill early, so the park's shuttles are a good option.

★ Highline Trail to Granite Park Chalet

Distance: 7.4 mi (11.9 km) to Granite Park Chalet, 11.4 mi (18.3 km) to The Loop
Duration: 5-6 hours
Elevation gain: 975 ft (297 m) up; 3,395 ft (1,035 m) down
Effort: Strenuous
Trail surface: Narrow, dirt, and rocky
Trailhead: Across Going-to-the-Sun Road from Logan Pass parking lot and shuttle stop

Many first-time hikers stop every 10 feet to take photos on this hike, which scares severe acrophobes with its exposed thousand-foot drop-offs. The trail drops from Logan Pass through a cliff walk above the Sun Road before crossing a flower land that gave the Garden Wall arête its name. At 3 mi (5 km), nearly all the elevation gain is packed into one

Granite Park Chalet Trails

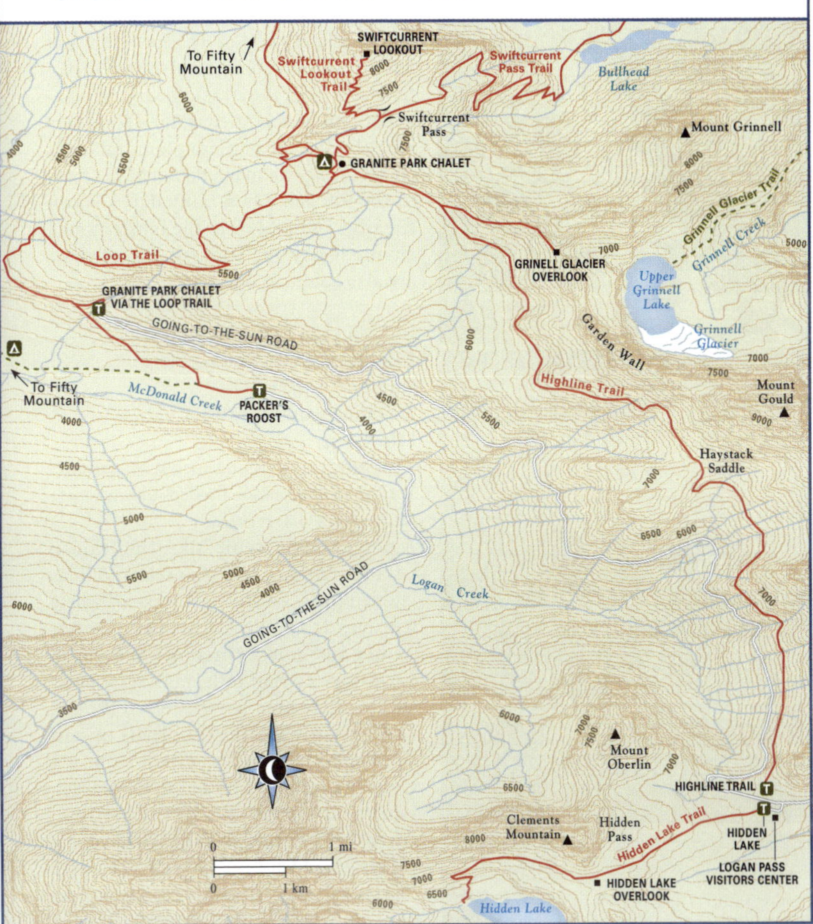

climb: Haystack Saddle appears to be the top, but it is only halfway. After the high point, the trail drops and swings through several large bowls before passing Bear Valley to reach Granite Park Chalet atop a knoll at 6,680 ft (2,036 m). Due to steep, snow-filled avalanche paths, the Park Service keeps the trailhead at Logan Pass closed usually into early July. New regulations are under consideration regarding the first section of the Highline: These may include making the trail one-way only from Logan Pass, adding an exit trail to Big Bend, and using a timed permit entry.

Stronger Highline hikers can add on side trails to Grinnell Glacier Overlook (a steep 1.6 mi/2.6 km round-trip) and **Swiftcurrent Lookout** (4.2 mi/6.8 km round-trip). To exit the area, some hikers opt to hike out over Swiftcurrent Pass to Many Glacier (7.6 mi/12.2 km) and catch shuttles; backpackers continue on to Fifty Mountain (11.9 mi/19.2 km farther) and

Goat Haunt (22.5 mi/36.2 km farther). Most day hikers head down The Loop Trail (4 mi/6.4 km) to catch the shuttle.

The chalet (July-early Sept.) does not have running water. Carry your own, filter water from the stream below the chalet, or purchase bottled water. Day hikers may also use the outdoor picnic tables or chalet dining room but do not have access to the kitchen. On a rainy day, a warm fire offers respite from the bluster and a chance to dry out. Sodas and candy bars are also sold.

Hidden Lake Overlook Trail

Distance: 2.7 mi (4.3 km) round-trip
Duration: 1.5 hours
Elevation gain: 540 ft (165 m)
Effort: Easy
Trail surface: Asphalt, boardwalk, dirt, gravel
Trailhead: Hidden Lake Overlook from west side of Logan Pass Visitor Center

A popular and scenic hike, the Hidden Lake Overlook Trail, also referred to as Hidden Lake Nature Trail, is paved where it leaves from the Logan Pass Visitor Center and quickly becomes boardwalk for just over a half mile, making it passable in all manner of weather. At the end of the boardwalk, the trail leads toward Bearhat Mountain and offers stunning views of Clements Mountain, the Garden Wall, and Mount Oberlin. Hikers will cross the Continental Divide before arriving at Hidden Lake Overlook at 1.3 mi (2.2 km). Sperry Glacier is visible on clear days, and wildlife encounters along the route are not uncommon.

Rocky Point

Distance: 1.4-1.6 miles (2.3-2.6 km) round-trip
Duration: 1 hour
Elevation gain: None
Effort: Easy
Trail surface: Dirt with roots and rocks
Trailhead: Fish Creek Campground Loop D or the start of the Inside North Fork Road

Top to bottom: trail to Iceberg Lake; Swiftcurrent Lake; Hidden Lake Overlook Trail

Apgar Lookout

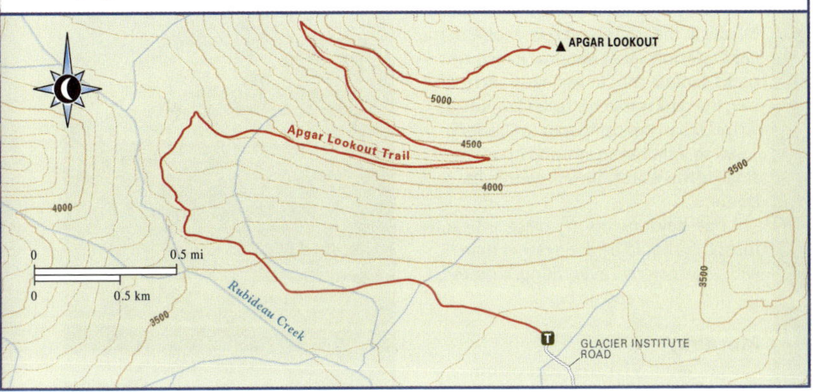

Rocky Point is a short interpretive romp along Lake McDonald's north shore through the 2003 Robert Fire and up a rock promontory. Places of heavy burn with slow regrowth alternate with lighter burn now clogged with lush greenery. Don't forget your camera: The view from Rocky Point looks up the lake toward the Continental Divide and grabs grand shots of Mount Jackson and Mount Edwards to the south. If the lake is calm, photos can capture stunning reflections. Snow leaves early and comes late to this trail, making it good for spring and fall hiking. From the promontory, make a loop back on the Lake McDonald Trail.

Apgar Lookout

Distance: 7 mi (11.3 km) round-trip
Duration: 4 hours
Elevation gain: 1,868 ft (569 m)
Effort: Moderate
Trail surface: Narrow, dirt with roots and rocks
Trailhead: End of Glacier Institute Road, 2 mi (3 km) from Going-to-the-Sun Road. Take the first left after the west entrance station at the Glacier Institute sign. At the first fork, follow the sign to the horse barn and veer left, crossing over Quarter Circle Bridge. Drive to the road's terminus at the trailhead.

Beginning with a gentle walk, the trail soon climbs steeply uphill toward the first of three long switchbacks (hike in the morning on hot days). As the trail ascends, some large burned sentinels stand as relics from the 2003 Robert Fire amid the thick growth of new lodgepoles pressing in on the trail that used to be a road. Snippets of views look down on the Middle Fork, Rubideau Basin, the railroad tracks, and West Glacier. Following the third switchback, the trail traverses the ridge, which has snow in June, to the rebuilt lookout. From this 5,236-ft (1,596-m) aerie, tall trees allow only partial views of the park's southern sector, Lake McDonald, and peaks of the Livingston Range. Park communication radio antennas clutter the summit, but at least they are clustered in one location.

Biking

East Glacier

There aren't many places in the country where you can hop on a bike, head to the nearest highway, and pedal through spectacular scenery in every direction. Although the inclines can be steep and the declines precipitous around East Glacier, the air is fresh and the mountain vistas unrivaled. The traffic—human and animal—needs to be minded.

For avid cyclists, it's possible to do a 137-mi (221-km) loop in and around the

One Day in Waterton Lakes National Park

Just north of Glacier, across the Canadian border in the southwest corner of Alberta, lies Waterton Lakes National Park (https://parks.canada.ca). Similar in terrain to Glacier, the park is much smaller (about 203 sq mi/526 sq km compared to Glacier's 1,600 sq mi/4,144 sq km) and houses a small town, Waterton Park, within its borders.

A one-day itinerary in a place as beautiful as this should be deep rather than wide. You can't do everything, so commit to what you do and go big.

Prince of Wales Hotel in Waterton Lakes National Park

Morning

The gorgeous **Visitors Reception Centre** (404 Cameron Falls Dr.; 403/859-5133; www.parks.canada.ca; 8am-4pm Mon.-Fri., 9am-5pm Sat.-Sun.) can provide you with plenty of information on the region. Spend some time in the center with the interactive exhibits learning about the region's natural and Indigenous history. The center is open year-round, but hours can vary by season.

From the center, head to Waterton Marina on the shores of Upper Waterton Lake, where you can take a 15-minute cruise with **Waterton Shoreline Cruise Company** (403/859-2362; www.watertoncruise.com; $32, no cash) across the lake to the Crypt Lake Trailhead. Those who are more excited about cruising the deepest lake in the Canadian Rockies than hiking can take a guided 135-minute cruise ($85) across the entire lake to the Goat Haunt Ranger Station and back. Passports are not required for passengers who are not staying longer than 30 minutes at Goat Haunt. Make sure to have packed plenty of water, a lunch, a swimsuit, and bear spray.

Afternoon

When you disembark from the boat to follow the **Crypt Lake Trail,** considered one of the best hikes in Canada, you'll hike a gentle grade through shady coniferous forest past a waterfall. At the second waterfall, the incline steepens and the trail is exposed. You hike along a ledge, up a ladder, and through a tunnel holding on to cables. The views are amazing, but it's not for the faint of heart.

Evening

Back on dry land, and with plenty of miles on your legs, one of the most photographed hotels in the world awaits. The **Prince of Wales Hotel** (Hwy. 5, Waterton Park; 844/868-7474; www.glacierparkcollection.com; CA$459-879) is a magnificent Swiss chalet-inspired lodge overlooking the lake and the town below. Although pricey, it's a great place to stay to have the full Waterton experience. If you're not staying the night, try to make it back from Crypt Lake in time for afternoon tea, and consider dinner at **Red Rock Trattoria** (107 Windflower Ave.; 403/859-2004; www.redrockcafe.ca; CA$18-55), a fabulous Italian restaurant, followed by a sunset stroll along the Waterton Lakeshore Trail.

park: Head southwest from East Glacier on US 2 to West Glacier, then over Going-to-the-Sun Road to St. Mary, then south on US 89 and Highway 49 back to East Glacier. Remember that bicycles are prohibited 11am-4pm daily June 15-Labor Day between Apgar Campground and Sprague Creek Campground. From Apgar to Logan Pass, bicycle traffic in both directions is prohibited 3pm-6pm daily late May-early September, so plan accordingly. In the vicinity of East Glacier, biking to the Two Medicine Valley, 12 mi (19 km) northwest of town, is also a popular route.

The closest place to rent bicycles is on the west side of the park, at Apgar Village, from **Glacier Outfitters.**

West Glacier

Biking in Glacier is not for the nonchalant. The climbs are treacherous, the edges precipitous, and the automobile traffic even worse. But the thrill of reaching the summit of Going-to-the-Sun Road, seeing how far you've come, soaking in the scenery, and whooshing back down again is unrivaled.

Still, as with any activity in Glacier, cyclists should be well aware of the conditions, restrictions, and potential hazards. Common sense prevails: Use helmets and reflectors; wear brightly colored and highly visible clothing; and watch for falling rocks, wildlife, and ice on the road. E-bikes are allowed if the motor is less than 750 watts (1 hp) and engaged only when pedaling. Bicycles are prohibited 11am-4pm daily June 15-Labor Day between Apgar Campground and Sprague Creek Campground. From Apgar to Logan Pass, bicycle traffic in both directions is prohibited 3pm-6pm daily late May-early September. It takes roughly 45 minutes to ride from Sprague Creek to Logan Creek, and 3 hours from Logan Creek to the summit of Logan Pass. Bicycles cannot be ridden on any of the hiking trails, other than on a few marked trails in Waterton Lakes National Park. For more information on restrictions and current road closures, check online (www.nps.gov/glac).

Glacier Outfitters

196 Apgar Loop; 406/219-7466; www.goglacieroutfitters.com; $60-135

Bicycles can be rented at Apgar Village from Glacier Outfitters. It rents e-bikes (ages 16 and up), hybrid road-mountain bikes, and bike racks for regular and e-bikes as well as Thule child trailers.

Horseback Riding

Swan Mountain Outfitters

406/387-4405; www.swanmountainglacier.com; $140-415

Guided horseback rides, from 1 hour to a full day, are available in good weather late May to mid-September at the corrals at Apgar, Lake McDonald, and Many Glacier from Swan Mountain Outfitters, the only outfitter that can offer trail rides inside the park. Options include 2-hour rides, 5-hour rides, and full-day trips. They also offer options for fish-and-ride day trips. Trail rides can be arranged late April-mid-October, and fishing trips are offered July-September. Rates do not include gratuities, which are encouraged. Reservations are required.

Boating

Glacier Park Boat Company

406/257-2426; www.glacierparkboats.com

Family owned since 1938, the Glacier Park Boat Company is the ultimate boating resource across the park. Reservations are recommended but not required. Same-day reservations are not available, but visitors can go to the selected tour or rental location to purchase same-day tickets.

East Glacier

The Glacier Park Boat Company rents rowboats ($32.50), single and double kayaks ($24.20-32.50), canoes ($32.50), and 8-horsepower motorboats ($45) by the hour. Excellent 45-minute cruises (tours $10.10-20.25) across Two Medicine Lake on the historic *Sinopah* take place at least four times daily mid-June to early September. The 2.5-hour guided hike to Twin Falls can be added at no extra cost.

St. Mary to Many Glacier

Boats are permitted on **St. Mary Lake,** but you'll have to bring your own as there are no rentals on-site. There are 90-minute **tours** ($40.50) available several times daily through the Glacier Park Boat Company. The tours depart from the Rising Sun boat dock, 6 mi (10 km) inside the east entrance on Going-to-the-Sun Road, and offer views of various waterfalls, Sexton Glacier, and Wild Goose Island. A 15-minute walk to Baring Falls is also an option on the St. Mary Lake cruise. Twice daily, the cruises can be combined with a guided hike to St. Mary Falls (less than 2 mi/3.2 km round-trip; 200-ft/61-m elevation gain) for a 3.5-hour outing.

In the Many Glacier area, **canoes/rowboats/double kayaks** ($32.50/hour) and **single kayaks** ($24.20/hour) are available to rent at **Swiftcurrent Lake,** adjacent to the Many Glacier Hotel. The Glacier Park Boat Company also provides **scenic cruises** ($40.50) on Swiftcurrent Lake and Lake Josephine. There are up to seven trips daily during summer, and cruises can be combined with guided hikes or used as a shuttle for hiking trips. A highlight for many is seeing the Grinnell Glacier on a cruise across Lake Josephine.

West Glacier

Before Going-to-the-Sun Road was completed, most of Glacier's adventurous visitors saw the park by boat. Today this nostalgic mode of travel offers benefits all its own. Both Lake McDonald and Bowman Lake offer excellent boating and fishing opportunities in the form of kayaking, canoeing, and even semi-restricted motorboating. Boat rentals are

kayaking on Swiftcurrent Lake

available at Apgar and Lake McDonald Lodge.

Hour-long **boat tours** ($27)—think sunset cocktail cruises in a historic wooden boat—are available on **Lake McDonald.** Rowboats and double kayaks ($32.50/hour), paddleboards ($24.20/hour), and 8-horsepower motorboats ($45/hour) can be rented on Lake McDonald at both the Lake McDonald Lodge and Apgar.

Fishing

While fishing permits or licenses are not required in Glacier National Park, it is imperative that anyone fishing abides by the regulations. A brochure can be picked up at any of the visitor centers or downloaded from the **National Park Service website** (www.nps.gov/glac/planyourvisit/fishing.htm). Several lakes, creeks, and rivers throughout the park are closed to fishing, and fishing for native species anywhere in the park must be catch-and-release only.

St. Mary Lake

Because of the altitude in Glacier, the water is colder, and some of the lakes in the park are sterile. St. Mary Lake is not especially productive water, but it sure is nice to stand in and soak up the scenery. There are some rainbow trout, brook trout, whitefish, and the rare bull trout in the lake for the patient angler. No bull trout may be kept. Shore fishing is possible, but the chances for catching increase significantly out in the deeper waters. St. Mary Lake can get rough quickly, with 2-3-ft (0.5-1-m) swells, so keep a constant eye on the conditions.

Many Glacier

In Many Glacier, presumably because of its proximity to the hotel and the road, the trout in crystal-clear **Swiftcurrent Lake** see the most action, but they seem to have wised up. Brook trout in the 10-in (25-cm) range are the most common catches here. **Lake Josephine** and **Grinnell Lake** have brook trout populations that seem more willing to go for flies.

Red Rock Lake

Some backcountry lakes are worth hiking into if fishing is the goal. Red Rock Lake, located along Swiftcurrent Creek, for example, is accessible by a fairly level 2-mi (3.2-km) hike and holds plenty of brook trout in the 10-12-in (25-30-cm) range. Dry-fly anglers will do best in the morning or evening, the same time bears are most active, but will have to go deep in the afternoons.

Rafting

Although there is no rafting inside the park, white-water outfitting services in West Glacier offer trips on the 87-mi (140-km) Middle Fork of the Flathead River. The North Fork of the Flathead, which forms the western boundary of the park, can be rafted as well.

Glacier Raft Company

106 Going-to-the-Sun Rd., West Glacier; 406/888-5454 or 800/235-6781; www.glacierraftco.com; half-day from $75-81, full-day from $145-161, half-day with riverside dinner $105-111

Glacier Raft Company offers everything from half-day and dinner floats to multiple-day expeditions. The company caters to all floaters, from novices to adrenaline junkies. They also offer horseback riding, fly-fishing, and kayaking.

Montana Raft Company

11970 US 2, West Glacier; 406/387-5555 or 800/521-7238; www.glacierguides.com; all-inclusive half-day from $81, full-day from $152

Montana Raft Company has some of the most well-rounded and knowledgeable guides in the area. Group numbers tend to be smaller (9 in a boat as opposed to 14), and the company offers an expansive range of options including rafting and horseback riding, overnight adventures, inflatable kayak trips, family-friendly day trips, raft and dinner trips, and scenic floats. Because of water conditions, in June the minimum age for rafters is eight; from July through the rest of the season, rafting is available to those ages six and up.

Wild River Adventures

11900 US 2 E., West Glacier; 406/387-9453 or 800/700-7056; www.riverwild.com; half-day from $80

Another noteworthy outfitter offering rafting trips in the region is Wild River Adventures. All-day trips, including lunch, are $153. The minimum age for rafters in May and June is 12, and six-year-olds and up can raft from July onward. They also offer evening dinner white-water rafting ($112), sport raft wild side tours ($110), inflatable kayak tours ($90 half-day), and custom overnight adventures ($545-840) on both the Middle Fork and North Fork for either one or two nights.

Cross-Country Skiing

When the white stuff blankets the park, cross-country skiers and snowshoers find themselves in a winter paradise. Many of the hiking trails double as ski and snowshoe trails, but nothing is groomed, so keen and constant orientation is critical.

Lower McDonald Creek

The Lower McDonald Creek trailhead is just south of McDonald Creek Bridge, and the trail is 2-3 mi (3-5 km) round-trip of gentle, forested terrain that parallels the creek in some spots.

Rocky Point Trail

Another mostly level but longer option is the Rocky Point trail, which is 6 mi (10 km) round-trip and rewards skiers with a phenomenal view of Lake McDonald. The trailhead is 0.2 mi (0.3 km) north of Fish Creek Campground.

Going-to-the-Sun Road

Since many of the roads in the park are unplowed and impassable for cars in winter, they make excellent ski trails. Going-to-the-Sun Road is one of the best, but due to avalanche danger, it can often be closed east of Avalanche Creek.

Izaak Walton Inn

290 Izaak Walton Inn Dr. off US 2, Essex, between East Glacier and West Glacier; 406/807-8540; www.logecamps.com

Although it's not in the park, one of the region's most beloved areas for cross-country skiing is the Izaak Walton Inn, which has repeatedly been named one of the best cross-country ski resorts in the Rockies. Thirty mi (48 km) of trails are groomed for skiers mid-December-late March, and the inn's proximity to the park invites backcountry travel. Ski rentals are available for classic, skate, and backcountry skis (rates to be determined).

Food

East Glacier Area

For a town with just over 300 year-round residents, East Glacier has good restaurants that cater to Glacier-bound visitors. Often the best way to select a spot to eat is to walk around and see where the wait is shortest.

Serrano's Mexican Restaurant

29 Dawson Ave.; 406/226-9392; www.serranosmexican.com; 5pm-9pm daily May-Memorial Day and Labor Day-early Oct., 5pm-10pm daily Memorial Day-Labor Day; $16-28

Serrano's Mexican Restaurant is inside the oldest house in East Glacier. Nothing is old-fashioned, however, about the menu: There are classic and delicious Mexican favorites alongside local offerings including grilled Montana flank steak and huckleberry tres leches cake. The cocktail offerings and beer list are extensive.

Two Medicine Grill

314 US 2 E.; 406/226-9227; www.seeglacier.com/two-medicine-grill; 6:30am-2:30pm daily summer; $7-18

Two Medicine Grill is a great spot for budget travelers. The menu has pretty standard fare for the region—bison burgers, homemade chili, chicken-fried steak—but the quality is excellent, and the staff are friendly and generous with advice and insights on the area. The huckleberry shakes are the stuff of legend, as is the double-crusted huckleberry pie.

Summit Mountain Lodge Steakhouse

16900 US 2; 406/226-9319; www.summitmtnlodge.com; 5pm-9pm Tues.-Sun. mid-June-late Sept.; $19-38

Getting rave reviews from locals and tourists alike is Summit Mountain Lodge Steakhouse, housed in an old train station with a beautiful outside dining area. The food is locally sourced whenever possible. There is a good wine list, and pairing suggestions are offered. Entrées include saltimbocca, grilled beef tenderloin, wild prawns piccata, salads, and pasta.

St. Mary to Many Glacier

Snowgoose Grille

3 Going-to-the-Sun Rd.; 406/732-4431; www.glacierparkcollection.com; 8am-9pm daily late May-late Sept., hours can vary so call ahead; $12-40

Without a doubt, the fanciest (and priciest!) place to go for a meal in St. Mary is the Snowgoose Grille in the St. Mary Village. This slightly modern take on the Western steakhouse offers steak frites, bison stroganoff, huckleberry salmon, and wild game gnocchi, as well as plenty of vegetarian options, for both lunch and dinner. There are burgers, soups, and salads too. There is also a breakfast buffet ($15-22) with all the usual suspects. The adjacent **Curly Bear Café** (11am-8pm daily; $12-18) is primarily a sandwich and ice-cream joint. Outside seating is available and highly desirable when the weather cooperates. The on-site **Triple Divide Coffee Company** serves up coffee, espresso drinks, boba, and pastries (6am-6pm daily).

Two Dog Flats Grill

1380 Wisconsin Ave.; 855/733-4522; www.glaciernationalparklodges.com; 6:30am-10am, 11am-2:30pm, and 5pm-10pm daily early June-early Sept.; $8-28

Two Dog Flats Grill at the Rising Sun Motor Inn & Cabins is operated by Glacier National Park Lodges. It offers standard fare, from burgers and chicken to steak and pasta, and is open for three meals daily during the season. Basic boxed lunches are available with no substitutions.

★ Park Café

3147 US 89; 406/732-9979; www.parkcafeandgrocery.com; 8am-7pm daily early-mid-June, 7:30am-9pm daily June 20-Aug., 8am-7pm daily Sept. 1-mid-Sept.; $12-26

The Park Café in St. Mary is staffed by people who know and really love Glacier National Park. The mantra here is "The Power of Pie." The pies—nine flavors daily—are worth every mile on the trail you'll need to work them off. The food is mostly American, from steaks and fish to outrageous baked potatoes, and for the most part as healthy as it is inventive and delicious. There's also a fantastic gift store and grocery on-site.

★ Two Sisters Café

3600 US 89, 4 mi/6 km north of St. Mary; 406/732-5535; www.twosistersofmontana.com; coffee shop 7:30am-3pm daily, café 4pm-9pm Sun.-Fri. June-Sept.; $5-29

Up the road in Babb is the Two Sisters Café, a colorful place that is worth the scenic drive along Lower St. Mary Lake. Although the decor is rather outrageous, the food is sublime—a hiker's dream come true. Entrées vary wildly from trout and waffles to the hand-cut bison tenderloin au poivre, from banh mi to barbecued pork. All are excellent, as is their famous Red Burger. The café serves grass-fed bison from the recently restored Blackfeet tribal herd. It's quite a story! And be sure to save room for dessert; their pies, like everything else, are out of this world.

Ptarmigan Dining Room

Many Glacier Hotel; 855/733-4522; www.glaciernationalparklodges.com; 6:30am-10am, 11:30am-2:30pm, and 5pm-9pm daily mid-June-mid-Sept.; $20-44

For those not cooking their own supper over a fire pan in Many Glacier, there are only a few options. The Ptarmigan Dining Room offers such flavorful entrées as pan-seared duck breast, bison tenderloin, burgers, and more. But perhaps the best part of the meal will be the lake and mountain view. For breakfast ($8-14) diners can choose from the buffet or order à la carte. Reservations aren't accepted—it's first-come, first-served only.

Swiss Lounge

Many Glacier Hotel; 11:30am-10pm daily, drinks until 11pm; $6-28

Lighter fare, including appetizers, burgers, salads, and cocktails, is available in Many Glacier Hotel's Swiss Lounge. The hotel also has a snack shop and espresso stand on-site.

'Nell's

855/733-4522; www.glaciernationalparklodges.com; 6:30am-10am and 11am-10pm daily mid-June-mid-Sept.; $10-23

In the Swiftcurrent Motor Inn & Cabins is a casual eatery, 'Nell's. It serves standard fare for three meals daily including all-day breakfast, pizza, sandwiches, and burgers, all of which can taste outstanding after a long day on the trail. Boxed lunches are available when ordered a day ahead.

West Glacier Area

Russell's Fireside Dining Room

288 Lake McDonald Lodge Loop; 855/733-4522; www.glaciernationalparklodges.com; 6:30am-10am, 11:30am-2:30pm, 5pm-9pm daily mid-May-early Oct.; $13-49

The ambience is the main attraction here, both the beauty of the lodge itself as well as the lakeside location. The food is fine—burgers and steaks and such—but it's the experience of dining in what feels like an old hunting lodge that makes a meal here special. There are full and continental breakfast buffets in this casual restaurant. Reservations are not accepted.

★ Belton Dining Room and Tap Room

12575 US 2 E.; 844/868-7474; www.glacierparkcollection.com; 5pm-10pm daily summer; $28-49

Even if you are not planning to stay at the Belton Chalet, the Belton Dining Room offers a rich dining experience in the historic 1910 chalet that is definitely worth a visit in this land of burgers and grilled cheese. The menu changes seasonally, and chef Earl offers innovative dishes incorporating fresh ingredients from local Montana growers and the chalet's own Flathead Lake orchard. For dinner you could sample heirloom tomatoes and burrata cheese, bison meatball, or drunken mussels. Entrées range from pasta with elk sausage and vegetarian red curry to steelhead trout, coffee-rubbed filet mignon, and classic rib eye steak.

Glacier Highland Restaurant

12555 US 2; 406/888-5427; www.glacierhighland.com; 7am-10pm daily July-Aug., off-season days and hours vary; $18-32

Glacier Highland Restaurant is an authentic West Glacier diner experience. Located just before the entrance to the park and across from the Amtrak depot, this is an easy stop if you are craving a 5-oz burger with all the toppings and fresh-cut fries. Hearty homemade soups and fresh-baked sweet treats are also on offer.

Eddie's Café & Mercantile

236 Apgar Loop Rd.; 406/888-5361; www.eddiescafegifts.com; 7am-9pm daily summer; $14-20

For breakfast and lunch with outdoor seating options in Apgar Village, Eddie's Café & Mercantile serves up excellent grub including oatmeal and breakfast sandwiches, bison burgers, and pulled pork.

Freda's

190 Going-to-the-Sun Rd.; 406/868-7474; 7:30am-9pm daily mid-May-Sept.; $8-17

The closest restaurant to the entrance at West Glacier is Freda's. Set in a classic Park Service-like building, the family-friendly restaurant offers casual dining with salads, burgers, ice cream, and an impressive beer and cocktail menu.

Polebridge Mercantile

265 Polebridge Loop; 406/888-5105; www.polebridgemerc.com; 7am-9pm daily Memorial Day-Labor Day, 9am-6pm daily Labor Day-last Sun. in Oct. and late Mar.-Memorial Day; $4-12

A long way down a dirt road in Glacier's North Fork Valley is a special off-the-grid spot that is worth every bump and then some. In business for more than 100 years, the remote Polebridge Mercantile offers world-class baked goods—don't leave without at least a couple of huckleberry bear claws—and a full deli in addition to groceries and gifts. Lodging in sweet cabins and gear rentals are also available.

Accommodations

East Glacier Area

★ Glacier Park Lodge

US 2 and Hwy. 49; 844/868-7474; www.glacierparkcollection.com; late May-late Sept.; $259-469

East Glacier has several small, kitschy motels that are ideal for a night or two before heading into the park, but they are not well suited for a week's stay. The alternative is the stately Glacier Park Lodge, which opened to guests in 1913. An Adirondack-style hotel commissioned by the Great Northern Railway, it was constructed of massive fir and cedar timbers. The local Blackfeet who watched the structure go up called it omahkoyis, or "big-tree lodge." The grounds are beautifully manicured—there's even a historic and very playable nine-hole golf course in addition to a pitch-and-putt. The 161-room hotel offers fine and casual dining, a cocktail lounge, an outdoor swimming pool, and a day spa. The rooms are modest but comfortable, and some are worse for the wear than others. Family rooms come with multiple beds.

Mountain Pine Motel

909 Hwy. 49, 1 mi/1.6 km north of US 2; 406/226-4403; www.mtnpine.com; May-Sept.; $120-400

Slightly off the main drag is the tidy and comfortable Mountain Pine Motel, with 25 units plus the Bear's Den cottage that sleeps up to eight.

Whistling Swan Motel

512 US 2; 406/226-4412; www.seeglacier.com; motel rooms $129-219, cabins $199-279

The Whistling Swan Motel is a long, skinny building that feels a bit like train cars—somewhat appropriate given that the Amtrak station is just across the street. The guest rooms are spotlessly clean and quite comfortable. Hosts Mark and Colleen are exceptionally hospitable and go out of their way to make every guest feel welcome and accommodated. This motel is also within easy walking distance of the local eateries and shops.

East Glacier Motel & Cabins

1108 Hwy. 49; 406/226-5593; $130-250

The East Glacier Motel & Cabins offers six motel units and 11 cabins at an excellent value.

Traveler's Rest Lodge

20987 US 2; 406/226-9143 summer or 406/378-2414 winter; www.travelersrestlodge.net; Apr. 15-Oct. 1; $169-229

On the east side of town, offering cute, park-style cabins complete with kitchenettes, gas fireplaces, and covered front porches, Traveler's Rest Lodge is a great choice. There are discounts for staying more than one night.

Bison Creek Ranch

20722 US 2; 406/226-4482; www.bisoncreekranch.com; from $200-275

Two mi (3 km) west of town on what used to be a dude ranch is Bison Creek Ranch, a lodge offering simple sleeping cabins and larger A-frames. The same family has been pouring heart and soul into the ranch for more than 70 years, and it shows in every detail from the artwork to the housekeeping. Pets are permitted for a $20 fee.

Summit Mountain Lodge

16900 US 2; 406/226-9319; www.summitmtnlodge.com; from $169

A few miles from town is Summit Mountain Lodge, which offers eight cabins with modern amenities. Single cabins (from $249) have one queen bed and a full kitchenette. Double units (from $199) have two queen beds and a living area. Family cabins (from $545) sleep 6, 8, and 10 people. The setting and the views are world-class. And the on-site steakhouse, housed in an old train station, is a special place for a memorable meal.

TOP EXPERIENCE

Hike-In Chalets

★ Granite Park Chalet

888/345-2649; www.graniteparkchalet.com; from $140 first person, $95 each additional person, optional linen and bedding service $40 pp

If you are willing to hike to your accommodations, Granite Park Chalet is a fantastic option. The last of the railroad chalets to be built, Granite Park Chalet is a hiker's hostel geared toward do-it-yourselfers. The rooms are private; hikers prepare their own meals and, although linens can be ordered ahead of time,

generally sleep in their own sleeping bags. The most popular trail into Granite Park is the 7.6-mi (12.2-km) **Highline Trail,** accessed from Logan Pass. A shorter 4-mi (6.4-km) trail through burned country and with a steep 2,300-ft (701-m) climb can be accessed from the Going-to-the-Sun Road switchback known as The Loop, which is in fact not a loop.

Sperry Chalet

888/345-2649; www.sperrychalet.com; $284 first person, $189 each additional person per room

The 17 rooms in Sperry Chalet burned to the ground in a 2017 wildfire, but the historic property was ambitiously rebuilt and opened in 2020. There are also a handful of workshops put on at Sperry Chalet each summer on topics including glaciers, high alpine ecology, and Glacier Park history that include two nights in the chalet. Still rustic—there is no heat, electricity, or running water—and only accessible on foot, Sperry offers beds with bedding and three informal meals with each night's stay. Nightly rates go down by $32 after the first night. The Sperry Trail starts at Lake McDonald Lodge and covers 6.7 mi (10.8 km) with significant elevation gain.

St. Mary to Many Glacier

Although options abound in both St. Mary and Many Glacier for hotels, motels, and cabins, there are not many budget-friendly choices. The prices seem to reflect the scenery, which is spectacular, rather than the amenities, which can be quite modest. Campgrounds and RV parks are more common, but small cabins can be found as well.

Cottages at Glacier

300 Going-to-the-Sun Rd., St. Mary; 406/309-4231; www.thecottagesatglacier.com; late May-Oct.; $595-985

The Cottages at Glacier offer views of St. Mary Lake and comfortable varying accommodations that can sleep up to nine. The price tag is steep, and there

Granite Park Chalet

is a 2-3-night minimum stay, depending on the cottage, but for those who want a full kitchen, Wi-Fi, and satellite TV, these cottages are excellent.

St. Mary Village

US 89 and Going-to-the-Sun Rd.; 844/868-7474; www.glacierparkcollection.com; mid-June-late Sept.; $189-499

In business for more than 75 years, St. Mary Village is a full resort with all the modern amenities. From tipis to cabins, tiny houses, and motel and lodge rooms, this resort has 127 guest rooms among six facilities.

Rising Sun Motor Inn & Cabins

Going-to-the-Sun Rd.; 855/733-4522; www.glaciernationalparklodges.com; mid-June-early Sept.; from $254

Adjacent to St. Mary Lake is the 1940s-era Rising Sun Motor Inn & Cabins, offering simple, clean, motel-style rooms and on-site dining.

★ Many Glacier Hotel

855/753-4522; www.glaciernationalparklodges.com; mid-June-mid-Sept.; from $279

In Many Glacier, the standout is clearly the Many Glacier Hotel, a historic Swiss chalet-style lodge built in 1915 by the Great Northern Railway. The hotel is right on the shore of Swiftcurrent Lake, and there is no limit to the natural beauty of the region or the number of ways in which to enjoy it. The hotel is being refurbished, wing by wing, but the rooms are still simple and charming; the steep prices speak more to the hotel's setting in the Many Glacier Valley than its amenities. There are no televisions in the rooms and the Wi-Fi is extremely limited. There is nightly entertainment and a wealth of activities that include boat cruises, ranger-led hikes, evening programs, Red Bus Tours, and horseback riding from the lodge. Many Glacier Hotel is 11 mi (18 km) west of Babb on Route 3/Many Glacier Road and can only be accessed through the Many Glacier entrance station.

Swiftcurrent Motor Inn & Cabins

855/753-4522; www.glaciernationalparklodges.com; mid-June-mid-Sept.

Nearby, the Swiftcurrent Motor Inn & Cabins is decidedly less grandiose and equally less expensive. But this place also has a history; it was established as a tipi camp in 1911 by the Great Northern Railway. The Swiftcurrent will be closed throughout 2025 for improvements. Check the website for a reopening date, room types, and rates. The Swiftcurrent Motor Inn & cabins are 12 mi (19 km) west of Babb on Route 3/Many Glacier Road.

West Glacier Area

The West Glacier area has a good selection of places to stay, but once inside the park, or even within view of it, accommodations do not come cheap. If you are on a tight budget, camping is the best option. The hotels listed are only open during the summer season, when Glacier is busiest.

Izaak Walton Inn

290 Izaak Walton Inn Dr. off US 2, Essex, between East Glacier and West Glacier; 406/807-8540; www.logecamps.com; $216-600

Avid cross-country skiers who want to take advantage of the park during the winter should head to the Izaak Walton Inn, a charming, old but recently overhauled railroad hotel that is on the National Register of Historic Places. Built in 1939, the inn changed very little until it was sold in 2024 to LOGE Camps, after which it got a significant update with hipster flair. In addition to cozy rooms in the lodge, guests can select from unique accommodations including family cabins and beautifully restored railcars.

Glacier Haven Resort & Inn

14305 US 2 E.; 406/888-5720; www.glacierhavenresort.com; $100-199

In Essex, 20 mi (32 km) from West Glacier and 35 mi (56 km) from East Glacier, is Glacier Haven Resort & Inn, which offers old-school, clean accommodations in addition to great home-style cooking. The resort is open from April to December and has an **RV park** (from $65/night).

Apgar Village Lodge & Cabins

Lake View Dr., West Glacier; 406/892-2525 or 844/868-7474; www.glacierparkcollection.com; $189-469

A reasonably priced motel in the West Glacier area is the Apgar Village Lodge & Cabins, 2 mi (3 km) east of West Glacier village at the south end of Lake McDonald. There are 28 cabins with Western decor that sleep up to eight, most with kitchens with stoves and refrigerators, and each with its own picnic table. Ask for a cabin on McDonald Creek; you can literally fish from your front door. There are also 20 modestly furnished, clean motel rooms, some overlooking the creek, with either a queen or two twin beds.

Village Inn at Apgar

1.3 mi/2.1 km from the entrance at West Glacier; 855/733-4522; www.glaciernationalparklodges.com; $257-516

On the shores of Lake McDonald, the Village Inn at Apgar is a quaint, 1950s motor inn with 36 rooms and a listing on the National Register of Historic Places. As one of the less expensive accommodations in the park given its waterfront location, it is typically booked a year in advance. The season runs late May-early October.

West Glacier Cabins & RV Park

350 River Bend Dr., West Glacier; 406/888-5580; www.glacierparkcollection.com; cabins from $469, RV sites from $185

Set near the Flathead River, in and behind the village of West Glacier with easy access to dining, shops, and the park entrance, West Glacier Cabins & RV Park offers one- and two-bedroom full-service cabins with kitchens, porches, and modern amenities including Wi-Fi and cable TV.

Glacier Highland Resort

12555 US 2 E.; 406/888-5427; www.glacierhighland.com; from $185

In West Glacier, just across the street from the Amtrak depot, is the Glacier Highland Resort, which offers 33 clean, rustic rooms. They're open May through October.

Lake McDonald Lodge

Going-to-the-Sun Rd., 12 mi/19 km from West Glacier; 855/733-4522; www.glaciernationalparklodges.com; $153-640

Lake McDonald Lodge was built on the lake in 1914 by furrier John Lewis and adheres to the Swiss chalet style of architecture. Though the lodge and cabins are showing their age, they outshine the 1950s motor inn on-site. The 82-room lodge emanates rustic charm and still has personal touches, such as Lewis's hunting trophies displayed in the lobby. Guests and visitors can sip cocktails on the sprawling veranda, a serene setting that affords a beautiful view of the lake. The guest rooms, all with queen beds, are rustic yet comfortable. There are also duplex to six-plex cabins.

★ Belton Chalet

12575 US 2 E.; 406/888-5000 or 888/235-8665; www.glacierparkcollection.com; rooms $290-380, cottages $389-440

The most memorable stay in West Glacier is at Belton Chalet at the west entrance to the park. This was the first hotel built by the Great Northern Railway in 1910. A National Historic Landmark, all 25 guest rooms come with a queen bed and private bathroom and are furnished with antiques, but without TV, phones, or air-conditioning. The two cabins on the grounds each have three bedrooms to accommodate up to six people. Although the lodge is mostly closed during the winter season, the cabins are available to rent throughout the year. The lodge is immediately adjacent to both the highway and the train tracks, so silence is not possible. A fabulous restaurant on-site offers innovative and satisfying meals. The incredibly friendly staff even offer wake-up calls for northern lights and bear sightings.

Camping

Glacier has 13 front-country campgrounds with more than 1,000 sites, at least some of which are open May to mid-October. With the exception of St. Mary and Fish Creek, half the individual and group sites at Apgar, and half the campsites at Many Glacier, all campgrounds are available on a first-come, first-served basis, with nightly fees ranging $10-23. You'll increase your chances of finding a site by showing up earlier in the day and scheduling your trip midweek rather than on the weekend. An excellent page on the National Park Service website (www.nps.gov/glac) shows updated availability at campsites across the park. For advance reservations at Fish Creek or St. Mary, contact the **National Park Reservation System** (877/444-6777; www.recreation.gov).

If your decision to camp is last-minute and you find yourself without such critical items as a tent or sleeping bag, **Glacier Outfitters** (196 Apgar Loop; 406/219-7466; www.goglacieroutfitters.com) can help with its stock of rentable items.

East Glacier Area

Two Medicine Campground

13 mi/21 km from East Glacier; 100 sites; mid-May-late Sept.; $30

Set on Two Medicine Lake, Two Medicine Campground is well developed with potable water, flush toilets, and an amphitheater for nightly ranger presentations. Outside the regular season, primitive camping ($20) is possible late September-late October. Reservations are required (www.recreation.gov).

Cut Bank Campground

21 mi/34 km from East Glacier; 14 sites; late May-mid-Sept.; $20

Farther north in a smaller and more secluded spot, the primitive Cut Bank Campground has 14 first-come, first-served sites, accessed 5 mi (8 km) down a dirt road from US 89. RVs are not recommended due to the nature of the road and the campground layout. Shuttles are only available from the highway.

St. Mary to Many Glacier

St. Mary Campground

148 sites; late May-mid-Sept.; $30

St. Mary Campground has 148 sites, including 22 sites that can accommodate RVs and truck-trailer combinations up to 35 ft (11 m), as well as water and flush toilets. It is the park's largest campground, only 0.5 mi (0.8 km) from the St. Mary Visitor Center, and has limited shade but superb views. Primitive camping ($20) is available early April-late May and mid-September through November. Reservations are required (www.recreation.gov). Winter camping is also possible December-March.

Rising Sun Campground

84 sites; mid-June-early Sept.; $20

Rising Sun is located halfway along St. Mary Lake in the shadow of Red Eagle Mountain. Sites are first-come, first-served. Some sites are exposed, while others are tucked into the trees. There are 10 RV sites, water, flush toilets, and showers.

Many Glacier Campground

109 sites; late May-late Sept.; $30

Not far from the Many Glacier Hotel, Many Glacier Campground has 109 sites (reservations required, www.recreation.gov), including 13 sites for RVs up to 35 ft (11 m), as well as water and flush toilets. The regular season is late May-late September, but primitive camping ($20) is available late September-October. The views are phenomenal, and the access to hiking and boating is amazing.

West Glacier Area

Apgar

1 mi/1.6 km northeast of the west entrance; late Apr.-late Sept.; $30

At 194 sites, Apgar is the largest campground and set in the trees along Lake McDonald.

Fish Creek

Camas Rd., 2.5 mi/4 km from Apgar Village; mid-May-early Sept.; $30

The second-largest campground in the park, Fish Creek has 187 sites. There are some trees here and views of Lake McDonald from some of the sites.

Whitefish

Given a great boost when the train was rerouted from Kalispell in 1904, Whitefish (pop. 8,915, elev. 3,036 ft/925 m) grew up around Whitefish Mountain (long called Big Mountain) and the sport of skiing, and today is Montana's largest year-round resort community. Although Whitefish is clearly a ski town, it is also an art town, a gateway to Glacier, a summer hot spot, and a great place to find gourmet cuisine.

Getting to Whitefish

From **West Glacier,** Whitefish is 30 mi (48 km) west on US 2, a 40-minute drive. From **Kalispell,** it's 15 mi (24 km) north on US 93, a 25-minute drive.

Amtrak (500 Depot St., Whitefish) runs the **Empire Builder** from Chicago to Seattle with daily stops in Whitefish in each direction.

Getting Around

There are multiple taxi options including **406 Rides of Northwest Montana** (406/309-1542; www.406rides.com) and **Wild Horse Limousine** (406/756-2290 or 509/220-0364 after hours; www.wildhorselimo.com). Shuttle service is available from **Airport Shuttle Express** (403/509-4799; www.airportshuttleexpress.com), **Arrow Shuttle** (406/300-2301; www.arrowshuttletaxi.com), and **Mountain Shuttle** (406/493-2345; www.mountainshuttlemt.com).

Adventure and Recreation

★ Skiing at Whitefish Mountain Resort

1015 Glades Dr.; 406/862-2900; www.skiwhitefish.com; $97

When it comes to skiing in Montana, it doesn't get much better than at Whitefish Mountain Resort, which offers 111 marked trails, 11 lifts, 2,353 ft (717 m) of vertical drop, and a 3.3-mi (5.3-km) run. When the snow conditions are just right, trees all across the top of the mountain look like enormous snow monsters. It's magical—or terrifying, depending upon your point of view. This is a *big* mountain, with serious skiing and family fun at its best. The mountain stays open year-round for hiking, mountain biking, zip-line tours, and an alpine slide, among other activities. In addition to offering regular 9am-4pm lift hours, it's also one of the few mountains in Montana that offer lighted night skiing (4pm-8:30pm daily; $30). Be aware that prices generally increase every year.

Cross-Country Skiing

Glacier Nordic Center

1200 US 93 W., Whitefish; 406/862-9498; www.glaciernordicclub.com; day passes $20

For cross-country skiers, groomed trails can be found at the Glacier Nordic Center on Whitefish Lake Golf Course. There are 7.5 mi (12 km) of skate and classic trails on gently rolling terrain, and lighted night skiing on 1.9 mi (3 km) of trails until 11pm. A Nordic shop (406/862-9498) on-site sells passes and rents gear for kids and adults by the half day, full day, or week. Private and group lessons are also available.

Hiking and Biking

3840 Big Mountain Rd., Whitefish; 406/862-2900 or 877/754-3474; www.skiwhitefish.com; 8am-6pm daily mid-June-early Sept., Fri.-Sun. only through late Sept.; $57 full day, $42 2 hours

In addition to having Glacier National Park as a backyard, both Kalispell and Whitefish have excellent hiking and biking trails. Among the adventures at **Whitefish Mountain Resort** are mountain biking opportunities for the hard-core and not-so-hard-core, who might prefer to limit rides to downhill only. There are more than 25 mi (40 km) of lift-accessed single-track and cross-country trails on the mountain.

Danny On National Scenic Trail

Distance: 8 mi (13 km) round-trip
Duration: 5 hours
Elevation gain: 2,037 ft (621 m)
Effort: Strenuous
Trail Surface: Dirt and rock, can be slippery
Trailhead: Danny On Memorial Trail #370, Whitefish Mountain Resort

For hikers, the Danny On National Scenic Trail winds 4 mi (6.4 km) from the base of the ski hill to the summit. The lift can be taken up or down to make the hike shorter and easier. It's a popular trail, and dog-friendly, so you'll likely have company as you hike. There is shade along the well-maintained trail, and huckleberries to pick in season.

Golf

Whitefish Lake Golf Club

1200 US 93 N.; 406/862-5960, 406/862-4000 for tee times; www.golfwhitefish.com; $63-93 for 18 holes, $38-60 for 9 holes, $54-66 for 18 holes on the South Course after 3pm

Public courses in Whitefish include the North and South Courses at the Whitefish Lake Golf Club, which offers

Whitefish in winter

discounts for booking within two days of play. Clubs ($30-45) and carts ($30-46) are available for rent.

Entertainment and Events

Downtown Farmers Market

1 Central Ave.; 406/407-5272; www.whitefishfarmersmarket.org; 5pm-7:30pm Tues. late May-late Sept.

In Whitefish, summer brings the Downtown Farmers Market, offering local produce and art, handmade crafts, prepared food, and entertainment.

Whitefish Arts Festival

Depot Park, Whitefish; 406/862-5875; www.whitefishartsfestival.org; July

Among the annual festivals celebrating local art, food, and culture is the Whitefish Arts Festival, usually held the first weekend in July in Depot Park.

Huckleberry Days Art Festival

Depot Park, Whitefish; 406/862-3501; www.whitefishchamber.org; Aug.

The Huckleberry Days Art Festival, held over three days in mid-August, celebrates the juicy purple berry with music, entertainment, an art fair, and lots of family fun.

Feast Whitefish

O'Shaughnessy Center, 1 Central Ave., Whitefish, across from the train station; 406/862-3501; www.feastwhitefish.com; May

In mid-May, Feast Whitefish is the region's premier food event. It includes a weeklong dinner series with exquisite nightly meals by regional chefs and a one-day distiller's fest that focuses on local vodkas, whiskeys, and other spirits by seven regional distilleries.

Whitefish Winter Carnival

www.whitefishwintercarnival.com; Feb.

Whitefish Winter Carnival is a silly and fun event meant to help locals survive the gray middle of winter, held annually in early February. Activities include an elaborate parade, penguin plunge, pie social, and beer curling.

Alpine Theatre Project

600 2nd St. E.; 406/862-7469; www.atpwhitefish.org

Despite its size, Whitefish has a remarkably savvy theater crowd, anchored by the Alpine Theatre Project, a highly respected repertory theater company with a reputation that reaches far beyond state lines.

Whitefish Theatre Company

1 Central Ave.; 406/862-5371; www.whitefishtheatreco.org

Whitefish Theatre Company offers an impressive season of events each year, including plays, concerts, professional dance, improv performances, workshops, camps, and films.

Shopping

The streets of downtown Whitefish are filled with bars, restaurants, spas, and notably, art galleries. **Whitefish Gallery Nights** (www.whitefishgallerynights.org) takes place the first Thursday evening of each month May-October. Nine galleries are involved, each sponsoring a different artist each night of the event. It's a great way to view art, meet the artists, sample good food, and experience the community.

Stumptown Art Studio

145 Central Ave.; 406/862-5929; www.stumptownartstudio.org; 10am-6pm Mon.-Sat., noon-5pm Sun.

Several galleries line Central Avenue, including Stumptown Art Studio, a marvelous gallery for buying, learning about, and even making art.

Imagination Station Toys

221 Central Ave.; 406/862-5668; www.montanatoys.com; 10:30am-5:30pm Mon.-Sat., 11am-4pm Sun.

Imagination Station Toys began about 25 years ago when the owners realized that they missed the toys of their youth. They stock up with the latest wooden toys from Europe, have a good selection of educational toys, and like to keep a lot of puzzles and board games on hand.

Sappari

215 Central Ave.; 406/862-6848; www.sappariwhitefish.shopsettings.com; 10am-6pm Mon.-Sat., noon-5pm Sun.

For a well-curated selection of clothing, housewares, jewelry, gifts, and Montana designers, head to Sappari.

Kettle Care Organics

3575 US 93; 406/257-6622; www.kettlecare.com; 9am-5pm Wed.-Fri.

Kettle Care Organics is committed to producing fine all-natural body-care products while remaining conscious of its carbon footprint. The ingredients come from its certified organic farm and are created, packaged, and labeled for sale on-site. A small showroom is stocked with products.

Food

Buffalo Café & Nightly Grill

514 3rd St. E.; 406/862-2833; www.buffalocafewhitefish.com; breakfast and lunch 7am-2pm Mon.-Sat. and 8am-2pm Sun., dinner 5pm-close Tues.-Fri.; $15-21

Its status as a resort town means that Whitefish has several excellent restaurants. One of the all-around best places to go for a hearty meal is the budget-friendly Buffalo Café & Nightly Grill. From old-fashioned milkshakes and blueberry granola pancakes to Mexican specialties and baby back ribs, this local favorite has mastered comfort food.

★ Loula's Café

300 2nd St. E., Whitefish; 406/862-5614; www.whitefishrestaurant.com; 7am-2pm daily; $7-16

When breakfast or pie (or any meal whatsoever) is on the docket, one should not overlook Loula's Café. Breakfast ($7-16) is everything from Yuppie Scrambles to Ski Bum Biscuits and Gravy, eggs Benedict, and breakfast burritos. Save room for pie. Lunch ($10-16) is a selection of burgers, sandwiches, soups, and salads. And pie. Don't forget the pie. If you happen to be in Loula's when the pies come out of the oven and you don't jump to buy at least one, you will regret it for the remainder of your trip. I'm not kidding. Eating a huckleberry cherry pie, straight from the box and still a bit warm, on the shores of Lake McDonald is a memory that will stay with you forever.

Wasabi Sushi Bar

419 E. 2nd St.; 406/863-9283; www.wasabimt.com; from 5pm Tues.-Sat.; $8-25

Although Montana is not known for its sushi, Whitefish residents could not live without Wasabi Sushi Bar, with classic nigiri and sashimi, a contemporary twist on sushi and tempura, and plenty of grill

Whitefish

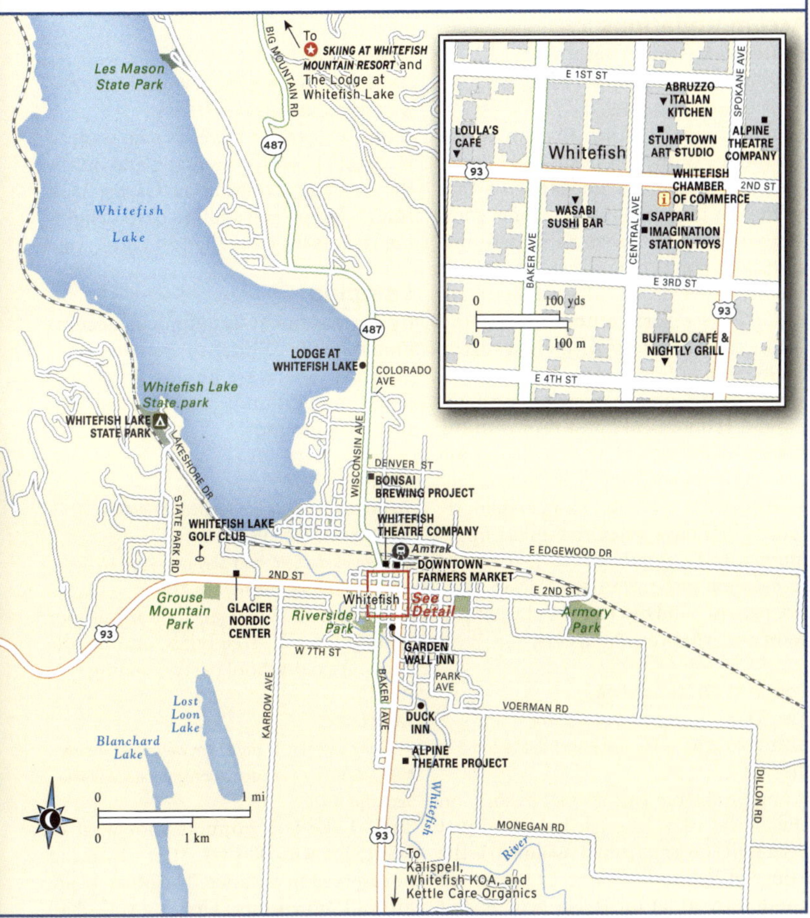

items that include steak, duck, scallops, fish tacos, and more.

Abruzzo Italian Kitchen

115 Central Ave., Whitefish; 406/730-8767; www.abruzzoitaliankitchen.com; 4pm-9pm Sun.-Thurs., 4pm-10pm Fri.-Sat.; $18-42

Open since 2017, Abruzzo Italian Kitchen focuses on quality ingredients and the simplicity of preparation. Everything is made from scratch. There are Italian cocktails and wine, wood-fired pizzas, salads, and entrées like wild boar ragu, spaghetti carbonara, chicken cacciatore, and, of course in Montana, steak.

Bonsai Brewing Project

549 Wisconsin Ave., Whitefish; 406/730-1717; www.bonsaibrew.com; noon-8pm Tues.-Sun.

Bonsai Brewing Project's tap list usually has more than 10 offerings, from blond ales, pale ales, and IPAs to brown ales, barleywine, and aged sour pale ales. Plus they have plenty of other selections in bottles. They serve snacks, salads, soul bowls, and tacos ($6-21).

Accommodations

Whitefish Mountain Resort

3889 Big Mountain Rd.; 406/862-2900; www.skiwhitefish.com; $217-479

Given its proximity to Whitefish Mountain, Whitefish Lake, and Glacier National Park, it's no surprise that Whitefish has an abundance of accommodations—but true to its resort-town vibe, beds don't come cheap. The largest and most diverse is Whitefish Mountain Resort, the resort community around Whitefish Mountain with eight different lodging options, 90 percent of which are condominiums that range from modest and economical guest rooms in the **Hibernation House** to five-bedroom townhouses (from $665). Rates are generally higher in winter, and particularly around holidays when five-night minimums can be required. Navigating the reservation system can be a feat, so practice patience and be clear about what you want and what your budget is.

Lodge at Whitefish Lake

1380 Wisconsin Ave.; 406/863-4000 or 877/887-4026; www.lodgeatwhitefishlake.com; $183-413

Another sizable full-service resort, on the shores of Whitefish Lake and just over 1 mi (1.6 km) from downtown, is the Lodge at Whitefish Lake. The attached condos are great for larger groups, but somewhat less romantic than the luxe lodge rooms. Immediate lake access is a disincentive to ever leave, and on-site restaurants keep guests well fed and happy.

Duck Inn

1305 Columbia Ave.; 406/862-3825 or 800/344-2377; www.duckinn.com; $153-384

Smaller options for lodging in the town of Whitefish include the riverfront Duck Inn, a rambling inn on the river with 15 rooms and suites, and a hearty breakfast to launch each day. There is a family room that sleeps six and three queen rooms with bunk beds that sleep four.

Garden Wall Inn

504 Spokane Ave.; 406/862-3440 or 888/530-1700; www.gardenwallinn.com; $225-395

A perfect spot for travelers who want to walk into town for shopping and meals, the charming five-bedroom Garden Wall Inn is chef-owned and has been delighting visitors for more than 30 years.

Camping

By far the most economical accommodations in Whitefish are the campgrounds. There are beautiful national forest campgrounds as well as two private campgrounds.

Whitefish KOA

5121 US 93 S., 2 mi/3 km south of Whitefish; 406/862-4242 or 800/562-8734; www.glacierparkkoa.com; mid-May-mid-Sept.; RV and tent sites $79-140, cabins $148-271

Whitefish KOA has an indoor/outdoor pool, mini golf, free bikes, and paddle boats. It's old-school party camping.

Tally Lake

913 Tally Lake Rd., 17 mi/27 km west of Whitefish; 406/646-1012; www.recreation.gov; late May-late Sept.; from $20

Tally Lake is a popular spot west of Whitefish with 38 sites, 21 of which can be reserved in advance. The other 17 are for walk-up visitors. There's a volleyball net and beaches, and each site has a picnic table, fire ring, and grill.

Whitefish Lake State Park

1615 E. Lakeshore Dr.; 406/862-3991 or 406/751-4590; www.fwp.mt.gov/whitefish-lake; park open year-round, campground with showers open May-Sept.; $12-42

Closer to town, Whitefish Lake State Park offers 25 waterfront tent and RV sites that go quickly at this beautiful, convenient spot. Sites can be reserved at www.montanastateparks.reserveamerica.com.

Information and Services

Whitefish Chamber of Commerce

505 E. 2nd St., Whitefish; 406/862-3501; www.whitefishchamber.org; 9am-5pm Mon.-Fri.

The Whitefish Chamber of Commerce includes the Whitefish Visitor's Bureau and is an excellent online resource for events, attractions, and more.

Logan Health Whitefish

1600 Hospital Way at the intersection of US 93 and Hwy. 40; 406/863-3528; www.logan.org

In Whitefish, Logan Health Whitefish is a private critical access hospital with a 24-hour emergency room and 25 patient rooms.

Kalispell

The town of Kalispell (pop. 22,761, elev. 2,956 ft/901 m) exists because of James Hill's Great Northern Railway and survives in spite of it. Freight and mercantile baron Charles Conrad founded the town of Kalispell when he convinced his friend Hill to run the railroad through it in 1891. By 1904, the Great Northern had abandoned its Kalispell route in favor of the more geographically amenable Whitefish line just 15 mi (24 km) to the north. The people of Kalispell were furious, but the town's economy survived thanks to Conrad's National Bank and the booming timber industry. Today it is still rather industrial—a nuts-and-bolts kind of town that serves as a natural supply and shopping center—and has some wonderful museums, parks, and an ideal location between Flathead Lake and Glacier National Park.

Getting to Kalispell

From **West Glacier,** Kalispell is 35 mi (56 km) southwest on US 2 and MT-206, about a 50-minute drive. From **Whitefish,** it's 15 mi (24 km) south on US 93, about a 25-minute drive.

Just south of Whitefish, Kalispell is the larger of the two cities and has commercial flights and bus service, along with taxi services.

The **Glacier Park International Airport** (FCA; 4170 US 2 E., Kalispell; www.iflyglacier.com) is served daily by Delta, Alaska, American, and United. Seasonal and twice- or three-times-weekly flights can be found on Sun Country, Jet Blue, Frontier, and Allegiant. There are on-site car-rental counters for **Avis, Budget, Hertz,** and **National/Alamo; Dollar,** (406/892-0009; www.dollar.com), **Enterprise** (406/755-4848; www.enterprise.com), and **Thrifty** (406/257-7333; www.thrifty.com) are off-site but near the airport.

Greyhound (2075 US 2 E., Kalispell; 406/755-7447) offers daily bus service in and out of Kalispell.

Getting Around

There are multiple taxi options including **406 Rides of Northwest Montana** (406/309-1542; www.406rides.com) and **Wild Horse Limousine** (406/756-2290 or 509/220-0364 after hours; www.wildhorselimo.com). Shuttle service is available from **Airport Shuttle Express** (403/509-4799; www.airportshuttleexpress.com), **Arrow Shuttle** (406/300-2301; www.arrowshuttletaxi.com), and **Mountain Shuttle** (406/212-2149; www.mountainshuttlemt.com).

Sights

Conrad Mansion National Historic Site

330 Woodland Ave., Kalispell; 406/755-2166; www.conradmansion.com; 10am-4pm daily May 15-Oct. 15, 10am-4pm Wed.-Sun. Dec. 4-31, 10am-4pm Tues.-Fri. Jan. 16-May 14; docent-guided tour $20, self-guided tour $15

Just a block from Woodland Park sits the palatial home of Charles Conrad, Kalispell's founder. The Conrad Mansion was completed in 1895 and the family made sure that residents of Kalispell felt some connection to the house: On Christmas Day of the year it

was finished, the Conrads invited people from around town who would otherwise have spent the holiday alone to share in their feast. The entire city was invited to a grand New Year's Eve ball a week later. Over the years, Alicia Conrad hosted famous parties, including a Halloween gathering just after a fire had burned through the roof of the mansion. After her death in 1923, the family continued to occupy the home until the mid-1960s. In 1974, Conrad's youngest daughter donated the residence to the city of Kalispell. The 26-room, nine-bedroom Norman-style mansion has been restored and is furnished with the family's original furniture. There is also a large collection of family clothing and three generations of children's toys. Special tours include historical fashion tours and the Lettie Conrad tour, which focuses on the mansion's original matriarch.

Hockaday Museum of Art

302 2nd Ave. E., Kalispell; 406/755-5268; www.hockadaymuseum.com; 10am-5pm Tues., 10am-4pm Wed.-Sat. summer, 11am-5pm Tues., 11am-4pm Wed.-Sat. Sept.-May; $8

The Hockaday Museum of Art was originally begun by local artists in the late

1960s, and today it is known for showcasing some of the region's most important art and artists. Visitors will find works by T. J. Hileman, John Fery, and Charles M. Russell, among others. It has the largest collection of Glacier Park art in the country and a large permanent collection dedicated to the Blackfeet Nation. Public tours are offered for free, with admission, on Thursday and Saturday at 10:30am. Hockaday hosts the **Arts in the Park** program each July, and the gift shop has a broad selection of original works, including jewelry, pottery, and prints by local artists.

Northwest Montana History Museum

124 2nd Ave. E., Kalispell; 406/756-8381; www.nwmthistory.org; 10am-5pm Mon.-Fri., 10am-3pm Sat. June-Aug., 10am-5pm Mon.-Fri. Sept.-May; $9

The Central School building opened in 1894 and is used by the Northwest Montana Historical Society as the Northwest Montana History Museum. The museum is dedicated to preserving the history of northwestern Montana and especially Kalispell. Permanent exhibits include a historical examination of the Flathead Valley, the growth of the logging industry in Montana, a historical look at recreation in Glacier National Park, and a fascinating look at Demersville, a once-active community in the Flathead and now a stretch of deserted road. The museum hosts walking tours of Kalispell during the summer, as well as free movie nights featuring classic films and free popcorn.

Adventure and Recreation

Hiking and Biking

Lone Pine State Park

300 Lone Pine Rd., Kalispell; 406/755-2706; www.stateparks.mt.gov/lone-pine; $8/vehicle nonresidents

Just 4 mi (6 km) southwest of Kalispell, Lone Pine State Park has a nature trail, 7.5 mi (12.1 km) of hiking and biking trails with scenic overlooks, and a year-round visitor center with flush toilets and a picnic shelter. A variety of programs—from yoga to full-moon hikes—are scheduled throughout the year. Young kids ages 4-7 will be excited about the **Junior Ranger Club,** where they can learn about the natural world through activities and games.

Entertainment and Events

Kalispell Farmers Market

777 Grandview Dr.; 406/260-5102; www.kalispellfarmersmarket.org; 9am-12:30pm Sat. early May-mid.-Oct.

With so much to do year-round in this part of the state, the calendar is always full. In northwestern Montana, summertime means farmers markets. Kalispell Farmers Market is held at Flathead Valley Community College.

Artists and Craftsmen of the Flathead Summer Outdoor Show

920 S. Main St., Kalispell; 406/201-9383; www.artistsandcraftsmen.org

Another market, which focuses on locally made arts and crafts, is Artists and Craftsmen of the Flathead Summer Outdoor Show, held over a summer weekend. They also put on an excellent market at the Flathead County Fairgrounds over a weekend in late November or early December.

Northwest Montana Fair & Rodeo

Fairgrounds, 265 N. Meridian Rd., Kalispell; 406/758-5810; www.nwmtfair.com; fair admission $8, special events ticketed separately

Perhaps the most anticipated event of the year is the Northwest Montana Fair & Rodeo, usually held in mid-August and kicked off with a parade. The nearly weeklong event includes local agricultural exhibits, a carnival, three nights of professional rodeo, and live entertainment.

Shopping

Western Outdoor

48 Main St., Kalispell; 406/756-5818 or 800/636-5818; www.westernod.com; 9:30am-6pm Mon.-Sat., 10:30am-4pm Sun. summer, 10am-6pm Mon.-Sat., 11am-4pm Sun. fall-spring

Western Outdoor boasts more than 2,500 pairs of boots and close to 1,500 hats in every size, shape, and style imaginable. If you've always wanted real cowboy duds, this is the place.

Montana Kite Sports

405 3rd Ave. E.; 530/356-2758; 11am-5pm daily

A perfect winter shop in Kalispell is Montana Kite Sports, which introduces the sports of "power kiting" and "ice boating" to the willing. Hours can change with the weather, so call ahead. In addition to sales, they offer lessons!

Brix Bottleshop

115 S. Main St.; 406/393-2202; www.brixbottleshop.com; 10am-6pm Mon.-Thurs., 10am-6:30pm Fri.-Sat.

Located in Kalispell's historic loading dock, Brix Bottleshop carries more than 300 rotating craft beers and a beefy selection of wines with handwritten description tags. There are gourmet food items and seasonal gifts.

Food

The Knead Café

21 5th St. E., Kalispell; 406/755-3883; 8am-3pm Tues.-Sat.; $7-16

The Knead Café is a Mediterranean-inspired breakfast and lunch joint that rightly calls itself a "spirited fusion of food, art, and music."

Hops Downtown Grill

121 S. Main St., Kalispell; 406/755-7687; Facebook @HopsDowntownGrill; 5pm-9pm Sun.-Thurs., 5pm-9:30pm Fri.-Sat.; $10-32

Hops Downtown Grill is known for its wide selection of craft beer and gourmet burgers. Chicken, lasagna, ribs, and steak round out the menu.

The DeSoto Grill

227 1st St. W., Kalispell; 406/314-6095; www.desotogrill.com; 11am-9pm Tues.-Fri.; $12-48

Where else can you order bison frites? Described as rockabilly barbecue, the DeSoto Grill is set in an old forge. While you can't go wrong with any of the barbecue, the elk sausage and smokehouse nachos are especially good.

Mercantile Steak

30 2nd St. E.; 406/609-0821; www.mercantilesteak.com; 5pm-9pm Tues.-Sat.; $29-68

A classic steakhouse with contemporary flair, Mercantile Steak is in the historic KM building with original Tiffany-style lamps, stained glass windows, and a copper tin ceiling. From rib roast stew and elk meatball Bolognese to airline chicken and gorgeous steaks, the menu is timeless. Don't skip the twice-baked potato.

Accommodations

Kalispell is definitely the best place near Glacier to find an assortment of more budget-friendly chain hotels and motels, but prices can rise when the town is packed with travelers en route to or from Glacier or Flathead.

Aero Inn

1830 US 93 S.; 406/755-3798; www.aeroinn.com; $125-250

Next to the airport, the Aero Inn has 61 no-frills guest rooms and is reasonably priced.

Blue & White Motel

640 E. Idaho St.; 406/755-4311 or 800/382-3577; www.blueandwhitemotel.com; $59-125

Another good value can be found at the 106-room pet-friendly Blue & White Motel, which, in addition to cool signage, has decent rooms, standard amenities, and a 24-hour restaurant next door (making it a hit with truckers).

Kalispell Grand Hotel

100 Main St.; 406/755-8100 or 800/858-7422; www.kalispellgrand.com; $245-285

For a more historic experience, try the pet-friendly Kalispell Grand Hotel downtown. This stately brick property is the last of eight hotels that once lined downtown.

Camping

There are camping options, both public and private, outside of Kalispell, but nothing for tent campers in town.

Montana Basecamp RV Park

1000 Basecamp Dr., Kalispell; 406/756-9999; from $99

The 50-acre (20-ha) Montana Basecamp RV Park is wide open and grassy and includes free Wi-Fi and access to laundry. Instead of sites, each RV has a yard with pavement, a fire pit, a picnic table, and mountain views.

Ashley Lake Campgrounds

North Shore Rd., off Ashley Lake Rd., 17 mi/27 km west of Kalispell; 406/758-5204; www.fs.usda.gov; Memorial Day-Labor Day; no fees for day use or overnight camping, 5-day stay limit

A good primitive option for tent campers is Ashley Lake Campgrounds, which offers 11 lakefront sites but no services other than a vault toilet.

Information and Services

Kalispell Chamber of Commerce

2 S. Main St., Ste. 205; 406/758-2800; www.kalispellchamber.com; 8am-5pm Mon.-Fri.

With Kalispell's rapidly growing population, the Chamber of Commerce promotes civic, industrial, and commercial progress.

Flathead Convention and Visitor Bureau

15 Depot Park, Ste. 1; 406/756-9091; www.fcvb.org; 8:30am-4pm Mon.-Fri.

This is the best place to go for updated info on festivals and the culture of the Flathead Valley.

Flathead National Forest Headquarters

650 Wolf Pack Way, Kalispell; 406/758-5208; www.fs.usda.gov/flathead; 8am-4:30pm Mon.-Fri.

The Flathead National Forest Headquarters has helpful information for campers and hikers.

Logan Health Medical Center

350 Conway Dr.; 406/752-1733; www.logan.org

The Logan Health Medical Center has a 24-hour emergency room and several walk-in clinics.

Logan Health Primary Care

1287 Burns Way and 160 Heritage Way, Ste. 202; 406/752-5111; www.logan.org; 8am-6pm Mon.-Fri., 9am-5pm Sat.-Sun.

Logan Health Primary Care has two walk-in clinics in Kalispell.

Glacier to
Bozeman
BUTTE

Highlights

★ **Hiking at Jewel Basin:** With 27 lakes, 35 mi (56 km) of trails, and no motorized vehicles or horses permitted, this is a hiker's paradise (page 233).

★ **CSKT Bison Range:** On a low, rolling mountain near the Mission Mountains, some 400 bison wander as they once did on one of the country's oldest wildlife refuges (page 244).

★ **Old Butte Historical Adventures:** Spend some time with one of the passionate and knowledgeable guides here, where you'll see history both above and below the ground (page 260).

★ **World Museum of Mining:** This museum, built atop the Orphan Girl mine yard, is packed with artifacts from more than a century of hard-rock mining (page 262).

★ **Museum of the Rockies:** Renowned for its impressive dinosaur collection, this museum is home to 300,000 objects in permanent and traveling displays, a planetarium, and an outdoor living history farm (page 274).

★ **Madison Buffalo Jump State Park:** A hike on this park's cliff can be both a lesson in Native American history and an exercise in solitude (page 276).

Glacier to Bozeman

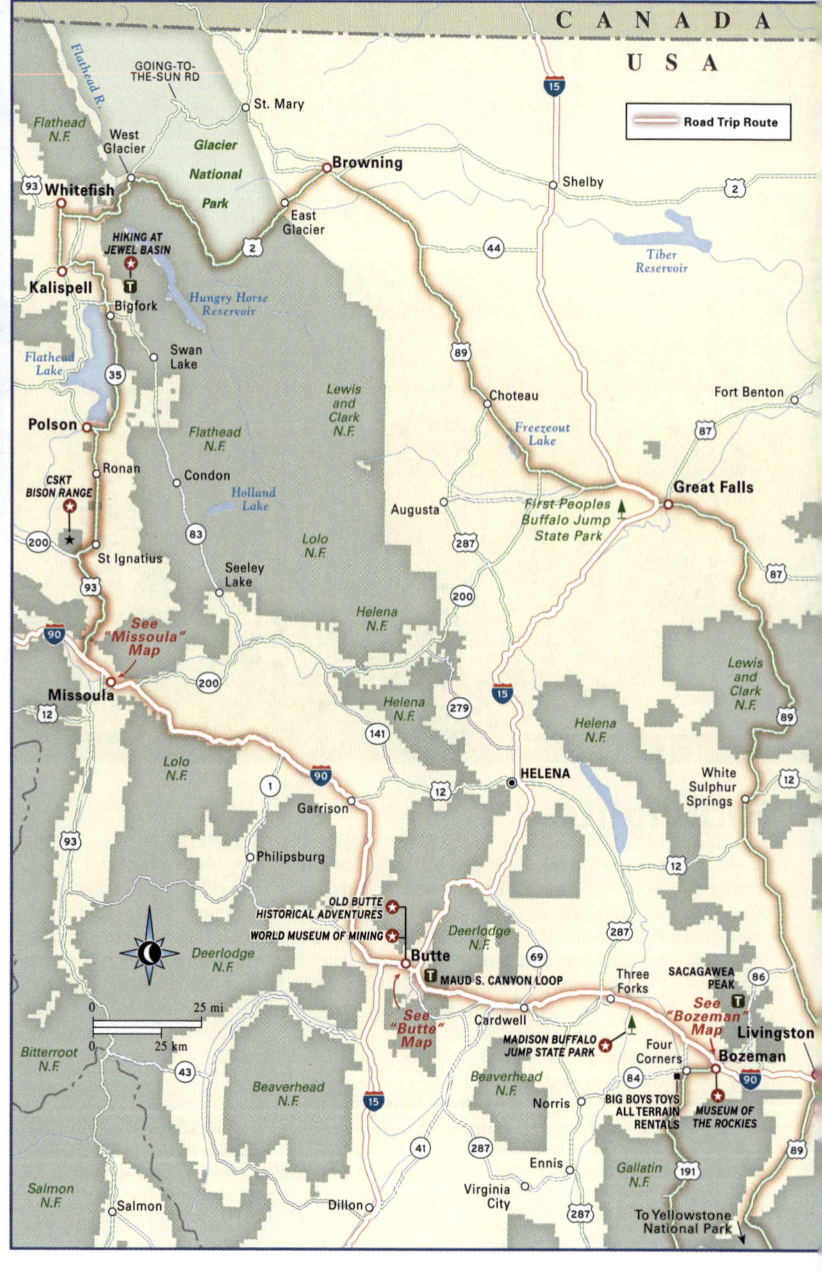

Driving From Glacier to Bozeman in Two Days

From Bigfork to Bozeman, the western route through Missoula is about 300 mi (483 km), south on US 93 and east on I-90, and about a 5-hour drive. There's plenty of nature to wet your feet and culture enough to whet your appetite.

Day 1

Wherever you wake up, start your day with a morning hike into the **Jewel Basin;** Twin Lakes is a good bet. Then refuel with a hearty meal at **Echo Lake Café** off of MT-83. Drive through **Bigfork**—stop for a coffee or some shopping if you like—and then wind along the east shore of **Flathead Lake** on MT-35. Make sure to stop and dip your toes in the water, and if it's cherry season, don't miss the chance to pick your own **Flathead cherries.**

Stop in to see the **St. Ignatius Mission** and then take a drive through the **CSKT Bison Range.** Continue down US 93 to **Missoula,** where you can enjoy a wood-fired pizza at **Biga Pizza** and settle in for the night at **The Wren.**

Day 2

In the morning, amble across the bridge for a pastry and espresso from **Le Petit Outre,** walk along Missoula's Riverfront Trail, and then hit I-90, heading eastward to **Butte.** In Butte, stop for a pasty at **Uptown Café** and visit the **World Museum of Mining.**

Continue on toward **Bozeman,** where you can grab dinner at **Revelry** and settle in for the night at **The Lark.**

Traveling from Glacier to Bozeman on the west side of the Rockies' spine—along Flathead Lake and through the Mission Valley to Missoula—this region of the state will put you amid lakes and cherry orchards and soaring peaks, wonderful territory for hiking, boating, and exploring. With the largest freshwater lake in the western US, and the wide-open space of the CSKT Bison Range, the Flathead and Mission valleys south of Glacier are also home to the lakeside towns of Bigfork and Polson. The hard part is not deciding what you want to see, but what you are willing to miss.

Missoula is a university town and a real city by Montana standards, with plenty of places to get a great meal and a comfortable bed. But there's culture here too, along with nightlife, downtown shopping, and a miles-long walking path beside the river, connecting the University of Montana campus to downtown. Active travelers can keep up the pace with a hike up the M or an adventure in the nearby Rattlesnake National Recreation Area.

Farther east, one of the state's best-known mining towns, Butte prospered and diversified, becoming one of Montana's most interesting and historically significant cities. Others, like Virginia City and Nevada City, all but disappeared before rising again as well-maintained tourist attractions. Indeed, history comes to life here.

The area around Bozeman is a playground, bursting with mountains to climb, rivers to fish, and trails to hike. While the main draw is the natural splendor and recreational opportunities, Bozeman—home of Montana State University—is an increasingly busy tourist hot spot with a lively arts scene and plenty of culinary and shopping options.

Alternate Route: Driving Down the Seeley-Swan Valley

For those looking for a more scenic route down the western side from Glacier to Bozeman, a single-lane highway through the Seeley-Swan Valley takes you through tall forests, along winding waterways, and past vast open ranchland in virtually the same amount of time as the main route via US 93 and I-90.You'll miss Polson and Missoula, but you'll have a chance to see how Montana used to be.

From West Glacier, head southwest on Highway 2 to Columbia Falls, where you'll go south on MT-206 for 13 mi (21 km) to MT-35, which will bring you to the edge of Flathead Lake and the resort town of **Bigfork.** Fuel up with a late breakfast or early lunch at **Echo Lake Café.**

From there, you'll drive east 5 mi (8 km) on MT-209 to US 83, which takes you down through the Seeley-Swan Valley nestled in the evergreen forest between the Swan and Mission mountain ranges. If you can, stop for lunch or a quick dip at the **Holland Lake Lodge** (1947 Holland Lake Lodge Rd., Condon; 406/754-2282; www.hollandlakelodge.com) and take a 3.2-mi (5.1-km) hike on the **Holland Falls National Recreation Trail** (1.5 hours; 750 ft/229 m elevation gain).

Continue south and east for 33 mi (52 km) on MT-141 and US 90 through Avon, Garrison, Deer Lodge, and Butte—where you can visit the **World Museum of Mining.** Continue east on I-90 54 mi (87 km) and, if time permits, you can have dinner at **Pompey's Grill** in the beautiful Sacajawea Hotel. From there it's just another 30 minutes' drive (31 mi/50 km) to Bozeman.

Planning Your Time

About halfway between Yellowstone and Glacier, **Missoula** is a natural stopping point along both east-west I-90 and north-south US 93. It's easier to get here by air than much of the state, but the city is also a great destination on its own. From boutique shopping and hip eateries near the **University of Montana,** to adventurous athletic pursuits in town and nearby, Missoula is Montana with an urban edge.

Between Missoula and Glacier, the stunning Flathead and Mission Valleys offer up plenty of history, remarkable wildlife refuges, and tiny but bustling villages lining the sandy shores of **Flathead Lake**—don't miss charming **Bigfork** with its galleries, eateries, and theater.

Butte is a fascinating destination, not so much for its present-day incarnation, which can be a bit rowdy and somewhat bleak, but for its older glory: the remarkable architecture that still stands, the underground city that is just coming to light, and the mines that made Butte the "richest hill on earth" and one of the country's largest cities west of the Mississippi for nearly 50 years. Butte is a marvelous place to spend at least a day, or more if you are interested in mining or history.

A host of other places in the region make great add-ons or stand-alone destinations. **Virginia City** and **Nevada City** are meticulously preserved ghost towns.

With its central location, ease of air or highway access, and abundance of accommodations, **Bozeman** is a superb launching point for the region. You could easily spend three days here, checking out the arts scene and nightlife and enjoying the spectacular recreational opportunities in every direction.

Best Restaurants

★ **Echo Lake Café, Bigfork:** This is the kind of place where you'll wait, happily, for generous portions of scrambles, crepes, and sandwiches, with homemade everything, from syrups and gravies to sauces and baked goods (page 236).

★ **Biga Pizza, Missoula:** Innovative and made from scratch, everything here is cooked in the wood-fired oven, from award-winning pizzas—like prosciutto and fig, or sweet potato, bacon, and maple chipotle—to mouthwatering calzones (page 257).

★ **Uptown Café, Butte:** In the heart of the mining city, this spot balances white-tablecloth elegance, sophisticated flavors, and good old Butte hospitality for a memorable meal (page 267).

★ **Woolzie's Willow Creek Café and Supper Club, Willow Creek:** Known for their mouthwatering ribs and chicken-fried chicken, this restaurant in the tiny town of Willow Creek is as charming as it is good (page 269).

★ **Star Bakery, Nevada City:** First opened in 1863, this bakery serves wonderful fresh-baked goods and comfort foods for three hearty meals a day (page 271).

★ **Little Star Diner, Bozeman:** This little gem has inventive dishes—think potato and porcini pierogi or sour cream donuts with rhubarb jam—lovely ambience, including a rooftop patio, and a killer Sunday brunch (page 284).

Bigfork

Arguably the most beautiful of the lakeside hamlets, Bigfork (pop. 4,953, elev. 2,979 ft/908 m) was named for its location along the fork of the Swan River. At the northeast corner of Flathead Lake, Bigfork has unlimited outdoor recreation opportunities, a handsome offering of live theater, art, fine dining, boutique shopping, and elegant accommodations. The feeling here is of an East Coast beach village 25 years ago—small, quaint, and lovely.

Getting to Bigfork

From **West Glacier,** Bigfork is 40 mi (64 km) south on US 2 and MT-35, a drive of about an hour. From **Kalispell,** Bigfork is 20 mi (32 km) south on US 93 and east on MT-82, a 25-minute drive.

From **Polson,** Bigfork is 35 mi (56 km) north on MT-35 (also known as the East Shore Route, as it parallels the eastern shore of Flathead Lake), a 45-minute drive.

Adventure and Recreation

★ Hiking at Jewel Basin

One of the best and most distinctive places in the state to hike is **Jewel Basin** (Forest Rd. 5392, 10 mi/16 km northeast of Bigfork; 406/387-3800; www.fs.usda.gov/recarea/flathead), a wilderness area with high peaks, lush forests, 27 lakes, and 35 mi (56 km) of dedicated hiking trails. Camping is permitted, and midweek hikes are better since the trails can be crowded on weekends.

Since there are so many trails, and more than 20 lakes to visit, a map is handy. The best map for the area is published by the **Glacier National Park Conservancy** (406/892-3250; www.glacier.org). Note that grizzlies frequent the area, particularly in late summer when the huckleberries are ripe.

Best Accommodations

★ **The Wren, Missoula:** Missoula's first and only boutique hotel—the sister hotel to Bozeman's Lark—opened in 2022 with 73 one-of-a-kind guest rooms featuring local art, comfortable amenities, and plenty of advice on all the adventures you can launch from Missoula (page 258).

★ **Copper King Mansion, Butte:** A stay at the historic Copper King, part museum and part bed-and-breakfast, is a delightful way to get to know the history of this mining city (page 268).

★ **Sacajawea Hotel, Three Forks:** A grand old hotel around which the town grew up, the updated Sacajawea is lovely and welcoming and boasts an outstanding restaurant (page 269).

★ **Nevada City Hotel & Cabins:** Overnighting in Nevada City in these rustic cabins and cozy Victorian-style rooms is like staying in an old-timey photograph (page 272).

★ **The Lark, Bozeman:** Local right down to the wonderful art on every wall, The Lark makes for an outstanding base camp for active, adventurous travelers (page 285).

★ **Kimpton Armory, Bozeman:** Modern, sleek, and ideally situated in the heart of downtown Bozeman, the Kimpton Armory is both modern and historic with plush amenities (page 285).

Black Lake

Distance: 8 mi (13 km) round-trip
Duration: 4 hours
Elevation gain: 1,500 ft (457 m)
Effort: Moderate to strenuous
Trail surface: Uneven dirt, rocks
Trailhead: Camp Misery Trailhead off Forest Service Road 5392

One of the best day hikes in the area is that into Black Lake at the base of Mount Aneas. It's a classically beautiful alpine hike with a tumbling creek rushing by, and two campsites at the lake.

Twin Lakes

Distance: 5.5 mi (8.9 km) round-trip
Duration: 3 hours
Elevation gain:1,473 ft (449 m)
Effort: Moderate
Trail surface: Dirt
Trailhead: Camp Misery Trailhead off Forest Service Road 5392

A relatively gentle up-then-downhill hike will take you to Twin Lakes, where you can fish and take in the high mountain beauty. There are all sorts of ways to incorporate peaks and make loops with several lakes on each one. But out-and-back works just fine too.

Boating

Flathead Raft Company

50362 US-93, Polson; 406/883-5838; www.flatheadraftcompany.com; from $69-100

Based south of Bigfork, out of Polson, Flathead Raft Company offers an assortment of boating adventures in the valley, from half-day white-water trips that cover 8 mi (13 km) on the Class II and III rapids of the Flathead River, to inflatable kayak and river-board trips, to flatwater floats through the Mission Valley, and both flat- and white-water fishing adventures on the Lower Flathead (from $600 for 2 people, 6-10 hours). This is an extraordinary way to cover some territory, stay cool, and experience the water culture of the valley.

Cherry Picking

Picking fresh, sweet Flathead cherries, or just eating them, is a perfect way to spend an afternoon. Several orchards dot the east side of the lake between Polson and Bigfork, so don't be shy about stopping at roadside stands to do a little taste-testing; in this valley, you can't go wrong. The primary harvest is late July-mid-August. The average season lasts just 7-10 days.

Try **Bowman Orchards** (19944 East Shore Rd./Hwy. 35, 10 mi/16 km south of Bigfork at mile marker 21.5 on the east shore of Flathead; 406/982-3246; 9am-6pm daily), a family-owned business since 1921 that grows a variety of cherries and sells both the fresh fruit and a number of delicious cherry products.

Flathead cherries

In addition to cherries, **Getmans' Orchards** (21848 East Lakeshore, Bigfork; 406/871-5499; www.getmanorchardandvineyard.com; call for pick times) grows apples, plums, pears, and peaches, all of which customers can pick in season.

Bigfork Outdoor Rentals

110 Swan River Rd.; 406/837-2498; www.bigforkoutdoorrentals.com

In Bigfork, you can rent ski boats (from $300-450 plus gas for 4 hours), WaveRunners (from $95/hour plus gas), and various size pontoon boats (from $450-495 plus gas for 4 hours) that seat 10-14 people. You can also rent skis, tubes, surfboards, and wakeboards (all $30-35) from Bigfork Outdoor Rentals and have all of it delivered to Flathead, Swan, and Echo Lakes.

Far West Boat Tours

7135 US-93; 406/844-2628; www.flatheadharbor.com; $35-45

For a scenic cruise across Flathead Lake or a Sunday live music or evening karaoke cruise, check out Far West Boat Tours out of Lakeside. During peak season they offer cruises daily at 1 pm, Sunday-Tuesday at 7pm, and every other Wednesday at 8pm. There's live music Sunday 7pm-9pm and karaoke every other Wednesday 8pm-10pm. Check the website or call for updates. Tickets are available online or in person.

Entertainment and Events

Bigfork Summer Playhouse

526 Electric Ave.; 406/837-4886; www.bigforksummerplayhouse.com; mid-May-Labor Day; $35

The repertory theater at Bigfork Summer Playhouse is a standout in the Northwest. For more than 65 years the company has been staging award-winning productions of musical classics like *Fiddler on the Roof, Dirty Rotten Scoundrels, Beauty and the Beast, The Little Mermaid*, and *Sugar Babies*.

Riverbend Concert Series

Everit Slider Park, downtown Bigfork; 406/837-5888; www.riverbendconcertsbigfork.com; 7pm Sun. late June-late Aug.; $5

Also running all summer in Bigfork is the Riverbend Concert Series, held every Sunday. The bring-your-own-seating concerts range in genres and bring some of Montana's best-loved musicians to the stage.

Festival of the Arts

406/837-5888; www.bigfork.org; 9am-4:30pm Sat.-Sun.

Held annually the first weekend in August, Bigfork's Festival of the Arts has been attracting visitors and artists alike since 1978 with more than 150 booths, food, and entertainment.

Shopping

In tiny Bigfork, art is the thing, so stop in at a few galleries during your visit. You could cover the entire town, easily, in a day.

ArtFusion

471 Electric Ave.; 406/837-3526; www.bigforkartfusion.com; 10am-5:30pm Mon.-Sat., 11am-5pm Sun.

Several artists have their own galleries in Bigfork to represent their work exclusively. Other galleries include the colorful and playful ArtFusion, representing more than 60 Montana artists, including ceramicists, painters, jewelers, and photographers.

Riecke's Bayside Gallery

482 Electric Ave.; 406/837-5335; www.rieckesbaysidegallery.com; 9am-5pm daily June-Sept., call for off-season hours

Riecke's Bayside Gallery has an astonishingly large collection of Montana and Northwest artists working in such media as jewelry, painting, mixed media, ceramics, glass, and fabric.

Food

★ Echo Lake Café

1195 Hwy. 83, Bigfork; 406/837-1000; www.echolakecafe.com; 6:30am-2:30pm daily; $9-18

For breakfast and lunch, the hands-down favorite in the Flathead Valley is the Echo Lake Café, where everything is homemade and fabulous. There's often a wait for a table. It's worth it.

Top to bottom: shopping in Bigfork; trail in Jewel Basin; Flathead Lake

Pocketstone Café

444 Electric Ave. #1; 406/837-7223; www.pocketstonecafe.com; 7am-2:30pm Tues.-Sat.; $10-18

Here's another place you should be prepared to wait in line with locals for a table. Right downtown, Pocketstone Café has all the breakfast specialties you could want, plus great sandwiches, burgers, salads, and soups for lunch.

Flathead Lake Brewing Company

116 Holt Dr.; 406/837-2004; wwwflatheadlakebrewing.com; noon-8pm Wed.-Sat.; $11-19

Flathead Lake Brewing Company serves casual but delicious fare—from seared scallops with beet puree to braised pork shank, rib eye, and house-made pizzas and pastas—in a festive environment.

Great Northern Gourmet

425 Grand Dr.; 406/837-2715; Facebook @Great-Northern-Gourmet; 5pm-8:30pm Tues.-Sat.; $15-39

For a casual bite, American small plates, soups, salad, and a diverse entrée lineup, Great Northern Gourmet offers lots of farm-fresh organic options, from a pupu platter to Maryland-style crab cakes, ruby snapper piccata, wild boar, and hunter's beef ragout.

Whistling Andy Distillery

8020 Hwy. 35, Bigfork; 406/837-2620; www.whistlingandy.com; 11:30am-9pm daily summer

Lovers of craft spirits will enjoy a tasting at Whistling Andy Distillery, where the whiskeys, gins, vodkas, rums, and more are handcrafted using local ingredients—from cherries to grains—for big flavor. In addition to tastings and tours (2pm and 4pm daily), the tasting room serves outstanding cocktails.

Accommodations

Luxuriousness and prices rise as you get closer to Bigfork. Depending on the size of your group, a vacation rental can be the most economical choice. In addition to listings on Airbnb, there are a few vacation rental companies in town, including **Stay Montana** (888/871-7856; www.staymontana.com/flathead-lake-vacation-rentals), which offers a variety of rentals around the lake.

Flathead Lake Resort

14871 Hwy. 35, Bigfork; 406/837-3333; www.flatheadlakeresort.com; $61-350

South of town, just a short walk from the pebbled shores of Flathead Lake, Flathead Lake Resort offers a variety of accommodations, some of them pet-friendly, from queen motel rooms to two-bedroom cabins, dry sleeping cabins, restored campers, plus RV and tent sites.

Islander Inn

14729 Shore Acres Drive, Bigfork; 406/837-5472; www.sleepeatdrink.com; $160-295

Just down the road is the funky Islander Inn, which boasts colorful and cozy boutique-style bungalows, each designed to reflect Anguilla, Crete, Jamaica, Maui, Wild Horse, Zanzibar, or Bali. A gift shop, bakery, and restaurant is on the property, so you may not want to leave.

Bridge Street Cottages

309 Bridge St.; 406/837-2785; www.bridgestreetcottages.com; $295-695

Right in Bigfork, the Bridge Street Cottages offers 13 luxury cottages, both on the river and in the trees. They are all nicely appointed and homey.

Averill's Flathead Lake Lodge

150 Flathead Lodge Rd.; 406/837-4391; www.flatheadlakelodge.com; weeklong all-inclusive trips from $5,985

For a phenomenal guest ranch experience, Averill's Flathead Lake Lodge is a historic family ranch set right on the water. Offering everything from sailing to horseback riding, fly-fishing to mountain biking, this ranch is classic and exceptional.

Camping

Wayfarers State Park

8600 Hwy. 35, 0.5 mi/0.8 km south of Bigfork; 406/837-4196; www.fwp.mt.gov/wayfarers; Apr.-Oct., water available May-Sept.; nonresident entrance fee $8, campsites $4-34

If you can get a tent site, camping is one of the best ways to stay as close to Flathead Lake as possible. Among the most popular is Wayfarers State Park, on the northeast shore of the lake near Bigfork, amid cliffs and rocky shoreline. Tall trees offer shade for the park's 30 sites, and RVs and trailers up to 40 ft (12 m) can fit.

Information and Services

Bigfork Area Chamber of Commerce and Visitors Center

Old Town Center, 8155 Hwy. 35; 406/837-5888; www.bigfork.org; 10am-2pm Mon.-Fri.

The Bigfork Area Chamber of Commerce and Visitors Center is on the east side of Flathead Lake.

Polson

Polson feels like the kind of town where there is almost always a fair going on or some other reason to celebrate. Historically the economy has been based on lumber, steamboat trade, and ranching. Founded around a trading post at the southern end of Flathead Lake in 1880, the town was named for David Polson, a local rancher who married a Nez Perce woman and who played the fiddle at dances and powwows across the region. Settlement from 1910 greatly increased the size of the town, and when much of the state was losing population during the Great Depression, Polson actually doubled in size with farmers who came to try their luck with the Flathead Irrigation Project and people seeking work at the Kerr Dam construction project.

Today Polson (pop. 5,478, elev. 2,931 ft/893 m) is a lakeside town, the heart of Montana's cherry-growing district, and the busiest town along Flathead Lake. Its proximity to the magnificent lake, the Flathead River, and the Mission Mountains makes Polson a natural playground.

Getting to Polson

From **Bigfork,** Polson is 35 mi (56 km) south on US 93 (also known as the East Shore Route), about a 45-minute drive.

From **St. Ignatius,** Polson is 30 mi (48 km) north on US 93, a 35-minute drive.

Sights

Miracle of America Museum

36094 Memory Ln.; 406/883-6804; www.miracleofamericamuseum.org; 9am-5pm daily; $10

An eclectic little museum, to say the least, the Miracle of America Museum likes to think of itself as the "Smithsonian of the West." Indeed, the founders were passionate collectors of Western artifacts, and the museum is packed to the rafters with more than 100,000 objects including moonshine stills, antique motorcycles, entire buildings, and military paraphernalia. The museum is kid-friendly, with coin-operated music machines and other curiosities children love. Behind the main building is the museum's Pioneer Village, which has 35 buildings spread across 4 acres (1.6 ha). There's a helicopter to play in, a replica of Laura Ingalls Wilder's sod-roofed home, and a couple of kiddie trains that still operate.

Adventure and Recreation

Boating

Polson offers rafting opportunities on the warm, clear lower **Flathead River,** plus equipment rentals and cruises across Flathead Lake.

Flathead Raft Company

50362 US-93, Polson; 406/883-5838; www.flatheadraftcompany.com; rafting $69-100, fishing from $600

Flathead Raft Company offers an assortment of boating adventures, from half-day white-water trips covering 8 mi (13 km) on the Class II and III rapids of the Flathead River, to inflatable kayak and river-board trips, to flat-water floats through the Mission Valley, and both flat- and white-water fishing adventures on the Lower Flathead. This is an extraordinary way to cover some territory, stay cool, and experience the water culture of the valley.

Flathead Lake Tours

Location specified for each tour; 406/546-7081; www.flatheadlakeboattours.com; 8am-8pm daily in season; $349-749

Flathead Lake Tours offers a variety of immersive tours taking in the beauty of the lake, from 2-hour morning tours to 3-4-hour guided tours of Wild Horse Island that can include a chance to explore the island's wilderness and encounter some of its wild horses and bighorn sheep.

Flathead Boat Company

50230 US 93 S., Polson; 406/883-0999 or 406/871-8445; www.flatheadboatcompany.com; $265-440 for 4 hours depending on boat size; $385-605 for 8 hours

Flathead Boat Company rents a variety of vessels for 4-hour to multiday rentals, from 19-22-ft (5-7-m) boats to Jet Skis ($100/hour).

Entertainment and Events

Polson Farmers Market

3rd Ave. W.; 406/675-0177; www.polsonfarmersmarket.com; 9am-1pm Fri. May-mid-Oct.

In Polson, the Polson Farmers Market features local produce, crafts, jewelry, photography, and more.

Mission Mountain NRA Rodeo

320 Regatta Rd.; 406/883-1100; www.polsonfairgroundsinc.com; June

The Mission Mountain NRA Rodeo is generally held in late June; the professional rodeo action and small-town fun always ensure a big crowd.

Flathead Cherry Festival

Main St.; 406/883-3667; www.polsonchamber.com; July

The biggest event of the year in Polson is probably the Flathead Cherry Festival. It has a fair-like environment and celebrates everything cherry, including pie-eating contests, seed-spitting contests, exhibitions, and entertainment throughout the weekend. The event is typically held at the end of July.

Shopping

Three Dog Down

48841 US 93; 406/883-3696 or 800/364-3696; www.threedogdown.com; 9am-5pm daily

A good place to stop in Polson for some warm Montana bedding is Three Dog Down, known in the region for custom-made comforters and pillows. Shopping here is a Montana experience—you can buy everything from soap to moccasins to saltwater taffy—and bargain hunters should know that singing the "Star-Spangled Banner" will earn you a discount.

Food

Betty's Diner

49779 US 93; 406/883-1717; www.bettysdiner.net; 7am-3pm Mon.-Sat., 6am-3pm Sun.; $6-16

Lovers of all things pink will delight in the pinkaliciousness at Betty's Diner. The goodness starts with breakfast, including specialties for "kids and old farts." Lunch includes such classic diner favorites as burgers, cheesesteaks, patty melts, and other sandwiches.

Mrs. Wonderful's Café

103b 3rd Ave. E.; 406/319-2080; www.mrswonderfulworld.com; 10am-2pm and 4pm-8pm Wed., 10am-2pm and 4pm-6pm Thurs., 10am-2pm and 4pm-8pm Fri.,10am-2pm Sat.-Sun.; $7-28

Mrs. Wonderful's Café serves locally grown and organic breakfast, lunch, and early dinner. There's also a store selling specialty foods and a gorgeous selection of wine, selected by an on-staff sommelier. On Wednesday nights, diners can build their own 10-inch pizzas; on Thursday nights it's wine flights and dinner, and Friday night is pasta night.

Cherries BBQ Pit

105 2nd St. E.; 406/571-2227; 11am-7pm Mon.-Sat.; $10-27

In Polson, Cherries BBQ Pit serves up tender and flavorful barbecue using—yep—Flathead cherries in a selection of ribs, pulled pork, brisket, chicken, and sandwiches with any of the meats. Kind of nice for a roadside barbecue joint with mostly outside dining or takeaway, Cherries also offers a delicious big salad and a kids' menu.

Glacier Brewing Company

6 10th Ave. E., Polson; 406/883-2595; www.glacierbrewing.com; noon-8pm Sun.-Thurs., 10am-8pm Fri.-Sat.

Glacier Brewing Company is a German-style ale house serving its own impressive line of beer and homemade soda. Hours change with the seasons and without advance notice but are posted on the Facebook page.

Accommodations

Mission Mountain Resort

3 minutes from Polson on Hwy. 35; 406/883-1883; www.polsonmtresort.com; holiday cabins from $175 for 2 people, $300 for 4 people

Plenty of choices for lodging exist in Polson and Bigfork, but a room with a view in these parts can get pretty expensive. Among the best bargains in the area is the rustic Mission Mountain Resort, a collection of cabins and lodge rooms on 75 acres (30 ha) set back from the lake.

Best Western KwaTaqNuk Resort and Casino

49708 US 93 E., Polson; 406/883-3636 or 800/882-6363; www.kwataqnuk.com; $115-285

The waterfront Best Western KwaTaqNuk Resort and Casino, which is owned and operated by the Flathead Nation, has 107 guest rooms and an extensive menu of activities that includes lake cruises, boat rentals, fishing tours, and plenty of gaming at the on-site casino. Pets are permitted for a $20 per night fee.

Camping

Finley Point State Park

31543 S. Finley Point Rd., 11 mi/18 km north of Polson, then 4 mi/6 km west on County Rd.; 406/887-2715; www.fwp.mt.gov/finley-point; Apr.-Oct.; $4-34

North of Polson on the southeast shore of Flathead Lake is Finley Point State Park, a secluded but developed campground in a conifer forest. When the water level is high enough, a boat launch and dock are available.

Yellow Bay State Park

23861 Hwy. 35, 15 mi/24 km north of Polson at mile marker 17; 406/982-3034; www.fwp.mt.gov/yelllow-bay; mid-May-mid-Sept.; $4-34

On the east side of Flathead Lake in prime cherry orchard country is Finley Point State Park, a popular day-use area.

There are only five campsites, open to tent camping only. Flush toilets are available mid-May-Labor Day.

Information and Services

Polson Chamber of Commerce

402 1st St. E.; 406/883-5969; www.polsonchamber.com; 9am-2pm Mon.-Fri., 10am-2pm Sat. Memorial Day-Labor Day, 10am-2pm Mon.-Fri. Labor Day-Memorial Day

The Polson Chamber of Commerce is an excellent resource for the south end of the Flathead Valley.

Ronan

Renamed by residents in 1883 for the first Indian agent, Major Peter Ronan, the town of Ronan (pop. 2,172, elev. 3,048 ft/929 m) was once part of the Flathead Reservation before it was opened to sale and settlement in 1910.

Ronan's history is marked by tragedy and travesty. In 1912, a fire erupted in an automobile garage on a particularly windy afternoon. Within hours, the entire town lay in ruins. In June 1929, a robbery at the Ronan State Bank made a group of seven robbers $3,000 richer. The group of twentysomethings went on a spree of robberies across the state with police always a few steps behind. Eventually all but the ringleader were caught and either killed during the pursuit or sent to prison. A woman who accompanied them, known dramatically as "the woman in white," was eventually found murdered in a Helena brothel.

Today Ronan is known for its proximity to two of the state's most beautiful wildlife refuges: the Ninepipe National Wildlife Refuge and, farther south, the CSKT Bison Range.

Ninepipe National Wildlife Refuge

www.fws.gov

Five mi (8 km) south of Ronan and just north of the CSKT Bison Range on land of the Confederated Salish and Kootenai Tribes, the Ninepipe National Wildlife Refuge is a waterfowl preserve.

Ninepipe National Wildlife Refuge

Established in 1921, these wetlands are at the base of the Mission Mountains and situated around a large reservoir. The marshlands are difficult to walk through, but good bird-watching is possible from the parking areas surrounding the reservoir. The refuge is situated on a popular migratory path for numerous birds, including mallards, gadwalls, great blue herons, and swans. It has become an important breeding and resting area for the Flathead Valley Canada goose population. The refuge is closed during waterfowl hunting season (fall) and the nesting season (spring). Signed access to the refuge is off US 93. Other roads allowing access to the area from US 93 are Olsen Road and Highway 212.

Ninepipes Museum of Early Montana

69316 US 93, Charlo; 406/644-3435; www.ninepipesmuseum.org; 10am-5pm Mon.-Fri., 10am-4pm Sat. Mar.-mid-Dec.; $9.95

The Ninepipes Museum of Early Montana is halfway between Missoula and Kalispell next to the Ninepipe National Wildlife Refuge. It documents daily life on the Flathead Reservation over the last 100-plus years and even includes a complete replica of a Native American camp. In addition to Native American life, the history of early trappers, miners, loggers, and ranchers is on display, including photos, artwork, costumes, and artifacts from people in these different walks of life.

St. Ignatius

The oldest town on the Flathead Reservation, and among the oldest settlements in the state, St. Ignatius (pop. 820, elev. 2,939 ft/896 m) is the site of the St. Ignatius Mission, first settled in 1854 by Jesuit priest Adrian Hoecken, who moved from Washington State to be closer to the Indigenous people he wanted to reach. The town grew quickly as nearly 1,000 Native Americans resettled near the mission, and in 1864 a group of nuns added schools and a hospital to the community.

The oldest building in the state, constructed in 1846, is at Fort Connah, just 6 mi (10 km) north of St. Ignatius on US 93. It is all that remains of the last trading post built in the United States by the Hudson's Bay Company. The post was in operation until 1871.

Getting to St. Ignatius

From **Polson,** St. Ignatius is 30 mi (48 km) south on US 93, a 35-minute drive. From **Missoula,** St. Ignatius is 40 mi (64 km) north on US 93, a 45-minute drive.

Sights

St. Ignatius Mission

300 Bear Track Ave.; 406/745-2768; https://stignatiusmission.org; 9am-7pm daily summer, 9am-5pm daily winter, mass 9am Sun.; free, donations accepted

The beloved redbrick chapel standing today on the St. Ignatius Mission was built in the 1890s, but the mission itself was settled as early as 1854 by Jesuit priest Adrian Hoecken and hundreds of Native Americans who set up camp near him. In 1864, a group of nuns from Montreal, the Sisters of Providence, came to the mission to open a boarding school for girls, a hospital, and eventually, with the help of Ursuline nuns, an orphanage, a kindergarten, and a school for boys. At its peak in the mid-1890s, some 320 children attended school at the mission. The boys' school was burned down by students in 1896, and when the federal government ceased aiding the mission, all schooling was turned over to the Ursuline Sisters. In 1941, they adopted coeducation. The school was shuttered permanently in the 1970s.

When you visit any of the missions and boarding schools attended by Native American children, it's important to recognize the stories that weren't heard for decades. St. Ignatius Mission and its schools were not immune to the

TOP EXPERIENCE

Powwows

There is some debate as to how powwows got their name. Some argue it comes from the word *pa-wa,* the Pawnee word for "to eat." Others suggest the word descends from the Algonquin word *pauau,* which suggests a gathering of people for celebration. Either way, powwows are a time for gathering, celebrating, and honoring traditions. Many contemporary powwows include dancing, singing and drumming contests, encampments, feasting, parades, and more.

Arlee Celebration Powwow

Reminders: When you're attending a powwow as a spectator, your role is to be a respectful observer. Photographs are often allowed, unless the announcer says otherwise, but it's always a good idea to ask before you snap a picture. Be sure not to use a flash in a dancer's face. Don't enter the dance floor unless you are invited to do so. Be mindful that food booths, raffle ticket sales, and arts and crafts booths defray the costs of the powwow, so support them when you can. Be patient and don't expect all the events to start when the program says they will. (Also see page 174.)

One of the most important events on the Flathead Reservation is the annual **Arlee Celebration** (www.arleemontana.com), which takes place over a few days around the Fourth of July at Arlee. The celebration has played out each year since 1898 with camping, competition dancing, drumming and singing, traditional games, and a host of food and arts and crafts vendors. Though the US government ban on "Indian doings" in the 19th and 20th centuries forbade such celebrations, Native Americans held the event on the Fourth of July so that the Army would see it as a patriotic display.

child abuse that plagued so many missions and Indian schools across North America. In 2011, 45 former students sued the Ursuline Academy/St. Ignatius Mission School for physical, sexual, and emotional abuse. The suit was resolved with a multimillion-dollar settlement in 2015. In 2018, the Jesuits West Province released a list of 111 members from 10 Western states—dating 1880-1982—who abused or might have abused children or vulnerable adults, 31 of them in Montana and some at Ursuline Academy/St. Ignatius Mission School. A 2020 Jesuit report showed that abusive priests were often assigned to rural Native American reservations and boarding schools in a cover-up strategy known as priest shuffling. Vigils have been held at the mission church to honor the Indigenous children who were taken from their families and forced to stay at boarding schools, and to recognize and name the intergenerational trauma that continues to affect Native American families and their communities.

The brick chapel was completed in 1894 with 58 original murals painted by Joseph Carignano, who worked in the kitchen and as a handyman for the mission. Carignano taught himself to paint and managed to complete the frescoes in only 14 months despite working on them only when he wasn't doing his primary job. The paintings tell the life story of St. Ignatius Loyola. In the summer of 2016, significant cracks in the frescoes were being monitored, and the church is trying to raise the money to preserve them.

In addition to the chapel, a small museum and gift shop can be found in the log house that was the original residence of the Sisters of Providence.

★ CSKT Bison Range

58355 Bison Range Rd., Charlo; 406/644-2211; www.bisonrange.org; 8am-6pm daily Nov.-Apr., 7am-8pm daily May-Oct., visitor center/gift shop closes one hour before gate; $20/vehicle

Established in 1908 when the population of bison across North America had dropped from upward of 30 million animals down to just a few hundred, the CSKT Bison Range (formerly the National Bison Range, and now named for the Confederated Salish Kootenai Tribes that manage it) is one of the oldest animal refuges in the country and well worth a visit. Its origins date back to a Qlispé (or Pend d'Oreille) man named Little Falcon Robe who gained permission from various tribal leaders to bring orphaned bison calves across the Continental Divide to the Flathead Indian Reservation. Those few calves prospered under Native stewardship and number 350 today. The 18,500-acre (7,487-ha) refuge is also home to white-tailed and mule deer, bighorn sheep, pronghorn, and elk.

There are two driving routes: the year-round **West Loop and Prairie Drive,** a short 5-mi (8-km) tour that takes about 30 minutes; and the 17-mi (27-km) one-way loop, **Red Sleep Mountain Drive,** that climbs about 2,000 ft (610 m) and takes close to 2 hours. The longer route, open in summer, is incredibly scenic and definitely worth the time. The roads through the refuge are gravel; no bicycles or motorcycles are permitted on them, but parking is available at the **visitor center** (8am-7pm daily in summer with shorter hours depending on daylight in fall, winter, and spring). Several short hiking trails leave from the day-use area as well as from Red Sleep Mountain Drive, which closes earlier in the day and entirely when snow blankets the range.

Before beginning your tour, stop in at the visitor center for informative displays, knowledgeable park rangers, and a large relief map of the refuge marked with small lights indicating where bison can likely be seen that day.

Shopping

Four Winds Indian Trading Post

US 93, 3 mi/5 km north of St. Ignatius; 406/745-4336; www.fourwindsindiantradingpost.com; 10am-6pm daily summer

The Four Winds Indian Trading Post is the oldest operating Indian trading post in the state. Opened in 1870, the Four Winds has long supplied local Native Americans with a variety of wares, including beads, face paint, animal hides, and dance bells. The store is authentic and sells traditional Native American crafts alongside history books and made-in-Montana products.

Food and Accommodations

Ninepipes Lodge

69286 MT-93; 406/644-2588; www.ninepipeslodge.com; $151-225

About 12 mi (19 km) up the road in Charlo is Ninepipes Lodge, set against the backdrop of the Mission Mountains and adjacent to the Ninepipes Reservoir.

It's a full-service resort with basic motel-style rooms and a great restaurant, **Allentown Bar & Restaurant** (7am-9am and 11am-close daily; $10-37), serving steaks, pasta, seafood, and salads. On warm nights, eat outside on the deck overlooking the kettle pond with unrivaled mountain views. There's also a sports bar on-site with excellent cocktails, including a Huckleberry Mule, and a fine selection of locally brewed beers.

Missoula

Given its site at the hub of five river valleys—the Jocko and Blackfoot Rivers to the north, the upper and lower Clark Fork east and west of the city, and the Bitterroot to the south—Missoula's longtime status as an important trade center makes perfect sense. About halfway between Yellowstone and Glacier National Parks, Missoula (pop. 73,489, elev. 3,200 ft/975 m) is on the way to just about everywhere in this part of the state.

In addition to its history of logging and paper milling, the other defining element of the city—the University of Montana—keeps Missoula young, vibrant, and relatively liberal. Perhaps because the school is best known for its creative writing, art, drama, and dance programs, Missoula is decidedly arts oriented.

Missoula offers outdoors enthusiasts options right in town—hike the M on Mount Sentinel, kayak the Clark Fork or bike its shores. There is world-class river fishing, hot-potting (the art of getting to and swimming in natural hot springs), mountain biking, and no end of places to hike.

Getting to Missoula

Driving

I-90 runs directly through Missoula, making it an easy destination by car. Missoula is 40 mi (64 km) south of **St. Ignatius** on US 93, a drive of roughly 45 minutes.

From **Butte,** Missoula is 120 mi (193 km) northwest on I-90, a drive of about 1 hour 45 minutes. Missoula is 200 mi (320 km) northwest of **Bozeman** on I-90, about a 3-hour drive.

Air

Just 4 mi (6 km) northwest of the university, **Missoula International Airport** (MSO; 5225 US 10 W.; 406/728-4381; www.flymissoula.com) is served by Alaska, Allegiant, American, Delta, Frontier, and United. On the first floor of the terminal are **Alamo, Avis, Budget, Enterprise, Thrifty,** and **Hertz** car-rental agencies. **Dollar** has shuttles to and from the airport. Most hotels offer free shuttle service to and from the airport; the **Airport Shuttler** (406/543-9416 or 406/880-7433; www.msoshuttle.com) also provides transportation into town.

Bus

The **Greyhound** bus station (1660 W. Broadway; 406/549-2339) has several buses in and out of town daily.

Getting Around

The **Mountain Line** (406/721-3333; www.mountainline.com; 6am-8:45pm Mon.-Fri., 9am-6pm Sat.; free) is the free municipal bus service; the city has worked hard to make this a zero-fare public transportation system.

For taxi service, call **Yellow Cab** (406/543-6644; www.yellowcabmissoula.com) or **Green Taxi** (406/728-8294), which only uses hybrid cars.

Sights

Carousel for Missoula and Caras Park

101 Carousel Dr.; 406/549-8382; www.carouselformissoula.com; 11am-7pm daily June-Aug., 11am-5:30pm daily Sept.-May (hours can change); $2

Aside from being a beautiful hand-carved carousel, one of the first built in the United States since the Great Depression, what makes the Carousel for Missoula so sweet is how it came to be. Local cabinetmaker Chuck Kaparich vowed to the city of Missoula in 1991 that if they would "give it a home and promise no one will ever take it apart," he would build a carousel by hand. As a child, Kaparich had spent summer days in Butte at the Columbia Gardens riding the carousel. For four years, he carved ponies, taught others to carve, and worked to restore and piece together the more than 16,000 pieces of an antique

Missoula

To Missoula Smokejumper Visitor Center and Jim and Mary's RV Park
To Rocky Mountain Elk Foundation Visitor Center and Snowbowl
MISSOULA KOA HOLIDAY
ENGLAND BLVD
Pleasant View Park
N RESERVE ST
W BROADWAY ST
MULLAN RD
Clark Fork
GREYHOUND
TOOLE AVE
West Broadway Island Natural Area
Silver Park
TAGLIARE DELICATESSEN
WYOMING ST
BOXCAR BISTRO
N RUSSELL ST
S 3RD ST WEST
S 5TH ST W
ZOO TOWN SURFERS
JOHNSON ST
STEPHENS AVE
S 14TH ST WEST
BROOKS ST
S RESERVE ST
S RUSSELL ST
MONTANA DEPARTMENT OF FISH, WILDLIFE & PARKS
SPURGIN RD
Big Sky Park
SOUTH AVE WEST
COMMUNITY MEDICAL CENTER
FORT MISSOULA
U.S. FOREST SERVICE
Bitterroot R.
COSTCARE WALK-IN CLINIC
Spartan Park
Playfair Park
ST. PATRICK'S HOSPITAL
THE DEPOT
MISSOULA FARMERS MARKET
N ORANGE ST
W SPRUCE ST
JAMES BAR
OWEN ST
W PINE ST
Missoula
N HIGGINS AVE
W BROADWAY ST
WOODY ST
OXFORD SALOON & CAFÉ
CHARLIE B'S
W FRONT ST
PLONK
PANGEA BAR & RESTAURANT/ STAVE & HOOP
MISSOULA ART MUSEUM
W MAIN ST
THE RHINO
BUTTERFLY HERBS
BIGA PIZZA
RYMAN ST
CAROUSEL DR
FACT & FICTION BOOKS
CLARK FORK MARKET
DESTINATION MISSOULA
CAROUSEL FOR MISSOULA & CARAS PARK
Caras Park
MONTGOMERY DISTILLERY
THE WREN
SCOTTY'S TABLE
BRENNAN'S WAVE
N PATTEE ST
THE TRAIL HEAD
SHAKESPEARE & CO.
S HIGGINS AVE
BETTY'S DIVINE
FAIR TRADE STORE
0 200 yds
0 200 m

To Rocky Mountain Elk Foundation Visitor Center
Pineview Park
RATTLESNAKE DR
200
LOLO ST
Bugbee Nature Preserve
W GREENOUGH DR
Mount Jumbo
See Detail
W SPRUCE ST
Greenough Park
90
ALLEGIANCE PARK
W BROADWAY ST
N VAN BUREN ST
McCormick Park
S ORANGE ST
Missoula
MISSOULA CHILDREN'S THEATRE
To Ron's River Trail
MONTANA NATURAL HISTORY CENTER
S HIGGINS AVE
200
DOUBLETREE BY HILTON
MISSOULA CHAMBER OF COMMERCE
MISSOULA EDGEWATER
LE PETIT OUTRE
12
BIG DIPPER ICE CREAM
Jacob's Island
CAMPUS DR
KETTLE HOUSE BREWING CO.
To Garnet Recreation Management Area
12
90
200
E BROADWAY ST
Clark Fork
W BECKWITH ST E
ROCKIN RUDY'S
M TRAIL ON MOUNT SENTINEL
University of Montana
K Williams Natural Trail Area
E BECKWITH AVE
MOUNT AVE
Bonner Park
S HIGGINS AVE
ARTHUR AVE
Mount Sentinel
0
600 yds
0
600 m

carousel frame. The town raised funds and contributed more than 100,000 volunteer hours. In May 1995 the carousel opened with 38 ponies, three replacement ponies, two chariots, 14 gargoyles, and the largest band organ in continuous use in the country.

The jewel-box building opens to the green of **Caras Park** in summer and keeps the cold out during the rest of the year. A fantastic adjacent play area, **Dragon Hollow** (9am-8pm daily summer, weather permitting), was built with the same remarkable volunteerism.

Missoula Art Museum (MAM)

335 N. Pattee St.; 406/728-0447; www.missoulaartmuseum.org; 10am-5pm Tues.-Wed. and Fri.-Sat., 10am-7pm Thurs.; free

With the tagline "Free Expression Free Admission," Missoula Art Museum brilliantly combines a 110-year-old Carnegie library with a contemporary glass, steel, and wood addition. The museum hosts solo and group shows, most of them by Montana artists and quite contemporary. And their own collections—from Montana Modernists to contemporary folk art—are fascinating. Don't miss the museum's impressive Contemporary American Indian Art Collection.

Fort Missoula

3400 Captain Rawn Way; 406/728-3476; www.fortmissoulamuseum.org; 10am-5pm Mon.-Sat., noon-5pm Sun. Memorial Day-Labor Day, noon-5pm Tues.-Sun. Labor Day-Memorial Day; $4

Originally established to protect settlers against Indian attacks, Fort Missoula was never used for its intended purpose. When no attacks occurred, the fort was used to house the African American 25th Infantry Bicycle Corps in 1888 and as an alien detention center for Italian Americans and Japanese Americans during World War II. The museum houses exhibits about the fort's history. The fort grounds (free) are open year-round. While the museum is housed in the fort's original buildings, more than 20 historical buildings—including a one-room schoolhouse, an 1860s church, and a homesteader cabin—have been relocated to the grounds.

Montana Natural History Center

120 Hickory St.; 406/327-0405; www.montananaturalist.org; 10am-4pm Tues.-Sat.; $5

The Montana Natural History Center was created by educators who wanted to work with schools and the public to help nurture an understanding and appreciation of nature. It offers workshops, including children's activities, as well as field trips and evening lectures conducted by local scientists and naturalists.

University of Montana

32 Campus Dr.; 406/243-0211; www.umt.edu

The University of Montana was founded in 1895 at the base of Mount Sentinel. To secure Missoula as the site of the state's university, city leaders bribed state legislators with 5 gallons of whiskey, a case of beer, a case of wine, and 350 cigars. Despite its shady beginnings, the university flourished as a liberal arts and research institution with a well-respected creative writing program. The university has a beautiful campus to explore. **University Center,** on the east side of the campus almost directly under the M on the hillside, is the hub of campus life. Wander in to grab a bite at the food court or peruse the bookstore. To find out what lectures, plays, concerts, or other entertainment is happening on campus, visit the website (http://events.umt.edu). In 2015, Jon Krakauer wrote a damning book that chronicled the stories of five women who reported rapes or attempted rapes at the University of Montana. The events, and the book, had an impact on the school, and enrollment continues to drop from 15,669 students in 2011 to 10,349 students in 2024.

Rocky Mountain Elk Foundation Visitor Center

5705 Grant Creek Rd.; 406/523-4500 or 800/225-5355; www.rmef.org; 8am-5pm Mon.-Fri.; free

Promoting the view that hunters are the most resolute conservationists, Rocky Mountain Elk Foundation Visitor Center has protected millions of acres of wildlife habitat across North America since 1984. The center does an impressive job of putting elk in the context of a wide range of wildlife and emphasizing the importance of habitat conservation. A favorite among hunters due to its wealth of trophy mounts, the visitor center is like a natural history museum, and in addition to a wooded walking trail on the property's 22 acres (9 ha), there are kid-friendly interactive exhibits and wildlife conservation films. Tours can be arranged by emailing in advance.

Missoula Smokejumper Visitor Center

5765 W. Broadway, 0.5 mi/0.8 km west of the Missoula airport; 406/329-4934; www.fs.usda.gov; 9am-5pm daily Memorial Day-Labor Day, by appointment Labor Day-Memorial Day; free admission, free tours daily in summer at 10am, 11am, 2pm, 4pm

Sharing space with the largest smokejumper training base in the country, Missoula Smokejumper Visitor Center is a fascinating place for those interested in wildfires and the firefighters who parachute in to battle them. There is a memorial to those killed on duty and a replica of a 1930s fire lookout; visitors on the 45-minute tour have access to the 1937 actual fire lookout.

Brennan's Wave

Next to Caras Park

Although there is no street address, everyone in Missoula knows where Brennan's Wave is. Located on the Clark Fork River next to Caras Park, this engineered white-water masterpiece was built in honor of Brennan Guth, a Missoula native and world-class kayaker who perished while paddling in Chile. Brennan's Wave hosts competitions and everyday paddlers looking for a thrill. The banks are always lined with spectators.

Adventure and Recreation

Rattlesnake National Recreation Area and Wilderness

406/329-3814; www.fs.usda.gov

Less than 5 mi (8 km) north of town, the 60,000-acre (24,280-ha) Rattlesnake National Recreation Area and Wilderness is fed by some 50 creeks and has 30 lakes, waterfalls, and many miles of trails, some of which lead up to McLeod Peak, the highest spot in the area at 8,620 ft (2,627 m). The area is a dream for hikers, runners, mountain bikers, campers, cross-country skiers, and anglers; it's home to deer, elk, coyotes, mountain goats, bighorn sheep, black bears, and more than 40 species of birds in spring and fall. Dispersed camping is permitted anywhere beyond the 3-mi (5-km) radius from the Rattlesnake's well-traveled main trailhead.

To get to the area from Missoula, take the I-90 Van Buren Street exit at the east end of town and travel 4.5 mi (7.2 km) north on Rattlesnake Drive.

Hiking and Biking

The flat riverfront trails along the north and south shores of the Clark Fork River are hugely popular with walkers, runners, and bikers. Leashed dogs are welcome on all of Missoula's trails.

Ron's River Trail

Distance: 2 mi (3.2 km) one-way

Duration: 1 hour

Elevation gain: 10 ft (3 m)

Effort: Easy

Trail surface: Asphalt, gravel

Trailhead: Access all along the trail including at Caras Park, Bess Reed Park, and Kiwanis Park on the river's north side

Ron's River Trail runs along the north side of the Clark Fork River and provides access to Caras Park, Bess Reed Park, and Kiwanis Park. The trail, graveled in places and paved in others, connects to other intersecting trails. It is easily accessible throughout town, but the most abundant parking can be found at Caras Park near the Carousel for Missoula. There are several pedestrian bridges between the north and southside trails, and the nearest one to Caras Park is on Higgins Avenue.

Kim Williams Nature Trail

Distance: 9.8 mi (15.8 km) round-trip
Duration: 3 hours
Elevation gain: 226 ft (69 m)
Effort: Easy
Trail surface: Asphalt, dirt, gravel
Trailhead: Park at Albertson's at Van Buren and 4th St. and cross the footbridge over the Clark Fork

Also traveling alongside the Clark Fork in Missoula, Kim Williams Nature Trail is a converted railroad bed near the base of Mount Sentinel (where you can hike the M) that winds through a 134-acre (54-ha) natural area in Hellgate Canyon. The trail is wide and level, and it is open to pedestrians, equestrians, and cyclists. It's also frequented by wildlife, so keep your eyes open. The trail runs through Hellgate Canyon and connects to the Deer Creek-Pattee Canyon Loop. From Ron's River Trail, this trail can be accessed easily from Jacob's Island Park near the Van Buren Pedestrian Bridge.

M Trail on Mount Sentinel

Distance: 1.6 mi (2.6 km) round-trip
Duration: 1 hour
Effort: Moderate
Elevation gain: 620 ft (189 m)
Trail surface: Dirt with rocky sections
Trailhead: Across from Aber Hall at 1111-1201 Campus Dr.

For a bird's-eye view of the city, hike up the historic M Trail on Mount Sentinel, which was established by University of Montana students in 1908. It is a popular trail, so there will be others huffing and puffing up the hill with you. There is no shade on this trail that climbs 620 ft (189 m) from bottom to top, so be prepared. There are 13 switchbacks on the west-facing slope, and the views over Missoula and the Bitterroot Valley at sunset are worth the sweat.

Skiing

Snowbowl

1700 Snowbowl Rd.; 406/549-9777 or 800/728-2695; www.montanasnowbowl.com; $75-80 full-day, $73 half-day

Twenty minutes north of Missoula, Snowbowl is a nice little ski hill with an average of 300 in (762 cm) of snow annually, 2,600 ft (793 m) of vertical drop, and a run that covers 2.6 mi (4.2 km). In summer, the mountain is open Friday-Sunday late June-mid-September for mountain biking ($22), disc golf ($10), and ziplining (from $47). The chairlift is open for scenic lift rides ($16) noon-5pm.

Garnet Recreation Management Area

30 mi/48 km northeast of Missoula on Garnet Range Rd. off MT-200; 406/329-3914; www.garnetghosttown.org; 9:30am-4:30pm daily year-round with limited access in winter; $10

There is no shortage of cross-country ski trails around Missoula. One unique destination is the BLM-managed Garnet Recreation Management Area, with 50 mi (80 km) of trails in a ghost town. In summer, hiking and mountain biking are popular. To get to Garnet, follow Highway 200 east of town and turn south at the Garnet Range Road, between mile markers 22 and 23, about 30 mi (48 km) east of Missoula. Follow the range road approximately 12 mi (19 km) to the parking area. The road is closed to vehicles January-April.

Fishing

A Classic Journey Outfitters

877/327-7878 or 406/880-0541; www.montanaflyfishingguide.com; $650 full-day float, $550 half-day float, multiday trips with lodging available

While access to the Clark Fork River right in town is easy, the river is still recovering from decades of pollution. Better bets are the Bitterroot, the Blackfoot, and Rock Creek. One guiding outfit that does them all is A Classic Journey Outfitters. Owner Joe Cummings grew up fishing on a ranch in nearby Stevensville and left to play professional football. But his heart has always been where the big, wild trout are. He and his guides fish year-round, have a passion for dry flies, and know the area backward and forward.

Tom Jenni's Reel Montana

406/539-6610 or 866/885-6065; www.tomjenni.com; $675 full-day for 1 angler, $775 full-day for 2 anglers

Another guide who is a phenomenal naturalist in addition to being a world-class fishing instructor is Tom Jenni of Tom Jenni's Reel Montana. Jenni grew up in Missoula and has been fishing its rivers for more than 40 years. He also offers multiday trips (from $1,300 pp for 2 days) up to four nights/five days.

Boating and Water Sports

10,000 Waves Raft & Kayak Adventures

802 W. Spruce St.; 406/240-9833; www.10000-waves.com; full-day trips from $99, half-day from $75

With five rivers in the vicinity, Missoula is a boater's town. There is even an artificial practice wave, Brennan's Wave, right in town for kayakers to play safely in. Try 10,000 Waves Raft & Kayak Adventures for everything from scenic rafting to white-water adventures, sit-on-top kayaks, and kayak instruction on numerous sections of the Blackfoot and Clark Fork Rivers. There are also overnight trips (from $495 for up to 4 people) on the Clark Fork and in the Alberton Gorge, as well as on the Blackfoot River. Rentals are available too, including kayaks, SUPs, tubes, and pack rafts.

Top to bottom: Brennan's Wave; skiing at Snowbowl; swimming in the Clark Fork

Zoo Town Surfers

1001 S. 4th St. W., Ste. 5, Missoula; 406/546-0370; www.zootownsurfers.com

Another local outfitter that specializes in all things white-water is Zoo Town Surfers. They offer scenic and white-water rafting trips ($70-145) and scenic kayak tours ($100-125) on the Clark Fork, in the Alberton Gorge, on the Blackfoot, and on Idaho's Lochsa River.

Horseback Riding

Dunrovin Ranch

5001 Expedition Dr., Lolo; 406/273-7745; www.dunrovinranchmontana.com

Less than 30 minutes south of Missoula in Lolo, Dunrovin Ranch offers experiences with an emphasis on community, education, science, and the arts. Animals are at the heart of Dunrovin, from the family of smooth-gaited Tennessee walking horses to "diva donkeys," beloved dogs, and ospreys and other wild animals that call the ranch home. Though Dunrovin offers lodging and the full guest ranch experience, it also offers riding opportunities for nonguests. Trail rides off the ranch are available to anyone older than eight, starting at 1.5 hours (from $135). Private rides can be arranged as well. Dunrovin Ranch also offers a historical ride for history buffs. Horsemanship lessons start at $135.

Spectator Sports

Missoula PaddleHeads Baseball

Allegiance Park, 700 Cregg Ln.; 406/543-3300; www.milb.com/missoula; from $9

At Ogren Field in **Allegiance Park,** the Missoula PaddleHeads, whose mascot is a moose, take on other Pioneer League teams in some great small-town minor league baseball. Missoula is known for its softball, so it's no surprise that the community shows up in force to watch their hometown PaddleHeads, whose name is also a nod to Missoula's active boating scene.

Entertainment and Events

Nightlife

Home to college students and artists, Missoula has no shortage of watering holes, and a brief walk will take you to establishments that are pulsing with activity.

Oxford Saloon & Café

337 N. Higgins Ave.; 406/549-0117; www.the-oxford.com; 24 hours daily

The Oxford Saloon & Café dates back to the 1880s and still offers live poker nightly at 8pm. Though it no longer serves brains and eggs, the Oxford still makes a pretty tasty Garbage Omelet.

James Bar

127 W. Alder St.; 406/721-8158; bar hours 5pm-10pm Mon.-Tues., 11:30am-11:30pm Wed.-Thurs., 11:30am-12:30am Fri., 11am-11:30pm Sat., brunch 11am-2pm Sat.-Sun., kitchen open reduced hours; $6-35

Complete with a Hunter S. Thompson quote etched on the outside of the building, James Bar is a classy joint for cocktails and good, local cuisine—including bison, crab, falafel, lamb sliders, and the best fries—instead of standard bar fare.

Top Hat Lounge & Casino

134 W. Front St.; 406/830-4640; www.logjampresents.com; 11am-10pm Mon.-Thurs., 11am-11pm Fri.-Sat.; $11-21

Music lovers will do well at the Top Hat Lounge & Casino, which has been bringing live music to Missoula since 1952. The tapas-style menu, including Korean street tacos and chicken and waffles, does not disappoint.

Plonk

322 N. Higgins Ave.; 406/926-1791; www.plonkwine.com; 3pm-midnight daily; $12-48

Mellower and upscale Plonk pairs exquisite wine, inspired cocktails, and elegant food with eclectic music. Too pricey for the average college student, Plonk tends to appeal to an older crowd.

Montana Wineries

Since 1984, when Tom Campbell Jr. and his father first started growing grapes along the shores of Flathead Lake, in Montana cherry territory, several other wineries have sprouted up across the state, primarily on its west side. Many have disappeared after hard winters and rough economies, but a handful are proving that Montana vintners have what it takes. There are several growers among the bunch, including some that opt for unconventional base fruits like cherries, huckleberries, apples, pears, currants, and rhubarb.

- **Ten Spoon Vineyard and Winery** (4175 Rattlesnake Dr., Missoula; 406/549-8703; www.tenspoon.com) is among the fastest-growing wineries in the state and has a marvelous origin story. Owner Connie Poten bought some pastureland in the Rattlesnake outside Missoula to protect open space. She met Andy Sponseller on a local preservation campaign, and their shared love of wine led to the backbreaking work that built the vineyard and set the stage for their subsequent success with more than 20 varietals, including Moonlight pinot noir, Ranger Rider Red, Flathead cherry dry, Farm Dog Red, and Sweet Talk Riesling.
- **Hidden Legend Winery** (1345 US 93 N., Ste. 5, Victor; 406/363-6323; www.hiddenlegendwinery.com) in the Bitterroot Valley specializes in honey-based mead with Montana twists like chokecherry and elderberry.
- **Trapper Peak Winery** (75 Cattail Ln., Darby; 406/821-1964), also in the Bitterroot Valley, produces an affordable selection of cabernet sauvignon, petite syrah, merlot, cabernet franc, and muscat using California grapes.

Montgomery Distillery

129 Front St.; 406/926-1725; www.montgomerydistillery.com; noon-8pm Mon.-Sat., 2pm-8pm Sun.

Montgomery Distillery is a family business that serves their award-winning whiskey, rye, vodka, gin, aquavit, and more in an elegant setting.

Stave & Hoop

223 N. Higgins, alley entrance; 406/493-0282; www.staveandhoop.com; 4:06pm-11pm Mon.-Thurs., 4:06pm-midnight Fri.-Sat.

A speakeasy that was built to pay homage to the 1896 building it's in, Stave & Hoop serves craft cocktails, beer, wine, and Montana comfort food, from flatbread and bacon-wrapped dates to elk burgers.

Kettle House Brewing Co.

605 Cold Smoke Ave., Bonner; 406/728-1660; www.kettlehouse.com; noon-8pm daily

East of Missoula, but worth the drive, Kettle House Brewing Co., home of the famous Cold Smoke, has a taproom where their year-round favorites and limited release brews can be sampled. Set on the river next to the Kettlehouse Amphitheater, the taproom has live music and a food truck to make beer drinking even more fun.

The Arts

Missoula Children's Theatre

425 E. Broadway; 406/728-7529 or 406/728-1911; www.mctinc.org

One of the state's most beloved theater companies, the Missoula Children's Theatre mounts several productions annually of such family favorites as *Hansel and Gretel* and *Snow White and the Seven Dwarfs* with children as cast members. Most significantly, MCT has become known for its performances in 16 countries around the world that include local children. The company arrives in town the Monday before a Friday performance, casting and rehearsing

Montana's Literary Treasure

Few states can boast a nearly 1,200-page, 5-lb tome dedicated to the literature that has defined the state. (The state's "Big Sky" moniker even came courtesy of A. B. Guthrie Jr.'s classic 1947 novel *The Big Sky.*) Montana's literary anthology, *The Last Best Place,* was published in 1988, and the state's literary status only continues to grow. This may partly be attributed to poet and professor **Richard Hugo,** who directed the University of Montana's renowned creative writing program from 1964 until his death in 1982. The less prosaic might ascribe the inordinate number of well-known authors and poets to things like the light, space, and quality of life here, or the long, cold winters and limited distractions.

A Few of Montana's Best-Known Writers

- **Wallace Stegner:** A historian, novelist, essayist, teacher, and conservationist, Stegner (1909-1993) wrote the semi-autobiographical *Big Rock Candy Mountain* and won the Pulitzer Prize for his 1971 novel *Angle of Repose.*
- **James Welch:** Growing up on the Blackfeet Reservation in Browning, Montana, James Welch (1940-2003) was a celebrated novelist, historian, and poet, best known for such works as "Fool's Crow" and "Winter in the Blood."
- **Dorothy Johnson:** Though many readers don't recognize her name, Dorothy Johnson's (1905-1984) short stories and novels are widely familiar: *The Man Who Shot Liberty Valance* and *A Man Called Horse* among them.
- **Rick Bass:** Inspired by the work of another beloved Montana writer, Jim Harrison, geologist Rick Bass (b.1958) moved to northwest Montana in the 1980s and has written more than 30 books, both fiction and non-, including his lauded collection of short stories, *For a Little While.*

local children to light up the stage (or the gym, as is often the case in small-town Montana). In Missoula, the company performs Broadway musicals and poignant comedies in its home performance space.

Festivals and Events

Weekly Summer Events

With an active, outdoorsy, and independent population, Missoula hosts weekly events during summer that encourage everything from outdoor dining to art appreciation. **Missoula on Main** (406/532-3240; www.missouladowntown.com/first-friday) is held 5pm-8pm on the first Friday of every month. Some 15-20 galleries open their doors, often to display new exhibitions, and they provide complimentary hors d'oeuvres and refreshments to art strollers. On Wednesdays, **Out to Lunch** (406/543-4238; www.missouladowntown.com; 11am-2pm Wed. June-Aug.) in Caras Park is a riverside performing arts picnic with local musicians and more than 20 food trucks. Also in Caras Park, **Downtown ToNight** (406/543-4238; www.missouladowntown.com; 5:30pm-8:30pm Thurs. June-Aug.) features live music, food vendors, and a beverage garden on Thursdays.

International Wildlife Film Festival

718 S. Higgins Ave.; 406/541-9364; www.wildlifefilms.org; late Apr.

Since 1977, the International Wildlife Film Festival has been celebrating

- **Debra Magpie Earling:** A member of the Bitterroot Salish tribe, Debra Magpie Earling (b. 1957) became the first Native American director of the university's creative writing program in 2016. Her novels *Perma Red* and *The Lost Journals of Sacajawea* address the often-interwoven triumphs and tragedies of Native women.

Literary Locales in Missoula

Montana's literary heritage courses through every corner of this community; one of the area's softball teams went by the name "The Montana Review of Books," which once had an outfield lineup with 12 published novels among them. Here are some places with a literary claim to fame.

- **Bookstores:** The city boasts some fabulous independent bookstores that promote and often host local writers, including **Fact and Fiction** (220 N. Higgins Ave.).
- **Writer hangouts: Charlie B's** (428 N. Higgins Ave.), a favorite haunt of the late James Crumley, has no sign, tinted windows, and a big wooden door. Crumley was also a regular at **The Depot** (201 Railroad St. W.). During his tenure at the University of Montana, Bill Kittredge and plenty of creative writing students frequented **Diamond Jim's Eastgate Casino and Lounge** (900 E. Broadway) just over the Van Buren footbridge from campus.
- **Bars in books: The Rhino** (158 Ryman St.) was identifiable in Jeff Hull's short stories and his 2005 novel. Probably the best known among Missoula's thirsty literary geniuses, Richard Hugo often wrote about bars—**The Dixon Bar** (Hwy. 200, Dixon), which is, for the moment anyway, still open; **Trixi's Antler Saloon** (Hwy. 200, Ovando); and more famously, the **Milltown Union Bar** (11 Main St., Milltown), which is now the Milltown Moose Lodge, home to the fraternal Moose club, and is virtually unrecognizable.

conservation and film with an eight-day event based at Missoula's famed Roxy Theatre. The event runs in late April, featuring wildlife films from around the globe.

Shopping

Souvenirs

The Fair Trade Store

519 S. Higgins Ave.; 406/543-3955; www.jrpc.org; 10am-6pm Mon.-Sat., noon-4pm Sun.

The Fair Trade Store is operated by the Jeannette Rankin Peace Center and promotes equitable and fair partnerships between producers and distributors of goods. There is a distinctive and colorful selection of merchandise from around the globe, including textiles, pottery, silver, and handmade cards.

Butterfly Herbs

232 N. Higgins Ave.; 406/728-8780; www.butterflyherbs.com; 9am-6pm Mon.-Fri., 9am-5:30pm Sat.-Sun.

In addition to being Missoula's oldest espresso bar, Butterfly Herbs is a fun and eclectic gift shop. It sells whole herbs, teas, coffee, and spices in bulk as well as soaps, lotions, handmade jewelry, candles, and other decorative goods.

Rockin Rudy's

237 Blaine St.; 406/542-0077; www.rockinrudys.com; 9am-9pm Mon.-Sat., 11am-6pm Sun.

Rockin Rudy's uses as a tagline, "A place. Sort of." More than just a place, Rockin Rudy's is *the* place in Missoula for music, posters, cards, gag gifts, jewelry, and on and on. Big and random, this place is part of Missoula culture.

Clothing and Gear

The Trail Head

221 E. Front St.; 406/543-6966; www.trailheadmontana.net; 10am-7pm Mon.-Fri., 9am-6pm Sat., 11am-6pm Sun.

The Trail Head is a part of the Missoula community and thrives by knowing the area as well as its activities and specific conditions. Trail Head staff participate regularly in volunteer efforts to preserve and enhance recreational opportunities in the region. The store has fantastic gear for nearly every activity in the area, including skiing, boating, camping, and climbing. Since 1974, great adventures have started here.

Betty's Divine

509 S. Higgins; 406/721-4777; www.bettysdivine.com; 10am-7pm Mon.-Sat., 11am-5pm Sun.

It would not be a trip to Missoula without visiting a thrift shop, and Betty's Divine is as good as it gets. There is an assortment of both vintage and vintage-inspired garb, and though the prices are not cheap, the quality is outstanding, as are the friendly service and the groovy tunes. It's a women-owned, women-run business that prioritizes financial, social, and environmental responsibility. Alongside their clothing, Betty's Divine sells shoes, jewelry, and records.

Bookstores

Fact and Fiction Books

220 N. Higgins Ave.; 406/721-2881; www.factandfictionbooks.com; 10am-6pm Mon.-Fri., 10am-5pm Sat., noon-4pm Sun.

In a famously literary town, Fact and Fiction Books is a Missoula institution and a good place to learn about local culture and regional authors.

Shakespeare & Co.

103 S. 3rd Ave.; 406/549-9010; www.shakespeareandco.com; 11am-6pm Mon.-Sat., 11am-5pm Sun.

For new books, postcards, cards, journals, gifts, and magazines, the independent Shakespeare & Co. is a real find on the Hip Strip.

Farmers Markets

Known as the Garden City, Missoula boasts three fabulous farmers markets, including the **Clark Fork Market** (101 Carousel Dr., next to Dragon Hollow; 406/880-9648; www.clarkforkmarket.com; 8am-1pm Sat. May-Sept., 9am-1pm Oct.), which offers an abundance of local produce, meat, and other products, including hot prepared food. There is live music 10am-12:30pm, and plenty of parking is available. The **Missoula Farmers Market** (Circle Square, north end of Higgins Ave.; 406/201-6902; www.missoulafarmersmarket.com; 8am-12:30pm Sat. May-Oct., 5pm-7pm Tues. June 19-Sept.) features more than 100 vendors of fresh local produce, flowers, eggs, honey, and more. The **Missoula People's Market** (inside the Iron Horse Bar & Grill, and outside on E. Pine and N. Higgins Ave.; 406/830-3216; www.missoulapeoplesmarket.org; 9am-1pm Sat. May-Sept.) has prepared food, plus art and crafts by local artisans.

Food

Missoula's dining scene offers more cultural diversity than much of the rest of the state, with plenty of sushi and global offerings, but its strong suit is still Rocky Mountain cuisine with the freshest local ingredients.

Tagliare Delicatessen

910 Wyoming St.; 406/613-7128; www.tagliaredelicatessen.com; 11am-6pm Mon.-Sat., 11am-5pm Sun.; $11-14

For the best deli sandwiches this side of Brooklyn, Tagliare's is the place. Their cured meats and cheeses are killer, as are the house-made sauces and fresh-baked bread. From the Zeppelin to the Megadeath and the New Edition to the Clash, each sandwich is made to order, or they are always happy for you to build your own. Their charcuterie trays are out of this world.

★ Biga Pizza

241 W. Main St.; 406/728-2579; www.bigapizza.com; 11am-9pm Mon.-Sat.; $12-22

For the best local pizza, you can't beat the wood-fired offerings from Biga Pizza. From the simple house pie with garlic oil, tomato sauce, fresh basil, and fresh mozzarella to the maple chipotle pizza with sweet potato and bacon, to the prosciutto di Parma with herbed mascarpone fig paste, toasted almonds, and mozzarella, its combinations are nothing short of mouthwatering. Gluten-free crusts are available, as are calzones, salads, sandwiches, and antipasti. Since there is often a line for dinner, ordering ahead online to pick up can be a good option.

Pangea Bar & Restaurant

223 N. Higgins Ave.; 406/493-1190; www.mtpangea.com; 11am-9pm Mon.-Thurs., 11am-10pm Fri.-Sat.; $16-45

A great spot for drinks and dinner is Pangea Bar & Restaurant, which won a Wine Spectator Award for Excellence. Their curries and fish are outstanding, as is the bison prime rib on Tuesdays. They also have a nice selection of burgers, flatbreads, and salads.

Scotty's Table

131 S. Higgins Ave., downstairs in the Wilma; 406/549-2790; www.scottystable.net; 11:30am-2pm and 5pm-9pm Wed.-Fri., 9:30am-1:30pm and 5pm-9pm Sat.-Sun.; $28-45

Among the best restaurants in Missoula is Scotty's Table, serving American bistro fare with a global twist. It's an upscale restaurant for the whole family—the gourmet kids' menu was inspired by the chef's own child. Entrées include mouthwatering cioppino and chicken schwarma, but the appetizers are enchanting—try the fried Brussels sprouts and cauliflower, mussels and fries, or local short ribs; you might not even make it to the main course.

Boxcar Bistro

875 Wyoming St., Ste. 101; 406/551-4166; www.boxcarmissoula.com; 4pm-9pm Tues.-Sat.; $21-58

Located in the Old Sawmill District, Boxcar Bistro is a charming mashup of Montana history, the luxury of the train travel era, plus French food and wine. The restaurant calls its fare "regional cuisine with a French backbone," and it's delicious. From caviar and oysters to filet mignon and duck confit, the menu is classic upscale bistro and the ambience is top-notch.

Le Petit Outre

129 S. 4th St. W.; 406/543-3311; www.lepetitoutre.com; 7am-4pm Mon.-Fri., 8am-4pm Sat., 8am-2pm Sun.

For real French pastries and espresso, visit Le Petit Outre, where there is almost always a line because no one wants them to be out of ham and cheese croissants when it's their turn to order. Le Petit makes beautiful bread, too.

Big Dipper Ice Cream

631 S. Higgins Ave.; 406/543-5722; www.bigdippericecream.com; 11am-11pm daily summer; and 2700 Paxson St., Ste. F; 406/926-1160; 11am-10pm Sun.-Thurs., 11am-10:30pm Fri.-Sat.

If you're just starting your Montana adventure, you'll need to get in shape for all the ice-cream offerings. A good place to start is Big Dipper Ice Cream, which has unexpected but out-of-this-world flavors like cardamom, El Salvador coffee, Mexican chocolate, and mango habanero sorbet in addition to the lip-smacking classics. Don't miss daily special flavors like cotton candy, Thai peanut curry (really), and Elvis (peanut butter, banana, chocolate chip, chocolate, and bacon). During summer, the walk-up window is open 11am-11pm daily, and there's almost always a line in the evening. Hours vary throughout the year at both locations, so call ahead or check the website.

Accommodations

As one of Montana's bigger cities, Missoula has plenty of lodging options. The old-school independent motels line much of East and West Broadway, while some of the newer chain hotels can be found on Reserve Street.

Gelandesprung Lodge at Snowbowl

1700 Snowbowl Rd.; 406/549-9777; www.montanasnowbowl.com; $77-147

Twenty minutes north of Missoula is the Gelandesprung Lodge at Snowbowl, a European-style ski-in ski-out lodge on the mountain and open throughout the ski season and on weekends in summer. Some rooms have private baths, others share a hall bath. For the ultimate family or friend reunion, you can rent the whole place ($1,161/night). Rates are announced seasonally, so call ahead or check online.

DoubleTree by Hilton Missoula Edgewater

100 Madison St.; 406/728-3100 or 800/222-8733; www.missoulaedgewater.doubletree.com; from $140 off-season, from $279 in-season

In the heart of Missoula on the banks of the Clark Fork River is the pet-friendly DoubleTree by Hilton Missoula Edgewater, an enormous hotel with all the amenities, including room service. Ask for a room facing the river.

★ The Wren

201 E. Main St.; 406/401-4400; www.wrenmissoula.com; $127-362

Ideally situated in the heart of downtown and uber pet-friendly, The Wren is a relatively new and hip hotel with spare, clean rooms and a great coffee shop downstairs.

Resort at Paws Up

40060 Paws Up Rd., Greenough; 406/244-5200; www.pawsup.com; luxury tents $2,798-5,581/night for 2 adults and 2 children

At the other end of the spectrum is an ultraluxe experience that will thin your wallet considerably. The five-star family-friendly Resort at Paws Up in Greenough, 32 mi (52 km) east of Missoula, is among the most glamorous spots in the state. There are luxury homes and luxury tents that are unimaginably elegant, with heated floors, electricity, king-size feather beds, a dining pavilion with your own personal chef, a camping butler, and nightly bonfires with s'mores. This is camping fit for a high-maintenance king. The food is exquisite, as is the spa, and the activities and adventures are limitless. The same company also runs the adults-only **the green o** (4069 Backcountry Rd., Greenough; 877/251-2841 or 406/244-4934; www.thegreeno.com; from $2,048/night for 2 adults) nearby.

Camping

There are only a handful of private campgrounds in Missoula, but the **Lolo National Forest** (406/329-3750; www.fs.usda.gov/lolo) has a wide range of campsites in beautiful settings, among them Lolo Creek, Ninemile, and Rock Creek. Camping is also permitted in certain sections of the **Rattlesnake National Recreation Area and Wilderness** (406/329-3814) beyond a 3-mi (5-km) radius from the main trailhead.

Missoula KOA Holiday

3450 Tina Ave.; 406/549-0881 or 800/562-5366; www.missoulakoa.com; year-round; from $61 tents, from $62 RVs, from $106 cabins w/o bath

For in-town convenience with RV-specific sites, try the Missoula KOA Holiday. The tree-lined property offers 200 RV and tent sites in addition to amenities like a heated pool, two hot tubs, bike rentals, mini golf, free Wi-Fi, nightly ice cream, and a café that serves breakfast daily in summer.

Jim and Mary's RV Park

9800 US 93 N.; 406/549-4416; www.jimandmarys.com; RV sites from $65 plus $3 pp over 12 years old, including water, sewer, electric, cable TV, and Wi-Fi

Offering 70 nice, shady sites just outside of town is the Good Sam-recognized Jim and Mary's RV Park. There are discounts for weekly stays.

Information and Services

Visitor Information

The **Missoula Chamber of Commerce** (825 E. Front St.; 406/543-6623; www.missoulachamber.com; 8am-5pm Mon.-Fri.) and **Destination Missoula** (101 E. Main St.; 800/526-3465 for travel consultation; www.destinationmissoula.org; 9am-7pm Mon.-Fri., 9am-5pm Sat., 10am-3pm Sun.) are both great sources of information for visitors.

The **US Forest Service** (26 Fort Missoula Rd.; 406/329-3511; www.fs.usda.gov/lolo) and the **Montana Department of Fish, Wildlife and Parks** (3201 Spurgin Rd.; 406/542-5500; www.fwp.mt.gov; 8am-5pm Mon.-Fri.) offices offer good information about hiking, camping, and fishing in the national forests.

Health and Emergencies

The main hospitals are **St. Patrick's** (500 W. Broadway; 406/543-7271) and **Community Medical Center** (2827 Fort Missoula Rd.; 406/728-4100), both of which have 24-hour emergency rooms. There are several walk-in urgent care facilities in town. The **CostCare Walk-In Clinic** (3031 Russell St.; 406/728-5841; www.costcare.com; 8am-6pm Mon.-Fri., 9am-2pm Sat.-Sun.) has several locations and expanded hours, including weekends.

Butte

Everyone in Montana is (or should be) rooting for Butte. Once the cosmopolitan moneymaking center of the state, Butte (pop. 36,068, elev. 5,700 ft/1,737 m) today is beat-up but still scrappy; "rough around the edges" is putting it mildly. The most far-reaching and present reminder of its former glory, other than the open-pit mining scars that rend the entire valley, are the car license plates that start with 1, Butte's rank in population when motor vehicles showed up on the scene.

But Butte is a remarkable place with the most compelling and diverse history in the state as well as fabulous old buildings just waiting for a renaissance. In fact, Butte is among the largest registered National Historic Landmark Districts in the country. Time in Butte gives visitors an incredible opportunity to learn about Montana's past and see firsthand what happens to a place when all of its natural resources are exploited as quickly as possible. Indeed, there is something of *The Lorax* in Butte, and something of *The Giving Tree.* But no copper king or corporation can rob this place of its fascinating past and modern-day spirit.

Getting to Butte

Driving

Butte is 120 mi (193 km) southeast of **Missoula** on I-90, a drive of about 2 hours.

From **Bozeman,** Butte is 85 mi (137 km) west on I-90, about a 90-minute drive. From **Helena,** it's 69 mi (111 km) south on I-15, a drive of just over an hour.

Air

The **Bert Mooney Airport** (BTM; 101 Airport Rd.; 406/494-3771; www.butteairport.com) in Butte is served by Delta Connection with daily flights to and from Salt Lake City. NetJets also serves the airport. The car-rental agencies at the airport are **Avis, Budget,** and **Hertz. Enterprise** (3285 Harrison Ave.; 406/494-1900; www.enterprise.com) has an off-site service center.

Bus

Bus service from **Greyhound** and **Rimrock Stages** (406/723-3287) is available at 1324 Harrison Avenue.

Butte

Getting Around

The Butte-Silver Bow Transit System (406/497-6515; www.buttebus.org; free) offers bus service 6:45am-6:15pm Monday-Friday and 8:45am-4:15pm Saturday. You can pick up a bus schedule at the public library or download a copy online. **Mining City Taxi** (406/723-6511) offers service 24 hours every day.

Sights

★ Old Butte Historical Adventures

117 N. Main St.; 406/498-3424; www.buttetour.info; scheduled tours 10am, noon, and 2pm Mon.-Sat., by reservation only Sun. Apr.-Sept., by reservation only Nov.-Mar.; $20-25

If you only have one day in Butte, take a tour put on by Old Butte Historical Adventures, which offers walking tours of Butte's underground city, complete with a speakeasy, a barbershop, and an old city jail. Other tours stay aboveground and visit the Myra brothel, Finntown, Tony's Tinshop, and the Cabbage Patch shantytown. Ghost tours, labor history tours, and ethnic culture walking tours can also be arranged. What makes these tours so compelling, other than the mind-blowing

history, is the passion and knowledge of the guides—you may just fall in love with Butte. Reservations are recommended; custom tours can be arranged for a minimum of four people (from $25 pp).

The Berkeley Pit

350 Shields Ave.; 406/723-3177; www.pitwatch.org; 9am-5pm daily June-Sept.

The first open-pit mine dug in pursuit of copper, the Berkeley Pit swallowed several of the underground mines along with entire neighborhoods as the Anaconda Company dug deeper and wider for smaller amounts of copper. In 1982, because of steadily falling copper prices, the Berkeley Pit shut down. The mines under the city and the pit itself immediately started to fill with water bearing the same acidity levels as lemon juice. The water depth surpassed 5,356 ft (1,633 m) and was continuously climbing, with 2.6 million gallons (9.8 million liters) flooding in every day until remediation started in 2019, when pumps began pumping out and treating about 3 million gallons (13.6 million liters) per day to prevent contamination of the region's water supply. The water itself is highly toxic and appears various shades of brown, blue, green, and red.

In 1995, a flock of snow geese landed in the Berkeley Pit and after several days 342 birds were found dead in the water. In 2016, more snow geese landed in the pit in a single day than often do in a year. Crews employed myriad ways to encourage the birds to leave after a short rest—fireworks, bird wailers, drones—but several thousand stayed for a few days and, sadly, perished as a result.

One curious creature that managed to live in and around the pit for years was a dog known by miners as "The Auditor." He greeted workers daily for 17 years but never came close enough for anyone to touch. The miners built him a shanty and left food and water, pointing to the dog as proof that there were indeed things able to withstand the toxicity of the Superfund site. The pit's unofficial mascot died in 2003, but not before the community raised enough money to commission a bronze statue of the mangy mutt, which is on display at the pit viewing stand.

Our Lady of the Rockies

Tours leave from 3100 Harrison Ave.; 406/782-1221; www.ourladyoftherockies.org; tours 10am, 2pm, and 6pm daily weather permitting June-Oct., gift shop 11am-4pm Mon.-Sat. June-Oct.; $28

High atop the crest of the Continental Divide is Our Lady of the Rockies, a 90-ft (27-m) statue of the Virgin Mary meant to watch over this predominantly Catholic town. Between 1979 and 1985, the statue was built and erected entirely by volunteers, many of them miners who had lost their jobs when the Berkeley Pit, Butte's last operating mine, closed down. Bob O'Bill, who worked for the Anaconda Mining Company for years, vowed that if his wife recovered from illness, he would hoist a statue of the Virgin Mary on the East Ridge overlooking the city. When the final piece was set in place by helicopter, Butte came to a screeching halt to watch in proud silence. Indeed, the statue is a reflection of this city's indomitable spirit. The roughly 2.5-hour tours leave from the gift shop in the Butte Plaza Mall on Harrison Avenue and include a trip inside the metal sculpture.

★ World Museum of Mining

155 Museum Way Rd.; 406/723-7211; www.miningmuseum.org; 9:30am-5:30pm daily Apr.-Oct., hours subject to change after Labor Day; $12

Off West Park Road, across from the Montana Tech campus, is the World Museum of Mining, which sits on the now-defunct Orphan Girl mine yard. It houses numerous exhibits and the mine yard is filled with a variety of equipment covering a century of use, including smelter cars and ore carts. When you purchase your entry ticket to the museum, you may also want to buy a ticket for the 1.5-hour **underground mine tours** (from $25). Visitors to the underground mine wear hard hats, cap lamps, and battery belts and descend 65 ft (20 m) into the mine. The tours are led by former mine workers who tell their personal stories. They also explain how equipment was used and how the ore was mined and removed from the pit. Combined tickets can be purchased for the museum and the underground tour. Children under five are not permitted on the underground tour.

A highlight of the museum is its **Hell Roarin' Gulch,** a full-scale, authentic reproduction of an 1890s mining town. There are 50 buildings on site, 15 of which are historic buildings that have been relocated to the museum. Visit a bank, general store, school, and Chinese herbalist whose shelves are stocked with original herbs and medicines. The buildings have been painstakingly re-created using as many antiques and original materials as possible. A rock and mineral room in the museum will delight rock hounds, and there's a remarkable doll and dollhouse collection.

Copper King Mansion

219 W. Granite St.; 406/782-7580; www.thecopperkingmansion.com; 10am-4pm daily May-Sept., by appointment Oct.-Apr., tours at 10am, noon, 2pm, and 3:30pm; $20

The Copper King Mansion is both a museum and bed-and-breakfast ($200-359). Guided tours (often hosted by a woman who grew up in the house) show off this 34-room Victorian home built in 1898 for the infamous King of Copper, William Andrews Clark. Considered one of the wealthiest men in the world, Clark could easily afford to import all the material for the house's construction as well as the European artisans needed to do the work. The cost to construct the mansion is estimated at around $500,000, which represents one-half day's revenue for Clark at the peak of his career.

Clark Chateau Museum

321 W. Broadway; 406/565-5600; www.clarkchateau.org; noon-4pm Thurs.-Sun. May-Aug., noon-4pm Fri.-Sat. Sept.-Apr., 1-hour tours at 1pm; $10 guided tour, $7 general admission

W. A. Clark's son, Charles, also commissioned a house in 1898. The Clark Chateau Museum is a replica of a château Charles had admired in France. Today the house is a period museum and Butte's community arts center. Up the gorgeous spiral staircase to the 2nd and 3rd floors is the museum's permanent collection, dedicated to showcasing the diverse cultural and ethnic heritage of the city. Two galleries offer current shows, and the exhibits change over the course of the season. Weekday tours can be arranged off-season by emailing clarkchateau@gmail.com.

Dumas Brothel Museum

45 E. Mercury St.; 406/351-9922; www.dumasbrothel.com; call for hours and admission prices

Top to bottom: World Museum of Mining; Mai Wah Museum; Copper King Mansion

Butte is home to the Dumas Brothel, "America's longest-running house of prostitution," which operated from 1890 to 1982. Now, Dumas Brothel Museum showcases the seedier side of the city's history. Naturally, the brothel is rife with ghost stories, including the tale of Madame Elenor Knott, who is often reported, and even photographed, in the building. The museum is usually open for tours every other Saturday 11am-6pm, but call before visiting, since restoration often requires closures. This is a labor of love in every way imaginable, like so much of Butte's restoration. Be flexible and patient—it's worth it.

Mai Wah Museum

17 W. Mercury St.; 406/723-3231 or 406/565-1826 off-season; www.maiwah.org; 10am-4pm Tues.-Sat. June-Sept.; $8

Mai Wah Museum is dedicated to documenting and preserving Butte's Chinese heritage. By 1910, Butte's Chinatown had more than 2,000 Chinese residents, and the 1914 directory listed 62 Chinese businesses including gambling parlors, noodle shops, herbalists, and grocery stores. The permanent exhibit tells the story of Chinese immigrants to the city who came for lucrative jobs in the mining industry 1860-1940. Other exhibits contain photos, artifacts, and interpretive materials. The museum is in the Wah Chong Tai and Mai Wah buildings, just off China Alley, the heart of Butte's Chinatown. Originally the buildings were a mercantile store and noodle shop that served as meeting places and a major point of social interaction for the Chinese immigrant community.

Adventure and Recreation

United States High Altitude Speed Skating Center

1 Olympic Way; 406/494-7570; free

A unique facility with an outdoor speed-skating rink and a training facility for Olympic athletes from all over the world, the United States High Altitude Speed Skating Center hosts various competitions and is open to the public. Since it's volunteer-run, hours can vary.

Stodden Park

Sampson St. and Utah St.; 406/494-3686 or 406/494-6200; www.co.silverbow.mt.us

Stodden Park tops the list of the many green spaces in town with a swimming pool, tennis courts, horseshoes, an awesome playground that celebrates the city's mining heritage, a nine-hole golf course ($17 for 9 holes, $26 for 18 holes), and **Ridge Waters Waterpark** (3103 S. Utah St.; 406/497-6585; noon-3pm and 4pm-7pm early June-early Sept.; $7), complete with a lazy river and two slides.

Hiking

Maud S. Canyon Loop Trail

Distance: 4 mi (6.4 km) round-trip
Duration: 2 hours
Elevation gain: 994 ft (303 m)
Effort: Moderate
Trail surface: Dirt
Trailhead: 4800 Saddle Rock Rd.

One of the best places to get a bird's-eye view of the city and meet the active locals is on the Maud S. Canyon Loop just east of town. The trail winds through open grasslands to the old railroad bed and into the Beaverhead-Deerlodge National Forest.

Entertainment and Events

Nightlife

Like a puckish teenager, Butte's reputation has always preceded it. This is a scrappy town where no one likes to back down. Even the most elegant older women love to tell of carrying pearl-handled revolvers every time they traveled into or through Butte. It's a fighting town, which means Butte is a drinking town.

M&M Bar and Cafe

17 N. Main St.; 406/299-2192; www.mandmbarandcafe.com; 8am-10pm Mon.-Thurs., 8am-midnight Fri.-Sat., 8am-2pm Sun.; $7-19

Butte has numerous bars, many of them

good ones, but the best one—the M&M Cigar Store—burned to the ground in May 2021. Opened in 1890, the M&M remained unlocked for more than 100 years, bearing witness to Butte's glory days from a front-row seat. There was once a bowling alley in the basement, a dining and drinking room on the 1st floor, and a gambling lounge upstairs. The cigars were added during Prohibition as a polite show of compliance, but the liquor was never locked up. In a 1970 *Esquire* article, Jack Kerouac wrote a poignant description of a late night spent at the M&M, summing it up: "It was the end of my quest for an ideal bar." But this is Butte. And no one gives up here. The new M&M reopened next door to the original bar and although the physical history is gone, the spirit of the place is alive and well. They serve breakfast, lunch, and dinner.

Silver Dollar Saloon

133 S. Main St.; 406/782-7367; 4pm-2am daily

The Silver Dollar Saloon is another legendary Butte watering hole, established on the border between Chinatown and the red-light district. The adjacent building was both a brothel and a boardinghouse for Chinese laborers. One of the hubs of the St. Patrick's Day festivities, the Silver Dollar is known for its live music offerings.

Quarry Brewing Company

124 W. Broadway; 406/723-0245; www.quarrybrew.com; 3pm-8pm Mon.-Thurs., 11am-8pm Fri.-Sat., 3pm-6pm Sun.

For a more family-friendly place with outstanding beer, try Quarry Brewing Company in the old Grand Hotel. Its five different German-style beers are brewed on-site, and kids will appreciate the play area, free popcorn, and homemade root beer and orange cream soda.

Jim's Bar

2720 Elm St.; 406/782-3431; 3pm-2am daily

Jim's Bar is kind of a biker bar, with plenty of fun and rowdy events such as biker rodeos and beach volleyball. Closing time is dependent on the number of customers.

51 Below Speakeasy

53 W. Park St.; 406/723-8928; www.theminershotel.com; 4pm-9pm Mon.-Wed., 4pm-10pm Thurs., 4pm-midnight Fri., 11am-midnight Sat.

The newest bar on the scene in Butte, and a really interesting one in how it pays homage to Butte's history, is 51 Below Speakeasy, located in the boutique Miner's Hotel, a building with fantastic, gritty history. The bar is intimate, as you would expect in a speakeasy, and they serve a huge selection of whiskey cocktails, plus signature cocktails with every other spirit under the sun. There are nine different varieties of Moscow Mule, for example.

The Arts

Main Stope Gallery

14 S. Dakota St.; 406/723-9195; www.mainstopegallery.com; 11am-5pm Wed.-Fri., 9am-2pm Sat.

For a selection of contemporary gems, try Main Stope Gallery, which sells pottery, paintings, photography, and other fine art by contemporary Montana artists.

Carle Gallery

226 W. Broadway; 406/723-3361; www.buttepubliclibrary.info; 9am-5pm Mon. and Fri.-Sat., 9am-7pm Tues.-Thurs.

Located on the 3rd floor of the Butte Public Library, the Carle Gallery pays tribute to Butte artist John Carle, known for his paintings of the city's buildings and people, and hosts monthly shows. The gallery also hosts rotating exhibits from the World Museum of Mining and Mai Wah Museum.

Mother Lode Theatre

316 W. Park St.; 406/723-3602; http://buttearts.org

Seeing an event at the Mother Lode Theatre is an event in itself. Built entirely with private funds by the Masons in 1923 as the 1,200-seat Temple Theatre, the glorious building was converted into a movie house during the Depression. As the mines were abandoned, so was the theater. In the 1980s, the only other theater in town was condemned and razed. True to form in Butte, people made it a priority to restore the building. Today, the Mother Lode provides performance space for the Butte Symphony, Montana Repertory Theatre, Missoula Children's Theatre, traveling Broadway productions, concerts, and numerous other events and organizations.

Silver Bow Twin Drive In

116054 S. Buxton Rd.; 406/782-8095; www.silverbowdrivein.com; spring-early-Sept.; $7

Since 1977, the Silver Bow Twin Drive In has been an absolute classic. There really isn't a better way to see a movie under the Big Sky. Two screens allow for a capacity of nearly 500 cars. Don't bring food with you—a concession stand (that until 1973 was at a drive-in theater in Deer Lodge) serves great popcorn and other old-school goodies including Tombstone pizza and ice cream. The audio can be found on your FM dial; a few portable radios are available to rent for those without a working car radio or who want to sit outside.

Shopping

Once home to 100,000 people and a number of copper kings, it's no surprise that Butte offers plenty of antiques shopping in the historic uptown.

Rediscoveries Vintage Clothing

83 E. Park St.; 406/723-2176; 11am-5pm Mon.-Fri., 11am-4pm Sat.

Several antiques stores are located uptown, including in the area bounded by Main, Montana, Granite, and Galena Streets. Rediscoveries Vintage Clothing on Park is packed with a little bit of everything, from trinkets and treasures to furnishings, jewelry, and clothes.

Whitehead's Cutlery

73 E. Park St.; 406/723-9188; www.whiteheadscutlery.com; 1pm-5pm Mon.-Sat.

Whitehead's Cutlery was founded in 1890 and is considered to be the oldest continuously operated family-owned small business in the state. Its founder, Joseph Whitehead, made his living by traveling to mining camps in the region selling and sharpening knives. His first grinder in Butte was powered by a St. Bernard that ran on a treadmill to run the wheel. While his own line of products expanded from knives to include straight razors, barber supplies, and hockey and figure skates, Joseph's son Edward collected knives and swords from around the world. The impressive collection is on display and worth a visit.

Second Edition Books

112 S. Montana St.; 406/723-5108; www.secondeditionbooks.com; 9am-5:30pm Mon.-Sat.

Another Butte treasure is Second Edition Books, a second-generation, family-run used bookstore. In addition to a great selection of Butte books, both common and rare, Second Edition Books carries a nice selection of books on Montana, mining, engineering, geology, Yellowstone, and Glacier. There is also a children's section.

Butte Stuff

116 W. Park St.; 406/299-2254; www.buttestuff.com; 10am-5:30pm Mon.-Wed., 10am-4pm Sat.

For Butte T-shirts (including "Long Live the M&M"), hoodies, hats, stickers, and other Butte souvenirs, try the appropriately named Butte Stuff, which sells Butte- and Montana-related glassware, T-shirts, coffee, cutting boards, dish towels, and more.

Headframe Spirits

21 S. Montana St.; 406/299-2886; www.headframespirits.com; 10am-8pm daily

If you lack space in your suitcase for antique treasures and have a taste for spirits, stop into Headframe Spirits, founded in

2010 but steeped in Butte history. You can sip and sample the Neversweat Straight Bourbon, Destroying Angel Whiskey, Anselmo Gin, High Ore Vodka, and Orphan Girl Bourbon Cream Liquor. This women-led steel to glass distillery was named Distiller of the Year for Artisan Spirits. Visit the elegant and family-friendly tasting room to sample some of their exquisite cocktails. It's really quite a fitting way to spend an afternoon in Butte.

Food

No other Montana town can match the culinary history and culture of Butte. The **Butte pasty,** inspired by the Cornish dish, is a flaky pastry filled with meat and potatoes for the ultimate miner's lunch; when in Butte, it is the thing to try.

Hummingbird Café

605 W. Park St.; 406/723-2044; www.birdcafe605.com; 9am-3pm Mon.-Thurs., 8am-3pm Sat.-Sun.; $5-18

The Hummingbird Café is a wonderful spot, and probably the best breakfast in town. They have incredible—and hearty—wraps and sandwiches, excellent omelets, and pancakes. For lunch, their sandwiches are colorful and delicious, piled high with fresh veggies. Salads are great too. There are loads of options here for vegetarians, vegans, and gluten-free diners.

Pekin Noodle Parlor

117 Main St.; 406/782-2217; 5pm-9pm Wed.-Sun.; $10-17

A James Beard Award-winning, fun, and historic establishment is the Pekin Noodle Parlor, Butte's oldest Chinese restaurant, open since 1911. The place is casual and utterly authentic with private booths hidden behind curtains. Everything is the color of a Creamsicle. Reading the menu is a lesson in history, and an evening in the parlor is time well spent. Hours can vary depending on the number of customers, so call ahead.

Casagranda's Steakhouse

801 S. Utah St.; 406/723-4141; www.casagrandassteakhouse.com; 5pm-9pm Sun.-Wed., 5pm-9:30pm Thurs.-Sat., wine bar from 4pm; $17-47

In a newly restored 1900s warehouse, Casagranda's Steakhouse serves outstanding cuts of meat, in addition to pasta, chicken, seafood specialties, and sushi. Every Thursday night is sushi night, but the hand-cut steaks, sourced locally and regionally, are unbeatable, with various preparations to choose from, including au poivre, demiglace, fungi, Oscar-style, and more. The full-service **Guido's Bar** is open at 4pm.

★ Uptown Café

47 E. Broadway; 406/723-4735; www.uptowncafe.com; 11am-2pm Mon.-Fri., 5pm-8pm Fri.-Sat.; $19-59

Long considered the best restaurant in Butte, the Uptown Café is a gourmet restaurant with sophisticated style and plenty of Butte spirit. The lunches are excellent, from beef stroganoff and Cajun chicken pasta to Butte pasties and Wiener schnitzel. But the dinners, on weekends only, are worth writing home about. From small plates—including clams Maison to beef skewers—to their excellent entrées including beef Wellington, Alaskan king crab legs, shrimp scampi, and chicken saltimbocca, you will not leave hungry.

Accommodations

Butte has its fair share of reliable chain hotels, but none of them capture the town's amazing history as well as the cool-but-not-fancy independent hotels and inns that can be found uptown.

Hotel Finlen

100 E. Broadway; 406/723-5461 or 800/729-5461; www.finlen.com; $133-222

In the heart of uptown Butte is another fantastic old building striving to achieve its former glory. Hotel Finlen was built in 1924 on the site of the old

McDermott Hotel, one of the grandest in the Northwest. Modeled after the Astor Hotel in New York City, the Finlen is a nine-story Second Empire building with a copper-shingled roof. Over the years, Hotel Finlen was visited by Charles Lindberg, Harry Truman, John F. Kennedy, and Richard Nixon. As is true of all of Butte, Hotel Finlen fell into disrepair and neglect as the mining economy dried up. The Taras family purchased the hotel in 1979 and has worked hard to restore the lobby and mezzanine, both of which are more beautiful than ever. The 30 guest rooms are basic, and the 25 guest rooms in the motor inn are dated; still, there is history here, and with some luck, a future.

Miner's Hotel

53 W. Park St.; 406/763-8928; www.theminershotel.com; $139-259

A 12-room boutique hotel that pays homage to the city's history, the Miner's Hotel is listed on the National Registry of Historic Places. Housed in the 1913 Miner's Savings and Trust Co., the building has a lot of history. At one point the hotel was a boardinghouse and was occupied at the same time by government Prohibition agent Carrol Olson and known bootlegger Henry Alexis. Each room is different, but they are all quite comfortable. Several of the rooms—including the one in the original vault—are below ground and do not have exterior windows. Also, there is no elevator in the hotel. The 51 Below Speakeasy offers craft cocktails in the basement of the hotel.

★ Copper King Mansion

219 W. Granite St.; 406/782-7580; www.thecopperkingmansion.com; $200-359

Those who fall in love with Butte have a tendency to get caught up in the saga of Butte's past and present, and the local inns have so much more history than any chain hotel. William Andrews Clark's Copper King Mansion is also a bed-and-breakfast. Guests sleep in accommodations ranging from the butler's room to the Clarks' master bedroom. Because it is a functioning museum, check-in is at 4pm and guests must check out by 9am to accommodate the tour schedule. Guided tours are free for guests, and a full breakfast is served in the formal dining room.

Tuscany on the Green

1 Green Ln.; 406/494-2625 or 602/577-2953; $225-575

For an adults-only stay with classic charm on the grounds of the Butte Country Club, Tuscany on the Green (formerly Toad Hall Manor) is an excellent choice. From a goblet of sherry or port upon arrival to feather beds, Jacuzzi tubs, and decadent breakfasts, this four-room property offers classic B&B style.

Information and Services

Visitor Information

Chamber of Commerce and Visitor Information Center

1000 George St.; 406/723-3177; www.buttechambersite.org; 9am-5pm Mon.-Sat. summer, 10am-5pm Mon. and Fri.-Sat. winter

The front of the Butte-Silver Bow Chamber of Commerce and Visitor Information Center is stocked with brochures, pamphlets, and tour information; in back, you can usually find a helpful chamber employee to answer questions. A terrific Butte online resource is www.visitbutte.com.

Health and Emergencies

The emergency room at **St. James Healthcare** (400 S. Clark St.; 406/723-2500; www.sclhealth.org) is open 24 hours every day.

Three Forks

Named for the three rivers that form the headwaters of the Missouri River, Three Forks (pop. 1,986, elev. 4,075 ft/1,242 m) was put on the map by Lewis and Clark in 1805. The town is rich in fur trapping and trading history and equally distinguished today by a tightly knit community and a mild climate that locals refer to as the "banana belt."

Entertainment and Events

The **Three Forks Rodeo** (www.threeforksrodeo.com) is held annually in mid-July at the fairgrounds and includes a parade, two nights of rodeo, plenty of food, and entertainment.

The town's **Christmas Stroll** is what every small town should aspire to: the crowning of a Christmas king and queen, fireworks, horse-drawn wagon rides, a community cookie exchange, and s'mores around the bonfire.

Accommodations

★ Sacajawea Hotel

5 N. Main St.; 406/285-6515; www.sacajaweahotel.com; rooms from $149, cottages from $300

For a historical treat in Three Forks, the Sacajawea Hotel is one-of-a-kind. Lovingly restored by the Folkvord family, local farmers who own the enormously successful Wheat Montana Bakeries, the Sac is a historic gem. There are 29 charming and comfortable rooms (starting at $149), some of which are pet-friendly, ranging from full beds to kings. And the seven new cottages (starting at $300) are elegant and private. The amenities are pretty plush, and the food is sensational.

Visit the Sac for a meal or just a cocktail at **Pompey's Grill** (4:30pm-9pm Mon.-Thurs., 4:30pm-10pm Fri.-Sat., 4pm-9pm Sun. on-season, closed Mon.-Tues. off-season; $28-62).

Willow Creek

Six mi (10 km) south of Three Forks, the small community of Willow Creek (pop. 211, elev. 4,153 ft/1,266 m) has plenty of charm. The creek that runs through town was originally named Philosopher's River by William Clark, but the town wisely renamed it and the town for the willows that grow along the banks.

Entertainment and Events

The town's half-dozen artists organize the **Willow Creek Art Walks** the third Friday of each month June-August. A local gallery not to be missed is **Aunt Dofe's Hall of Recent Memory** (102 Main St.; 406/285-6996; 1pm-4pm Sat.-Sun. or by appointment, hours may vary in summer), which supports the work of contemporary local artists.

Food

★ Woolzie's Willow Creek Café and Supper Club

21 Main St.; 406/285-3698; 4pm-9pm Wed.-Sun.; $20-42

Across the street from Aunt Dofe's, Woolzie's Willow Creek Café and Supper Club draws diners from far and wide for its quaint ambience and savory cuisine, including the best ribs in the valley—maybe the whole state. You can't go wrong with the daily specials—everything is made from scratch.

Detour: Virginia City and Nevada City

Seventy-five mi (121 km) southeast of Butte are Virginia City and Nevada City, two thriving ghost towns left over from Montana's glorious gold-mining era. In May 1863, a party of six prospectors left Bannack after a string of bad luck. While they set up camp for the night along Alder Creek, the men discovered what would become one of the richest gold deposits in North America. Nine camps grew up along the creek almost overnight, the largest of which would be named Virginia City.

Within a year, the town had upward of 10,000 residents and became the first territorial capital. It was also the site of the state's first newspaper, the first public school, and the first Masonic lodge. The town's history is intertwined with the Vigilantes of Montana, the group that would hang Sheriff Henry Plummer, among others, in 1864.

By 1875, much of the mining activity

in the region had abated, and Virginia City's population had dwindled to less than 800. Over the years, as new technologies developed, including the mining dredges, the area was mined over and over for traces of what might be left. Still, between 1863 and 1889, some $90 million worth of gold had been extracted from the region. Today, that amount of gold would be worth $40 billion.

In 1961, Virginia City was designated a National Historic Landmark and protected as an important historic site. Since then, many of the buildings have been restored to function as shops, restaurants, and a hotel. The display of artifacts in both Virginia City and Nevada City constitutes the largest collection of Old West memorabilia outside the Smithsonian. The population of 198 people works hard to re-create the atmosphere of Virginia City at its peak.

There are **train rides** on a 1910 locomotive between the cities, and an abundance of living history exhibits scattered around the sites. Plenty of services—accommodations and restaurants—are available for visitors who plan to stay.

Sights

Alder Gulch Shortline Railroad

413 W. Wallace St.; www.virginiacitymt.com; late May-early Sept.; $8-10

Connecting Virginia and Nevada City, this 15-minute-long open-air train ride gives visitors a chance to enjoy the scenery and learn about the towns. Tickets are sold first-come, first-served and cannot be reserved. Trains depart weekdays from Virginia City on the hour from 11am-6pm, and from Nevada City on the half-hour from 10:30am-5:30pm. On weekends, trains start running 1 hour earlier. There are no rides in bad weather.

Nevada City Museum

1578 MT-287; www.virginiacitymt.com; $10-12

This open-air museum includes 100 beautifully restored buildings that were erected between 1863 and the early 1900s.

Nevada City

On weekends in summer, the town comes alive with living history interpreters in period dress, giving visitors a vivid picture of life in a frontier mining town.

Entertainment and Events

Throughout the summer, nightly cabaret entertainment at **Brewery Follies at Gilbert Brewery** and nightly 19th-century melodrama courtesy of the **Virginia City Players at the Opera House** entertain visitors.

Virginia City Players

338 W. Wallace St., Virginia City; 406/843-5314 or 800/829-2969, ext. 2; www.virginiacityplayers.com; $25-30

For more than six decades, the illustrious Virginia City Players have been entertaining the crowds at the Virginia City Opera House with turn-of-the-20th-century-style melodrama and variety acts. They generally offer three shows over the course of the summer season and also play silent movies on one of only two operating photoplayers in the world. Weekday shows are 1 hour and weekend shows are 2 hours. Reservations are strongly encouraged.

Brewery Follies

200 E. Cover St., Virginia City; 800/829-2969, ext. 3; www.breweryfollies.net; $25, adults only

For more outlandish theater and comedy geared strictly to adults, the Brewery Follies at the Old H. S. Gilbert Brewery offers the unique setting of a restored 1864 brewery with bawdy entertainment and excellent microbrews.

Food and Accommodations

This is not plain-burger-and-fries country (although the beef in southwestern Montana is notably good).

Bob's Place

304 W. Wallace, Virginia City; 406/843-5292; www.bobsplacemt.com; $5-33

Far from the fanciest joint in town, Bob's is a great spot for a hearty meal. They serve pizza, salads, sandwiches, and wraps—don't miss the house-made pesto and hummus. And check out Bob's pottery while you wait for your meal.

★ Star Bakery

1570 Hwy. 287, Nevada City; 406/902-9025; www.starbakerymt.com; 8am-sold out Thurs.-Sun. Memorial Day-Labor Day; $15-30

The Star Bakery has been serving food since 1863 when it was a hot spot with miners. Today the clientele is more family-oriented, and the exquisite assortment of baked goods and quick breakfasts appeal to everyone. They also have a full espresso bar and sell their renowned pies to-go.

Wells Fargo Steakhouse

320 W. Wallace St., Virginia City; 406/843-5556; 5pm-9:30pm Mon.-Sat. mid-May-mid-Sept.; $15-32

There is fine dining at Wells Fargo Steakhouse, a stately building with tall tin ceilings and a grand horseshoe bar. In addition to gourmet cuisine like pork scallopini, brick chicken, and, of course, mouthwatering steaks, the Wells Fargo often hosts live music in its ballroom-size dining room.

Fairweather Inn

305 W. Wallace St., Virginia City; 406/843-5377 or 800/829-2969, ext. 5; www.aldergulchaccommodations.com; June-mid-Sept.; $114-189

For a historical lodging experience with plenty of charm, this building from 1863 offers 14 guest rooms, 6 of which have en suite baths; the others share facilities. Don't expect to find a bed larger than a double here.

★ Nevada City Hotel & Cabins

1578 US 287, Nevada City; 800/829-2969, ext. 5; mid-May-late Sept.; from $209

The Nevada City Hotel & Cabins has a rustic exterior with slightly more elegant interiors. All the guest rooms have private baths, and two Victorian suites have their own balconies. The cabins are true sod-roofed pioneer cabins that have been updated with comfortable accommodations and modern amenities. Both this hotel and the Fairweather Inn offer ideal access to all the sights in Virginia City and Nevada City plus some local discounts.

Information and Services

In addition to the two visitor centers at either end of the Alder Gulch Shortline Railroad, you can get more information from the **Montana Heritage Commission** (300 W. Wallace, Virginia City; 406/843-5247; www.montanaheritagecommission.mt.gov). The **Virginia City Chamber** (111 Wallace St., Virginia City; 406/843-5555 or 800/829-2969; www.virginiacity.com) is available by phone during the off season.

Bozeman

Bozeman is lost. Ask anywhere around the state and that's what long-time Montana residents will tell you. Walk downtown on a sunny afternoon, or try to get a table at a restaurant or a parking space at the airport, and you might come to the same conclusion. With the Montana State University anchoring it and a geographical setting that has always appealed to outdoors enthusiasts and nature lovers, over the last 30 years Bozeman (pop. 59,050, elev. 4,820 ft/1,469 m) has grown from a cow town to a town of wine bars, high-end hotels, suburban sprawl, and traffic jams. The housing crisis here touches everyone but the very rich. And there are plenty of those folks here now. Whereas Bozeman used to be an ag community, a place where a 6am counter stool at the Cowboy Café was at the center of things, today it is a vacation mecca, an escape from hotter places, a place where you can see a woman on the sidewalk in January in fuzzy mules, a fur coat but no pants, cell phone glued to her head, waiting for her toy Chihuahua to pee. "Bozangeles," some call it, both ironically and not. The character of this town has changed. And not for the better, locals would argue. But who can blame them for coming? For the wide-open space and access to public land, the laid-back lifestyle, and the beauty. Oh, the beauty.

That said (and it's plenty, I know), the historic downtown is still the heart of this community and attracts crowd-wary locals for numerous special events. A growing number of excellent restaurants and bars appeal to everyone from broke and thirsty college students to whiskey and wine connoisseurs. A handful of galleries and some unique shops round out downtown's offerings.

Although the city is expanding exponentially and is always on the list of Montana's fastest-growing cities, the original draw—nature—is still intact, for now. Bridger Bowl and Big Sky are excellent alpine skiing destinations nearby. The Gallatin, Madison, and Yellowstone Rivers, three blue-ribbon trout streams, are also nearby. And there are literally hundreds of hiking and biking trails, enough to satisfy the most hard-core enthusiast.

Getting to Bozeman

Driving

Off I-90, Bozeman is easily accessible by car. It is 85 mi (137 km) east of **Butte** on I-90, about a 90-minute drive. From **Helena,** it's 100 mi (161 km) southeast on US 287 and I-90, a drive of about 1 hour 40 minutes. From Bozeman, it's 89 mi (143 km) south on US 191 to the west entrance of Yellowstone National Park at **West Yellowstone,** about a 1-hour-45-minute drive, and 78 mi (126 km) southeast on I-90 East and US 89 South to **Gardiner,** which is roughly an 80-minute drive.

Air

Bozeman Yellowstone International Airport (BZN; 406/388-8321; www.bozemanairport.com) is 8 mi (13 km) northwest of downtown Bozeman in the nearby town of Belgrade. Delta, Alaska, American, Allegiant, Frontier, Jet Blue, Southwest, Sun Country, and United all offer regular nonstop service to and from major US cities, including Salt Lake City, Minneapolis, Seattle, Atlanta, Chicago, Denver, Houston, Las Vegas, Los Angeles, New York, Phoenix, Portland, Nashville, Charlotte, Boston, Newark, and San Francisco.

Bus

Greyhound travels to almost 40 towns and cities in Montana from the bus depot (1500 N. 7th Ave.; 800/451-5333) at Walmart Supercenter.

Getting Around

From the airport, the Comfort Suites, Homewood Suites by Hilton, Hilton Garden Inn, Element, and several others offer shuttle service. Car-rental agencies are at the airport too; the car-rental center is next to the baggage claim. **Alamo, Avis, Budget, Enterprise, Dollar, Hertz, Thrifty, Enterprise, Go Rentals,** and **National** have on-site counters.

The only ground transportation provider within the terminal, **Karst Stage** (406/556-3540 or 800/287-4759; www.karststage.com) offers daily bus service in winter to Big Sky, West Yellowstone, and Mammoth Hot Springs. Shuttles are by reservation only in non-winter months.

Greater Valley Taxi (406/388-9999) has a courtesy phone next to the baggage claim area. **Bozeman Airport Taxi** (406/451-3231; www.bozemanairporttaxi.com) offers reliable service from the airport and around town. **Lone Peak Transportation** (406/995-4895 or 888/454-5667; www.lonepeaktransportation.com; from $250 one-way to Big Sky Resort or Mountain Clubs, from $65 to Bozeman, from $150 to Livingston, $300 to Gardiner) provides private van and SUV transportation to, from, and around the region, as does **Big Sky Bound** (406/539-3828; www.bigskyboundshuttleandtransportation.com; $250 one-way between Big Sky and the airport 8am-8pm). **Lyft** and **Uber** also serve the Bozeman area.

Sights

Historic downtown Bozeman is interesting architecturally and compelling culturally. It is without a doubt the heart and soul of the city, and more often than not it is the gathering point for the most celebrated events, including **Bite of Bozeman, Music on Main, Crazy Days,** various parades, and **Christmas Stroll.** Businesses have faced some stiff competition from big-box stores on the perimeter of town, and there is significant turnover in retail and restaurants,

but local residents support downtown in meaningful ways, even starting a petition campaign to fight to keep staple businesses, like the Owenhouse Ace Hardware, on Main Street. For a list of businesses and a calendar of weekly, annual, and special events that really showcase Main Street, visit www.downtownbozeman.org.

★ Museum of the Rockies

600 W. Kagy Blvd.; 406/994-2251; www.museumoftherockies.org; 9am-5pm daily; $20, $4 planetarium show

Best known for its paleontology exhibit curated by dinosaur guru Jack Horner, Museum of the Rockies is a resource for the entire state. The museum tackles 500 million years of history, no small feat, with permanent exhibits that reflect Native American culture, 19th- to 20th-century regional history, an outdoor living history farm (open only in summer), a planetarium, and, of course, the dinosaurs.

The **Siebel Dinosaur Complex** includes hundreds of fossils and an array of life-size reproductions. The traveling

exhibitions vary—think polar obsession, the villas of Oplontis near Pompeii, *National Geographic*'s 50 greatest photos, and even chocolate—but typically offer excellent contrast to the permanent exhibits.

The **Martin Children's Discovery Center** upstairs offers a great space for schoolchildren to play in hands-on Yellowstone exhibits. They can camp in a tent, listen for the eruption of Old Faithful (beware—it's loud, surprising, and often scary for little ones), recline in an eagle's nest, play house in a log cabin, fish for magnetic fish, and dress up as a park ranger or firefighter. For kids with vivid imaginations, this may be the highlight of the museum. In addition, the museum offers several engaging classes for children and excellent day camps for elementary-age kids.

Gallatin History Museum

317 W. Main St.; 406/522-8122; www.gallatinhistorymuseum.org; 10am-5pm Tues.-Sat. summer, 11am-4pm Tues.-Sat. fall-spring; $10

Touted as the place "where history and Main Street meet," Gallatin History

Museum is housed in Bozeman's 1911 county jail. The museum shared space with prisoners from 1979-1982 before the current jail was completed. It boasts a comprehensive permanent collection of items that reflect Bozeman's early history, including an 1870s homesteader's cabin, an agricultural room, historical photographs, and a sheriff's room with plenty of artifacts and exhibits related to crime and punishment in the Old West. The Silsby Fire Engine, a top-of-the-line engine in the late 1800s, is a favorite exhibit for kids. The museum offers maps for various self-guided tours of the area.

Emerson Center for the Arts and Culture

111 S. Grand Ave.; 406/587-9797; www.theemerson.org

Operated as an elementary school from 1918-1991, Emerson Center for the Arts and Culture, or The Emerson, as it's known, is the nucleus of Bozeman's robust arts scene. More than 30 studios, galleries, boutiques, and art-related businesses reside in the building in addition to Crawford Theater and **Sidewall Pizza.**

★ Madison Buffalo Jump State Park

6990 Buffalo Jump Rd., 7 mi/11 km south of Logan off I-90; 406/285-3610; www.stateparks.mt.gov; sunrise-sunset daily; $8/vehicle nonresidents, $4/walk-in, bicycle, or bus passenger

Farther afield but well worth the visit is Madison Buffalo Jump State Park. Used by Indigenous tribes through the region some 2,000 years ago (and as recently as 200 years ago), long before horses were brought to North America, buffalo jumps are a testament to human ingenuity. A small, covered interpretive display explains how Native Americans persuaded bison up the hill and off the cliff to their deaths, but the real lesson comes from hiking the trail (watch for rattlesnakes and cacti, both of which love the sun here) and exploring the site independently. Tipi rings can be identified, as can eagle-catching pits. Splinters of bison bone have been found at the base of the cliff. Aside from the compelling history of the area, the views from the top are magnificent.

Adventure and Recreation

Hiking

There is an abundance of hiking in and around Bozeman, from developed dog-friendly trails right in town to longer jaunts in Bridger and Gallatin Canyons, including a 21-mi (34-km) trail that runs from the mouth of Bridger Canyon to the Fairy Lake Campground near the end of it. South of town is **Hyalite Canyon,** an excellent recreation area with loads of trails, including one that is wheelchair-friendly, as well as opportunities for fishing, boating, climbing, camping, and winter sports.

Peets Hill

Distance: up to 2.3 mi (3.7 km) round-trip
Duration: 45 minutes
Elevation gain: 246 ft (75 m)
Effort: Easy to moderate
Trail surface: Dirt
Trailhead: Parking lot at base of Peets Hill on Church, or easily accessible from Bozeman Public Library at 626 E. Main St.

Just behind the Bozeman Public Library is Peets Hill, the city's most popular in-town spot for a hike and a great place to watch the sun set over town. A quick cruise up the hill leads you to a network of trails, a chance to commune with just about anyone and their dog, and ultimately to **Lindley Park** and the historic **Sunset Hills Cemetery.**

M

Distance: 1.9 mi (3.1 km) round-trip
Duration: 1.5 hours
Elevation gain: 820 ft (250 m)
Effort: Moderate to strenuous
Trail surface: Dirt
Trailhead: College M Trailhead on Bridger Canyon Rd. across from Bozeman Fish Technology Center (4050 Bridger Canyon Rd.)

Accessed from a small parking lot on the west side of Bridger Drive, across the road from the Bozeman Fish Technology Center, the M is hard to miss. There is a steep route up (20-30 minutes) or a longer, gentler route (45 minutes-1 hour), making mix-and-match loops a possibility.

Sacagawea Peak

Distance: 4.5 mi (7.2 km) round-trip
Duration: 4 hours
Elevation gain: 1,975 ft (602 m)
Effort: Strenuous
Trail surface: Dirt with rocky sections and scree
Trailhead: Sacagawea Peak at Fairy Lake Campground

From the Fairy Lake campground (23 mi/37 km north of Bozerman on MT-86, then 5 mi/8 km west on the bumpy Fairy Lake Road) this trail takes hikers up almost 2,000 ft (610 m) over 2 mi (3.2 km) one-way to Sacagawea Peak, the highest point in the Bridger Range at 9,665 ft (2,946 m). The trail winds through conifer forest and climbs several rocky switchbacks. At 8,963 ft (2,732 m) is the **Bridger Divide,** with signed turnoffs to Hardscrabble Peak (9,575 ft/2,918 m), North Cottonwood Creek, Corbly Creek, and Sacagawea to the south. Follow the trail to the left and watch for mountain goats. From the summit, there are views in every direction. The there-and-back hike is only 4.5 mi (7.2 km), but with so much elevation gain, it can easily take 3-4 hours. For hikers who want to keep going (and can set up shuttle vehicles), between the Bridger Divide junction and Sacagawea Peak is a junction for the 19.9-mi (32-km) **Bridger Mountains National Recreation Trail,** running along the spine of the Bridger Range all the way to the M trailhead.

Top to bottom: Madison Buffalo Jump State Park; Hyalite Canyon; Palisade Falls

Palisade Falls

Distance: 1.1 mi (1.8 km) round-trip
Duration: 45 minutes
Elevation gain: 249 ft (76 m)
Effort: Easy
Trail surface: Asphalt
Trailhead: Palisade Falls up Hyalite Canyon

South of town is another excellent recreation area, **Hyalite Canyon** (south on S. 19th Ave. to Hyalite Canyon Rd.), one of the most popular in the state. There are excellent opportunities for boating on the reservoir, fishing in Hyalite Creek, and hiking on various trails, including Palisade Falls Trail, which is paved for wheelchair access. Other recreational opportunities include mountain biking, ice climbing, and backcountry skiing in winter.

Skiing

Bridger Bowl

15795 Bridger Canyon Rd.; 406/587-2111; www.bridgerbowl.com; 9am-4pm daily during ski season; full day $82-97, discounts for online tickets and multiday tickets, $25 all ages for beginner lifts only

One of two nonprofit ski areas in Montana, Bridger Bowl is 16 mi (26 km) north of Bozeman and offers 2,000 acres (809 ha) of terrain for a lot less than you would pay at Aspen or Vail, especially if you get tickets online. Multiple-day tickets and ski school options are available, and there are 75 marked trails and eight lifts to get you on the mountain, including **Schlasman's,** which summits the ridge, an area long known as an "earn your turns" mecca. Though the area is hugely popular with locals and a seat in the cafeteria can be hard to find at lunchtime, lift lines are rarely longer than 10-15 people. The mountain offers diverse terrain but is slightly more geared to advanced skiers, with 42 percent of the trails rated "expert." In summer, trails are open to hikers and bikers.

Crosscut Mountain Sports Center

16621 Bridger Canyon Rd.; 406/586-9690; www.crosscutmt.org; 9am-4pm daily; from $30, multiday discounts

Just north of Bridger Bowl is Crosscut Mountain Sports Center, a wonderful place for cross-country novices and racers alike. Crosscut boasts 16 mi (26 km) of groomed trails suitable for both classic and skate skiers, and it's also hosted numerous competitions, including the US Olympic Qualifying Championship and national NCAA events. In summer, Crosscut transforms its trails into excellent hiking and mountain biking terrain. Rentals, lessons, and private adventures are available.

Lindley Park

E. Main St. and Buttonwood Ave.

In downtown Bozeman, Lindley Park offers groomed cross-country ski trails courtesy of the Bridger Ski Foundation. The best place to park is the northwest parking lot of Bozeman Deaconess Hospital (915 Highland Blvd.). Season passes can be purchased online (www.bridgerskifoundation.org; $75) and day-use donations can be made in boxes at various trailheads.

Bangtail Bike & Ski

137 E. Main St.; 406/587-4905; www.bangtailbikes.com

Buttons, which are the wear-on-your-jacket equivalent of a ski pass, can be purchased at locations in town, including Bangtail Bike & Ski, an excellent cycle and Nordic ski shop that also rents cross-country skis.

Fishing

Bozeman is a trout lover's paradise, with several blue-ribbon streams nearby. The **Gallatin, Jefferson,** and **Madison Rivers** flow through the valley, forming the headwaters of the Missouri River in aptly named Three Forks (31 mi/50 km west of Bozeman on I-90).

6X Outfitters

406/586-3806; www.6xoutfitters.com; wade or float trips from $425 for 1-2 people, from $525 for 3-4 people, $40-140 private water rod fee

Guiding since 1979, Al Gadoury of 6X Outfitters is widely considered to be among the region's best outfitters, particularly when it comes to spring creeks and private water. Though he does not have a storefront and offers guided excursions only, his shore lunches (think grilled moose burgers) are second to none.

Montana Troutfitters

1716 W. Main St.; 406/587-4707; www.troutfitters.com; 7am-7pm daily; from $695 full-day wade or float trips for 1-2 anglers

Montana Troutfitters has been guiding fly-fishing excursions since 1978 and offers online fishing reports and gear.

Floating the Madison River

In a college town with an active and outdoorsy population, floating the rivers is a popular pastime. The calm and relatively warm Madison River is easily the most popular, followed by the slightly more remote **Jefferson River.**

From Big Boys Toys, drive 30 minutes west on Highway 84 (also known as Norris Rd.) to the Warm Springs access. Float time down to Black's Ford is 2-3.5 hours, depending on the time of year and water flow. If you only have one vehicle, make sure to arrange a shuttle through the rental shop. Try to schedule your float on a weekday, if possible, or early in the morning on the weekend if you don't want to get caught up in the college booze-cruise flotilla.

Big Boys Toys All Terrain Rentals

25 New Ventures Dr. off of Norris Rd.; 406/587-4747; www.bigboystoysrentals.com; $12-40, discounts for 3 or more days

For a half-day float on the Madison, rent a 3-6-person raft or inner tubes from Big Boys Toys All Terrain Rentals. Or rent kayaks, stand-up paddleboards, canoes, and drift boats.

Entertainment and Events

Nightlife

Plonk

29 E. Main St.; 406/587-2170; www.plonkwine.com; 3pm-midnight Sun.-Wed., 3pm-1am Thurs.-Sat.

In downtown Bozeman, Plonk is an elegant wine bar known as much for its tapas and desserts—start with the cheese board or ploughman's platter—as for its global selection of more than 600 wines. The atmosphere integrates 100-year-old architecture, contemporary original works of art, minimalist urban design, and an eclectic collection of well-played vinyl records. In summer, the crowd spills outside to a handful of sidewalk tables and a patio in back.

Bar IX

311 E. Main St.; 406/551-2185; www.bar-ix.com; 11am-2am daily, kitchen 11:30am-8:30pm daily

Also downtown, Bar IX is both industrial and rustic, and it's usually hopping. Its happy hour specials and Bucket Nights are well known locally.

Pub 317

321 E. Main St.; 406/582-8898; www.pub317.com; 11am-2am daily

Appealing to Bozeman's athletic crowd, Pub 317 is one of the few bars that host running races. Twice each year, the Irish pub sponsors 10K or half-marathons that end back at the bar. There's usually live Irish music on Sunday, live bluegrass on Tuesday, and trivia nights on Wednesday.

Sky Shed

24 W. Mendenhall St.; 406/551-7703; www.skyshedbar.com; 2pm-11pm daily in season

Giving visitors the idea that Bozeman really is the town of *Yellowstone* fame, Sky Shed towers over the city on the roof of the Kimpton Armory hotel. There is nothing old-school or Old West about this bar, but the 360-degree view from every seat is unmatched.

Rocking R Bar

211 E. Main St.; 406/587-9355; www.rockingrbar.com; 11am-2am daily

Popular with the college (and alumni) crowds, Rocking R Bar has been a favorite hangout since the 1940s. There is plenty of sidewalk seating when the weather permits, and the 20 TVs, four pool tables, and dartboards offer entertainment in this loud bar.

Haufbrau House

22 S. 8th St.; 406/587-4931; 11am-2am Mon.-Sat., 1pm-2am Sun.

Not exactly downtown, but not far, Haufbrau House is a favorite with college students and hosts live music nightly. It looks and smells like a dive, but the open mic nights are fun and the burgers are tasty.

Mountains Walking Brewery

422 N. Plum St.; 406/219-3480; www.mountainswalking.com; 11:30am-8pm daily

For an upscale brewpub experience on Bozeman's hip north side, Mountains Walking Brewery has outstanding beer, brewed on-site, and lots of organic farm-to-table food, including wood-fired pizzas and small bites like crispy Brussels sprouts, plates of candied bacon, pecorino truffle fries, beer-brined wings, tacos, and more.

Theater

Broad Comedy

406/522-7623; www.broadcomedy.com

For a relatively small Rocky Mountain town, Bozeman has a decent number of theater offerings. Among the most popular is Broad Comedy, which produces irreverent and side-splitting satire by a female cast (geared to mature audiences only). The company has achieved global recognition and plenty of YouTube followers. If you are in town when the company is performing, most often at the Emerson Center for Arts & Culture (111 S. Grand), be there.

Montana Shakespeare in the Parks

www.shakespeareintheparks.org, free

One of the state's most beloved troupes, Montana Shakespeare in the Parks is based out of Montana State University and travels all over the state bringing outdoor (when weather permits) and free Shakespearean theater to parks and even cow pastures in small, underserved communities. The company has been bringing the Bard to the people since 1973. Bill Pullman is one of the company's most famous alumni. You can always catch a glimpse of them at Bozeman's Sweet Pea Festival, but going to see them anywhere in Montana or Wyoming is worth doing.

Music

Thanks to eager audiences provided by the university and growing community, Bozeman has a lively music scene.

Opera Montana

406/587-2889; www.operamontana.org

Since 1978 Opera Montana has been producing two professional shows annually in spring and fall that feature world-class performers and conductors with a local chorus and orchestra. They also offer a musical each spring and special events throughout the year. Until Bozeman gets a proper performing arts center, performance locations vary by show.

Bozeman Symphony Orchestra and Symphonic Choir

406/585-9774; www.bozemansymphony.org

Under the dynamic young conductor Norman Huynh, Bozeman Symphony Orchestra and Symphonic Choir presents several performances each season, starting in September, that range from late Renaissance pieces through the 20th century. Most concerts happen at the Willson Auditorium (404 W. Main St.), but symphonic choir performances are held at churches around town.

Live from the Divide

627 E. Peach St.; 406/624-3321; www.livefromthedivide.com

Live from the Divide celebrates the songwriters of American Roots music with frequent performances in their century-old brick and wood studio that seats only 50 lucky music lovers. Check the online calendar.

Logjam Presents

506 N. 7th; 406/830-4640; www.logjampresents.com

Hosting plenty of shows at both The ELM (506 N. 7th) and The Rialto (10 W. Main St.), Logjam Presents brings tons of concerts to town year-round, including some big-name performers like Lainey Wilson and Yung Gravy.

Festivals and Events

Although Bozeman residents joke about the "nine months of winter and three months of houseguests," people take summertime recreation seriously, and the town of Bozeman (www.downtownbozeman.org) has created numerous ways to celebrate outside.

Sweet Pea Festival of the Arts

Lindley Park at E. Main and Buttonwood; 406/586-4003; www.sweetpeafestival.org; Aug.; from $30

Held annually the first full weekend in August, Sweet Pea Festival of the Arts is Bozeman's answer to Mardi Gras. No one is parading around half-naked—this is Montana, after all—but there is plenty of food (don't miss the tater pigs, a Sweet Pea classic), live music, theater, dance, an arts and crafts fair, both juried and open art shows, and a flower show. Events leading up to the festival include **Chalk on the Walk** (Tues. before Sweet Pea), **Bite of Bozeman** (Wed. before Sweet Pea), and the **Children's Run and Sweet Pea Parade** (Sat. morning of Sweet Pea). Packed into three days, the nearly 50-year-old festival draws more than 15,000 visitors annually.

Summer SLAM Festival

Bogert Park at 325 S. Church St.; 406/219-7773; www.slamfestivals.org; Aug.; free

Founded in 2011, in response to the increasing competition and expense for local artists to get into Sweet Pea, SLAM Fest, which stands for Support Local Artists and Music, runs in Bogert Park the same weekend. Like a smaller and free version of Sweet Pea, SLAM hosts 50-plus artists and artisans from around the state, plus live music, readings, dance, food, and a beer garden.

Music on Main

6:30pm-8:30pm Thurs. July-Aug.; free

Music on Main is an opportunity for folks to gather downtown on closed-off streets and enjoy live music, food vendors, and early evening activities for kids.

Bozeman Farmers' Market

Lindley Park; www.bozemanfarmersmarket.org; 5pm-8pm Tues. June-Sept.; free

Bozeman Farmers' Market includes everything from produce, art, and crafts to gourmet food trucks, entertainment, and activities (like reverse bungee jumping and rock climbing for kids). The park can be packed, so plan to stay in immediate contact with little ones. For a more relaxing evening, bring a blanket and park yourself away from the masses.

Big Sky Country State Fair

901 N. Black Ave.; 406/582-3270; www.406statefair.com; $10; July

Another annual event worth checking out is the Big Sky Country State Fair, held at the county fairgrounds the third week in July, which offers food, carnival rides, entertainment, animals, and traditional contests. Where else can your kid ride a sheep or wrestle a piglet?

Wild West Winter Fest

Gallatin County Fairgrounds; 901 N. Black Ave.; mid-Feb.

Geared to the heartiest locals and visitors, Bozeman's mid-February Wild West

Winter Fest offers a celebration of the cold with family-friendly events including a petting zoo, skijoring, an art show, live music, and food.

Christmas Stroll

Downtown; 406/586-4008; www.downtownbozeman.org; first Sat. in Dec.

Bozeman's Christmas Stroll brings the town out the first Saturday of December to eat, shop, and enjoy the festive season downtown with the streets closed off to vehicles. From his horse-drawn wagon, Santa lights the town's hideous and beloved "Christmas spiders" from Willson Avenue to Rouse.

Shopping

Like most regional hubs in Montana, Bozeman offers an abundance of shopping opportunities for every taste and budget level. **Downtown Bozeman** (www.downtownbozeman.org), however, is by far the best place to go for unique items and pure charm.

Country Bookshelf

28 W. Main St.; 406/587-0166; www.countrybookshelf.com; 9:30am-6:30pm daily

The Country Bookshelf is Bozeman's most beloved bookstore and the state's largest independent bookstore. It is especially geared to local and regional authors, many of whom are willing to show their affection for the place with readings and book signings.

Vargo's Jazz City & Books

6 W. Main St.; 406/587-5383; 10am-7pm Mon.-Fri., 10am-6pm Sat., 11am-5pm Sun.

On the same block is Vargo's Jazz City & Books, an excellent place to get lost. The shop specializes in slightly more obscure books, CDs, and vinyl, both new and used. It's also the best place in town to get greeting cards.

HeyDay

7 W. Main St.; 406/586-5589; www.heydaybozeman.com; 10am-7pm Mon.-Sat., 10am-5pm Sun.

Touted as a shop "for the everyday celebration," HeyDay specializes in home decor and gifts with Montana flair. From gardening to personal grooming, cooking, and entertaining, this stylish little shop is sure to delight.

Montana Gift Corral

237 E. Main St.; 406/898-2034; www.giftcorral.com; 9am-7pm Mon.-Fri., 9am-6pm Sat., 10am-5pm Sun.

For gifts that could only come from Montana—including locally made jewelry, specialty food gift baskets, and souvenirs—Montana Gift Corral is the place to go.

The River's Edge

612 E. Main St.; 406/586-5373; www.theriversedge.com; 8am-6pm daily summer, 9am-5:30pm Mon.-Fri. and 9am-5pm Sat. fall, winter, and spring

The River's Edge is one of Bozeman's oldest and most venerated fly-fishing shops. Now owned by gear manufacturer Simms, the fly shop is packed with gear, clothing, flies, and more.

Schnee's

35 E. Main St.; 406/587-0981; www.schnees.com; 9am-6pm Mon.-Sat., 10am-5pm Sun.

For hunters and outdoors enthusiasts, downtown Bozeman offers top-of-the-line shopping. Occupying two restored 1903 storefronts is an outstanding shoe store and something of a Bozeman institution. Poised to make shoe snobs out of nearly anyone, Schnee's sells everything from locally made bombproof hunting boots to a selection of very hip street shoes and sandals. It also sells clothes and accessories, leather bags, and hunting and fishing gear, and takes its 100 percent satisfaction guarantee very seriously.

Visions West Contemporary

34 W. Main St.; 406/522-9946; www.visionswestcontemporary.com; 10am-5:30pm Mon.-Sat.

Visions West Contemporary is a dynamic space that focuses on contemporary artists in the West.

Montana Trails Gallery

7 W. Main St.; 406/586-2166; www.montanatrails.com; 10am-6pm daily

For an exquisite collection of historic and contemporary Western art, Montana Trails Gallery is a worthwhile stop, even if you're just looking. They curate some of the best-known artists—from Frederic Remington and Charlie Russell to Clyde Aspevig and Carrie Ballantyne.

Food

If you have recently traveled through rural Montana, Bozeman seems like a foodie mecca. With everything from sushi to tapas, the town affords diners much more than the burgers and steaks for which the state is so well known (although there is an outstanding selection of those as well).

Coffee Shops and Cafés

Western Café

443 E. Main St.; 406/587-0436; www.thewesterncafe.com; 6am-2pm daily; $5-15

As Bozeman has evolved from its ranching and agricultural heritage, many of the classic diners have been lost to trendier eateries, but one has stood the test of time. The Western Café is an old-timer's classic for breakfast and lunch, including its famed chicken-fried steak and cinnamon rolls. If you want to sit in a place and feel how Bozeman used to be, this is the spot.

Community Food Co-op

908 W. Main St.; 406/587-4039; www.bozo.coop; 8am-9pm daily, deli and hot bar open 11am-7pm; $5-15

The Community Food Co-op is a cornerstone of the community and is not only convenient but also offers an excellent hot bar, salad bar, and sandwich and smoothie counter. Everything the co-op does—gourmet and often locally produced groceries, prepared foods, and a coffee shop, juice bar, and bakery—is done brilliantly. The homemade soups are excellent, as is the salad bar and just about everything in the sprawling deli case. Exotic hot lunches and dinners are often available at a good value.

Feed Café

1530 W. Main St.; 406/219-2630; www.feedcafebozeman.com; 7am-2pm daily; $10-16

Another fantastic place for a big, healthy meal is Feed Café, serving gourmet breakfast sandwiches, egg dishes, soup, salads, and lunch sandwiches in the big red barn.

Jam!

25 W. Main St.; 406/585-1761; www.jamonmain.com; 7am-3pm daily; $5-20

Right downtown, the super-casual and always popular Jam! serves hearty breakfasts and lunches, ranging from crab cake Benedict and chicken and biscuit Benedict (there's even a flight of three favorite Benedicts!) to pulled pork omelets, sweet and savory crepes, every kind of pancake, and beet and root hash. Breakfast is served all day, but this place is always hopping so be prepared for a wait. They also serve beer and wine if it's *that* kind of brunch.

Wild Crumb Bakery

600 Wallace St.; 406/579-3454; www.wildcrumb.com; 7am-3pm Wed.-Sun.

On the hip north side of town, the Wild Crumb Bakery is one of the favorite bakeries in Bozeman, as indicated by the constant line out front. They don't serve espresso (you can get a great cup a few steps away at **Treeline Coffee Roasters**), but their artisan breads and pastries are beyond compare. Try the orange pecan sticky buns or the ham and gruyère croissant. You know what? Try anything: a tart, a cake, a loaf of challah. You will be back.

Casual Eateries

Sidewall Pizza Company

207 W. Olive St.; 406/570-0730; 11am-9pm Tues.-Sun.; $15-23

A few steps off Main Street, tucked into the Emerson Center for the Arts and Culture, Sidewall Pizza Company has lots of shareable appetizers, salads, and pizzas with bases that range from garlic sauce to basil pesto, chicken, and crushed tomato sauce. The little pepperonis on crushed tomato sauce are especially good.

Hooked Sushi

119 E. Main St.; 406/577-2332; www.hookedmt.com; 4pm-9:30pm Sun.-Thurs., 4:30pm-10pm Fri.-Sat.; $14-30

Hooked Sushi is a great spot for sushi and other comfort foods like ramen, fish or shrimp tacos, and more. The Ring of Fire roll is a favorite.

Revelry

24 N. Tracy; 406/404-1400; www.revelrymt.com; 11am-10pm Mon.-Fri., 10am-10pm Sat.-Sun.; $15-42

Revelry is a festive place for food and drinks, indoors or out, with lots of hearty pastas, sausages, burgers, sandwiches, salads, steak, and pizza.

Montana Ale Works

611 E. Main St.; 406/587-7700; www.montanaaleworks.com; 4pm-9:30pm daily; $14-45

On the east end of town, Montana Ale Works combines a hip eatery with a popular smoke-free bar and pool lounge. The menu offers inventive takes on Western staples like burgers and steaks, and the atmosphere, in a rehabbed 100-year-old railroad warehouse, is energetic and suitable for everyone from toddlers to grandparents; it can be loud at any time of the week, so a separate dining room is a good option for those with noise issues.

Ted's Montana Grill

105 W. Main St.; 406/587-6000; www.tedsmontanagrill.com; 11am-10pm daily; $16-52

In the historic Baxter Hotel downtown is Ted's Montana Grill. The flagship restaurant of local part-time resident and unequivocal philanthropist and land steward Ted Turner, everything is made from scratch, and each meat cut is available in bison or beef. The apple cobbler is extremely good, as are the inventive burgers.

Fine Dining

Shan

109 E. Oak St., #1J; 406/577-2222; www.shanrestaurants.com; 4:30pm-9:30pm Tues.-Sat.; $16-26

Considered by the 2024 James Beard Awards to be one of the 10 best new restaurants in the country, Shan combines southwest Chinese and northern Thai flavors with Montana ingredients in a perfect melding of mountain cultures. Inspired by the inviting Japanese izakaya and fueled by the knowledge owners Jarrett Wrisley and Candice Lin gained while eating and cooking across Asia for 20 years, this is a rare place indeed. Casual and not overly pricey, it can be hard to get into (they open reservations two weeks in advance and typically they are booked in minutes) unless you're willing to show up at 4:30 and maybe stand in line. But from the chicken khao soi to the lamb dumplings and the bison mapo tofu to the sticky tamarind ribs, the food is like nothing you've ever tasted.

★ Little Star Diner

548 E. Babcock St.; 406/624-6463; www.littlestardiner.com; 5pm-9pm Tues.-Sat.; $25-45

Little Star Diner boasts a frequently changing menu—including bison chorizo tacos, braised pork tamales, soup, farm-grilled butter chicken, and all varieties of kamut noodles—with lots of local produce and meats. With lovely ambience both on the rooftop and in the intimate dining room, this is a good spot for a special meal.

Feast Raw Bar & Bistro

270 W. Kagy Ave.; 406/577-2377; www.feastbozeman.com; 5pm-9pm daily; $24-70

Another spot for fresh, creative cuisine is not far from the Museum of the Rockies. Feast Raw Bar & Bistro specializes in sustainably sourced and globally inspired cuisine. A raw bar serves everything from daily ceviche and bison carpaccio to raw oysters and a shellfish tower. Shared plates include Vietnamese chicken wings, crispy Brussels sprouts, and steamed mussels.

Accommodations

For a long time, Bozeman's accommodations were lacking in charm, for a town with seemingly sophisticated tastes. That's changed with the addition of several contemporary hotels downtown. Still, for those willing to look, there are numerous and diverse offerings, from roadside motels to upscale chains, cozy vacation rentals, and, farther afield, a historical gem.

RSVP Hotel

510 N. 7th Ave.; 406/404-7999; www.rsvphotel.co; from $311

Another property that's long on charm and located in the growing midtown district is RSVP Hotel, a boutique hotel set in a restored roadside motel. There's a fantastic breakfast and lunch restaurant on-site (**The Farmer's Daughters**) and a music venue, **The ELM,** immediately next door. Owned by two sisters who grew up on a wheat farm just west of Bozeman, the hotel gets every detail right and is warm, inviting, and fun.

★ The Lark

122 W. Main St.; 866/464-1000; www.larkbozeman.com; $179-366

Newer is better in Bozeman when it comes to hotels, and the closer you are to downtown, the closer you are to the action. The Lark considers itself a pet-friendly base camp and works hard at getting guests out of its modern, art-filled rooms and into the wilds around Bozeman. A map room helps with planning, and motel employees are called guides. Still, your time inside The Lark will be a pleasure with 67 unique rooms in two buildings—the original motel and the 2018 hotel—each filled with work by local artists. Kids will love the bunk room, and everyone will appreciate the heart-of-downtown location, which is within walking distance to everywhere. In summer, look out for the **Airstream Ice Cream** truck just outside the hotel.

★ Kimpton Armory

24 W. Mendenhall St.; 406/551-7700 or 833/549-0847; www.armoryhotelbzn.com; from $499

By far the fanciest hotel in downtown Bozeman is the Kimpton Armory, which was built in Bozeman's cool old armory and opened in 2020. It's a full-service hotel with elegant rooms (including your own Peloton in some of them!), a sophisticated restaurant (**Fielding's**: 7am-1:30pm daily, 5:30pm-9pm Tues.-Sat.; $23-45) serving American regional cuisine, and a big-city-chic rooftop bar.

Treasure State Hostel

27 E. Main St.; 406/624-6244; www.treasurestatehostel.com; dorm bed from $32, private room from $52

Offering an ideal location right downtown, and the cheapest rooms anywhere, Treasure State Hostel is a find in Bozeman. Just 20 minutes from Bridger Bowl and an hour from Big Sky, the hostel is popular with skiers.

Bozeman Cottage Vacation Rentals

406/580-3223; www.bozemancottage.com

Bozeman Cottage Vacation Rentals offers a broad array of properties to meet individual preferences for location, price, size, and style—from a lodge near Bridger Bowl to downtown cottages and riverfront cabins. There are plenty of pet-friendly offerings, and last-minute bargains can be had for those inclined to wing it.

Information and Services

Downtown Bozeman Visitor Center

8 E. Main St.; 406/586-4008 or 406/556-5001; www.downtownbozeman.org; 10am-5pm Mon.-Sat.

Downtown shoppers can find an abundance of information, including real estate offerings from ERA Landmark, at the Downtown Bozeman Visitor Center.

Bozeman Health Deaconess Hospital

915 Highland Blvd.; 406/585-5000; www.bozemanhealth.org

Bozeman Health Deaconess Hospital has a 24-hour emergency room.

B2 Urgent Care

1006 W. Main St., Ste. E; 406/414-4800; www.bozemanhealth.org; 8am-7pm daily

B2 Urgent Care is open daily until 7pm for walk-in patients.

Essentials

Getting There

Getting to Bozeman

Car

Off I-90, Bozeman is easily accessible by car. It is 142 mi (229 km) west of **Billings,** 202 mi (320 km) southeast of **Missoula,** and 85 mi (137 km) east of **Butte.** The driving distances are slightly farther from Wyoming: **Jackson** is 215 mi (345 km) south and **Cody** is 214 mi (345 km) southeast of Bozeman.

Car and RV Rental

A number of car-rental agencies are at the airport; the car-rental center is located next to the baggage claim. **Alamo, Avis, Budget, Enterprise, Dollar, Hertz, Thrifty,** and **National** have on-site counters.

There are a handful of places in Bozeman where RVs can be rented, including **Cruise America RV Rental** (Big Boys Toys, 69 New Ventures Dr.; 406/587-4747; www.cruiseamerica.com), **Blacksford** (20777 Frontage Rd.; 406/384-6758; www.blacksford.com), and **C&T Motorhome Rentals** (27612 Norris Rd.; 406/587-8610; www.ctrvrentals.com).

Air

Bozeman Yellowstone International Airport (BZN; 406/388-8321; www.bozemanairport.com) is 8 mi (13 km) northwest of downtown Bozeman in the nearby town of Belgrade. Delta, Alaska, American, Allegiant, Frontier, JetBlue, Southwest, Sun Country, and United all offer regular nonstop service to and from major US cities, including Salt Lake City, Minneapolis, Seattle, Atlanta, Chicago, Denver, Houston, Las Vegas, Los Angeles, New York, Phoenix, Portland, Nashville, Charlotte, Boston, Newark, and San Francisco.

Bus

Greyhound travels to almost 40 towns and cities in Montana from the **bus depot** (1500 N. 7th St.; 800/451-5333) at Walmart Supercenter.

Getting to Billings

Car

As the largest city in Montana, Billings is an easy driving destination. It's along I-90 and I-94 begins just outside the town. Billings is 142 mi (229 km) east of **Bozeman** and 60 mi (97 km) northeast of **Red Lodge.** In Wyoming, **Cody** is 106 mi (171 km) away.

Car and RV Rental

At the Billings airport, **Enterprise, Thrifty, Dollar, Hertz, Alamo, Avis, Budget,** and **National** have on-site car-rental counters.

In Billings, RVs can be rented at **Cruise America RV Rental** (Taylors Choice Auto, 720 Central Ave.; 406/245-9800; www.cruiseamerica.com) and **Montana Happy Campers Travel Trailer & RV Rentals** (5101 US 87 N.; 406/384-3775; www.montana-happycampers.com).

Air

Billings Logan International Airport (BIL; 1901 Terminal Cir.; 406/247-8609 or 406/657-8495; www.flybillings.com) is situated atop the rimrocks off I-90 at the 27th Street exit. Delta, United, Allegiant, Alaska Airlines, American, and Cape Air offer regular flights.

If you arrive early at the airport or have some time to spare before you are picked up, visit the **Peter Yegen Jr. Yellowstone County Museum** (1950 Terminal Cir.; 406/256-6811; www.pyjrycm.org; 10:30am-5:30pm Mon.-Sat.; free). Once outside the terminal, follow the road around the west parking lot; the museum is on the right before the airport exit. The museum has artifacts and exhibits highlighting the history of the northern plains from early Native American influence through westward expansion and mining up to the 1950s. There's even a two-headed calf! The museum's deck provides a splendid view of the city below.

Bus

The **Greyhound bus terminal and ticket offices** (1830 4th Ave. N.; 406/245-5117; www.greyhound.com) are open 24 hours a day year-round.

Getting to Jackson Hole

Car

The major routes into Jackson Hole—including US 89/191/287 from Yellowstone and Grand Teton National Parks, US 26/287 from the east, Highway 22 from the west over Teton Pass, and US 189/191/89 from the south—can all be closed for weather in winter, particularly over Teton Pass. There is no car traffic in the southern portion of Yellowstone during the winter. For Wyoming **road reports** (www.wyoroad.info), call 800/996-7623.

Jackson is 240 mi (386 km) south of Bozeman, 177 mi (285 km) southwest of Cody through Yellowstone National Park, and 275 mi (443 km) northeast of Salt Lake City. Keep in mind that while distances through the national parks may be shorter in actual mileage, the time is often extended by lower speed limits, traffic congestion, and animal jams. In addition, most of the park roads are closed in winter, and car travel is not possible between Bozeman and Jackson or between Cody and Jackson. Driving distances around the parks increase significantly.

Car and RV Rental

The airport has on-site car rentals from **Enterprise, Avis/Budget, Hertz,** and **National. Alamo, Dollar, Thrifty,** and **Leisure Sports** are available off-site with complimentary shuttles.

In Jackson, RVs can be rented from individuals (like VRBO, but for RVs) on **Outdoorsy** (www.outdoorsy.com). High-end, pet-friendly campervans are available for rent from **Moterra Campervans** (1565 W. Berger Ln.; 307/200-7220; www.gomoterra.com). Travel trailers and other vehicles are available to rent through **Jackson Hole Adventure Rentals** (1060 S. Hwy. 89; 307/733-5678; www.jhadventure.com).

Air

The only airport within a national park, **Jackson Hole Airport** (JAC; 1250 E. Airport Rd.; 307/733-7682; www.jacksonholeairport.com) is served year-round by Alaska, American, Delta, and United. Schedules change seasonally but include regular flights from Salt Lake City, Denver, Seattle, Chicago, Charlotte, Minneapolis, Dallas, Houston, Phoenix, San Francisco, and Los Angeles.

Bus and Shuttle

Alltrans/Jackson Hole Express (4125 US 89; 307/733-3135 or 800/443-6133; www.jacksonholealltrans.com) offers shuttles between Jackson Hole, eastern Idaho, and Salt Lake City.

Greyhound (105 Buffalo Way; www.greyhound.com) is operated here by Salt Lake Express and leaves from under the canopy at the USPS mailbox outside Albertsons.

Getting to Missoula

Car

I-90 runs directly through Missoula, making it an easy destination by car. Missoula is 115 mi (185 km) west of Helena and the same distance south of Kalispell, 120 mi (193 km) northwest of Butte, and about 200 mi (320 km) northwest of Bozeman.

Car and RV Rental

On the 1st floor of the airport are **Alamo, Avis, Enterprise, Thrifty,** and **Hertz** car-rental agencies. **Dollar** has shuttles to and from the airport.

RVs can be rented at **Cruise America RV Rental** (12787 US-93, Lolo; 406/273-4994; www.cruiseamerica.com). RVs can be also be rented from individuals (like VRBO, but for RVs) on **Outdoorsy** (www.outdoorsy.com).

Air

Just 4 mi (6 km) northwest of the university, **Missoula Montana Airport** is served by Alaska, Allegiant, American, Delta, Frontier, Sun Country, and United. On the 1st floor of the terminal are **Alamo, Avis, Budget, Enterprise, Hertz, National,** and **Thrifty** car-rental agencies. **Dollar** has shuttles to and from the airport. Most hotels offer free airport shuttle service; the **Airport Shuttler** (406/880-7433; www.msoshuttle.com) also provides transportation into town.

Bus

The **Greyhound bus station** (1660 W. Broadway; 406/549-2339) has several buses into and out of town daily.

Getting to Great Falls

Car

Great Falls is situated directly off I-15, allowing easy access by car. It is 218 mi (355 km) northwest of **Billings,** 186 mi (300 km) north of **Bozeman,** 155 mi (250 km) northeast of **Butte,** and approximately 90 mi (145 km) from **Helena** (to the south).

Car and RV Rental

The airport's on-site car-rental companies are **National/Alamo, Avis/Budget, Enterprise,** and **Hertz.**

Share programs can often connect renters with privately owned RVs. Options include **RV Share** (www.rvshare.com) and **Outdoorsy** (www.outdoorsy.com).

Air

The **Great Falls International Airport** (GTF; 2800 Terminal Dr.; 406/727-3404; www.flygtf.com) is southwest of the city. It is served by Alaska Airlines, Allegiant, Delta, and United.

Bus

Greyhound Bus Lines (326 1st Ave. S.; 800/231-2222; www.greyhound.com) offers service to other major towns and cities in Montana from the Great Falls Transit Center.

Getting to Kalispell

Car

Kalispell is easily accessible by car. It's 117 mi (188 km) north of **Missoula** at the junction of US 2 and US 93. From **Whitefish,** Kalispell is 14 mi (22 km) south on US 93, a 25-minute drive. Kalispell is 33 mi (53 km) from the west entrance to Glacier National Park and 88 mi (142 km) from the entrance at East Glacier.

Car and RV Rental

There are on-site car-rental counters for **Avis, Budget, Hertz,** and **National/Alamo. Dollar** (406/892-0009; www.dollar.com), **Enterprise** (406/755-4848; www.enterprise.com), and **Thrifty** (406/257-7333; www.thrifty.com) are off-site but near the airport.

In Kalispell, RVs can be rented through RV share programs including **RV Share** (www.rvshare.com), **Outdoorsy** (www.outdoorsy.com), and **RVnGO** (www.rvngo.com). In **Whitefish**, high-end, pet-friendly campervans are available for rent from **Moterra Campervans** (5644 US 93; 307/200-7220; www.gomoterra.com).

Air

The **Glacier Park International Airport** (FCA; 4170 US 2 E., Kalispell; www.iflyglacier.com) is served daily by Delta, Alaska, American, Allegiant, and United, with seasonal service from Sun Country and Avelo.

Bus

Greyhound (2075 US 2 E.; 406/755-7447) offers daily bus service into and out of Kalispell.

Train

Amtrak (500 Depot St., Whitefish) runs the **Empire Builder** from Chicago to Seattle with daily stops in Whitefish in each direction.

Road Rules

Rental cars are available at the major airports. If you plan on renting a car, it's a good idea to reserve one well in advance. Unless you will be driving entirely on paved roads, which is doubtful, a high-clearance or all-wheel-drive vehicle is a good idea. Many Forest Service campgrounds are located along gravel roads, and anytime you venture off the beaten path, you're bound to encounter some type of gravel or dirt road. In the winter, all-wheel drive is a must. And be aware that rock chips on the windshield are common occurrences at any time of year. Make sure your insurance will cover it, or consider paying for added insurance from the car-rental agency.

Distances between settlements can be great in this region. As a rule of thumb, planning ahead is critical. Don't wait until your gas light is on to fill up your tank, and make sure your spare is inflated. Carrying emergency gear is recommended. A sleeping bag, water, headlamp, matches, and some food are the bare minimum for winter travel. Rest areas—even on major highways and interstates—can be hundreds of miles apart. Most major towns and cities have reliable mechanics and car dealerships, but don't expect to find parts for your old Porsche roadster in very many places.

In general, the **speed limit** is 80 mph (129 km/h) on interstates (65 mph/105 km/h on interstates within urban areas) and 70 mph (113 km/h) during daylight (65 mph/105 km/h at night) on most two-lane highways. Many two-lane roads have numerous turnouts where slower-moving vehicles can pull over and let cars pass. Locals are used to driving faster on these roads, so if you're getting tailgated, just pull over and let them go by. Increasingly, passing lanes are being incorporated into many state highways, particularly on roads over mountain passes. Be aware that Montana has a "move over law" that requires drivers to slow down and change lanes for stopped emergency or maintenance vehicles. Courtesy would suggest you do the same for any vehicle stopped alongside the road. Also new under the current governor is a law allowing motorcyclists to "lane split," which allows them to pass stopped or slow-moving traffic.

Travel Maps

Free road maps can be found at visitor centers and rest areas, while an excellent supplement is the **Delorme Gazetteer series** (www.delorme.com), available at bookstores and in many gas stations. These oversize companions are a must for those venturing off the beaten path, as they include topographic data, Forest Service roads and trails, camping and hiking information, fishing areas, scenic drives, and more. Sporting goods stores offer more specialized maps, from national forests and wilderness areas to Bureau of Land Management lands and mile-by-mile river guides. The free road maps you get when you enter the national parks are sufficient to use during your stay.

Traveling by Bicycle

This region has many options for those cycling through. Numerous back roads and accessible campgrounds make for some fun trips, but be prepared for long-distance rides and not much company. Both the Wyoming and Montana transportation websites (www.wyoroad.info, www.mdt.mt.gov/travinfo) offer excellent information for cyclists. You can order a **Montana Bicycle Touring Packet** online, as well as download maps and road grade information from each site. In Wyoming, information can also be found on www.cyclingwyoming.org. The Montana-based **Adventure Cycling Association** (800/755-2453; www.adventurecycling.org) offers self-contained and supported bicycle tours in Montana and in Yellowstone and Grand Teton National Parks.

Road Conditions and Closures

In general, interstates and major highways are in good condition across the region, although short summers mean road construction can be expected at any time of the day—or night, in some cases. State highways are often narrow and winding, not compatible with drowsy or inattentive drivers. Wildlife is a concern on any road, particularly at dusk and dark, and fallen rocks can be a problem in mountainous areas. For Wyoming road conditions, the **Wyoming Department of Transportation** (888/996-7623; www.wyoroad.info) has a wealth of information. Montana information can be found through the **Montana Department of Transportation** (800/226-7623; www.mdt.mt.gov/travinfo).

Winter Travel

Winter driving in Montana and Wyoming takes special care, focus, and—at times—lots of caffeine. Roads can be rendered impassable in a matter of minutes by snow and wind, and mountain passes are especially susceptible to fast-changing conditions. Because of the area covered, it may take a while before snowplows clear the roads. And be extremely cautious when driving behind or toward a snowplow, as visibility can be diminished to nothing. Be aware that because of wildlife, salt is rarely used on roads in Montana and Wyoming. Instead, the roads are graveled to provide better traction in icy conditions. Loose gravel often translates into cracked or chipped windshields, so drive with caution, and never get too close to a graveling truck.

Snow tires are a must in many places, and carrying emergency supplies is strongly recommended. A good emergency kit includes a shovel, a first-aid kit, jumper cables, a flashlight, signal flares, extra clothing, some food, water, a tow strap, and a sleeping bag. Don't rely on your cell phone to save you—although service is improving, there are many dead zones across the region.

Both states' transportation websites (www.wyoroad.info, www.mdt.mt.gov/travinfo) have links to current and projected weather patterns, and toll-free information numbers are updated regularly. It's a good idea to carry these numbers in your car. Occasionally weather information can be found on the AM band of your car radio—you'll notice signs along roads indicating when this is possible.

National Park Passes

With three of the country's most popular national parks in Montana and Wyoming, this is where many visitors begin and end their journey. **Glacier National Park** (www.nps.gov/glac) falls entirely within Montana, and the Canadian **Waterton Lakes National Park** (www.pc.gc.ca) is directly across the border, sharing some of the same trails. Although most of **Yellowstone National Park** (www.nps.gov/yell) is in Wyoming, three of the park's entrances are in Montana. South of Yellowstone in Wyoming is **Grand Teton National Park** (www.nps.gov/grte). The entrance fee in the summer for each park is $35 for automobiles, which is valid for seven days. An America the Beautiful national parks and federal recreation lands annual pass, which permits entrance to more than 2,000 federal recreation sites, costs $80. Campground and other lodging fees are extra. Annual passes for any of the three parks are $70.

Each state also has numerous national monuments, historic sites, trails, and recreation areas that fall within the National Park System. Consult the National Park Service website (www.nps.gov) for more information on these areas.

Practical Details

Canadian Crossings and Customs

Of the many roads that cross into Canada from Montana, only two of the 13 border crossings are open 24 hours daily year-round—US 93 (Roosville) and I-15 (Sweetgrass/Eureka)—and both are very busy. Wait times to enter Canada midsummer can be several hours, but travelers can go online (www.cbsa-asfc.gc.ca) to see the current wait times at each crossing and to sign up for border alerts. US citizens are now required to carry passports (or passport cards) when crossing into Canada; Canadians entering the United States must have a passport, or a NEXUS card, or an Enhanced Driver's License (EDL), or an Enhanced Identification Card (EIC). Citizens of other countries must show their passports and appropriate visas and may be asked to prove that they have sufficient funds for their length of stay.

Tourist Information

Both states have excellent information available for those interested in traveling to the region. Most chambers of commerce and visitor centers (listed for each town in this book) are good sources when driving around, but the online sites are where you should start your research. For Wyoming, visit **Wyoming Tourism** (307/777-7777; www.travelwyoming.com) for the latest information. You can check out the various towns, attractions, and events, as well as order a **free vacation guide.**

For Montana, the **Montana Office of Tourism** (800/847-4868; www.visitmt.com) is the state's official tourism organization for vacation information and to order the annual free **Montana Guidebook.** Montana has divided the state into six different tourism regions, and specific booklets are available for each one.

Communications and Media

Cell Phones

Although Montana and Wyoming may be remote, cell phone coverage is overall very good and getting better each year. That being said, rural and mountainous areas may have spotty coverage, and plenty have none at all. Verizon is the main carrier, although AT&T is increasingly available.

Internet Access

Many coffee shops and public libraries have computers available for internet access, and most larger towns have business centers with computers and fax machines. High-speed internet connections are generally available, but the service is often slower and more problematic compared to larger metropolitan areas. Wireless internet is frequently offered at coffee shops, libraries, hotels, and other public places.

Food

One thing is certain: This is meat-and-potatoes country, which can be great for those craving a good steak, as you can find one in almost every town. Locally raised beef can be found on the menus of many restaurants, and bison is becoming increasingly popular. If you haven't had it, it's highly recommended. A good bison burger or tenderloin is hard to beat, but if you are asked how you like it cooked, never ask for anything more than medium. Wild-game dishes, mostly elk and venison, are also found at finer establishments, with pheasant and other regional game occasionally on the menu. If you enjoy trying new fare, this can be an exciting option.

With all the meat on the menu, you would think that vegetarians would be out of luck when dining out, but surprisingly, options abound, especially at higher-end restaurants. The "eat local" campaigns are in full swing out West, and many of the best restaurants get as much of their food as possible from local and regional growers. Despite the region being seriously landlocked, seafood is no longer necessarily a bad idea. Fresh seafood is flown in from Hawaii or Seattle daily in many places, and it is generally pretty good. There are even fresh sushi bars in Montana and Wyoming, and some are darn tasty. Innovative cuisine can be found in every major town, but certainly Jackson, Bozeman, Bigfork, Whitefish, and Missoula stand out.

Does either state have a well-known meal? Well, not really. Montana is famous for its huckleberries and Flathead cherries, so a good pie or milk shake is a must. Pasties in Butte are considered indispensable regional cuisine, and Rocky Mountain oysters (calf testicles) are usually breaded and fried—not exactly gourmet, and not exactly popular or necessarily worth trying. Delicious Indian tacos load the ingredients onto fry bread, and good Mexican and Chinese restaurants can be found throughout the region. Other regional specialties in both states include wild game, chicken-fried steak, chili, and trout.

You'll also see the standard fast-food establishments, especially near the interstates, but avoid these and try a local restaurant instead. You'll find the best food at the most random of places—and it will certainly be a more interesting culinary and cultural experience. And remember, folks out here are friendly—if you stop and ask someone about the best place in town, they will usually point you in the right direction and will probably know the owner.

If you are traveling the back roads and small towns and get tired of ordinary bar-type food (burgers, burgers, and more burgers), consider a quest to find the best chicken-fried steak or the best piece of pie. Sometimes a personal challenge can relieve the boredom of limited options. Plus, who doesn't want an excuse to eat homemade pie for breakfast, lunch, and dinner?

Accommodations

Because Montana and Wyoming are both big destinations for visitors, it's no surprise that a wide variety of lodging options are available, from standard hotels and motels to luxury resorts and guest ranches. Generally speaking, all lodging is more expensive in the summer (except for those nearby ski resorts), and rooms fill rapidly—advance reservations are a must, especially around special events like the Livingston Roundup. Rooms, cabins, and even campgrounds in the national parks fill up several months—if not longer—in advance. Rooms in national parks can generally be reserved one year in advance. Shoulder seasons (spring and fall) offer reduced rates and thinner crowds, while rooms at the ski resort lodges fill up fast in the winter but may be more open during the summer.

Most larger towns have numerous chain motels, which are typically clustered around the interstate exits. Gateway towns to Yellowstone and Grand Teton National Parks also have chain hotels, as well as a number of mom-and-pop motels sprinkled around town. Travelers used to standard hotels will be happy with these choices, but those who seek a unique experience will want to try the smaller boutique. It just depends on whether you would rather stay in the usual Super 8 or sleep in a room that once accommodated Ernest Hemingway or Annie Oakley. An excellent resource is **Historic Hotels of the Rockies** (www.historichotels.org).

There are a number of bed-and-breakfasts in Montana and Wyoming in the higher-traffic tourist areas. Many are located on the banks of a river or nestled in the pine trees and often make great escapes from the busier hotel atmosphere. A comprehensive listing can be found at **BnBFinder** (www.bnbfinder.com). Very few hostels exist in Montana and Wyoming, but **Hostels.com** (www.hostels.com) has a list of what might be available.

Historic Hotels Beyond Park Boundaries

So much is written about the glorious hotels inside the parks that have not only shaped the visitor experience for more than 100 years, but gave rise to a unique form of architecture known as "parkitecture." The Old Faithful Inn, Jenny Lake Lodge, and Lake McDonald Lodge are outstanding examples. Because securing lodging at these beautiful old hotels can be challenging and expensive, we've come up with a list of lovely historic hotels outside the parks.

Yellowstone National Park

- Just 30 minutes north of Yellowstone, in the mountains of **Paradise Valley, Chico Hot Springs Resort** (www.chicohotsprings.com) dates back to old mining days. It is one of the region's favorite resorts thanks to its cozy rooms, outstanding dining, natural hot springs pools, abundance of year-round activities, something of a Hollywood vibe, and even its resident ghost.

- The closest lodging to Yellowstone's east entrance is **Pahaska Tepee** (www.pahaska.com), which was Buffalo Bill's original lodge in the Rockies, built in 1904. Today there are classic and modern cabins on the property.

Grand Teton National Park

- Not only does the **Triangle X Ranch** (https://trianglex.com) sit inside the boundaries of the park for the most extraordinary setting imaginable, but the ranch lodge is the original Turner family home. Its cabins housed valley families for generations before providing cozy accommodations for guests.

- **The Wort Hotel** (www.worthotel.com) in downtown **Jackson Hole** was opened as a glamorous lodging place in 1941, but its origins go back farther to its use as a corral and livery stable. Today, the elegant hotel is on the National Register of Historic Places and continues to be the heart of this town.

Glacier National Park

- **Belton Chalet** (www.glacierparkcollection.com) is an iconic lodge just outside the park in **West Glacier.** Built by the Great Northern Railroad, as were so many of Glacier's glorious buildings, the hotel opened in 1910 and underwent an award-winning restoration in 1999.

- Built in 1939 by the Great Northern Railroad as lodging for its workers, the Tudor Revival **Izaak Walton Inn** (www.izaakwaltoninn.com) in **Essex** is about halfway between the entrances at East and West Glacier. Charming rooms are set in the recently remodeled lodge, as well as in cabooses, luxury railcars, cabins, and an old schoolhouse.

Guest ranches range from traditional horse-and-cowboy dude ranches to luxury "glamping" (a portmanteau of *glamorous* and *camping*) resorts that offer spa services and high-end cuisine. Two excellent resources for those seeking a real Western working vacation are the **Montana Dude Ranchers' Association** (888/284-4133; www.montanadra.com) and the **Wyoming Dude Ranchers' Association** (888/996-9372; www.wyomingdra.com). Many of these are focused on horseback riding, fly fishing, and family activities and often booked in weeklong blocks. In the winter, some offer cross-country skiing, snowshoeing, or dogsledding.

Higher-end guest ranches are increasingly popular in Montana and Wyoming, offering guests a chance to experience a rustic atmosphere with upscale amenities. These are typically set in remote locations with beautiful surroundings and are private, in some cases gated from public access. Prices range from several hundred dollars to $1,000 or more per night.

Cabins and other vacation rentals are ideal for travelers looking for that Western cabin experience. These can range from rustic—just beds, no plumbing—to luxurious—down comforters, a rock fireplace—and are perhaps the best way to stay. Sites like **Airbnb** (www.airbnb.com) and **VRBO** (www.vrbo.com) offer private homes and cabins for rent, while many resorts provide nightly cabin rentals. For Forest Service cabins and fire lookout towers—which can be quite primitive but are set in phenomenal locations—travelers can check availability and make reservations at www.recreation.gov.

Plenty of RV and tent camping sites in Montana and Wyoming are available. RV campers will find private campgrounds in most towns, and most national forest campgrounds have room for all but the longest RVs. It's generally legal to camp on national forest land, unless you see a sign indicating that overnight camping isn't allowed. For something closer to backcountry experience without hoofing it, drive on a Forest Service road until you find a nice campsite, pull over, and set up camp. Not only can it be quite scenic, it's also free.

Health and Safety

While medical services and health care in many of the larger Montana and Wyoming towns are excellent—and in some cases on par with bigger cities—it's important to remember that when traveling around, you'll mostly likely be far away from emergency medical services. Rural and mountainous highways are especially troublesome, as cell phone coverage can be spotty. Most small towns have a local clinic, and services are available in the national parks. Refer to specific areas of the text for emergency numbers, and remember that calling 911 doesn't always work in many rural areas.

In general, **weather, altitude,** and **insect bites** pose the greatest risk traveling here. The summer sun can get extremely hot, and it is easy to get dehydrated, so make sure to drink plenty of water during the day. Hiking—and just walking, for some people—can be a strenuous activity as the altitude increases. It's best to carry plenty of food and water, and take your time getting to your destination. Always let someone know where you are going and when you plan to be back. The earliest and most obvious sign of altitude-related health problems is a headache, and the best remedy is drinking water and moving to a lower elevation if possible.

The common insect nuisances are mosquitoes and ticks. Montana and Wyoming mosquitoes rarely carry diseases, but they can be annoying at certain times during the summer. While West Nile virus is becoming an increasing threat to livestock across the West, human infection is less common. Still, it's a good idea to carry bug repellent with DEET, especially when hiking or camping near water. Ticks can pose a small threat of Rocky Mountain fever or Lyme disease, and they seem to have become more pervasive in the last 10 years or so. It's a good idea to check every part of your skin after a day of hiking or fishing outdoors—places where you might encounter underbrush, dense trees, and grassy meadows. If you find a tick with its head stuck in your skin, pull gently with tweezers or your fingers until the tick works its way out. Don't forget to check your pets too.

A common backcountry ill is **giardia,** sometimes called "beaver fever," a microscopic parasite that lives in mountain streams and can wreak havoc in your intestinal tract. Always avoid drinking unfiltered or untreated water directly from streams, rivers, springs, or lakes. It may look pristine where you are, but you can't see the herd of cattle upstream. Carry a water filter or water-purifying tablets (iodine or similar products), and you'll have nothing to worry about.

If you're camping or staying in a cabin where mice have been active, **hantavirus** can be a concern. Hantavirus is a potentially fatal disease caused by contact with rodent droppings, particularly those of deer mice. Symptoms include fever, muscle aches, coughing, and difficulty breathing. Campers should avoid sleeping on bare ground, and avoid cabins with signs of rodents. For more information, visit the Centers for Disease Control and Prevention (www.cdc.gov).

Winter poses different types of health concerns, namely **hypothermia** and **frostbite.** If someone shows any signs of hypothermia—uncontrollable shivering, slurred speech, loss of coordination—get them out of the wind and inside immediately. If you're camping, a dry sleeping bag is your best bet. It's a good idea to dress in layers, avoid cotton clothing, always bring a hat, and—most important—make good decisions *before* you put yourself in a situation where you could be stranded in the wind and cold. If you're outside in the winter, a sign of frostbite is the whitening and hardening of the skin. The best way to warm the affected area is with other skin, but avoid warming it too quickly because thawing can be quite painful.

Weather

The old saying is a tad cliché but often true: If you don't like the weather in Montana or Wyoming, just wait five minutes. What this means to the traveler is that weather in this part of the West can change dramatically in an unbelievably short amount of time. In summer, extreme heat can dehydrate the human body rapidly, and in winter, extreme cold can render your body useless in a matter of minutes. Sudden changes in weather can happen at any time of the year in mountainous areas. It can snow, sleet, hail, and rain at a moment's notice. If you're heading into the backcountry or getting ready for a three-day river float, check the forecast, but don't rely on it; plan for the worst with extra gear and plenty of food and water.

In general, Montana and Wyoming have a semiarid climate. There is enough moisture at certain times of the year, but summers are typically dry and warm, with July-August being the hottest months. Mountainous areas see heavy snowfall during the winter (to the delight of skiers), while the eastern part of both states can seem downright desert-like much of the year.

Wildlife

Although many people visit Montana and Wyoming for the abundant wildlife, with so much human interaction, safety is a real concern. A general rule of thumb is *never* to approach wildlife, no matter what the situation. Each year people are hurt or killed because they ignore this basic rule. Not only are they putting themselves in harm's way, but they are often precipitating imminent doom for the animal. The old adage, "A fed bear is a dead bear," can be applied universally to wildlife. The problem of humans getting too close to animals, particularly in Yellowstone National Park, gets plenty of coverage these days on Instagram (@touronsofyellowstone and @touronsofglacier), YouTube, and the evening news. Do not become a cautionary lesson for other travelers.

Safety in Bear Country

Grizzly bears and black bears live in many parts of Montana and Wyoming, and although encounters are rare, it is necessary to learn what to do in case it happens to you. It is also important to know how to avoid the situation in the first place. No method is foolproof, but with caution and attentiveness you can avoid most of the common mistakes that lead to bear encounters.

When out in the backcountry, it's the unexpected bear encounter you really want to avoid. The best way to do this is to let the bears know you are present. Make noise in areas of dense cover and blind spots on hiking or biking trails. Immediately move away from any animal carcass you come across, as there may be a bear nearby protecting it. Avoid hiking or biking at dawn or dusk, and travel in larger groups; the more of you there are, the more likely a bear will sense you and move away. Be aware that dogs can provoke bears and bring them right to you. And, of course, never leave food out.

If you're camping in an area frequented by bears, look for signs (waste, overturned rocks, decimated fallen timber, claw marks and hair on trees) around the campsite. Because bears are attracted to all kinds of odors—food, toothpaste, soap, deodorant—your cooking, eating, and food storage area should be at least 50 yards (46 m) from your tent. It's tempting to bring tasty items like sausage, ham, tuna, and bacon with you, but these smell good to bears too. Freeze-dried foods are your best bet. Store foods in airtight bags and be sure to hang all food at least 12-15 ft (4-5 m) off the ground and away from tree trunks. Some designated campsites have bear storage containers or food storage poles.

Carrying **pepper spray** (sold in most sporting goods stores, but it's worth noting that at the Grizzly and Wolf Discovery Center in West Yellowstone, you can buy bear spray at cost) is a must in bear country, and it has been proven useful in fending off bear attacks. These sprays only work at close range (10-30 ft/3-9 m) and can quickly dissipate in the wind or sometimes blow back in your face. Carry the spray in a holster or on a belt across your chest for easy access. It's important to note that these spray canisters are not allowed on commercial airplanes, they expire after a certain date, and they should not be left in a very hot place like a closed car. Also, test your container every now and then in light or no wind to make sure it works.

If you happen to encounter a bear, try not to panic or make any sudden moves. Do not run—bears can run more than 40 mph (64 km/h) in short bursts—and do not try to climb a tree. Make yourself visible by moving out into the open so the bear can identify you. Avoid direct eye contact with the bear; talking in a low voice may convince the animal that you are human. If the bear is sniffing the air or standing on its hind legs, it's most likely trying to identify you. If it's woofing and posturing, this could be a challenge. Stand your ground if the bear charges; most charges are bluffs, where the bear will stop short and wander away.

If a grizzly does charge and knocks you to the ground, curl up in the fetal position with your hands wrapped behind your neck and your elbows tucked over your face. Keeping your backpack on may offer some protection. Remain as still as possible, as bears will often only sniff or nip you and leave. This is considered playing "active dead." If the bear rolls you over, as it will likely try to do, roll yourself back over on your stomach and keep your neck as protected as possible. Remain on the ground until you know the bear has vacated the area.

In general, black bears are more common and seem to have more interaction with people. In many places they can be a nuisance—getting into garbage, breaking into homes—but don't think that they are not dangerous. Black bears will generally try to avoid you and are easily scared away, but if you encounter an attacking or aggressive bear, this usually means it views you as food. In this case, most experts recommend fighting back with whatever means possible: large rocks or sticks, and plenty of shouting.

It's a rare event when a bear attacks sleeping campers in tents at night, as tragically happened at the Soda Butte campground near Cooke City in July 2010 and in Ovando in 2021, but if you find yourself in that situation, defend yourself as aggressively as you can. In these circumstances, bears are viewing you as prey and may give up if you fight back. Never play dead in this case, and to thwart off an attack, always keep pepper spray and a flashlight handy.

Before you go into the backcountry, brush up on your **bear identification.** You can't tell what kind of bear you see by its color alone. Grizzlies are often larger and have a trademark hump at the top of their neck. Grizzlies also have more of a dish-shaped face profile, compared to a straighter profile of black bears.

Other Wildlife

Although bears get more press, there are other animals that you need to be aware of when traveling around Montana and Wyoming. **Moose** are prone to sudden charges when surprised, especially females traveling with young. If you travel through Yellowstone National Park, you'll encounter numerous **bison.** Although it may be tempting to walk up to them, avoid doing so. While they are not vicious, bison can charge if provoked and maim or even kill visitors every year. Statistically, bison injure more people in Yellowstone than any other animal. Be aware that these lumbering beasts can sprint the length of a football field in six seconds and can leap a 6-ft (2-m) fence. Likewise, **elk** in the park can seem downright docile, but do not approach them. They too have attacked, stomped, and gored visitors who got too close.

Mountain lions generally keep a low profile, but as humans encroach on their habitat, encounters are becoming more frequent. Most attacks have been on unattended children. If you happen to find yourself in a situation with a mountain lion, be aggressive and fight back if necessary, or throw rocks and sticks to try to make it go away.

Rattlesnakes can be found in the central and eastern parts of Montana and Wyoming, especially in the drier prairies. Rattlesnake bites are rarely fatal (less than 4 percent when antivenin is used in time), and the snakes generally avoid humans. Be careful where you step when hiking around these areas, and pay attention if children are with you. If you surprise or step on a rattlesnake—chances are you'll hear its trademark rattle before you see it—it may coil and strike. Any bite from a rattlesnake should be regarded as a life-threatening medical emergency that requires immediate hospital treatment.

With all of the incredible wildlife-viewing opportunities around Montana and Wyoming, it can be easy for some people to get complacent when taking pictures or hiking around. Treat all wildlife with respect and care, and never feed or approach any type of wild animal. If you are lucky enough to see these critters, observe them in their natural habitat and then carry on. The last thing you want is to become a meme. Or worse, a statistic.

Traveler Advice

Access for Travelers with Disabilities

For the most part, Montana and Wyoming comply with state and federal guidelines for accessibility. Most hotels offer accessible rooms, and the national parks and even some state parks feature accessible trails. However, it's important to remember that many parts of both states are rural, and some features may be outdated, less accessible, or nonexistent. For both Montana and Wyoming, a list of trails that are easy to navigate and accessible to most wheelchairs is available at **Accessible Nature** (www.accessiblenature.info). Another resource for travelers with disabilities is **Rocky Mountain ADA** (800/949-4232; www.rockymountainada.org). In the national parks, wheelchair accessibility information can be found on the park websites.

Women Traveling Alone

Overall, Montana and Wyoming can be exciting for a woman traveling alone. For the most part, the West is full of independent and strong women, and you won't seem out of place because of your gender in most areas. A cursory Google search turns up a wealth of stories and blogs of women chronicling their solo travels across Montana and Wyoming. The reality is that most of these women are probably white and the experience could be very different for a woman of color.

Of course, there is always the occasional weirdo, so if a place or a person makes you uncomfortable, the best thing to do is just leave. Use the same precautions and common sense that you would at home. Even in a quaint mountain town, it's probably not safe to be out, wandering alone, in the middle of the night. Places like Bozeman, Billings, Missoula, and even Cheyenne have growing unhoused populations that often take up residence in parks. It's worth noting that bear spray can be just as effective on a creepy dude as it is on a curious grizzly.

LGBTQ+ Travelers

It's safe to say that many people in Montana and Wyoming are socially conservative, and queer public displays of affection are not entirely common, although they are becoming more so. You shouldn't necessarily anticipate discrimination or hostility if you are LGBTQ+, but you'll want to be aware of your surroundings. In general, "don't ask, don't tell" is the safest policy to assume when traveling here. And, as is expected, urban areas are often friendlier to LGBTQ+ travelers.

That being said, there are thriving—although often underground—gay communities in many Montana and Wyoming towns, particularly college towns like Missoula, Bozeman, and Laramie. Two excellent resources for LGBTQ+ travelers are the **Western Montana LGBT Community Center** (406/543-2224; www.gaymontana.org) and the **University of Wyoming's Rainbow Resource Center** (307/766-3478; www.uwyo.edu/RRC). **Wyoming Equality** (307/778-7645; www.wyomingequality.org) is an organization whose vision is "a Wyoming where the dignity and humanity of all LGBTQ Wyomingites are celebrated and protected."

Travelers of Color

Both Montana and Wyoming are about 85 percent white, with Latino, Native American, multiracial, Black, and Asian people accounting for the rest of the population, according to the 2020 US census. With so few people of color in both states, Black people and other minorities tend to be cautious when traveling in this part of the country, according to Judith Heilman, former executive director of the Montana Racial Equity Project (www.themtrep.org). And for good reason: There are still a lot of sundown towns in both states, where people of color may not feel welcome or even safe. This doesn't mean you should expect to be intimidated or harassed, but it does mean you will have to be alert and aware of your surroundings.

The United States has a terrible record when it comes to land management and racial equity. People of color have been excluded from national parks—dating back to the founding of the National Park Service (NPS) in 1916 and the enforcement of segregation through Jim Crow laws—and other green settings for generations. Even though the country is becoming more diverse, parks, green spaces, and conservation spaces—which Montana and Wyoming have in abundance—remain white and somewhat elitist. An NPS poll taken in 2018 shows that even though people of color make up 42 percent of the US population, only 23 percent of visitors to the national parks were people of color, and only 6 percent identified as Black. There are a multitude of social and economic reasons why this is true, and the NPS is committed to addressing the racial disparity—by marketing to nonwhite communities, training staff on racial sensitivity, and working to hire rangers from more diverse backgrounds.

It follows that people of color are underrepresented in Montana and Wyoming, two mostly white states with vast expanses of public land, and thus face real questions of both comfort and safety. The Montana Racial Equity Project, based in Bozeman, encourages travelers of color to be alert and aware, and to document (and film, whenever possible) any mistreatment. Generally speaking, the larger towns in both states have more people of color and thus may feel safer and more welcoming. It's not a bad idea to connect with communities—and there are several—that can offer insider advice for your specific destinations. A remaking of the *Green Book*, a travel guide published 1936-1967 that identified businesses that were friendly to African American customers, the **Inclusive Guide** (www.inclusivejourneys.com) is an online community that lists safe and welcoming spaces for anyone who faces discrimination. There are also Instagram and Facebook pages targeted to people of color in the great outdoors. Outdoor Afro, Latino Outdoors, Brown People Camping, Natives Outdoors, and Black People Who Hike are but a few examples. **On She Goes** (www.onshegoes.com, @onshegoes) is a travel website created by and for women of color. And **Travel Noire** (www.travelnoire.com), which has more than 100 articles that reference Montana or Wyoming, is a digital media company geared to millennials of the African Diaspora. BIPOC journalist James Edward Mills started the **Joy Trip Project** (www.joytripproject.com), which focuses on outdoor recreation. There's an excellent list of antiracism resources on the site related to justice, equity, diversity, and inclusion of BIPOC in parks and green spaces. One such site is **Diversify Outdoors** (www.diversifyoutdoors.com), which promotes diversity in outdoor recreation and conservation.

Resources

Suggested Reading

History

Black, George. *Empire of Shadows: The Epic Story of Yellowstone*. New York, NY: St. Martin's Griffin Press, 2013. Historian George Black weaves together the American passion for exploration, the violence of the Indian Wars, and the "civilizing" of the frontier to tell the origin story of Yellowstone National Park.

Clayton, John. *Wonderlandscape: Yellowstone National Park and the Evolution of an American Cultural Icon*. New York: Pegasus Books, 2017. Using iconic figures—including painters, naturalists, and entrepreneurs—as the storytelling mechanisms, John Clayton paints a fascinating cultural picture of the park.

Djuff, Ray and Chris Morrison. *Glacier's Historic Hotels & Chalets: View With a Room*. Helena, MT: Farcountry Press, 2013. Whether or not you are lucky enough to get one of the rooms in this book on your stay, you will love reading about how these magnificent hotels and chalets came to be.

Guthrie, C. W. *Glacier National Park, The First 100 Years*. Helena, MT: Farcountry Press, 2008. A marvelous volume compiled to celebrate the park's centennial in 2010, this book features exquisite photos and artwork in addition to compelling history.

Righter, Robert W. *Crucible for Conservation: The Struggle for Grand Teton National Park.* Moose, WY: Grand Teton Natural History Association, 1982. This gripping history makes one grateful that things worked out the way they did.

Saunders, Richard L., editor. *A Yellowstone Reader: The National Park in Folklore, Popular Fiction, and Verse.* Salt Lake City: University of Utah Press, 2003. This volume offers a core sample of historical literature that spans the late 19th century through the 1980s.

Watry, Elizabeth. *Women in Wonderland: Lives, Legends, and Legacies of Yellowstone.* Helena, MT: Riverbend Publishing, 2012. Whether they were just passing through or dedicating decades of their life to America's first national park, these women—rangers, scientists, interpreters, and entrepreneurs—shaped Yellowstone's physical and cultural landscape.

Whittlesey, Lee. *Death in Yellowstone: Accidents and Foolhardiness in the First National Park.* Lanham, MD: Rowman & Littlefield Publishers, 2nd edition, 2014. This book dives into the more than 300 tragic, and often gruesome, deaths in Yellowstone since the 1830s.

Natural History

Johnsgard, Paul A., and Thomas D. Mangelsen. *Yellowstone Wildlife: Ecology and Natural History of the Greater Yellowstone Ecosystem.* Boulder, CO: University Press of Colorado, 2013. With stunning images by Mangelsen and detailed natural histories of the animals that call the park home, this is an outstanding book for wildlife lovers.

McIntyre, Rick. *Rise of Wolf 8: Witnessing the Triumph of Yellowstone's Underdog.* Vancouver, BC, Canada: Greystone Books, 2019. Written by the man who has probably seen more of Yellowstone's wolves than anyone, this book tells the riveting tale of one of the park's best-known wolves.

Murie, Margaret, and Olaus Johan Murie. *Wapiti Wilderness.* Boulder, CO: University Press of Colorado, 1985. A magnificent read by two of the region's now deceased but beloved conservationists, the chapters alternate between his work studying elk and her descriptions of their fascinating life together.

Murphy, Tom. *The Light of Spring: The Seasons of Yellowstone.* Livingston, MT: Crystal Creek Press, 2003. One of the park's best-known photographers, Murphy's gorgeous Yellowstone seasons series offers an exquisite and intimate portrait of the park's rebirth each year.

Phillips, Michael K., and Douglas W. Smith. *The Wolves of Yellowstone.* Stillwater, MN: Voyageur Press, 1996. Rife with fabulous color photos and intimate details by the two men who oversaw the project, this book tells the story of the wolves' reintroduction to Yellowstone in 1995.

Olsen, Jack. *Night of the Grizzlies.* Moose, WY: Homestead Publishing, 1996. Perhaps better read *after* your camping trip in Glacier, this is the account of a 1967 night in which two campers were killed in Glacier in two different locations by two different bears.

Turner, Jack. *Teewinot: A Year in the Teton Range*. New York, NY: St. Martin's Griffin Press, 2001. Written by a legendary climber, this memoir is a 40-year love letter to the mountains he climbed in his youth.

White, Christopher. *The Melting World: A Journey Across America's Vanishing Glaciers*. New York, NY: St. Martin's Press, 2013. A call to action, this book chronicles the first extinction of a mountain ecosystem from the perspective of Glacier scientist and ecologist Dan Fagre.

Williams, Terry Tempest. *The Hour of Land: A Personal Topography of America's National Parks*. London, England: Picador Press, 2017. Beloved writer Terry Tempest Williams gives us this personal and literary celebration of our nation's national parks, amid a world in which nature and beauty and wildness are disappearing.

Yellowstone Forever. *Yellowstone Official Guide*. Gardiner, MT: Yellowstone Forever, 2019. An indispensable resource for visitors to the park, this recently updated guide offers everything from reservation advice to human and geologic history, wildlife viewing, maps, and even a field guide section. You will want this in the car and in your day pack.

Recreation

Arthur, Jean. *Top Trails: Glacier National Park: Must-Do Hikes for Everyone*. Birmingham, AL: Wilderness Press, 2014. Writer and storyteller Jean Arthur has been hiking Glacier for 30 years—often in the company of rangers, historians and Blackfeet guides—making her book equal parts trail guide and cultural history.

Lomax, Becky. *Moon Best of Yellowstone & Grand Teton: Make the Most of One to Three Days in the Parks*. Berkeley, CA: Avalon Travel, 2023. This is the ultimate guide to what to see and how to see it in these two national parks.

Nystrom, Andrew Dean, and Bradley Mayhew. *Top Trails Yellowstone & Grand Teton National Parks: 46 Must-Do Hikes for Everyone*. Birmingham, AL: Wilderness Press, 2017. A National Outdoor Book Award winner, this guide covers wonderful hikes from 0.5-mi (0.8-km) jaunts to 30-mi (48-km) treks by an author who lived in the park and hiked every trail at least once.

Watters, Ron. *Winter Tales and Trails: Skiing, Snowshoeing and Snowboarding in Idaho, the Grand Tetons and Yellowstone National Park*. Pocatello, ID: Great Rift Press, 1997. Both a classic and a necessity for winter adventurers, this guide blends advice with great stories. You'll wish Ron were along for the trip.

Internet Resources

Montana Fish, Wildlife & Parks
www.fwp.mt.gov
This official state site is useful for finding state parks, fishing and hunting information, and other recreational opportunities.

Montana Office of Tourism
www.visitmt.com
Searchable by region and town, places to go, things to do, and a variety of other user-friendly options, the website is superbly organized and easy to navigate.

Montana Traveler Updates
www.mdt.mt.gov/travinfo
The best resource for up-to-date road information comes courtesy of the Montana Department of Transportation.

National Park Service
www.nps.gov
The NPS website is helpful for making plans to visit any of the national parks.

Recreation.gov
www.recreation.gov
This government-run site allows visitors to make reservations at public campgrounds.

U.S. Forest Service
www.fs.fed.us
The Forest Service's website is helpful for pursuing recreational opportunities—including multiuse trails, campgrounds, and cabin rentals—throughout Montana and Wyoming.

Wyoming State Parks, Historic Sites, and Trails
www.wyoparks.state.wy.us
Useful information on parks, recreation, and historic preservation.

Wyoming Travel and Tourism
www.travelwyoming.com
The state's comprehensive offering for visitors, this is a great place to find information on towns, accommodations, travel ideas and itineraries, shopping, and dining.

Wyoming Travel Information
www.wyoroad.info
Up-to-date road information provided by the Wyoming Department of Transportation.

Wyoming Game and Fish Department
http://wgfd.wyo.gov
The website offers much of what visitors need to know about fishing and hunting in the state.

Index

D

E

F

G

M

N

O

PQ

R

S

T

INDEX

UV

W

Y

LIST OF MAPS

Front Map

Welcome to the Yellowstone, Grand Teton & Glacier Road Trip

Yellowstone National Park

Grand Teton National Park

Rocky Mountain Front

Glacier National Park

Glacier to Bozeman

PHOTO CREDITS

All photos © Carter G. Walker except; title page photo: Arlene Waller | Dreamstime.com; page 4 © Bennymarty | Dreamstime.com; page 7 © (top) Wyoming Office of Tourism/Andy Austin; (bottom) Valentin Armianu | Dreamstime.com; page 8 © Sean Beckett | Dreamstime.com; page 11 © (top) Kelly Vandellen | Dreamstime.com; (bottom) Jim Lambert | Dreamstime.com; page 12 © Jeffrey Kreulen | Dreamstime.com; page 13 © Radkol | Dreamstime.com; page 14 © (top) Coltonstiffler | Dreamstime.com; (bottom) Maksershov | Dreamstime.com; page 15 © Dfikar | Dreamstime.com; page 18 © (top right) Karen Foley | Dreamstime; (bottom) Hpbfotos | Dreamstime.com; page 20 © (top) David Burke | Dreamstime.com; (bottom) Tino Woodburn; page 24 © (top left) Paul Lemke | Dreamstime.com; (top right) Brizardh| Dreamstime.com; (bottom) Valentin Armianu | Dreamstime.com; page 27 © Tom Branting | Dreamstime.com; page 28 © (top left) Arlene Hochman Waller | Dreamstime.com; (bottom) Steve Boice | Dreamstime.com; page 33 © Galyna Andrushko | Dreamstime.com; page 34 © Jo Ann Snover | Dreamstime.com; page 45 © (top) Coltonstiffler | Dreamstime.com; (middle) NPS/Jacob W. Frank; (bottom) Pongpol Wathakul | Dreamstime.com; page 50 © Davidhoffmannphotography | Dreamstime.com; page 54 © NPS/Jacob W. Frank; page 56 © (top) Pongpol Wathakul | Dreamstime.com; (middle) Ronniechua | Dreamstime.com; (bottom) Darren Patterson | Dreamstime.com; page 62 © (top) Brina bunt | Dreamstime.com; (middle) NPS/Jacob W. Frank; (bottom) NPS / Jacob W. Frank; page 75 © (top) lainhamer | Dreamstime.com; (middle) Amy Lutz | Dreamstime.com; (bottom) Mkopka | Dreamstime.com; page 77 © Mkopka | Dreamstime.com; page 80 © Tloventures | Dreamstime.com; page 85 © Mkopka | Dreamstime.com; page 93 © (top) Vince937 | Dreamstime.com; (middle) Thierrydehove | Dreamstime.com; (bottom) Haydn Adams | Dreamstime.com; page 96 © Pdamai | Dreamstime.com; page 97 © Sean Beckett | Dreamstime.com; page 107 © (top) Roberto Lo Savio | Dreamstime.com; (middle) Randy Harris | Dreamstime.com; (bottom) Steven Hardin | Dreamstime.com; page 111 © (top) Leonid Andronov | Dreamstime.com; (middle) Jorn Vangoidtsenhoven | Dreamstime.com; (bottom) Johan Elzenga | Dreamstime.com; page 121 © (top) Kwiktor | Dreamstime.com; (middle) Linda Mohammad; (bottom) Linda Mohammad; page 127 © ScenincMedia | Dreamstime.com; page 131 © (top) F11photo | Dreamstime.com; (middle) Steven Cukrov | Dreamstime.com; (bottom) Dan Mckenzie | Dreamstime.com; page 136 © (top) Michael Turner | Dreamstime.com; (middle) Jaimie Tuchman | Dreamstime.com; (bottom) Anita Rundell | Dreamstime.com; page 144 © Montana Dept. of Commerce; page 145 © Kushnirov Avraham | Dreamstime.com; page 152 © (top) Philip Bird | Dreamstime.com; (middle) Miroslav Liska | Dreamstime.com; (bottom) LMSwanson | Dreamstime.com; page 155 © Mkopka | Dreamstime.com; page 159 © (top) George Dodd | Dreamstime.com; (middle) Glenn Nagel | Dreamstime.com; (bottom) Kathy Russell | Dreamstime.com; page 161 © Cheri Alguire | Dreamstime.com; page 167 © (top) Joe Sohm | Dreamstime.com; (middle) Tloventures | Dreamstime.com; (bottom) Tloventures | Dreamstime.com; page 170 © Tloventures | Dreamstime.com; page 176 © NPS/Tim Rains; page 177 © Katinka2014 | Dreamstime.com; page 189 © (top) Alexey Kamenskiy | Dreamstime.com; (middle) NPS/Jacob W. Frank; (bottom) NPS/Jacob W. Frank; page 202 © (top) NPS/Tim Rains; (middle) Tracey Taylor | Dreamstime.com; (bottom) Brizardh | Dreamstime.com; page 204 © Brandon Smith | Dreamstime.com; page 206 © Brizardh | Dreamstime.com; page 213 © Kelly Vandellen | Dreamstime.com; page 218 © Ronniechua | Dreamstime.com; page 228 © Jonathan Cohen | Dreamstime.com; page 229 © Joneppard | Dreamstime.com; page 235 © Montana Dept. of Commerce/Donnie Sexton; page 236 © (top) Francisco Blanco | Dreamstime.com; (bottom) Adeliepenguin | Dreamstime.com; page 241 © Victoria Ditkovsky | Dreamstime.com; page 243 © Radkol | Dreamstime.com; page 251 © (top) Dspataro | Dreamstime.com; (middle) Montana Dept. of Commerce/Tim Kemple; page 263 © (top) Radkol | Dreamstime.com; (middle) Tloventures | Dreamstime.com; (bottom) Tloventures | Dreamstime.com; page 270 © Shannon Brassard | Dreamstime.com; page 277 © (top) Cheri Alguire | Dreamstime.com; (middle) Flashon Studio | Dreamstime.com; (bottom) Sue Smith | Dreamstime.com; page 287 © Tristan Brynildsen | Dreamstime.com.

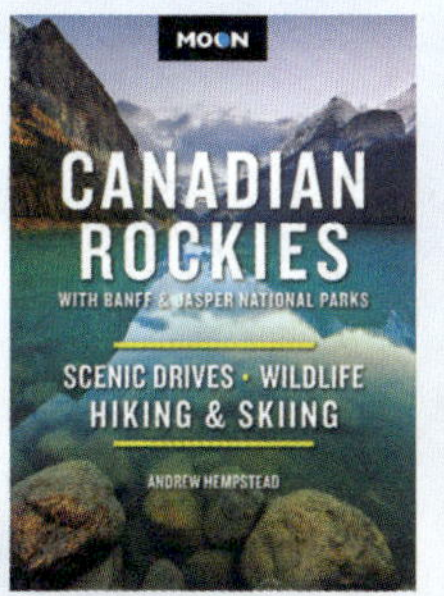

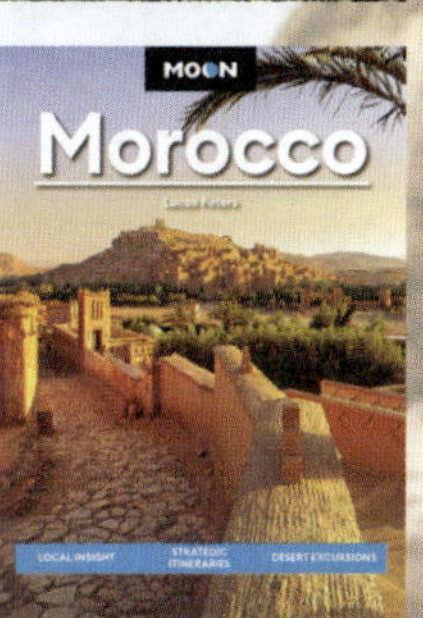

More Great Travel Guides from Moon

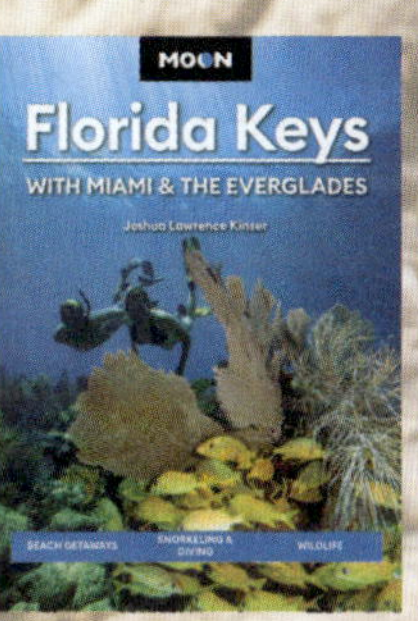

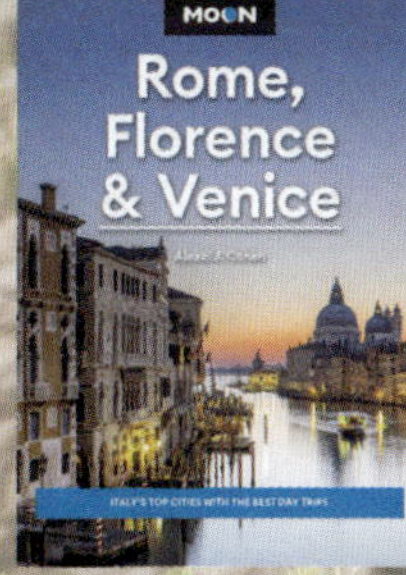

ROAD TRIP GUIDES

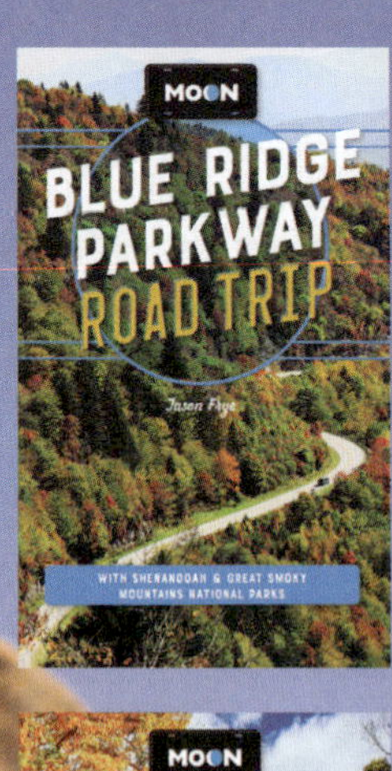

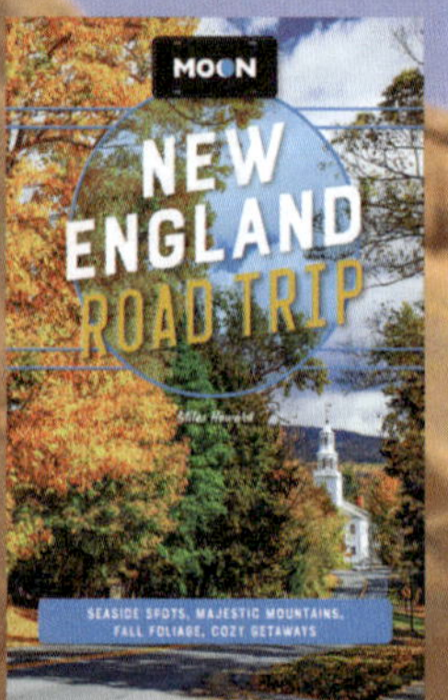

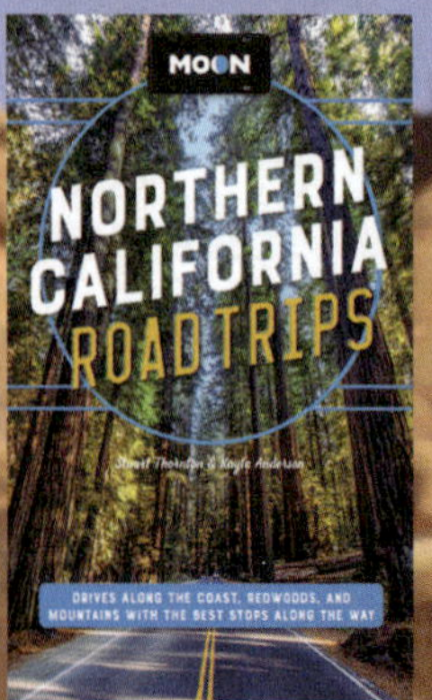

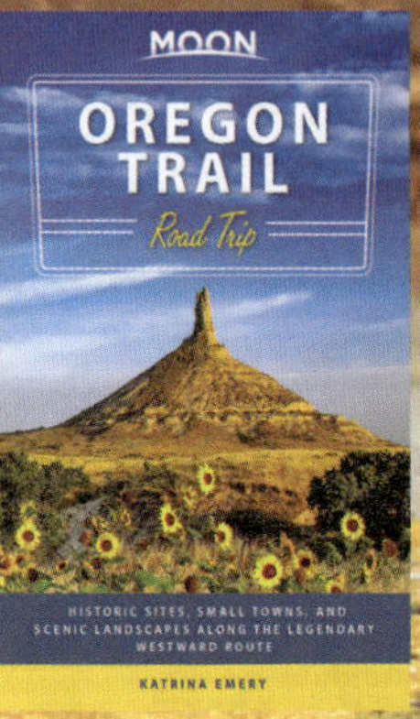

MOONTRAVELGUIDES.COM
ROADTRIPUSA.COM

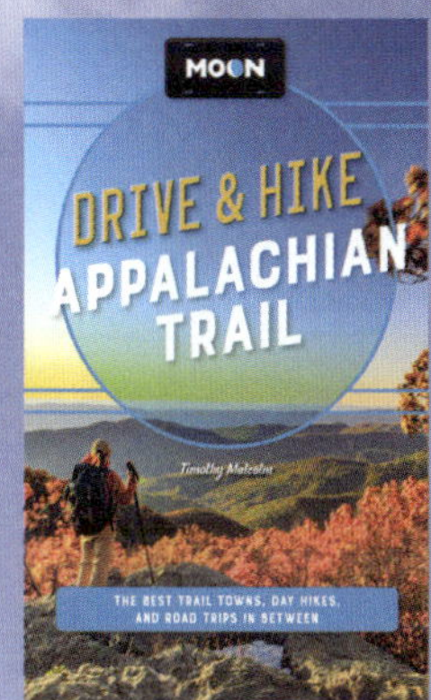
MOON
DRIVE & HIKE
APPALACHIAN TRAIL
Timothy Malcolm
THE BEST TRAIL TOWNS, DAY HIKES, AND ROAD TRIPS IN BETWEEN

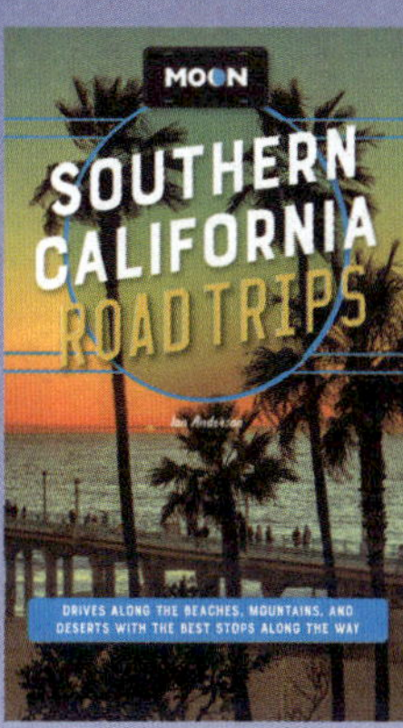
MOON
SOUTHERN CALIFORNIA
ROAD TRIPS
DRIVES ALONG THE BEACHES, MOUNTAINS, AND DESERTS WITH THE BEST STOPS ALONG THE WAY

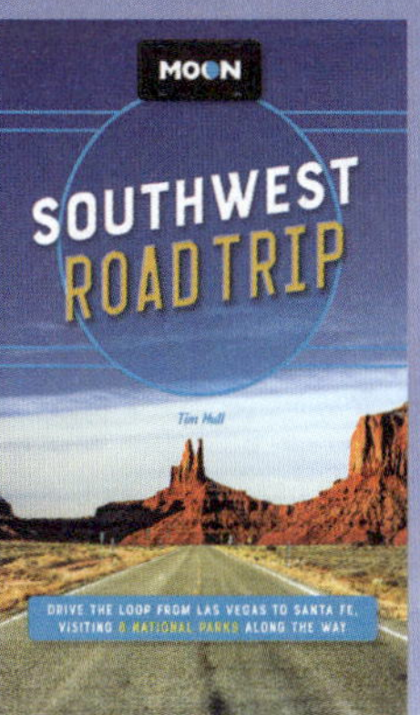
MOON
SOUTHWEST
ROAD TRIP
Tim Hull
DRIVE THE LOOP FROM LAS VEGAS TO SANTA FE, VISITING 8 NATIONAL PARKS ALONG THE WAY

MOON
ROUTE 66
ROAD TRIP
Jessica Dunham
DRIVE THE CLASSIC ROUTE FROM CHICAGO TO LOS ANGELES

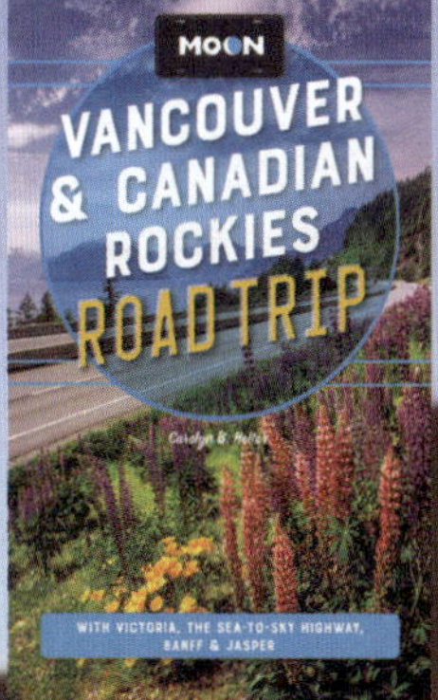
MOON
VANCOUVER & CANADIAN ROCKIES
ROAD TRIP
WITH VICTORIA, THE SEA-TO-SKY HIGHWAY, BANFF & JASPER

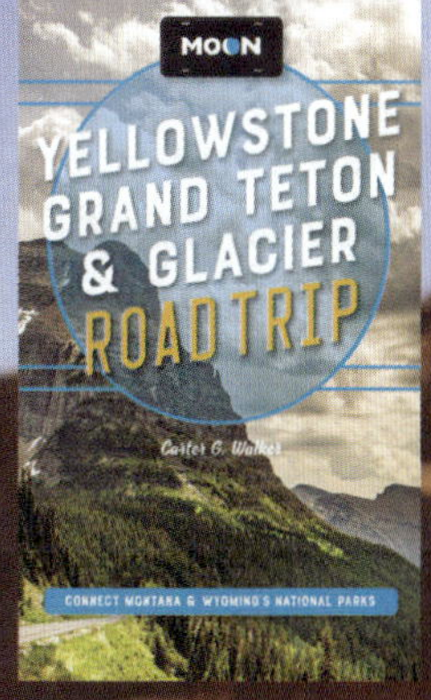
MOON
YELLOWSTONE GRAND TETON & GLACIER
ROAD TRIP
Carter G. Walker
CONNECT MONTANA & WYOMING'S NATIONAL PARKS

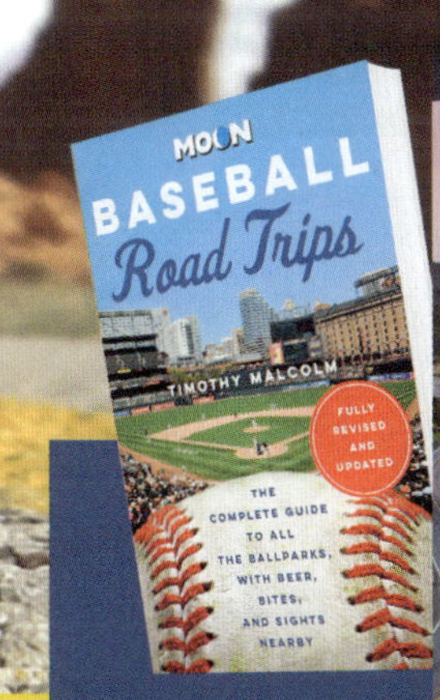
MOON
BASEBALL
Road Trips
TIMOTHY MALCOLM
FULLY REVISED AND UPDATED
THE COMPLETE GUIDE TO ALL THE BALLPARKS, WITH BEER, BITES, AND SIGHTS NEARBY

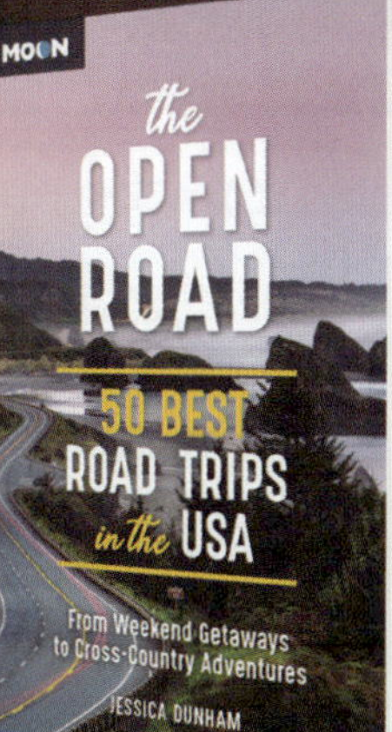
MOON
the OPEN ROAD
50 BEST ROAD TRIPS in the USA
From Weekend Getaways to Cross-Country Adventures
JESSICA DUNHAM

MOON
Road Trip USA
CROSS-COUNTRY ADVENTURES ON AMERICA'S TWO-LANE HIGHWAYS
Jamie Jensen

Latin America

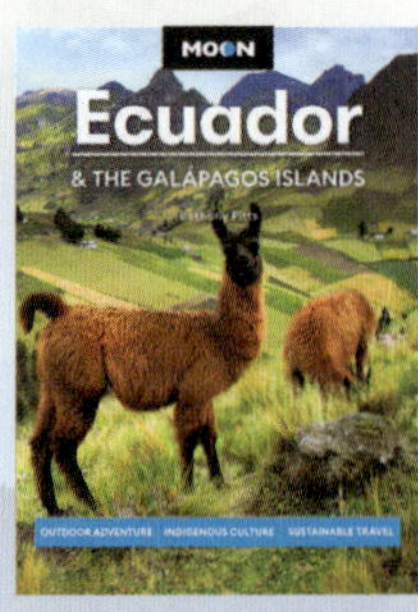

Europe, Africa & Asia

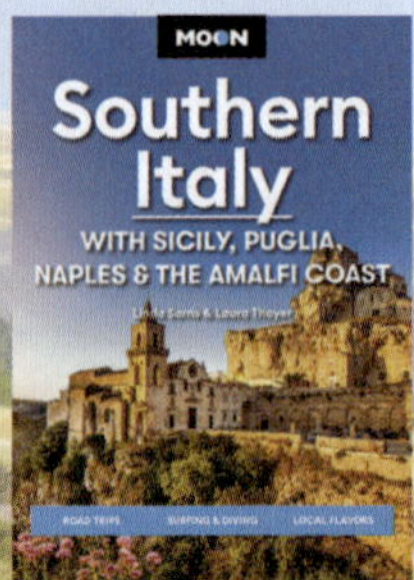

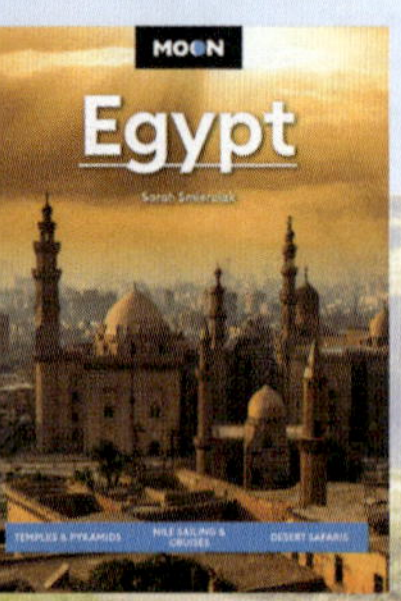

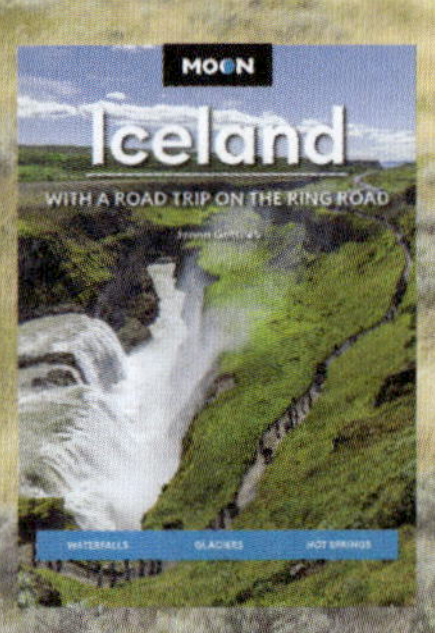

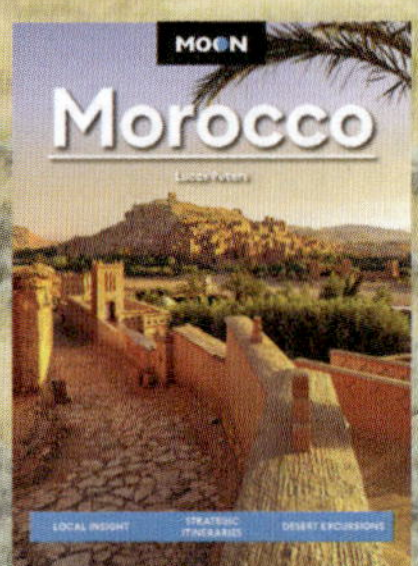

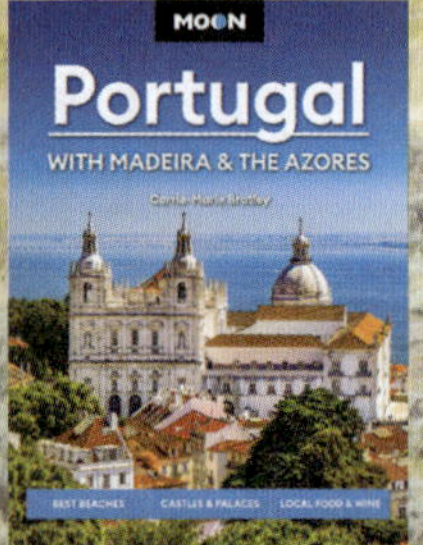

MOONTRAVELGUIDES.COM | @MOONGUIDES  

United States

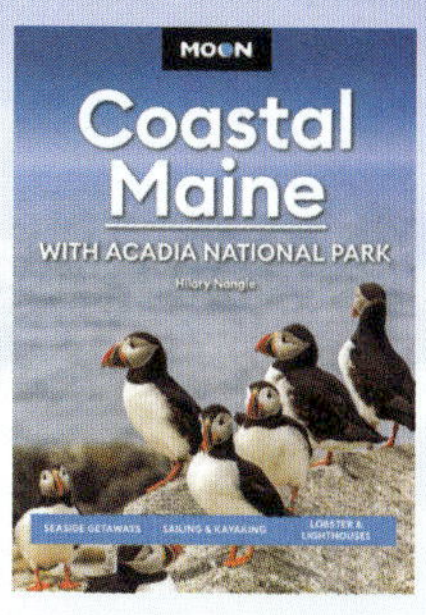

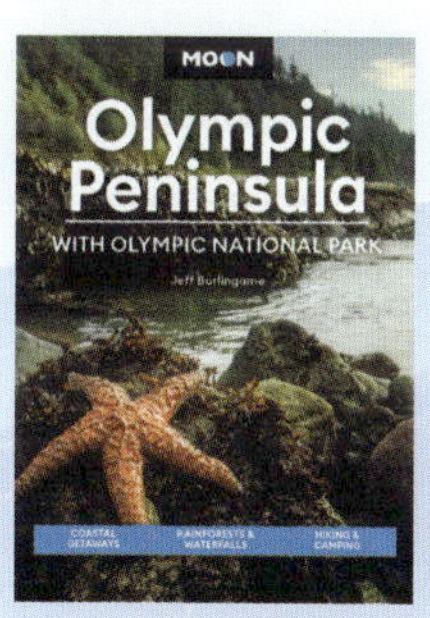

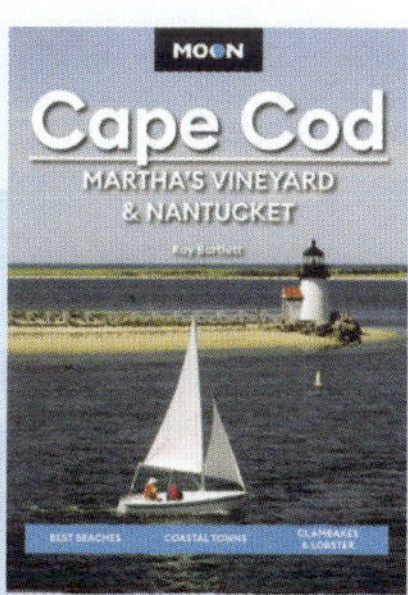

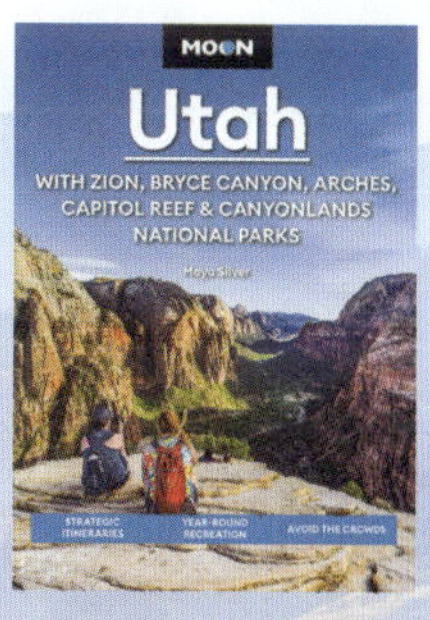

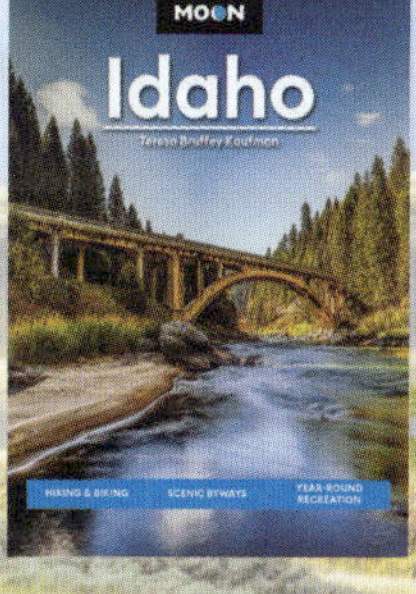

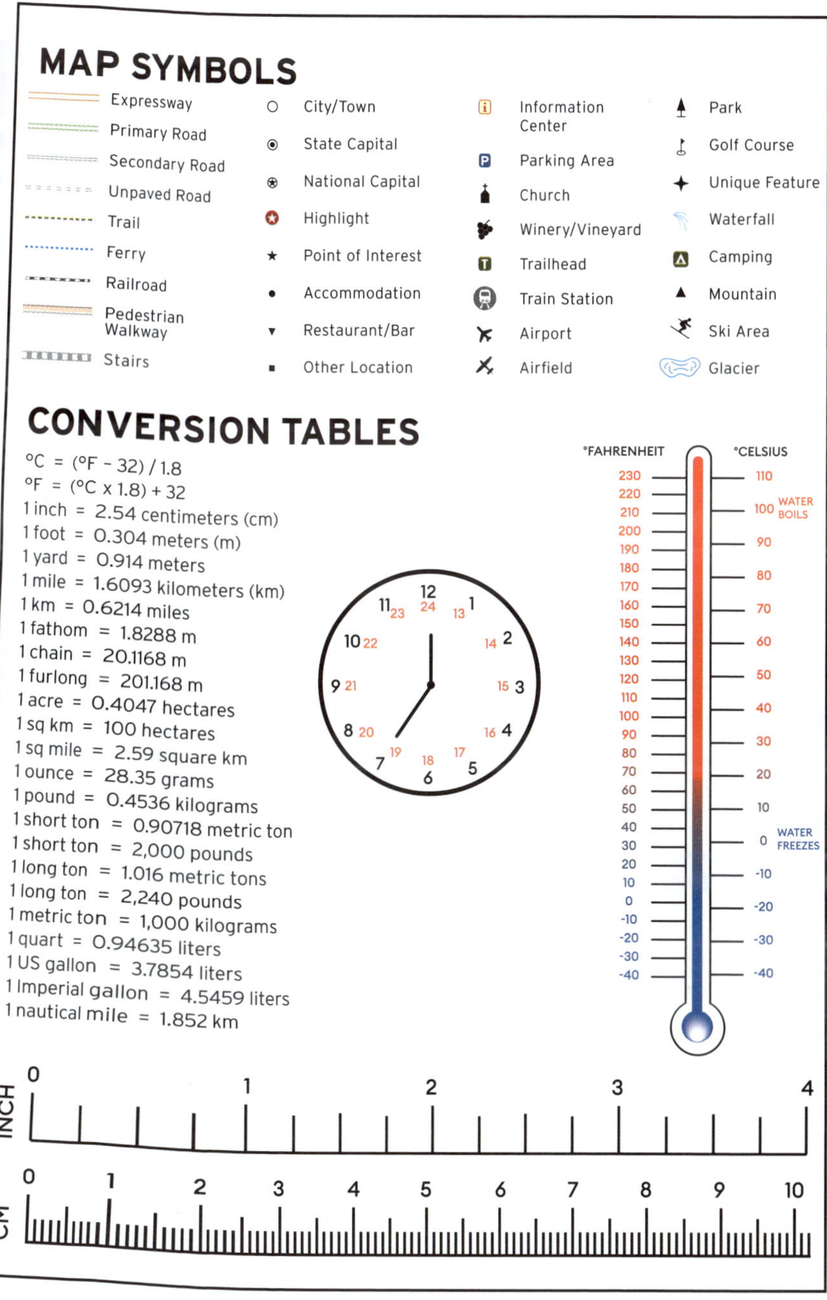

MAP SYMBOLS
Expressway
Primary Road
Secondary Road
Unpaved Road
Trail
Ferry
Railroad
Pedestrian Walkway
Stairs
City/Town
State Capital
National Capital
Highlight
Point of Interest
Accommodation
Restaurant/Bar
Other Location
Information Center
Parking Area
Church
Winery/Vineyard
Trailhead
Train Station
Airport
Airfield
Park
Golf Course
Unique Feature
Waterfall
Camping
Mountain
Ski Area
Glacier
CONVERSION TABLES
°C = (°F - 32) / 1.8
°F = (°C x 1.8) + 32
1 inch = 2.54 centimeters (cm)
1 foot = 0.304 meters (m)
1 yard = 0.914 meters
1 mile = 1.6093 kilometers (km)
1 km = 0.6214 miles
1 fathom = 1.8288 m
1 chain = 20.1168 m
1 furlong = 201.168 m
1 acre = 0.4047 hectares
1 sq km = 100 hectares
1 sq mile = 2.59 square km
1 ounce = 28.35 grams
1 pound = 0.4536 kilograms
1 short ton = 0.90718 metric ton
1 short ton = 2,000 pounds
1 long ton = 1.016 metric tons
1 long ton = 2,240 pounds
1 metric ton = 1,000 kilograms
1 quart = 0.94635 liters
1 US gallon = 3.7854 liters
1 Imperial gallon = 4.5459 liters
1 nautical mile = 1.852 km
°FAHRENHEIT
°CELSIUS
WATER BOILS
WATER FREEZES
INCH
CM

MOON YELLOWSTONE, GRAND TETON & GLACIER ROAD TRIP
Avalon Travel
Hachette Book Group, Inc.
555 12th Street, Suite 1850
Oakland, CA 94607, USA
moontravelguides.com

Editor: Rachael Sablik
Managing Editor: Hannah Brezack
Copy Editor: Jessica Gould
Graphics and Production Coordinator: Rue Flaherty
Cover Design: Toni Tajima
Interior Design: Darren Alessi
Map Editor: Karin Dahl
Cartographers: Abby Whelan and Kat Bennet
Proofreader: Brett Keener

ISBN-13: 979-8-88647-167-0

Printing History
1st Edition — 2019
3rd Edition — March 2026
5 4 3 2 1

Front cover photo: Going-to-the-Sun Road, Glacier National Park © Brian Welker / Alamy Stock Photo

Printed in China by RR Donnelley